Cases in International Relations

Fifth Edition

DONALD M. SNOW

Professor Emeritus
University of Alabama

Longman
Boston   Columbus   Indianapolis   New York   San Francisco   Upper Saddle River
Amsterdam   Cape Town   Dubai   London   Madrid   Milan   Munich   Paris   Montreal   Toronto
Delhi   Mexico City   Sao Paulo   Sydney   Hong Kong   Seoul   Singapore   Taipei   Tokyo

Acquisitions Editor: Vikram Mukhija
Editorial Assistant: Beverly Fong
Senior Marketing Manager: Lindsey Prudhomme
Production Manager: Fran Russello
Project Coordination, Text Design, and Electronic Page Makeup: George Jacob/Integra
  Software Services, Ltd.
Cover Design Manager: Jayne Conte
Cover Illustration/Photo: Vladimir Koletic/*Veer.com*
Printer and Binder: Courier Companies, Inc.

Library of Congress Cataloging-in-Publication Data

Snow, Donald M.,
  Cases in international relations : portraits of the future / Donald M. Snow.—5th ed.
    p. cm.
  Includes index.
  ISBN-13: 978-0-205-00582-6
  ISBN-10: 0-205-00582-9
  1. International relations.   I. Title.
JZ1242.S658 2012
327—dc22

                                                    2010041807

                    1 2 3 4 5 6 7 8 9 10—CRS—13 12 11

Longman
is an imprint of

www.pearsonhighered.com

ISBN-13: 978-0-205-00582-6
ISBN-10:   0-205-00582-9

BRIEF CONTENTS

Detailed Contents   v

Preface   ix

PART I   Conflict and Cooperation   1

CHAPTER 1   Sovereignty: The Legality and Impact of Invading
                  Iraq   3

CHAPTER 2   Resource Scarcity: Oil, the Lubricant That
                  Corrodes   21

CHAPTER 3   Limits on International Cooperation: War Crimes, the
                  International Criminal Court, and Torture   43

CHAPTER 4   Irresolvable Conflicts: The Israeli-Palestinian
                  Impasse   62

PART II   National and International Security   85

CHAPTER 5   Asymmetrical Warfare: The Case of Afghanistan   87

CHAPTER 6   Proliferation: The Case of North Korea   107

CHAPTER 7   Pivotal States: Confronting and Accommodating
                  Iran   126

CHAPTER 8   Peacekeeping: Humanitarian Disaster and
                  International Responses in Darfur   146

PART III   International Political Economy   167

CHAPTER 9   Free Trade: From ITO to WTO and Beyond   169

CHAPTER 10   Regional Integration: The European Union Faces the
                  Future   187

CHAPTER 11   Rising Powers: China and India   206

CHAPTER 12   Extending Globalization: From G-7 to G-20   222

PART IV   Human Security   243

CHAPTER 13   Global Warming: Facing the Problem after Copenhagen   245

CHAPTER 14   International Migration: The U.S.-Mexican Border   263

CHAPTER 15   Failed and Failing States: The Case of Pakistan   285

CHAPTER 16   Terrorism: The Changing Global Threat   305

Index   327

DETAILED CONTENTS

Preface   ix

Part I   Conflict and Cooperation   1

CHAPTER 1   Sovereignty: The Legality and Impact of
Invading Iraq   3

The Concept of Sovereignty   5

The Assault on Sovereignty Outside the United Nations: The Iraq
Precedent   12

CHAPTER 2   Resource Scarcity: Oil, the Lubricant That Corrodes   21

The Problem of Petroleum Scarcity   25

Petroleum Scarcity and Conflict   32

CHAPTER 3   Limits on International Cooperation: War Crimes, the
International Criminal Court, and Torture   43

The Problem of War Crimes   46

War Crimes Applied and Cooperation Applied: The International
Criminal Court and Torture   52

CHAPTER 4   Irresolvable Conflicts: The Israeli-Palestinian
Impasse   62

Irresolvable Conflicts   63

The Israeli-Palestinian Conflict   66

The Peace Process   71

The Current Impasse   78

Part II   National and International Security   85

CHAPTER 5   Asymmetrical Warfare: The Case of Afghanistan   87

Asymmetrical Warfare: New/Old War   90

Case: The Afghanistan War   98

CHAPTER 6   Proliferation: The Case of North Korea   107

The Proliferation Problem   108

The Proliferation Problem Applied: The Case of North Korea   117

CHAPTER 7   Pivotal States: Confronting and Accommodating Iran   126

Iran: A Pivotal State   128

Dealing with Iran   137

CHAPTER 8   Peacekeeping: Humanitarian Disaster and International Responses in Darfur   146

Humanitarian Disasters   148

The Peacekeeping Response   149

Peacekeeping in Darfur   158

Part III   International Political Economy   167

CHAPTER 9   Free Trade: From ITO to WTO and Beyond   169

Institutionalizing Trade   172

Is Institutionalized Free Trade a Good Idea?   177

CHAPTER 10   Regional Integration: The European Union Faces the Future   187

The Regional Integration Process   189

The European Union Experience   194

CHAPTER 11   Rising Powers: China and India   206

Rising Powers   207

China and India as Rising Powers   208

CHAPTER 12   Extending Globalization: From G-7 to G-20   222

Controversies and Dynamics   224

The Developmental Dimension   230

From G-7 to G-20   234

Part IV Human Security 243

CHAPTER 13 Global Warming: Facing the Problem after Copenhagen 245

The Road to Kyoto—And Beyond? 248

Warm and Getting Warmer: But How Much? 254

CHAPTER 14 International Migration: The U.S.-Mexican Border 263

Parameters of Immigration 264

The U.S.-Mexican Border Problem 273

CHAPTER 15 Failed and Failing States: The Case of Pakistan 285

The Nature and Problem of Failed States 287

Pakistan: A Failed State? 294

CHAPTER 16 Terrorism: The Changing Global Threat 305

What is Terrorism? 307

Evolving Terrorism since September 11 313

Dealing with Terrorism: The GWOT 316

Index 327

PREFACE

When the last edition of this book appeared in early 2009, international relations were dominated by two factors: the new incumbency of Barack Obama as president of the United States, and the economic recession that had begun on Wall Street the year before and was in danger of spreading worldwide. Both these events, of course, were basically American, but they were also universally important, reflecting the continuing dominant role of the United States in international relations.

The two phenomena were quite different in character and presumed impact. The election of Obama was, in many ways, heralded more effusively in other countries than it was in the United States, and there was a mood and anticipation that the new American president would lead the way to a more cooperative, less conflictual global scene. The economic upheaval emitting from the United States, on the other hand, was a much more worrisome event, and the prevailing concern was how much the negative effects would be in the other parts of the globe. These signs of change seemed to radiate from the backdrop of conflict and violence evidenced in the ongoing contest with terrorism and shooting conflicts in places like Iraq and Afghanistan.

The promise and dread of 2009 are now two years in the past, and they are still unfolding, if not in ways that were entirely anticipated. The horizon influence of the Obama presidency has been far less great than its champions heralded it would be. Great expectations often prove excessive in the crucible of reality, and the dreams that the Obama presence seemed to promise have yet to be realized. The new era of cooperation in international affairs, for instance, has not produced progress on the problem of global warming, in movement toward an enduring peace between the Israelis and the Palestinians, nor in resolving the contentious relations between the United States and North Korea or Iran. The economic malaise has indeed spread about the globe, infecting particularly the European Union (the Greek crisis of 2010 as prime example), but the global economy is also clearly in a process of readjustment, most notably in the continuing rise of China and India as world economic powers and in institutional recognition of that status through the replacement of the Group of Seven (G-7) by the Group of Twenty (G-20) as the prime international economic consultative mechanism.

The fourth edition assessed many of these dynamics, all of which have changed to some extent since then. Part of the burden of this volume, which has sought through its various editions to spotlight changing global trends, is to update and modify the discussion of situations with regard to a variety of evolving matters, from the international humanitarian disaster in Darfur to the global warming summit in Copenhagen in December 2009 to the ongoing gyrations of the U.S.-North Korean conflict over the proliferation of nuclear weapons. At the same time, this new fifth edition seeks to expand on past editions by incorporating new perspectives and problems that have emerged in the intervening two years between editions.

While there has been significant change in the international condition, of course, much remains familiar. The United States, for instance, is still engaged in two wars, one of which (Iraq) is winding down, while another (Afghanistan) continues amid controversy regarding its worth or the prospects of success. All this occurs within the context of the volatile Middle East and ongoing problems associated with terrorism, Iran, Pakistan, and Israel, all of which are continuing subjects of consideration in these pages.

The intention of this volume is to present material that is readable, under-standable, relevant, illustrative, and important to the reader and the instruc-tor assigning this book. By avoiding an excess amount of technical jargon and consciously trying to engage the reader with the material, the hopeful result is an enjoyable and understandable read. The cases were largely chosen because of their relevance to both the world in which we all live and the illustration of the important principles covered in these pages. The intent is a volume that is both valuable and important to understanding contemporary international relations.

NEW TO THIS EDITION

Each edition of *Cases in International Relations* has been different from its pred-ecessor in at least three distinctive ways. First, in order to accommodate dynam-ics that have appeared or been accentuated since the last edition, the author has added more contemporary cases and concepts. To keep the book manageable in length, each addition has been matched by scrapping or amending a case from the previous edition. Second, each edition has seen updating, modifying, and even replacing the case applications from the previous edition, and this has been done in this edition as well. Third, there has been some reordering and restructuring of the order of cases within and between sections of the book.

Substantively, three entirely new chapters have been added. In order to deal with the changing nature of the global economic system, Chapter 12, "Extending Globalization," has been added. It emphasizes the movement by the dominant economic powers (the G-7) voluntarily to a new consultative system expanded to include prominent members of the so-called developing world in the form of the G-20. This change comes in tandem with the exten-sive revision of Chapter 11, "Rising Powers," to examine the two most promi-nent new members of G-20, China and India. Chapter 14, "International Immigration," deals with the worldwide movement of people from one coun-try to another, an emphasis tied to the American domestic concern with the security of the U.S.-Mexican border. Arising from the international repercus-sions of the violence in southwest Asia, Chapter 15, "Failed States," examines the problems caused by and associated with the loosening of governmental control over territory, with particular attention to Pakistan. To accommodate these additions, two chapters ("Democratic Peace" and "International Disasters") have been eliminated, and two chapters, one devoted to China and the other to India and Venezuela, have been merged into Chapter 11.

In addition to these entirely new chapters, four others have received extensive modification or refocusing. Chapter 5, "Asymmetrical Warfare," brings more sharply into focus the unique character and challenge of this form of warfare and applies that challenge to the American and allied effort in Afghanistan. Chapter 8, "Peacekeeping," has been modified to emphasize more sharply the underlying humanitarian disasters that motivate such efforts and the general inadequacy of these endeavors, as illustrated vividly by Darfur. Chapter 13, "Global Warming," examines the great hope for progress that surrounded the December 2009 world conference in Copenhagen and how and why that conference failed to make substantial progress toward a follow-on to the Kyoto protocols. Chapter 16, "Terrorism," expands its coverage to include newly prominent forms the terrorist threat takes, notably the rise of so-called "protean" terrorist organizations and lone wolf terrorists.

Although it runs the risk of some oversimplification, the most important of the changes in this edition can be summarized as follows:

- An emphasis on change in the international economic order, accentuated by the emergence of the G-20 and the rise of India and China as world economic powers;
- An examination of the problem of international migration as a global problem, the current Mexican border case being one example of a broader issue;
- An introduction to instability in potential "failed states" and its impact on international relations;
- A much clearer and more focused examination of asymmetrical warfare and the perils of involvement in these kinds of conflicts;
- An updated and focused examination of the issues that divide Israel and its neighbors and friends and which demonstrate the difficulties of irresolvable conflicts;
- A new emphasis on the evolving nature of the terrorist threat and the emergence of new problems like those associated with lone wolf terrorists.

The structural rearrangement of the book begun in the last edition has been continued. Chapter titles identify the concept being explored as the primary title in each chapter, with the case application as the subtitle. The table of contents has also been rearranged in two ways. The format of four parts introduced in the last edition has been retained, with each section containing four chapters dealing with the general topic of the part. The order of the parts was changed in the last edition to bring the table of contents more into line with standard core texts in the field, and this feature has been retained as well. The organization by parts is as follows: Conflict and Cooperation, National and International Security, International Political Economy, and Human Security.

Part I, "Conflict and Cooperation," consists of chapters dealing with sovereignty and intervention and the impact of the American invasion of Iraq on those concepts (Chapter 1); resource scarcity as a source of ongoing conflict among states (Chapter 2); the collision of sovereignty and limits of cooperation in the areas of war crimes and international norms regarding torture (Chapter 3); and conflicts that are extremely difficult to resolve, like the Israeli-Palestinian conflict (Chapter 4).

Part II, "National and International Security," looks at problems affecting the security of states and the international order. Topics include asymmetrical warfare as a dominant feature of the future (Chapter 5), the proliferation of weapons of mass destruction and especially nuclear weapons (Chapter 6), the influence of important, pivotal regional powers like Iran (Chapter 7), and peacekeeping (Chapter 8).

Part III, "International Political Economy," shifts the focus of the cases to the economic realm. Topics include the concept and evolution of free trade (Chapter 9); the evolution of the most economically integrated region of the world, the European Union (Chapter 10); rising economic powers like China and India (Chapter 11); and the changing dynamics of an expanded and extended globalized world in the form of G-20 (Chapter 12).

Part IV was renamed "Human Security" in the fourth edition to reflect its emphasis on problems that are international in scope and that have a direct impact on people and their well-being and safety, and this designation has been retained. Topics include global warming efforts following the Kyoto accords (Chapter 13), international immigration (Chapter 14), the failure or potential failure of states to maintain effective control of their territory (Chapter 15), and terrorism and efforts to reduce it (Chapter 16).

FEATURES

What distinguishes this effort from other supplementary texts in the field? One answer is that all the essays included in the volume are original papers written by the author specifically for this volume. The reason for doing so was to allow for more timely coverage of ongoing situations than is possible with the publication lag time of scholarly journals and their availability to readers and other compendia. It also allows casting the cases in a common format that makes it easier to compare and contrast the contents of the various cases. In addition, journal articles are written for academic peers rather than more-or-less lay students, meaning they are generally rendered in language and theoretical trappings that are less than accessible to student readers. Finally, writing original articles facilitates updating and modifying materials as events and dynamics change, which hopefully adds to the freshness, accuracy, and timeliness of the materials contained in these pages. Presenting the most contemporary set of portraits possible has certainly been a major purpose of this and earlier editions.

A word about what this book is—and is not—is appropriate at this point. It is a case book, presenting a series of individual instances of dynamics and trends within the international arena. The effort is neither inclusive nor encyclopedic; it covers selected concepts and events, not the universe of international concerns. A series of 16 important, underlying concepts and principles of the international system have been chosen and discussed, and the discussion of these principles has been applied to contemporary, important, and interesting real-life examples. The result is not a systematic overview of the international system or its history, which is the province of core textbooks in the field. Likewise, it does not offer a unifying theoretical explanatory framework of international politics, a task that more specialized books purporting grand "theories" of international relations propound. Rather, the intent is to introduce and apply some basic concepts about international relations and how they apply in real situations.

The book's pedagogy reflects this approach. Each of the cases begins by identifying a particular problem or dynamic of the international system (indicated as the main chapter title). After describing the concept, it applies that concept to an actual case. Thus, for instance, Chapter 8 begins with the concept of peacekeeping and how it has evolved in the contemporary system and applies it to the current tragedy in Darfur, where an operation described as peacekeeping has been anything but what the concept of peacekeeping suggests. Each case concludes with a series of questions for study or discussion and a bibliography of contemporary articles and books useful to the intended readers of the book and some suggested Web sites for additional reference.

SUPPLEMENTS

Longman is pleased to offer several resources to qualified adopters of *Cases in International Relations* and their students that will make teaching and learning from this book even more effective and enjoyable.

Passport for International Relations

With Passport, choose the resources you want from MyPoliSciKit and put links to them into your course management system. If there is assessment associated with those resources, it also can be uploaded, allowing the results to feed directly into your course management system's gradebook. With over 150 MyPoliSciKit assets like video case studies, mapping exercises, comparative exercises, simulations, podcasts, *Financial Times* newsfeeds, current events quizzes, politics blog, and much more, Passport is available for any Pearson introductory or upper-level political science book. Use ISBN 0-205-10924-1 to order Passport with this book. To learn more, please contact your Pearson representative.

MySearchLab

Need help with a paper? MySearchLab saves time and improves results by offering start-to-finish guidance on the research/writing process and full-text access to academic journals and periodicals. Use ISBN 0-205-10916-0 to order MySearchLab with this book. To learn more, please visit www.mysearchlab.com or contact your Pearson representative.

The Economist

Every week, *The Economist* analyzes the important happenings around the globe. From business to politics, to the arts and science, its coverage connects seemingly unrelated events in unexpected ways. Use ISBN 0-205-00257-9 to order a 15-week subscription with this book for a small additional charge. To learn more, please contact your Pearson representative.

The Financial Times

Featuring international news and analysis from journalists in more than 50 countries, *The Financial Times* provides insights and perspectives on political and economic developments around the world. Use ISBN 0-205-07392-1 to order a 15-week subscription with this book for a small additional charge. To learn more, please contact your Pearson representative.

Longman Atlas of World Issues (0-205-78020-2)

From population and political systems to energy use and women's rights, the *Longman Atlas of World Issues* features full-color thematic maps that examine the forces shaping the world. Featuring maps from the latest edition of *The Penguin State of the World Atlas*, this excerpt includes critical thinking exercises to promote a deeper understanding of how geography affects many global issues. Available at no additional charge when packaged with this book.

Goode's World Atlas (0-321-65200-2)

First published by Rand McNally in 1923, *Goode's World Atlas* has set the standard for college reference atlases. It features hundreds of physical, political, and thematic maps as well as graphs, tables, and a pronouncing index. Available at a discount when packaged with this book.

The Penguin Dictionary of International Relations (0-140-51397-3)

This indispensable reference by Graham Evans and Jeffrey Newnham includes hundreds of cross-referenced entries on the enduring and emerging theories, concepts, and events that are shaping the academic discipline of international relations and today's world politics. Available at a discount when packaged with this book.

Research and Writing in International Relations (0-205-06065-X)

With current and detailed coverage on how to start research in the discipline's major subfields, this brief and affordable guide offers the step-by-step guidance and the essential resources needed to compose political science papers that go beyond description and into systematic and sophisticated inquiry. This text focuses on areas where students often need help—finding a topic, developing a question, reviewing the literature, designing research, and last, writing the paper. Available at a discount when packaged with this book.

ACKNOWLEDGMENTS

The result of this endeavor is a new stack of portraits of the future that the reader hopefully will find both broad and enriching. This edition of the book, like the original, is dedicated to my good friend and colleague, the late D. Eugene Brown. Gene and I met in 1989 at the U.S. Army War College, where we both served as visiting professors and shared an office for two years before he returned to his permanent home at Lebanon Valley College in Annville, Pennsylvania, and I returned to the University of Alabama in Tuscaloosa. In the ensuing decade, we were collaborators on several book projects; *Cases in International Relations*, which was mostly Gene's idea, was to be a continuation, even culmination, of those efforts. Unfortunately, Gene left us before the original project was complete. His shadow remains, I hope with a smile on his face.

I would like to thank the reviewers who made useful comments on this revision: Ted Blair, Diablo Valley College; Gloria Guevara, Ventura County Community College; David Hauser, West Virginia University; Remonda Kleinburg, University of North Carolina-Wilmington; Pedro dos Santos, University of Kansas; Samuel S. Stanton, Grove City College; Steven Walker, Northwest College; and Clarence Wallace, Angelo State University.

DONALD M. SNOW
PROFESSOR EMERITUS
UNIVERSITY OF ALABAMA

Conflict and Cooperation

Although the dynamics of the international system are in a more or less constant state of flux, some issues, problems, and themes recur across time. A major theme of international relations has been the existence of a state of conflict among the countries of the world and the dynamic tensions between conflict and cooperation as the principal approaches by which countries attempt to manage or settle their differences. The four studies in Part I address various aspects of that dynamic tension.

Chapter 1, "Sovereignty," addresses the concept of sovereignty, the bedrock principle of international relations for at least the last 300 years. Sovereignty means exclusive political authority over territory and people, and maintaining and protecting national sovereignty is a core value of the members of the international system. Intervention into the affairs of states, most extremely employing military force, directly challenges the sovereignty against those who are the objects of that force. The case application deals with the ramifications for the concept of sovereignty of the American invasion and occupation of Iraq, an event that clearly violated Iraqi sovereignty.

Chapter 2, "Resource Scarcity," examines a major source of conflict in international relations, the competition for scarce resources. The examination represents an extension and application of principles raised in Chapter 1, since the pursuit of scarce resources is one of the reasons why states cling to sovereignty and demonstrate a willingness to engage in sometimes extreme actions in the quest for scarce resources deemed vital to the state. The case concentrates on the problem of access to petroleum energy, a vital resource in increasingly short supply and over which states vigorously compete for access and control.

Chapter 3, "The Limits on International cooperation," deals with why it is often difficult to induce cooperation between states, even in an area, such as war crimes, where such cooperation would seem mutually advantageous to all states and the international order. The chief barrier in this case, as in other instances, is sovereignty, and the case examines how this bedrock principle impedes cooperation about what kinds of actions are permissible and impermissible during or leading up to war. A modern judicial body, the International Criminal Court (ICC), has been created to try alleged violations of war crimes, and one of the areas of war crimes currently under scrutiny is the use of torture, which is a war crime when committed during war and is thus within the purview of the ICC. Despite condemnation of war crimes, major countries, including the United States, resist the application of these cooperation-based efforts on the grounds of intrusions on national sovereignty.

Chapter 4, "Irresolvable Conflicts," looks at the problem caused by disagreements between states and entities that are so fundamental that there appears to be no way to create solutions acceptable to parties—to engage in cooperative resolution of conflicts. While there are relatively few of these irresolvable conflicts in the international arena, those that exist are particularly vexing and upsetting to international peace and stability. The most famous contemporary case is the confrontation between the Israelis and the Palestinians over the disposition of the territory they both claim in the Holy Land.

Sovereignty: The Legality and Impact of Invading Iraq

PRÉCIS

The principle of sovereignty, or supreme authority, has been the bedrock principle of operation of the international system since the end of the Thirty Years' War in 1648, a process known as the Peace of Westphalia. Over time, sovereignty has come to reside in the governments of states, where it is generally conceded to exist today. One of the most controversial areas involving sovereignty is its relationship to war and whether sovereignty permits acts of war under different circumstances. Because war is a primary result of the international system that has evolved around the principle of sovereignty, it has never been without critics who would prefer a more peaceful order. The effort to internationalize war crimes, the topic of the next chapter, is one aspect of that criticism.

The issue of sovereignty has come under particularly close scrutiny as one consequence of the U.S. invasion of Iraq in March 2003. The invasion clearly involved the violation of Iraqi sovereignty and thus raised legal and moral questions about whether the invasion was justified. This case will examine the invasion of Iraq and its impact on sovereignty as imbedded in international legal prohibitions and allowances to use force.

The American invasion and occupation of Iraq that is currently winding down has been controversial on many grounds, including its legality and its impact on the practices of states in the international system. Both of these areas of contention revolve around the question of whether the United States' action represented a fundamental challenge to the most basic principle of the international system, state sovereignty.

For more than 350 years, the bedrock principle of international relations has been the evolving concept of sovereignty, and more specifically, the idea of state sovereignty. Although its philosophical roots extend back farther, this concept was first introduced formally in a book written in the sixteenth century by the Frenchman Jean Bodin as the philosophical underpinning for the consolidation of power by Europe's monarchs, and in particular, the authority of the king of France. With the settlement of the extraordinarily brutal, religiously based Thirty Years' War in 1648, the triumphant secular monarchs of northern Europe adopted the concept as part of asserting their independence from papal authority.

State sovereignty, the idea that state governments have supreme authority in the international system and that there can be no authority superior to the state, has been a first principle by which international relations is organized ever since. The primacy of sovereignty has never lacked its critics, either in terms of the concept's validity or its philosophical and practical implications. Nevertheless, the principle has endured, and governments cling tenaciously to their possession of sovereignty.

Sovereignty has always done more than provide the philosophical underpinning of international relations. The idea—even the necessity—of possessing and protecting sovereignty has formed the basis of much state action, and particularly the geopolitical task of protecting the state from its enemies. The idea of a "national security state" that became a popular depiction during the Cold War was based in the need to protect the state's supreme authority over its territory from predators that threatened that authority. Among the defenders of this notion, the United States has stood out for its staunch defense of the sanctity of state sovereignty.

The sacrosanct status of unfettered sovereignty is being increasingly questioned. Part of the assault has come from the traditional critics of sovereignty; for instance, opponents of war who argue that armed conflict is an integral, inevitable, and regrettable consequence of a world in which sovereignty reigns. From this view, dismantling sovereignty is the necessary prerequisite for world peace. At the same time, the rise of other concerns such as human rights collides with state sovereignty. Why? Because a major historical justification for mistreatment of individuals and groups within states is that sovereign states possess absolute authority over their citizens, and that how states act within their sovereign jurisdiction is strictly their own business. This is roughly the position that the Russian government has taken with regard to its treatment of Chechnya during the attempted Chechen secession during the 1990s and into the 2000s. More indirectly, but no less fundamentally, the Bush doctrine's assertion of an American "right" to attack foes preemptively, as in Iraq, represents a de facto denial of the sovereignty it seeks to preserve.

Indifference toward humanity in the guise of sovereignty may seem incredible in contemporary terms, but it is an idea that was virtually unchallenged as little as a half century ago. Take a real example. When the war crimes trials at Nuremberg were being organized, there were questions about what crimes the Nazi defendants could be charged for committing. The leading U.S. jurist at the trials, a member of the U.S. Supreme Court, offered the official view that the Nazis could be charged with killing non-German citizens on German soil, but not with exterminating German Jews, because, as German citizens, they could treat them any way the Germans saw fit. The position was not particularly controversial at the time (partly because as a practical matter, there were plenty of war crimes with which to charge the defendants).

The bloody internal conflicts in places like the Balkans and parts of Africa have challenged the idea that state sovereignty provides an unfettered license for governments to do as they please to their citizens or, where governments are incapable or nonexistent, not to protect portions of their populations from ravage. Using the United Nations as a vehicle to justify actions, the international system has, on numerous occasions that will almost certainly continue into the future, intruded itself into these situations in order to prevent further abuse and to protect citizens.

The collision of traditional conceptualizations of sovereignty with the evolution of the post–Cold War world generally is thus a major question in international relations, a question of whether the world and its values are changing so much that the principle of sovereignty must be modified or abandoned to adjust to a new reality. One aspect of that reality is the collision between sovereignty and the assertion of an international right or need to intervene in civil wars within states or, more recently, to pursue international terrorists. The outcome of the ensuing debate will help answer the broader question of the role of sovereignty in the twenty-first century and is thus the focus of this case study.

What role does sovereignty play in defining what acts by states are permissible or impermissible in the international environment? Do the sovereign rights that states possess allow them to act as they wish and remain immune from international repercussions? Or, are there overriding considerations that permit states to violate the sovereignty of others in ways such as the physical invasion of one state by another? Examining these questions requires looking first at the content and evolution of sovereignty and some major criticisms of sovereignty in theory and action. That discussion will form the context for - examining the U.S. invasion and long occupation of Iraq, in terms of both its legality and the precedent it may serve for future interpretations of sovereignty.

THE CONCEPT OF SOVEREIGNTY

The basic concept of sovereignty has three distinct elements that collectively define what it means to possess sovereignty. The first element is legitimate authority. Authority is simply the ability to enforce an order; the qualifier "legitimate" means that authority is invested with some legal, consensual basis. Put another way, sovereignty is more than the exercise of pure force.

The second element of sovereignty is that it is supreme. What this means is that there is no superior authority to the possessor of sovereignty; the sovereign is the highest possible authority wherever the sovereign holds sway. The third and related element is that of territory; sovereignty is supreme authority within a defined physical territory. Since the Peace of Westphalia, the political state came to embody the territorial definition of sovereignty. Thus, states (or countries) have supreme authority over what occurs within their territorial boundaries, and no other source of authority can claim superior jurisdiction to the sovereign.

Before turning to why sovereignty has developed the way it has as a concept, it is worthwhile briefly to look at the consequences of these characteristics politically. In the *internal* workings of states, sovereignty is the basis of the political authority of state governments; the idea of supreme authority provides the state with the power to order its own affairs and the government to create and enforce that order. When the concept of sovereignty was first developed, this internal application was the emphasis. *Externally,* in the relations between states, this same sovereignty creates disorder, because there can be no superior authority to the sovereign within the defined territory of states. The result is *anarchy,* or the absence of government (political authority) in the relations among states. Thus, sovereignty has the schizophrenic effect of creating order and disorder, depending on the venue in which it is applied.

Early Origins and Evolution

The anarchical consequence was not so clear when Bodin formally enunciated the concept of sovereignty in his 1576 book *De Republica*. Bodin decried the inability of the French monarchy to establish its authority throughout the country, since lower feudal lords instead claimed what amounted to sovereignty over those realms—especially through charging taxes (tolls) to cross their realms. Bodin countered with the idea of sovereignty, which he defined as "supreme authority over citizens and subjects, *unrestrained by law.*" (Emphasis added.) The added and italicized element, Bodin felt, was necessary to avoid the unifying monarch being hamstrung by parochial laws in his quest to establish the power of the French monarchy. This part of the definition has fallen from common conceptions of sovereignty, but its implications remain and are part of the ongoing controversy central to this case: If the sovereign is above the law, then nothing he or she does can possibly be illegal, at least when committed within the sovereign jurisdiction over which the sovereign reigns.

When Bodin enunciated the principle of sovereignty, he was unconcerned about it as a maxim for international relations. This is not surprising in that the period of its gestation was a time when monarchs were consolidating their holds on what became the modern states of Europe and the modern state system. Given that all these states were absolute monarchies, it is further not terribly surprising the presumption quickly evolved (aided by philosophical publicists like Thomas Hobbes) that sovereignty resided with the monarch (which, among other things, helps explain why monarchs are sometimes referred to as sovereigns).

The concept of sovereignty was extended to international relations as the state system evolved and the structure of the modern state emerged and solidified. Hugo Grotius, the Dutch scholar generally acknowledged as the father of international law, first proclaimed state sovereignty as a fundamental principle of international relations in his 1625 book *On the Law of War and*

Peace. By the eighteenth century, the principle was well on its way to being in place, and by the nineteenth it was an accepted part of international relations.

By the nineteenth century, the content of sovereignty had evolved from its original context. Because virtually all countries were still ruled by more or less absolute monarchies (the fledgling, and not very important, United States, revolutionary France, and slightly democratizing Great Britain being the exceptions), the idea of absolute state sovereignty was the rule, and this principle governed both domestic and international relations. From the view of the international system, a prevailing way to describe international politics was in terms of something called the *billiard ball* theory. The idea, never to be taken entirely literally, was that state authority resembled an impermeable billiard ball, and that international relations consisted of these impermeable objects bouncing against one another, causing them to change course in their international behavior from time to time. Important to the theory, however, was that the balls were impermeable, which meant that nothing in international interactions could affect what went on within the balls, for instance, how states treated their citizens. Under this principle, it was simply impermissible for states to interfere in the internal affairs of other states, no matter how distasteful or disgusting domestic practices might be.

Even during its heyday, this conceptualization was not universally accepted. In fact, conceptual challenges tended to be grouped around two related questions that continue to be important. How much authority does the sovereign have in the territorial realm over which it is exercised? Within whom, or what body, does sovereignty reside? Different answers have decidedly different implications for what sovereignty means in the relations among states.

As sovereignty was originally formulated and implemented, the answer to the first question was that sovereignty is absolute, that the possessor has total authority over his or her realm. This interpretation flows from, among other sources, the idea that the sovereign is "unrestrained by law," to repeat Bodin's term. The contrary view emerged during the eighteenth and nineteenth centuries and reflected the growing notion of political rights asserted in the American and French Revolutions, each of which claimed the sovereign's powers were limited and could be abridged. Among the primary publicists of this view were the English political philosopher John Locke and his French counterpart, Jean-Jacques Rousseau.

The assertion that there are limits on sovereignty reflects the second question: Where does sovereignty reside? It is a question about the basis on which that authority is legitimately claimed by those who seek to wield power within their political jurisdictions. The traditional view was that sovereignty resides in the state. In the sixteenth and seventeenth centuries when sovereignty was taking hold as an organizational principle, this meant the king or queen had sovereignty, because the monarch was the unchallenged head of government. It was what is now called a "top-down" concept; the government exercised sovereignty over the population, whose duty it was to submit to that authority.

Beyond the philosophical positions taken by Locke and Rousseau, the contrary argument had its base in, among other places, the American Revolution. A major theme of the American complaint against the British monarch was his denial that the colonists had *rights* in addition to obligations. From that assertion, it was a reasonably short intellectual odyssey to the assertion that the *people,* not the state (or monarch) were the possessors of sovereignty. Under the notion of what became known as *popular sovereignty,* the idea was that the people, as possessors of sovereignty, ceded some of that authority to the state in order to provide the basic legitimacy for the social and political order. Ultimately, however, sovereignty resides with individual citizens, who can grant, withhold, or even, in some interpretations, rescind the bestowing of authority to the state.

These distinctions are more than abstract, academic constructs. Their practical meanings and implications become particularly clear if one combines the two ideas in matrix form.

Sources and Extent of Sovereignty			
		Extent of Sovereignty	
		Absolute	*Limited*
Source	State	(Cell 1)	(Cell 3)
	Individuals	(Cell 2)	(Cell 4)

The idea that sovereignty is absolute can be associated with authoritarian governance of one sort or the other. Traditional authoritarian regimes derive their claim to authority on the combination of absolute sovereignty and the state locus of authority (Cell 1). The populist/fascist regimes in Italy and Germany that arose between the world wars combine absolutism with some popular, individual base, Cell 2 (both regimes originally came to power popularly). On the other side of the ledger, the idea that sovereignty is limited is associated with democratic regimes. The idea of state sovereignty derived from the people is the backbone of traditional western democracy (Cell 3). When the conferral of sovereignty to the state is denied and maintained by subnational individuals or groups, the result can be the kinds of instability one associates with many of the unstable regimes in the developing world (Cell 4). Much of the debate about intervention in the internal affairs of states derives from the situation depicted in Cell 4. If one accepts the notion that sovereignty resides with individuals, then the possibility of legitimate interference on behalf of those sovereign individuals can be argued to override the sovereignty of the state.

Objections to Sovereignty

The idea and consequences of sovereignty have come under increasing assault as the twentieth century evolved toward the twenty-first century. Two broad categories of criticism, however, relate directly to the question of international intervention in the affairs of states and thus have direct relevance to our task of examining the impact of intervention on sovereignty. Both are attacks on the operationalization of the concept.

The first critique is aimed at absolutist conceptions of sovereignty. Critics of this argument maintain that sovereignty in application has never been as absolute as sovereignty in theory. The myth of the impenetrability of states by outside forces, including other states, is no more than a fiction to buttress the principle. States have always interfered in the internal affairs of other states in one way or another. The billiard ball theory is not, in the scientific sense, a theory at all, but instead a false hypothesis.

According to this argument, not only has sovereignty never been as absolute as its champions would assert, but it is becoming increasingly less so. A major reason for this dilution derives from the scientific revolution in telecommunications, which is making national borders entirely more penetrable from the outside, a trend anticipated more than a half century ago by Sir Anthony Eden in a speech before the British House of Commons on November 22, 1954: "Every succeeding scientific discovery makes greater nonsense of old-time conceptions of sovereignty."

Those "old-time" conceptualizations refer, of course, to state-centered, absolutist interpretations of sovereignty. Forces such as the spread of the Internet, economic globalization, the emergence of a homogenized commercial and popular culture around the world, and the desire to embrace the globalized world system all make the factual content of total sovereign control by governments over territory increasingly suspect. One must ask, however, whether this factual dilution of sovereign control extends to the "right" of the international system to infringe on the sovereign ability of the state to treat its citizens in ways that the international community disapproves. Is the spread of popular global culture, for instance, any kind of precedent to assert the rightfulness of forceful interposition by foreign troops into civil strife or to effect domestic change?

The other objection to absolute sovereignty has to do directly with the consequences of a system based in state sovereignty. Once again, a number of assertions are made about the pernicious effects of this form of organization on the operation of the international system. Two of them will be explored here.

The first, and most commonly asserted, objection to state sovereignty is its legitimization and, in some constructs, even glorification of war as a means to settle disputes between states. In a system of sovereign states, after all, there is no authority to enforce international norms on states or to adjudicate or enforce judgments resolving the disputes that arise between them, except to the extent states voluntarily agree to be bound by international norms or, ironically, can be forced to accept international judgments. If states cannot agree amicably on how to settle their differences, then they must rely on their own ability to solve favorably the disagreements they have.

The principle involved is known as *self-help*, the ability to bring about favorable outcomes to differences, often at the expense of the other state. This resolution becomes an exercise in *power* (the ability to get someone to do what he would not otherwise do), and one form of power available to states is military force. In situations that states deem to be of sufficient importance to settle with armed force, war may be the conflict resolution means of choice. In a system of self-help, there is thus no alternative to possessing, and in some instances using, armed force to get your way.

Despite the fact that all member states of the United Nations have renounced the waging of war as a means to resolve conflict (they are not called *wars* anymore), the resort to force is understood and accepted in international practice (with some reservations). A fairly large number of analysts, including many scholars and practitioners of international relations, however, decry this situation, because they abhor war and would like to see it end. Because sovereignty and the legitimate recourse to war are closely related, therefore, they welcome its dilution and replacement as an international principle.

The other, more contemporary, objection to the consequences of sovereignty is the power it gives governments over their people. In an international sense, governments still are, after all, legally "unrestrained" by international norms in dealing with their own populations, except, once again, to the extent that states have voluntarily limited their rights by signing international agreements. Historically, the notion that governments could do horrible things to their citizens was abhorred by many in the international community, but the right to such behavior was unchallenged on the basis of sovereignty. The phrase "Patriotism is the last refuge of a scoundrel," first uttered by the English author Samuel Johnson in 1775, could easily be paraphrased as, in international terms, "sovereignty is the last refuge of a scoundrel."

Whether this is good or bad is debatable. Governments strongly support sovereignty because it preserves the ability to conduct affairs without undue interference from outside. Unfortunately, the greater the protection of internal actions, the greater is the potential for abuse. In those cases in which abuse results in atrocity and human suffering, calls for outside intervention arise as a challenge to that sovereign authority.

The sanctity of this concept of sovereignty began to erode with the global reaction to the reality of the Holocaust that surfaced after World War II. The active revival of this objection came at the end of the Cold War. Scoundrel-like behavior did not, of course, go into hibernation during the Cold War (Pol Pot and the Khmer Rouge in Cambodia guaranteed that), but condemnation—and especially proposing action to combat it—tended to get entangled in Cold War politics. Could, for instance, the United Nations have proposed a peacekeeping mission to Cambodia in 1975 (when the Khmer Rouge seized power and began their slaughter), when the fighting and killing involved two communist factions, each aligned with a different communist superpower (China and the Soviet Union), each of which had a veto in the Security Council? Of course not!

The Assault on Sovereignty Through the United Nations

Since the end of the Cold War, traditional concepts of sovereignty have been increasingly questionable, both intellectually and practically through a series of actions organized by the United Nations. To borrow a term from military tactics, these attacks on sovereignty emanating from actions have not constituted a "frontal assault." None of the actions authorized by the UN Security Council directly challenged the concept of state sovereignty or aligned itself explicitly with a particular interpretation of the concept. Rather, they have been justified under Chapter VII of the UN Charter, which gives the council the authority to determine threats to or breaches of the peace and to authorize responses, including the use of military force.

The assault on sovereignty has thus been conducted indirectly and inductively. It began when the Security Council authorized a peacekeeping force (UNOSM I) to go to Somalia on December 3, 1992. The official reason for the mission was to alleviate human suffering (the threat of massive starvation) due to a five-year-long drought and a civil war, one consequence of which was that international relief efforts to get food to the afflicted were being interrupted by the combating factions. The motivation for the mission was hence humanitarian, to alleviate suffering in what would subsequently be referred to as a major humanitarian disaster.

The United Nations action was a major precedent in at least two ways that were influenced by the unique circumstances in Somalia at the time. First and possibly most important, it was a mission authorized and implemented without any consultation with the government of the country to which it was dispatched. The idea that the United Nations would in effect invade a member state presumably for its own good was a major change of policy for the international community working through the world body.

Circumstances on the ground in Somalia made this an easy course to take. The government of Somalia was not consulted before the intervention because *there was no legal government to consult.* Since the overthrow of Siad Barre the previous year, Somalia had been in a state of anarchy, and the overall objective of the civil war was to install one clan leader or another to form a new government capable of rule. The United Nations could not negotiate with any leader, because intervention in a civil war at the invitation of any party is illegal under international law. The United Nations in effect skirted the issue by invoking Chapter VII of its Charter and using its provisions to determine a breach of the peace had occurred and to take appropriate action to restore the peace. One could argue, although no one did publicly at the time, that the absence of a government meant there was no sovereign territory involved; the issue was officially ignored.

The second precedent was that this was the first occasion when the Security Council interpreted its jurisdiction to include purely humanitarian crises. Without going into the legislative history of the Charter, it is clear that the framers meant for Chapter VII to be invoked primarily in the case of cross-border invasions by states (interstate wars). The Persian Gulf War effort of 1990–1991 was the prototype the framers had in mind. Although the United Nations had (rather unhappily) intervened in a civil war in the former Belgian Congo (later Zaire, now the Democratic Republic of Congo), the decision to engage in humanitarian intervention in a civil war in a country for which the term *failed state* was later coined represented a major change of direction.

The involvement raised the question of what it meant to the overall nature of the international system if the world body could simply ignore the sovereignty of its members. It did so by deed, not by explicit acknowledgement that this was its intent or its effect.

THE ASSAULT ON SOVEREIGNTY OUTSIDE THE UNITED NATIONS: THE IRAQ PRECEDENT

On June 30, 2009, citizens of Iraq celebrated "National Sovereignty Day." The occasion was the formal withdrawal of American combat troops from the Iraqi cities they had occupied since the American conquest and occupation of the country in 2003, an event that had "interrupted" Iraqi sovereignty (the description is provided by Wikipedia). This event was hardly noted in the United States, which of course had provided the interruption of Iraqi sovereignty but did not like to describe the occupation in those terms. Jeremy Scahill, an opponent of the war, terms the occasion a "fake holiday." Yet, the declaration and celebration highlighted both that the American attack violated Iraqi sovereignty and that the Iraqis were (and are) anxious to reassert that status.

The American invasion has been controversial on a number of grounds largely concerned with whether it was necessary or whether it did, or eventually will, accomplish its purposes. Lurking behind these questions, however, is a more fundamental systemic concern: Did the invasion represent an illegal, precedent-setting assault on the very principle of sovereignty of which the United States has been the most ardent defender?

The Bush administration argued the invasion was not illegal, and thus indirectly against any negative precedent on the sovereignty question, on two debatable grounds. One was the principle of preemption, which says that a state can legally attack another whenever it faces an imminent threat that can be thwarted by preemptive action. The other is the authorization to use force under Article VII of the UN Charter. Alleged Iraqi possession and intention to use weapons of mass destruction in support of terrorism formed the justification for preemption. UN Security Council Resolution 1441, which demanded Iraqi compliance with weapons inspections and warned of unspecified consequences (that did not specifically include force) were used to justify Chapter VII. A large portion of the international community denied both claims.

The assault on sovereignty and challenges to international law represented by the American invasion must be placed in their international context. Two factors stand out. The first is the fluidity and change ushered in by the post–Cold War world. While the Cold War was a very dangerous environment because it contained the possibility of general nuclear war, it was also a reasonably orderly system wherein the major powers knew where and when they could and could not intervene in the affairs of third party states based on Cold War impacts such as the prospects for escalation of any contemplated action. This calculation provided a barrier to intervention except within the acknowledged spheres of influence of the superpowers, thereby creating an informal boundary around when and which countries' sovereignty might be breached by outside intervention. This was not much comfort to states within spheres of influence who might suffer intervention (the Dominican Republic or Czechoslovakia, for instance), but it did provide some protection for states outside those spheres. The end of the Cold War removed that barrier and made more states "eligible" for potential actions against them, including actions breaching national sovereignty.

Second, the terrorist attacks of 9/11 created an urgency and intensity that tended to sweep aside the theoretical and legal barriers to action. The "war on terror" (see Chapter 16) was cast as a life-or-death struggle against an opponent that honored no rules of civilized conduct, and the lawlessness and atrocity of the enemy made restrictions based in legal restraints unacceptable and even unmanly. The mentality of the time suggested that if the alternatives were counter-terror measures or less effective measures bounded by conventions, it was the boundaries that would suffer. Extraordinary circumstances justified extraordinary actions.

These factors help to frame the environment in which a decision to invade Iraq that most experts consider to have been illegal and certainly a direct violation of sovereignty could occur. To understand these dynamics, the discussion moves to the intervention response that was so common in the years leading up to the invasion of Iraq and then to the decision itself and its legality and impact on international relations.

The Intervention Response

The pattern of international response to intervention questions beginning in the 1990s has not been uniform. The international community has been willing to act forcefully in places like the Balkans, but not in Africa (Darfur, discussed in Chapter 15, is a particularly poignant example), for instance. Similarly, the major powers heaved a sigh of relief when nearby Australia agreed to provide the bulk of the resources for the International Force in East Timor (INTERFET) in 1999. American intervention was supported in Afghanistan but was far short of universal in Iraq.

When some sort of response is deemed unavoidable, the common mechanism for authorizing an international response has been to take it to the Security Council of the United Nations for a United Nations Security Council Resolution (UNSCR) under Chapter VII. The precedent for this route was Somalia, which in turn was the outgrowth of the successful use of UNSCRs in the Persian Gulf War. The effect, on an ad hoc basis, was to legitimize violations of states' sovereignty. But how?

First, because most of the world's countries are members of the world body, passing a resolution serves as a kind of statement of world opinion, a legitimating action indicating the support of the international community. The second, and more controversial, purpose of the use of UNSCRs is to create a kind of legal basis for intervention in civil wars. Intervention in civil wars violates traditional international law and, especially when done without invitation, is clearly a violation of the sovereignty of the country where the intervention occurs.

The UN Charter, however, does authorize the United Nations to act in the name of peace. Articles 39 and 42 (both part of Chapter VII) create the authority. Article 39 states, "The Security Council shall determine the existence of any threat to the peace, breach of the peace, or act of aggression and shall make recommendations or decide what measures shall be taken . . . to maintain or restore international peace or security." Article 42 makes the military option explicit: "[T]he Security Council . . . may take such action by air, sea or land forces as may be necessary to maintain or restore international peace and security." These provisions appear to refer to *international* rather than internal disputes. Earlier in the Charter, Article 2 (7) makes an ambivalent statement to that effect: "Nothing contained in the present Charter shall authorize the United Nations to intervene in matters which are essentially within the domestic jurisdiction of any state or shall require the members to submit such matters to settlement under the present Charter; but this principle shall not prejudice the application of enforcement measures under Chapter VII." One can use this language to justify intervening in a country's civil strife under two apparent circumstances: if there is a question about whether there is a domestic institution with jurisdiction; or if one determines that whatever is happening within a given country constitutes a threat to or breach of "international peace and security."

Why would the members of the United Nations go through all this trouble to justify interfering in internal matters? At least part of the answer has to be that it is a way to avoid the direct assault on national sovereignty that such actions involve. The UN Charter is quite explicit in its defense of the "territorial integrity or political independence of any state" [Article 2 (4)], or in other words, its sovereignty. The organization cannot directly admit that it is violating sovereignty without violating its own constitution, and its members, by signing the Charter, have also agreed to the sanctity of sovereignty. And yet violating sovereignty is exactly what the members do when they pass UNSCRs favoring intervention in the internal affairs of countries and then dispatch their troops to foreign shores to enforce those decrees. Manipulating the Charter effectively finesses the underlying issue of the violation of sovereignty by making intervention appear to be an expression of international will.

How long can the sovereignty issue effectively be skirted? The answer would appear to be not indefinitely. The reason for this assertion is the length of the missions and the conflicts they produce with native populations, who over time may see UN peacekeeping missions as unwelcome, rather than helpful, intrusions. The same is certainly true in situations like the American occupation of Iraq.

The American Response and the Legality of Invading Iraq

The legitimacy of outside intervention in the affairs of countries has come into question in the United States most dramatically over Iraq. The primary reasons for questioning have been political and practical. The issue has two facets. In the 2000 presidential election campaign, Republican George W. Bush came out strongly against the use of American forces in peacekeeping operations. The reason was practical: These deployments had arguably placed a strain on declining manpower and financial resources that could be devoted to more traditional military priorities. The implication was clear: Such interventions should be strictly limited or avoided in the future. Yet, the new president had been in office for less than nine months before the terrorist attacks of September 11, 2001, opened the window for new interventions—possibly protracted—in Afghanistan and later in Iraq. President Bush even embraced state building in postwar Afghanistan, an idea he had previously rejected for other places like Kosovo.

The original position changed. Questions of Afghan sovereignty were not raised in the deliberations over that intervention, although the administration later made a point of "restoring" Iraqi sovereignty in June 2004. The sovereignty question has never been raised very publicly in discussions of American intervention in Iraq. Does this mean there is a reluctance to open a Pandora's box of problems if the relationship is addressed directly? Is there a fear of raising a question that might produce a negative answer? Or is the question simply unimportant?

In some ways, the invasion of Iraq was simply the culmination of trends inherited from the 1970s. The breakdown of the Cold War had left the United States as the remaining superpower more-or-less unilaterally seeking to create a new world order for an increasingly unruly, contentious body of states. The attacks of 9/11 enraged the United States and most of the rest of the world and reminded everyone the world was still a dangerous place, parts of which required subduing. In that atmosphere, the United States deputized itself to restore order where it deemed it necessary to do so. Then President Bush declared in his 2004 State of the Union address that the protection of U.S. interests overrode all other concerns; indeed, the United States would no longer ask for "permission slips" before it acted.

The invasion of Iraq was the emotional culmination of this process. At the time (and to a large degree since), questions of international legality and sovereignty precedent were hardly raised in a very muted debate about the *policy* wisdom of the action (for a discussion, see Snow, *What After Iraq?*). In retrospect, however, it is possible and prudent to raise questions about the broader implications of the action. Was the invasion legal under international law? What effect does it have on the principle of sovereignty?

The requirements to legalize a military action are specified in the UN Charter, to which all signatory states (including the United States) are obliged to conform. The most basic statement is found in Article 2 (4): "All members shall refrain in their international relations from the threat or use of force against the territorial integrity or political independence of any state." As J. L. Brierly and other legal scholars point out, the exceptions are narrow and specific. The Charter specifies two circumstances in which the use of force is justified, both under Chapter VII: Actions with Respect to Threats to the Peace, Breaches of the Peace, and Acts of Aggression. The first is as part of enforcing a UNSCR authorizing the use of force against a state "to maintain or restore international peace and security." This use of force is included in

Article 42 of the Charter. The other use, specified in Article 51, entails "the inherent right of individual and collective self-defense if an attack occurs."

On their face, neither of these requirements was met before the U.S. invasion. The United States did not have an Article 42 mandate to use armed force on behalf of the United Nations, and it had clearly not been the victim of an armed aggression by Iraq prior to the invasion (indeed, if anyone could clearly justify the use of force under Article 42, it was the Iraqis).

The United States government did attempt a legal defense of its actions under both articles. It invoked UNSCR 1441 from November 8, 2002, which threatened "serious consequences" if Iraq failed "full compliance" with a list of demands centering on UN inspections of Iraqi weapons facilities (looking for weapons of mass destruction, or WMD). Resolution 1441 did not, however, specifically authorize the use of force specified in Article 42, and American and British efforts to obtain such permission failed.

The Bush administration also claimed authority under Article 51. Their device was the so-called Bush Doctrine of *preventive war*, which justifies the use of force when a preemptive attack is planned by an enemy. This is an extension of the legal justification of so-called preemption. Most interpretations argue that preemption is justified only when an attack is imminent; an enemy massing its troops on one's border is an obvious case in point. Jeffrey Record makes this point explicitly: "preemptive attack is justified if it meets Secretary of State Daniel Webster's strict criteria, enunciated in 1837 and still the legal standard, that the threat be 'instant, overwhelming, leaving no choice of means and no moment of deliberation. Preemptive war has legal sanction . . . Preventive war has none . . . This makes preventive war indistinguishable from outright aggression.' "

Almost all analysts—foreign and domestic—outside the Bush administration have concluded the U.S. legal position is questionable at best. UNSCR 1441 does not clearly authorize an Article 42 action (most argue it clearly does not), and the doctrine of preventive war is a statement of U.S. policy, not law. One leading U.S. neoconservative, Richard Perle, admitted the legal deficiency in a backhanded fashion: "I think in this case international law stood in the way of doing the right thing."

Unless one is willing to argue that international law is unjust in a general sense regarding the resort to violence, Perle's comment is enigmatic. Admitting that international law lacks an effective enforcement mechanism for dealing with those who break it, does that mean that whenever law gets in the way of state policy it is permissible to ignore that law? Such a position would be difficult to justify for a country which professes an abiding commitment to the rule of law.

In legal fact, the United States committed an illegal act of aggression against Iraq. Given the tenor and circumstances of the time, one can argue "so what?" as many defenders of the decision in effect have done.

But what of the precedential impact of the invasion? At heart, the U.S. invasion represented a violation of Iraqi sovereignty, and the UN Charter provisions on the legality of intervention are based in the defense of sovereignty, largely at the insistence of one of sovereignty's fiercest defenders, the United States. What does it mean when the world's most ardent supporter of the concept of sovereignty ignores or contravenes that principle?

Whether admitted openly or not, international intrusion into the domestic politics of states, no matter how objectionable or horrific the behavior of states may be, reflects a far different conceptualization of sovereignty than the one that reigned for the first 300 years of the modern state system. Had one asked in 1946 whether it was permissible to mount Operation Restore Hope in Somalia without the permission of the Somali government, the answer would have been overwhelmingly negative. The explanation would have been that such a mission would have been a direct violation of Somalia's sovereignty. The conception of sovereignty reflected in that argument, of course, would have been the traditional definition based in state sovereignty as an absolute and exclusive possession.

The unintended effect of recent interventions like Iraq has been to move the rationale for outside interference into alignment with the conceptualization of sovereignty based in the individual and the limited grant of individual sovereignty to the state. In terms of the meaning of sovereignty, there can be no other rationale for violating state sovereignty other than saying that state sovereignty *is no longer an inviolable principle of international relations.* To make that assertion, in turn, it is necessary to locate sovereignty somewhere else, such as in individuals and groups whose rights are being violated and to whose rescue international efforts are directed to support higher international values like the eradication of terror. The alternative, ironically, is to admit that violations of sovereignty such as the invasion of Iraq are illegal. In that case, the United States was a law breaker, but the principle of sovereignty of which it is a staunch defender is left relatively intact.

No state makes the justification of their participation in United Nations or other peacekeeping activities or for Iraq-style interventions in these terms. Why not? The answer is simple and straightforward: No state is willing to admit to the dilution of the concept of state sovereignty because to do so concedes its own sovereignty is potentially diminished in the process; sovereignty is too much a bedrock of national jurisdiction to make such an admission. And no state will admit that its ability to control what occurs within its territory may not be absolute but may, in fact, be subject to internationally imposed limits. Nowhere is that sentiment held more fiercely than in the United States.

The idea that no outside force should have the ability to interfere in internal American affairs can be dated back certainly to the Revolutionary period and the very negative view of governmental power held by most supporters of the American Revolution, and it remains an untouchable first principle that, if suggestions of its possible breach are raised, brings howls of protest. The result is schizophrenic but long-standing. The United States asserts the absolute nature of American national sovereignty, but has for a long time been willing in effect to ignore the sovereignty of others when it served American purposes. The numerous U.S. interventions in Central America and the Caribbean in the nineteenth and early twentieth centuries were nothing more than gross violations of the sovereignty of countries like Nicaragua, Panama, and Haiti. In some ways, the United States was simply acting as a large power in its "domain," the Western Hemisphere. Its profession of principles about sovereignty and its actions were, however, hardly consistent with one another.

The United States, of course, is not alone in this hypocrisy. The Russians (as Soviets), after all, invaded and occupied Afghanistan during the 1980s, a clear violation of Afghan sovereignty, and then turned around during the 1990s and used the absolutist rationale for sovereignty to argue that it was nobody's business but their own how they dealt with the uprising in Chechnya while simultaneously concurring in UNSCRs that violated the sovereignty of several other countries.

The unfolding two-stage U.S. withdrawal from Iraq has reignited the question of whether the Americans had any legal right to be there in the first place. Implementation of the Status of Forces Agreement (SOFA) --technically, the "Agreement between the United States and the Republic of Iraq on the Withdrawal of United States Force from Iraq and to the Organization of Their Activities during Their Temporary Presence in Iraq," according to the International Institute for Strategic Studies-- caused the Iraqis to declare National Sovereignty Day, a reminder that the Iraqis find the question lively and relevant.

The second stage of the withdrawal, which calls for the removal of all U.S. forces from Iraq by the end of 2011, is underway as a means to complete the process of restoring Iraqi sovereignty rhetorically begun in 2004 (when the restoration was declared but occupation continued). Because that process is ongoing, "the new Iraq is only now emerging as a sovereign international actor," according to Parker. The details (even the timing) of the final withdrawal remain contentious but are largely defined in sovereignty terms by the Iraqis. As Yaphe puts it, "It is popular to bash America and to insist on Iraq's rights as a sovereign nation-state." As negotiations on final terms move forward, Yaphe adds, "No Iraqi political leader, cleric, or tribal sheikh can afford to be seen as capitulating to American demands trading away Iraqi sovereignty."

The United States is on thin conceptual ice if it tries to resist Iraqi demands based on its sovereignty. By invading that country, the United States simply ignored that it was ignoring a principle that it holds dear when applied to interfering with the United States. Doing this is not unique to the United States. Power often trumps principle in these situations: The powerful do what they can, and the weak endure what they must, to paraphrase the old saw. The United States forced Iraq to endure what it could not avoid.

CONCLUSION

The United States may decide to forego future interventions on pragmatic bases such as interests or costs, thereby making the erosive effect of such actions on sovereignty a moot point. The general international trend toward asserting the legitimacy of human rights and the need to punish terrorists and others who threaten American interests and the international order (by no means always the same thing), however, makes abstinence on these grounds unlikely. The alternate justification for abstinence is based in its effects on sovereignty and in violations of international legal obligations based in sovereignty. If international interference in the often chaotic affairs of states occurs, eventually the question of the impact on sovereignty will have to be confronted directly and decisions made by the international community as to how much of the principle of state sovereignty it is willing to jettison in the name of humanity. The outcome is yet to be determined.

STUDY/DISCUSSION QUESTIONS

1. What is sovereignty? How is the question of the American war against Iraq a sovereignty question? Explain.
2. With which conception of sovereignty do you agree? Are, in other words, the rights of states more important than the rights of individuals and groups within states? How would the international system be different without the supremacy of state sovereignty?
3. Does American participation in military operations in countries torn by civil war or allegedly involved in terrorism violate American principles, such as our position on sovereignty? Or should the question of our participation be made on pragmatic grounds rather than on principles? If you were in a position to do so, how would you advise President Obama when the next intervention is proposed at the United Nations or elsewhere?
4. Under the UN Charter, when is it permissible to interfere in the sovereign affairs of states? Did the United States seek to invoke these conditions to justify the invasion of Iraq? How? Did the arguments succeed?
5. The American withdrawal process from Iraq has reentered the sovereignty question into the situation. In terms of the two-step withdrawal process, how has sovereignty been worked back into the discussion? Elaborate.
6. Based on the Iraq precedent, should questions of violating sovereignty be important concerns for the United States in contemplating other possible interventions? Is it hypocritical to defend U.S. sovereignty but to ignore the sovereignty of others? Can this apparent contradiction be reconciled? How important is it to do so?

READING/RESEARCH MATERIAL

Bodin, Jean. *Six Books on the Commonwealth*. Oxford, UK: Basil Blackwell, 1955.

Brierly, J. L. *The Law of Nations*. 6th ed. New York: Oxford University Press, 1963.

Burkeman, Oliver and Julian Borger. "War Critics Astonished as US War Hawk Admits Invasion Was Illegal." *The Guardian* (online), November 20, 2003. (http://www.guardian.co.uk/uk/2003/nov/20/usa.iraq/print)

Cusimano, Mary Ann, ed. *Beyond Sovereignty*. Bedford, MA: Bedford St. Martin's, 1999.

Grotius, Hugo. *The Rights of War and Peace: Including the Law of Nature and Nations*. New York: M. W. Dunne, 1981.

Hashami, Sohail H, ed. *State Sovereignty and Persistence in International Relations*. University Park, PA: Pennsylvania State University Press, 1997.

Hobbes, Thomas. *Leviathan*. Oxford, UK: Clarendon, 1989.

International Institute for Strategic Studies. "Reconciling Iraqi Sovereignty." *Strategic Comments* (online) 15, 10, December 2009.

Kantor, Arnold and Linton F. Brooks, eds. *U.S. Intervention Policy for the Post–Cold War World.* New York: The American Assembly, 1994.

Lewis, Charles and Mark Reading-Smith. "False Pretenses: Iraq: The War Card." Washington, DC: Center for Public Integrity, 2008.

Locke, John. *Two Treatises on Government.* New York: Cambridge University Press, 1988.

Lyons, Gene M. and Michael Mastanduno, eds. *Beyond Westphalia: State Sovereignty and International Relations.* Baltimore, MD: Johns Hopkins University Press, 1995.

Parker, Sam. "Is Iraq Back?" *Current History* 108, 722 (December 2009), 429–431.

Record, Jeffrey. *Dark Victory: America's Second War against Iraq.* Annapolis, MD: Naval Institute Press, 2004.

Rousseau, Jean-Jacques. *The Collected Works of Jean-Jacque Rousseau.* Hanover, NH: University Press of New England, 1990.

Scahill, Jeremy. "Iraq's 'National Sovereignty Day' Is U.S.-Style Trademark Hype." *Huffington Post* (online), June 30, 2009.

Snow, Donald M. *What after Iraq?* New York: Longman, 2009.

———. *When America Fights: The Uses of U.S. Military Force.* Washington, DC: CQ Press, 2000.

——— and Eugene Brown. *International Relations: The Changing Contours of Power.* New York: Longman, 2000.

Steinberg, James B. "Real Leaders Do Soft Power: Learning the Lessons of Iraq." *Washington Quarterly* 31, 2 (Spring 2008), 155–164.

Yaphe, Judith S. "Iraq: Are We There Yet?" *Current History* 107, 713 (December 2008), 403–409.

Resource Scarcity: Oil, the Lubricant That Corrodes

PRÉCIS

The desire, even necessity, to control scarce natural resources, and conflict over those resources, are as old as human history and have acted as a major source of conflict in the international order through time. Major wars have been fought over access to precious gems, metals, food, and exotic spices, to name a few examples. In the contemporary world, the most well-publicized resource conflict has been over access to the oil reserves of the Persian Gulf region. The conflict over petroleum, the lubricant that corrodes, is a continuing source of conflict and disorder.

This case examines the general parameters of the problem as it appears early in the twenty-first century, when the primary resources competitions center on access to adequate supplies of petroleum. The problem of petroleum scarcity is likely to remain ubiquitous for the near and medium futures. As the world approaches peak oil capacity, demand continues to grow and will do so until the transition to alternate energy sources reduces demand for oil. As the dynamics of petroleum scarcity continue to provide a challenge to international cooperation, international conflicts and competitions over sources of oil in places like the Caspian Sea and Iraq will remain major subjects of international concern.

Conflict and war over the ability to control, monopolize, or deny access to valued resources is as old as recorded human history. Men have fought and died, armies have swept across countless expanses, and empires and states have risen and fallen in the name of precious resources. Whether it was control of the silk route across Asia or the exotic foodstuffs of the Spice Islands, the diamonds and gold of southern and central Africa,

El Dorado in the new world, or the petroleum wealth of the Middle East, the struggle for natural, scarce, and valuable resources has been a recurrent theme of human history and the relations between individuals and groups.

How will this historic theme be enacted in the early twenty-first century? What is striking is that the resources over which there is the most competition are also among the most basic resources for the human condition. At the head of the list is water (more specifically, potable water). With 70 percent of the earth's surface covered in water, water per se is hardly a scarce resource, but water that is usable for human purposes (drinking, bathing, agriculture, etc.) is in shortage selectively in the world, and as global population grows, those shortages will likely spread. The other scarce resource and the one to which this chapter is devoted is petroleum, which has become the world's most basic source of energy. Whether there is indeed a global shortage of oil is debatable, but petroleum that is easily available for consumption (energy production) is currently close to the point of scarcity.

As has always been the case, resource scarcities are politically important, because political decisions, domestically and internationally, help define scarcities and responses to them. Where resources are in short supply, the political, including geopolitical, competition between those who have adequate or surplus supplies and those who do not can become acrimonious and the source of conflict among the haves and the have-nots. The worldwide demand for petroleum is growing and will likely continue to do so despite the search for alternate energy sources. As long as demand is increasing and those who can supply those demands can exercise some level of control over how much of the resource is made available to whom, there will be continued controversy when the possessors attempt to maximize the leverage their possession provides and those who desire the resource attempt to find ways to ensure that they (if not necessarily others) receive all they need.

When a situation of resource scarcity exists among those—in this case countries of the world—that want or need that resource, there are four possible means of allocating the resource. First, some method can be found to increase supply so that all claimants can have all the resource they need or want, scarcity disappears and so does the basis of conflict. The problem with this solution is that increasing supply usually results in lower prices, a situation that is unattractive to producers selling the resource. If their narrow (normally nationally defined) interests prevail, they will prefer scarcity of supply, since that condition drives prices up.

If existing suppliers are reluctant to make more supply available, how can supplies be made more plentiful? Finding new sources of petroleum, for instance, is the most obvious way to increase supplies, but it faces two difficulties. One is that easily (i.e., cheaply) available supplies are increasingly difficult to find and exploit, and the trend will be toward more difficult and expensive sources as time goes by. Next, although no one knows exactly how much untapped petroleum exists below the earth's surface, most estimates are that peak oil, the point at which half of the nonrenewable resource has been used up, has been or soon will be reached, meaning diminished and shrinking supplies in the future.

The second, and opposite, approach is to decrease demand for a resource so that the equipoise between availability and usage is reestablished at a lower level of consumption. In the case of oil, however, this solution is bedeviled by the fact that demand is actually growing worldwide at the same time supply is leveling off or declining. In July 2008, for instance, the U.S. market was hit by a double challenge. Indian automaker Tata announced it would begin production of the new Nano automobile (see Chapter 11), with the aim of providing "millions" of Indians with access to personal transportation powered by gasoline. At the same time, PEMEX, the Mexican state-owned petroleum company, announced reductions in the amount of crude oil it could make available to American gasoline company Valero because of depletion of Mexican oil fields. Demand increases, supply declines.

The third option is substitution. The most important current uses of petroleum energy are for power generation and transportation, and the question is whether alternatives to petroleum can be found and commercialized to lessen dependence on burning petroleum. Some of the alternatives become attractive because they substitute other physical means of energy generation for the carbon dioxide–generating byproduct of petroleum refinement. In the area of energy production, substitute means include nuclear power generation and alternative technologies such as wind and solar power, but each raises questions: storage and disposal of radioactive by-products from nuclear reactors and the adequacy of power generated by windmills or solar panels, for instance. Transportation substitutes include alternate propulsion hybrids (e.g., ethanol and biodiesel) or even non–petroleum-based forms of propulsion (e.g., hydrogen fuel or electricity), but these do not provide instant solutions and are themselves controversial. Is there, for instance, a net energy consumption gain or loss of propelling automobiles with gasoline or through energy expended to produce electricity for that propulsion? A number of technologies are likely to contribute to the transition from the dominance of petroleum as an energy source to some future solution, but their immediate adequacy is uncertain.

If the other three options fail, then a power struggle remains, pitting the suppliers against the consumers over how much petroleum will be available at what price: the summer 2008 spike in oil prices offered a harbinger of just how ugly that competition can be. It may also, however, pit consumers against one another in terms of access to particular sources of supply. At this level, international relations over petroleum could be at their most corrosive, as states scramble into complex political situations to try to secure their access to petroleum reserves at one another's expense. If peak oil is passed before substitution reduces demand substantially (a likely outcome), the prospects for violent resolution of conflicts will increase as well.

The epicenter of the petroleum scarcity conflict is, unsurprisingly, in the Middle East. Part of the reason is because petroleum is inextricably tied to the region, meaning that world access to the amounts of petroleum that countries need is, to some extent, tied to the vicissitudes of Middle Eastern politics (e.g., the current situation in Iraq). Increased demand for petroleum has already made the oil market much more competitive and resulted in increased leverage and influence for petroleum exporters, a situation unlikely to improve in the near term, since all of the supply-side alternatives that will produce more forms of energy are some years from coming on line.

In a recent *Current History* article, David L. Goldwyn summarizes the situation: "Energy insecurity is greater today than it has been in nearly 30 years. The global oil market is more fragile, more competitive, and more volatile. The global demand for oil is strong, powered by global economic growth, especially in China and the rest of developing Asia. Global supply has been restrained."

The structure of the contemporary petroleum problem is changing. According to 2006 figures, oil production was at approximately 85 million barrels a day, whereas consumption hovered around 83 million barrels per day (one can marginally quibble with the exact numbers, but the basic dynamic holds). This means the oil market is extremely "tight," in the sense that a relatively small increase in demand or decrease in supply could make oil a scarce commodity in supply/demand terms. As Leonardo Maugeri points out, this situation is the result of a 20-year trend: "Between 1986 and 2005, the world's spare oil production (the amount produced beyond current demand) dropped from about 15 percent to between 2 and 3 percent of global demand." That margin is shrinking: the two million barrels per day of "spare" production reported in 2006 may already be a deficit. Figures from the International Energy Agency, for instance, showed a projected *deficit* of production of about 1.4 million barrels a day (mb/d) for early 2010 (demand of 87.2 mb/d and supplies at 85.7 mb/d).

There are two major dynamics that affect this tight—and increasingly tightening—market and produce notable problems. The first is that the situation is bound to get worse. The reason, Daniel Yergin argues in a 2006 *Foreign Affairs* article, is that "the last decade has witnessed a significant increase in the world's demand for oil, primarily because of the dramatic increase in developing countries, in particular China and India." Both countries are net oil importers. According to figures provided by Infoplease for 2004, China produces about 3.62 million barrels a day and consumes 6.5 million barrels; about 45 percent of its total is thus imported. According to David Zweig and Bi Jianhai, in 2004 China "accounted for 31 percent of global growth in oil demand," and this figure is likely to continue to grow, although the impact of that growth is a matter of disagreement. (Maugeri, for instance, maintains "even sustained Chinese consumption growth would have only marginal effects on an otherwise normal global petroleum market.") China is currently the world's third-largest importer of petroleum, and this situation is likely to get worse rather than better in the future. India reflects this same trend on a smaller scale. Though Indian oil production is expected to increase to about 3 million barrels a day by 2010, there is a current gap of nearly 1.5 million barrels a day that India must import, a problem Indian growth can only make more acute.

In addition to increased demand, there is the leverage that oil producers realize they can exercise because of the tightness of the oil market. In 2004 figures, 14 countries produced 2 million barrels or more a day, meaning if any one of them suspended production of that amount for a sustained period of time, the effects could be profound, because, as Thomas L. Friedman points out, the more prices rise and the possibilities of manipulation of supply exists, "the less petrolists are sensitive to what the world thinks or says about them." He defines petrolist states as "states that are both dependent on oil production for the bulk of their exports and have weak state institutions or outright authoritarian governments." Azerbaijan, the major subject of the oil mini-case, and Iran are among the states he cites as examples of this phenomenon.

These introductory remarks help frame the question of petroleum scarcity as a global source of conflict and as a policy problem for most world states, including the United States. The discussion will begin by examining the current and predicted situations surrounding global oil and its place in possible global futures. As the world rapidly moves beyond peak oil production to a future of increasing demands and dwindling supplies, the alternative solutions to the petroleum crisis will be examined. One outcome is that the global competition for remaining supplies will likely intensify, corroding and making more conflicting the relations between the contenders for these resources. Two situations, the oil reserves of the Caspian Sea littoral—notably Azerbaijan—and the oil reserves of Iraq, will be highlighted as the case examples of the corrosive effects of petroleum.

THE PROBLEM OF PETROLEUM SCARCITY

The importance of petroleum derives from the centrality of its usage to modern society, including the worldwide trend toward globalization. Some scarcities, obviously enough, are more important than others. A shortage of cinnamon, for instance, would be distressing to the many people who regularly use it as a spice, but a sharp rise in price or reduction in supply would not be catastrophic: people would simply decrease their consumption without life-changing or life-threatening consequences.

Oil is different. Since oil overtook the burning of wood as the primary worldwide means of energy generation early in the twentieth century, world dependence on it has gradually increased to the point of almost total dependence for such basic needs as power provision and transportation. The resource struggle over petroleum is, from this vantage point, largely a struggle over managing the transition from petroleum as the world's primary energy source to alternate sources that assume the vital roles oil plays in contemporary world societies. The magnitude of this impact can be seen by viewing the problem from a series of perspectives.

The Importance and Value of Oil

Petroleum is a unique commodity with multiple uses. Current concerns center on its value as an energy source through burning it and converting it to energy.

Petroleum-based energy, energy from natural gas in its various states (liquid and gaseous), and coal, are the major fossil fuels burned to produce energy worldwide, and the three fuels are the major contributors to global warming, thus making a reduction in their usage desirable from an ecological standpoint. Petroleum is, however, so central to global energy use that a precipitous decline would have catastrophic economic and life-sustaining consequences.

Worldwide dependence on petroleum-based energy is not accidental. At the end of World War II, the international community was faced with the replacement of energy sources and generation facilities destroyed or crippled during the war. The problem was especially acute in Europe and Asia (notably Japan). The conscious solution was to rebuild the energy systems based on petroleum as the primary energy source. The premises of this decision included the abundant availability of petroleum at a low, controllable price, since most oil production was controlled by Western oil companies (the so-called "seven sisters"). Cheap, abundant supplies led to the conversion of energy systems to oil. In 1945, these assumptions were realistic, but they no longer are.

Both assumptions are now questionable. Petroleum that can be extracted in great quantities at minimal costs is rapidly disappearing, and those supplies are no longer controlled by oil companies that can manipulate the prices of oil. Instead, a major consequence of the forming of the Organization of Petroleum Exporting Countries (OPEC) has been the nationalization of oil assets by producing countries. According to Kurlantzik, national oil companies now control nearly four-fifths of the oil produced and Western companies control about one-tenth. These changes affect both availability (supply) and price. They also mean that the competition for petroleum has become state-centered, with buyers forced to deal with the governments of producing states, which can broker the competition for their scarce resource. These governments, mindful that their supplies are exhaustible, are also motivated to maximize the revenue they receive for their oil.

As already noted, petroleum is vital as a source of energy for economic activity and transportation. The single most important international indicator of economic (especially industrial) activity is energy consumption, meaning that the use of energy and economic vitality are inextricably intertwined. In turn, this means the well-being and prosperity of people in all countries are tied to how much energy they produce and consume and, to the extent energy production is tied to petroleum, to access to petroleum. Similarly, since most transport is based in petroleum sources, the world's transportation systems— by land, air, and sea—are also dependent on petroleum energy.

The uses of petroleum go well beyond its use as an energy source, including more economically valuable uses. Petroleum is, after all, the basic commodity used in the petrochemical industry, from which a wide variety of products, most prominently those made of plastic, are derived. The Shah of Iran, as quoted by Fleischman, once elaborated on this basic fact shortly before his overthrow. "There is a limited amount of petroleum in the earth. Oil is used for making plastics and other products." Many of these products are more valuable than produced energy. Based on this calculation, Reza Pahlevi concluded, "Oil is too valuable to burn. When we run out, what will we do? Fight each other for the last drop?"

Oil and Energy Cycles

Oil is the second source of energy to dominate human consumptive usage. For all of human history prior to the discovery of oil and its application to energy, wood was the dominant source. With the commercial exploitation of oil, it became the energy source of choice for most of the twentieth and into the twenty-first century. For most of this period, the popular underlying assumption was that petroleum would remain abundant more or less indefinitely, even though it was a nonrenewable resource.

Scientists have known now for some time that oil will eventually be depleted. As Hirsch pointed out in a 2007 U.S. Department of Energy study, "For decades, the world has consumed increasingly more oil than it has been finding. Because oil is a depleting natural resource, world oil production will reach a maximum, called the 'peak,' after which production will go into decline." The exact point at which the peak will be reached is the subject of controversy: a substantial number of scientists believe that the peak has been reached or is nearby, while a few others believe it will occur sometime in the future. At any rate, there is no doubt that such a peak will be achieved, and once it is, the availability of petroleum will gradually decline.

Controversy about the achievement of the peak and its consequences is largely based on two uncertain calculations. One is the amount of petroleum left to be discovered: current estimates top out around 1.3 trillion barrels of untapped discovered oil, and there is undoubtedly more. Hirsch argues that projections are marred by three uncertainties: proprietary interests of oil companies in keeping secret the amount of oil they do or want to control; state secrets in the major oil-exporting countries; and politically or economically biased estimates. All contribute to uncertainty and thus are the basis for disagreement about the future. The second calculation is the rate of exploitation and depletion of oil still in the ground. Extrapolations into the future require estimating the demands that worldwide consumers will make; obviously, the greater the demands, the shorter the period of time before the world approaches the total depletion of whatever reserves remain. Short-term estimates of demand and usage are generally unfavorable, given the increased demands of countries like China and India, as noted earlier. Generally speaking, more optimistic estimates emphasize the likelihood of larger undiscovered sources and/or reduced consumption rates than do more pessimistic projections.

The notion and proximity of peak oil production serves as a reminder that the petroleum-dominated energy cycle will not last indefinitely. Once peak oil production has been achieved and passed (if it has not already), the downward side of the normal curve will mean that production will gradually decrease as supplies dwindle and reduced discoveries of new sources fails to keep up with current consumption. While scientists may disagree on exactly *when* and *at what rate* this decline will occur, no one seriously doubts that it *will* occur.

Energy cycles are generally depicted as overlapping, normal bell curves. As the downward side of wood usage progressed, for instance, the upward side of the bell curve of petroleum usage increased. While these phenomena occur, the world is in a process of energy transition from primary reliance on one source of energy to another. The transition from wood to petroleum was a relatively orderly process because oil was generally recognized as the rising dominant fuel. The problem is different now, because there is no agreed successor source. Some scientists believe that the ultimate solution will be nuclear fusion, the physical process by which the sun produces energy. If harnessed, fusion-based energy would be virtually inexhaustible, since it involves the fusing together of heavy hydrogen atoms found in abundance in sea water. Methods for harnessing this energy source are unavailable for the foreseeable future. In the interim, alternatives like wind, solar, and nuclear fission are available, but none of them likely has the potential, individually or in combination, to replace petroleum.

The Petroleum Outlook

The prognosis regarding petroleum scarcity is bleak. World demand increases as more states demand more of it, and their voracity can cancel out the attempt to reduce worldwide demand through conservation. At the same time, production will decline as ready, economically viable sources are depleted. Remaining reserves, as well, will likely be concentrated in certain geographical areas, adding a geopolitical element to the equation.

The location of the remaining petroleum becomes more important as it becomes a progressively scarcer commodity. At the point where petroleum demand exceeds supply, two things will likely happen. One, already experienced in 2008, is that the price of remaining petroleum will rise, perhaps greatly. The other is that some claimants to that supply will be denied a portion of the petroleum they desire, an unacceptable outcome that states will go to great lengths to prevent. At best, countries will unite to reduce demand so that possible shortages during the energy transition will be minimized. At worst, there will be more or less open competition for those supplies with geopolitical implications.

Using figures from the *Oil and Gas Journal* published in *The 2010 World Almanac and Book of Facts,* known reserves as estimated in January 2006 are being displayed. The exact figures should not be considered sacrosanct but merely an indication. By geographic area, they are depicted in Table 2.1

Some of these figures should not be surprising. Over half the world's known oil reserves are in the Middle East, which also contains four of the five countries with the largest reserves (Saudi Arabia, Iran, Iraq, and Kuwait, in that order), but, as the Hirsch study points out, this probably represents most of the total Middle Eastern oil (discovered and undiscovered), since the discovery of new oil in the region has been far below production since the 1960s. The

| TABLE 2.1 |

World Oil Reserves, January 2006

Region	Reserves (in billions of barrels)	Percent of World Total
North American	213	16
Central, South America	103	8
Europe	16	1
Middle East	739	56
Eurasia	99	7
Africa	114	9
Asia and Oceania	33	3

only country to break into the top five with these countries is Canada, which ranks second in the world according to these figures. The Canadian case, however, also points to the fragility of the numbers, since 174 billion barrels of Canada's estimated 178.8 billion barrels is in the form of oil variant in oil sands, the extraction of which is more expensive than that of conventional oil (the same is true for the large shale oil deposits in the American West, notably the oil shale cliffs around Rifle, Colorado).

These figures also do not suggest either the extent or location of undiscovered oil, much of which may lie either beneath the world's oceans and seas or under the North or South poles. If there are vast, or even significant, reserves waiting to be found, their discovery will prolong the transition period and allow for a more orderly movement away from petroleum energy either toward the interim technologies or the long-term solution, fusion. These discoveries will not cancel the transition, but merely delay when the world runs out of oil or reaches the point where it no longer wants to use what petroleum remains for purposes more productive than burning. The current problem, as American billionaire oilman T. Ross Pickens puts it, is not one "we can drill ourselves out of."

Petroleum and Politics: The Lubricant that Corrodes

The growing scarcity of petroleum has major political implications, some of which are already evident in the contemporary environment. It affects the rate and direction of globalization, which is both an economic and political phenomenon. It reinforces the emergence and existence of so-called "petrolist" regimes in countries that are large petroleum producers. Finally, the search for reliable, secure sources of petroleum to cushion the energy transition will cause countries and groups within countries to engage in increasingly conflicting behaviors, including the use of violence.

Petroleum Scarcity and Globalization. One of the less recognized elements of the comparative advantage that undergirds free trade and thus the movement toward economic globalization is transportation of goods and services from sources of production to consumer markets. Whatever it costs to move a good or service to a market is, in other words, part of the value of that good, and to the degree that transportation adds to the cost of an otherwise cheaper product, it erodes the comparative advantage an imported good may have over a domestic equivalent. When transportation adds so much burden to a foreign good that it costs consumers as much or more than the domestically produced equivalent, then comparative advantage is lost altogether. According to Rohter, transportation costs, in other words, serve as an effective, if not an official, barrier to trade and thus to the expansion of globalization across international borders, a factor already being felt today.

The petroleum crisis of summer 2008 provided what may become a harbinger of this phenomenon in action. In the globalizing economy, the transportation methods most affected by rising costs in fuel are air and sea shipment and travel. The rise in oil prices to nearly $150 a barrel caused the cost of aviation fuel to rise and resulted in a variety of rate increases and surcharges among the world's airline companies; their net effect was to make it more expensive to fly, and this suppressed the number of people taking commercial aircraft journeys. Since the free movement of people (and their expertise) across boundaries is a pivotal aspect of globalization, the effect of reduced airline travel on the globalizing economic process, while not yet directly measurable, cannot be nonexistent.

The more dramatic impacts are on the transport of goods. Domestically within the United States, the brunt of rising gasoline prices was felt directly in the costs of goods shipped primarily by surface trucking, notably perishable foods, but also products found generally on store shelves. Internationally, the added costs of shipping across the major oceans of the world added enough to the price of goods and services in trade to create at least a temporary slowing of "outsourcing" and reliance on foreign goods and services.

It is too early to tell how much of a longer-term impact rising petroleum prices will have on globalization, but two observations are almost certainly true. One is that increasing demand and decreasing supply will continue to push petroleum energy prices generally upward, thus adding to transportation costs and reducing comparative advantage for goods and services moved internationally. This impact will be especially true of transport by sea and air, since, compared to ground systems, there are relatively fewer efforts currently underway to free shipping from petroleum sources of propulsion. The second is that these distortions of free trade (through increased added costs) will have some deflating effect on globalization. Clearly, short-term fluctuations in oil prices will accentuate or dampen these effects on a day-to-day basis, but there is every reason to believe the trend will be toward increasing prices, and the question is not if, but how much, difference that will make.

Domestic Effects: the Petrolists. As world petroleum markets tighten, those who control large amounts of petroleum will have an advantageous position in setting the terms for its extraction—including price and levels of flow. One result is the rise of so-called "petrolist" regimes like Russia and Venezuela, whose governments effectively bribe their populations into accepting less than democratic rule by providing economic benefits based on petroleum revenues. Oil wealth and political openness and democracy do not, as Friedman observed and Kurlantzik confirms when defining petrolism, necessarily coincide.

Using the same data already alluded to regarding oil reserves globally, this relationship becomes obvious. The 12 countries with the largest known oil reserves as of January 2006 are (with known reserves in billions of barrels in parentheses): Saudi Arabia (266.8), Canada (174.8), Iran (132.5), Iraq (115), Kuwait (104), United Arab Emirates (97.8), Venezuela (79.8), Russia (60), Libya (39.8), Nigeria (35.9), the United States (21.8), and China (18.3). These figures fluctuate marginally from year to year based on revisions of estimates, but basically they have held across time. Of these 12 states, only 2 are totally democratic countries (Canada and the United States), while all the others rank in Freedom House figures as either partially free or not free. In most of the countries that are less than free, economic benefits have been used to prop up regimes that are unpopular or whose popularity is based on dispensing petroleum-derived benefits.

This dynamic will not necessarily change greatly as the effects of petroleum scarcity grow. In a few places, like Russia (now the world's second largest exporter), where current exploitation is already driving down reserves and suggesting the need to reduce flow, the trend could be reversed somewhat. At the same time, in the five Middle Eastern countries that stand with Canada at the top of the list, the rates of discovery of new oil are very low. As the Hirsch study states: "Nowhere has the fall in oil discoveries been more dramatic than in the Middle East, where they plunged from 187 billion barrels in 1963–1972 to 16 billion barrels during the decade ending in 2002." If it is true that a great deal of the remaining oil to be found is beneath oceanic continental shelves and under polar ice masses, those countries contiguous to the poles (and with the strongest claims to sovereignty over or prime access to the poles or the shelves) are likely to be at some advantage in the future.

Geopolitical Struggle and Conflict. As supply and demand for petroleum approach equipoise, countries will increasingly try to calculate ways to bolster their own petroleum security by trying to control access to promising sources, even if their attempts come into conflict with the interests of others. Creating a cushion of guaranteed energy availability could become particularly critical if a precipitous downward momentum follows the crest of peak oil production before or during the transition to alternate energy sources. As the competition for remaining sources becomes more intense, behavior will become more cutthroat, and one way to hedge one's bets on the future is to try to control sources wherever possible. In this situation, the goal of states will be *energy security*—"access to energy sources that are reliable and reasonably affordable," in Roberts' terms.

There is nothing new about petroleum as the source of conflict, even violent conflict. A major concern of both the Allies and Axis during World War II was the control of Middle Eastern oil fields, and the ability of the Allies to deprive the Germans of this fuel source was a pivotal element in the defeat of the Axis in Europe; the Axis countries all but ran out of fuel for war machines requiring POL (petroleum, oil, and lubricants). In the mid-1960s, one of the wars on the Asian subcontinent between India and Pakistan was largely ignited when there was *suspicion* (which proved false) that there might be oil under an otherwise useless but contested piece of ground known as the Rann of Kutch.

Geopolitical competition for oil sources continues to this day, and as the petroleum "crunch" gets worse, it could accelerate and intensify. New players like China and India are now participants in the competition, joining more traditional Western consumers of petroleum. Depending on where new sources of oil are found (and how much of it there is in various locations), this competition could become quite intense and largely determine international conflict in the future.

With no particular claim of being representative, the study turns to a thumbnail sketch of two possible examples of resource scarcity contretemps in the future. One, which is controversial, is the question of access to Iraqi oil resources (the fourth largest in the world) and the relationship of that access to the causation and outcome of the Iraq War. The other, of somewhat longer standing, is the competition for the oil reserves of the Caspian Sea littoral, especially Azerbaijan.

PETROLEUM SCARCITY AND CONFLICT

As petroleum becomes scarcer, leverage and power will naturally increase for those who have control over it. This would not be a major problem if those who consumed the oil were also those who produced it, but that is not the case. With the exception of the vast oil tar sands of Canada, the exploitation of which is difficult and expensive, most of the world's known oil is in remote locations where political conditions are not always favorable to the consumers. The Middle East is an ongoing testament to the difficulties that exist when those who have and those who want a resource are not entirely aligned with one another politically or otherwise.

These problems will get worse in the future, unless major new sources of oil are found within the sovereign confines of the major consuming countries (under the continental shelves off the east and west coasts of the continental United States or Alaska, for instance) that increase global supply, or there is a dramatic reduction in consumption and thus demand. Since such possibilities are abstract and available as solutions sometime in the future (if at all), the quest for oil security must center on control or secure access to known oil sources.

Iraq and the Caspian Sea oil fields offer two contemporary examples of how that competition could work out. Iraq has some of the largest untapped sources of oil in the world, and control of it is a considerable geopolitical prize. Because of its importance, access or control of Iraqi oil has been suggested by some observers (including Iraqis) as the real reason for the U.S.

invasion and conquest of that country. Not far to the east of Iraq, a spirited geopolitical competition has been ongoing since the 1990s for control over the production and transport of oil from the Caspian Sea oil fields to world markets—a competition that has focused on Azerbaijan.

Iraqi Oil

Most recent discourse about the Iraq War in the United States has centered on determining when conditions are appropriate for an American troop withdrawal from that country. This analytical process accelerated during the 2008 American presidential campaign, which included strong suggestions from the government in Baghdad that it would like to see those withdrawals begin sooner rather than later. The Status of Force Agreement (SOFA) approved by both countries in December 2008 requires that American forces be removed from Iraq by the end of 2011. Whether or what kinds of American presence there will be after 2011 remains unclear.

Buoyed by the apparent success in the reduction of violence and casualties of the 2007 American "surge" in Iraq (for which the surge may or may not have been responsible), the "end game" process has diverted attention from the question of whether the United States should have been in Iraq in the first place. The original reasons given for the invasion—the existence of weapons of mass destruction and ties to terrorists (see Snow, *What After Iraq?*)—have proven either false or incapable of being demonstrated. Subsequent arguments—most recently to deter Iranian adventurism—have not enjoyed wide acceptance. The public remains undecided as to what the reasons were and skeptical that they justified war.

The oil issue in Iraq provides a link between the motivation to go to war and the desired conditions at war's end. The "oil card" is the idea that the true underlying motivation for going to war was to gain access to or control over Iraqi oil resources. It is not an argument widely discussed in the literature on Iraq, and it was not an explanation admitted by any member of the Bush administration on the decision to go to war or the conditions for leaving. Indeed, the Bush administration denied throughout its tenure that oil was a factor in the decision to topple the Iraqi government. Many Iraqis believe the United States invaded and conquered their country to snatch their oil. Without taking sides one way or the other, the bare bones of an oil motivation can, however, be laid out.

Iraq has the fourth largest oil reserves in the world, with a known stockpile of 115 billion barrels and estimates of as much as 200 billion barrels, as discussed in Deutch, et al. It is one of the largest virtually untapped resources in the world, because of the historic inefficiency of the Iraqi government-controlled oil operation. As Holt points out: "A mere two thousand oil wells have been drilled across the entire country; in Texas alone there are more than a million." Moreover, Iraqi oil is located at a comparatively shallow depth and thus can be extracted at a relatively low cost (between $1.50 and $3 a barrel), and it has a low sulfur content, making it "sweet" oil.

The United States was excluded from access to this source of oil between 1972 and the 2003 invasion. In 1972, the Iraqi government nationalized the oil fields and evicted the American-British companies who had operated those fields while paying the Iraqis a fee for usage. In the years leading up to the invasion, the government of Saddam Hussein had reopened the question of access and was discussing possible deals with, among others, the Russians and the Chinese. The Americans were not part of this negotiation.

Was gaining control of Iraqi oil a plausible reason for invading and conquering the country? This supposition really comprises two questions. The first involves access to control over Iraqi oil, and it is certainly a worthwhile goal of American foreign policy to gain access to such a rich resource, particularly as a hedge against the uncertain future discussed in these pages. The other question is if that interest justified going to war with Iraq, and the answer is more debatable.

Whether or not Iraqi oil acquisition was worth going to war depends on two debatable propositions. The first revolves around the kind of war one envisaged. Clearly, a short, decisive, relatively bloodless, and inexpensive campaign (the kind the Bush administration advertised and envisioned in its initial run-up) was clearly more "worth it" than the long, protracted, bloody, and expensive war the United States got. The Bush administration at one point claimed the United States would be substantially out of Iraq within 129 days of the invasion; had that been true and the outcome control over or guaranteed access to Iraqi oil, a strong case can be made that it would have been worth the price. Whether or not that access is worth the actual costs incurred is much more questionable.

The other question is if the use of the military instrument is the appropriate tool for gaining control of oil. In an age of asymmetrical warfare (see Snow, *National Security for a New Era,* third edition), there are few quick and decisive military outcomes, making the use of force of questionable utility. Whether or not the use of military force is internationally acceptable is the other aspect of the question: the American invasion has been condemned by almost all other countries.

The idea of oil access or control as a primary reason for the war does, however, connect going in and getting out of Iraq. Gaining control of Iraqi oil is a more traditional, realist goal than others the Bush administration used for going to war, and if it could be achieved at an acceptable cost in treasure and blood, it could be justified as acceptable. Had, for instance, victory *actually* been achieved when President Bush stood on the deck of the *USS Lincoln* with the "Mission Accomplished" banner behind him on May 1, 2003, then gaining a level of oil security in the process might well have been an acceptable proposition. That it was not could, under these assumptions, be attributed to a mistaken assessment of the actual cost of the war, not the reasons for launching it.

Similarly, the question of withdrawal takes on a different meaning if the underlying mission was control of Iraqi oil. A major part of the equation of troop egress is how many and what kinds of Americans will remain after combat troops depart. If the withdrawal is designed to reestablish total Iraqi control over their territory (clearly the goal from an Iraqi viewpoint), the more total the withdrawal the better. In that case, the residual American presence would be minimal: civilian contractors to help rebuild the country and some forces to protect them, for instance. If, however, part of the reason for a residual force is to make certain the Iraqis do not renege on any agreements that may be reached to insure continuing American access to Iraqi oil, then the presence probably needs to be larger and more potentially menacing.

Part of this scenario worked itself out in the summer of 2009, when the Iraqi government negotiated its first petroleum contracts since the American invasion. The negotiations covered access to oil fields in the Shi'a dominated southern part of the country, which encompasses about half of Iraqi production and potential. In these negotiations, no contracts were awarded directly to American companies, and most of the contracts were awarded to firms based in countries that had been hostile to the American invasion. The United States accepted these outcomes gracefully, despite the imputation that they might symbolize a repudiation of the American presence. The reason may be that the U.S. government expects much more favorable treatment when contracts are let for the other half of Iraqi oil in the northern part of the country—fields in Kurdistan and the disputed area around Mosul. These contracts had not been let as of this writing.

The oil card has thus not been played out. No one within the American government is likely to admit that Iraqi oil played a major role in the decision to invade and occupy Iraq, and gaining that control may have been a residual benefit at most in the eyes of decision makers. As World War II suggests, however, invading and occupying a foreign country because of its petroleum wealth is certainly not unknown in world history. The question is if that was the case this time, and if it worked.

The Caspian Sea Oil Fields

One of the ways to break dependence on Persian Gulf oil has led the world's oil consumers to look, among other places, at the small Soviet successor state of Azerbaijan, as well as Kazakhstan. Azerbaijan's capital, Baku, sits on the banks of the Caspian Sea (which is actually a salt lake and the world's largest inland body of water), under which some of the richest deposits of petroleum and natural gas left in the world lie. According to Maugeri, "the proven reserves of Azerbaijan and Kazakhstan stand at about 18 billion barrels, but these countries' total recoverable reserves are estimated to range between 70 and 80 billion barrels" (about the amount of Venezuelan resources). The largest of these deposits are about 60 miles offshore from Baku, making it the focus of concerted exploration and exploitation.

Azerbaijan and Kazakhstan are the two most important Caspian Sea littoral states (other than Russia) with claims to Caspian oil and natural gas (the others are Uzbekistan and Turkmenistan). The situations of the two states are similar but not identical. Kazakhstan is currently the larger exporter, ranking nineteenth globally in 2008 at slightly over 1.3 million barrels a day. Its known reserves are estimated at 30 billion barrels (eleventh largest in the world). Because of its location, Kazakhstan has also negotiated and begun constructing a pipeline to China, but the bulk of its eventual exports, like those of Azerbaijan, will be westward (westward options are catalogued in a Department of Energy report listed in the Web sites at the end of this chapter). These alternatives are essentially the same as those for Azerbaijan. Currently, Azerbaijan is not a major exporter, with about a half-million barrels a day going out of the country (twenty-ninth in the world) and proven reserves of seven billion barrels (nineteenth in the world). Azerbaijan, however, has a more interesting geopolitical situation that will thus be the focus of this case.

The existence of Caspian Sea petroleum is nothing new. In fact, oil was discovered in the area in the second half of the nineteenth century, and by the beginning of the twentieth century, the region supplied most of Russia's oil needs (Imperial Russia completed its annexation of Azerbaijan in 1828). Although Azerbaijan declared its independence in 1918, it was absorbed into the Soviet Union in 1920. During the period when it was a republic of the Soviet Union, Azerbaijan was clearly not an alternative source of petroleum for an increasingly addicted West, however, because of the nature of the Cold War competition and thus Western unwillingness to become dependent on Soviet-controlled petroleum reserves.

The demise of the Soviet Union opened the floodgates for Western entrepreneurs to be drawn to Baku and elsewhere along the shores of the Caspian Sea. When Azerbaijan declared its independence from the Soviet Union on August 30, 1991, the oil companies were not far behind, engaging in a flood of speculation and exploration that many veteran oilmen say had not been seen since the opening of the Texas oil fields in the early 1900s. By the mid-1990s, the Caspian Sea fields were widely being extolled as the means by which the developed world would break the stranglehold imposed by the Persian Gulf oil-producing states. Oil production led to an economic boom of sorts in the early 2000s, but the global economic downturn of 2008 resulted in decreased demand and less "petrodollars."

Why is this the case? There is certainly no lack of interest among Western governments and the private oil companies in exploiting and bringing to market the petroleum riches lying beneath the Caspian Sea, and there are no major technical or engineering barriers present either. But there are geopolitical problems: One is the political instability of the region; another is the geopolitics of piping the riches to market because of competing routes with different advantages and barriers.

Regional Instabilities.   Five states have claims to parts either of the oil or natural gas under or surrounding the Caspian basin. The three northern states (Azerbaijan, Kazakhstan, and Russia) have agreed to a division of the resource contiguous to their shores, but the oil from Azerbaijan still does not flow freely. The reason it does not is most clearly exemplified by the political situation in Azerbaijan.

The major geopolitical liability for Azerbaijan centers on two enclave areas that are points of major contention between Muslim Azerbaijan and neighboring Christian Armenia, Nagorno-Karabakh and Naxcivan (sometimes known as Nakichevan). Of these two disputes, the ongoing conflict over Nagorno-Karabakh has been the more serious and has created the most difficulties for Azerbaijan generally and for exploiting the oil in particular.

Nagorno-Karabakh is an enclave with a majority Armenian population that is located physically in Azerbaijan. There has been a long history of accusations by residents of the enclave that they have been mistreated by their Muslim rulers, and this has accompanied unease with being physically separated from their Armenian brethren, as the accompanying map shows.

The contest over the status of Nagorno-Karabakh, which was treated as an autonomous region within Azerbaijan by the Soviets, goes back to the latter days of the Soviet Union. In 1988, the Armenians petitioned Moscow to cede Nagorno-Karabakh to Armenia and were rebuffed by the Soviets. When Azerbaijan declared its independence, it announced that the region would lose its autonomous status and become an integral part of Azerbaijan, an action that sent residents into opposition. War broke out between secessionists from Nagorno-Karabakh and Azerbaijan, and Armenian troops entered the fray in support of the ethnic Armenians. By August 1993, Armenian forces had occupied the area and had also taken control of the corridor linking Nagorno-Karabakh to Armenia. A ceasefire was arranged in 1994, but the issue has never been permanently settled. In the meantime, Armenia remains in control of one-sixth of Azerbaijani territory that constitutes Nagorno-Karabakh and the corridor, and the possibility that fighting will resume remains an ever present likelihood in this undeclared war.

The fighting over Nagorno-Karabakh has left two legacies with which Azerbaijan must struggle. Of the most immediate concern are Azerbaijani refugees from the war zone. It is estimated that the refugees number over a million, which is the largest percentage of refugees (as a part of the population) in any country in the world, and most of them live in the most wretched of conditions within Azerbaijan. Getting the oil to market and hence gaining the revenues that oil will put into government coffers has the potential greatly to ease this problem.

The other legacy is the danger of renewed violence, which affects thinking about where pipelines can be constructed to get the petroleum to the West. The Armenians have made no secret that they are in a physical position to disrupt any lines going near Armenian territory and that they would not be reluctant to engage in disruption if they feel they need to.

The Pipeline Problem

The problem of exploiting the Caspian Sea oil and gas fields is not technical in nature; rather, it is almost entirely political, or, more specifically, geopolitical.

Map 2.1 Map of Azerbaijan and surrounding areas (Armenia, Chechnya, and Turkey)

In the decade or so since the demise of the Soviet Union, the major global oil companies have descended on the Caspian region, generously laden with Western expertise and funds, and have transformed the rickety petroleum industry run by the communists into a modern Western-style operation.

The problem is finding a way to get the oil safely and securely to market, which will help relieve some of the world's dependence on the Middle East. To this point, there have been three proposals for an Azerbaijani pipeline to the West; none of them meet the dual criteria of security and avoidance of the Persian Gulf. The three routes under consideration go through Russia, Turkey, and Iran. Each is flawed in some political manner.

The Russian pipeline would run across Azerbaijan's northern boundary with Russia and would make its way to the Black Sea, from which it could then be shipped to Western markets. As might be imagined, the Russians are very strong advocates of this route, because they would be able to charge a duty on the petroleum as it is transshipped across Russian territory, thereby providing needed money to aid the transformation and development of the Russian state. The Russian "solution" raises two objections. The first is that the Russian government has proved so inept and corrupt that it would likely squander the revenues or have them skimmed off by corrupt officials or other criminal elements in the country. Former Russian President Vladimir Putin is a classic petrolist, because he used Russia's oil revenues from the Caspian Sea and elsewhere to aid the imposition of authoritarian measures by the regime. Whether his successor, Dmitry Medvedev, will prove any better in this regard remains unknown. More fundamentally, however, the pipeline route traverses the rebellious province of Chechnya. The Russians realize that no one is going to endorse a pipeline scheme that could be held hostage by rebellious Chechens, and Chechen terrorism cools a good deal of the enthusiasm for this solution for getting Azerbaijani oil to market. The alternative route, through Georgia to the Black Sea (through which roughly one million barrels flow each day) was made problematical by Russia's invasion of Georgia in August 2008.

The Turkish solution has the same kind of problem. The idea here is to build a pipeline across Turkey that would connect to the country's existing oil refineries in the northwest part of the country (which, unfortunately, has been the site of major earthquakes in the past few years). The oil would then be shipped through the Black Sea into the Mediterranean and to market. The geopolitical problem is that the Turkish pipeline would have to be built across or adjacent to Armenian territory, thereby enmeshing it in the volatile relations between those two states. Azerbaijan has no direct border with Turkey. The shortest route to Turkish soil from Azerbaijan is through Armenia (and possibly Nagorno-Karabakh, depending on how a route might be fashioned), which is clearly untenable as long as the conflict between the two states exists. The alternatives would be to go around Armenia to the south through Iran, which hardly solves the problem of dependence on the Persian Gulf, or through Georgia. Georgia itself has been unstable, with Abkhazian secessionists periodically causing problems that have led to a Russian army occupation of parts of the country, and it is doubtful the Armenians would hesitate to violate Georgian soil to damage the pipeline if they felt the need to do so.

The Prospects. Because the dual criteria of pipeline security and lessening dependence on Persian Gulf oil have not been met, the Caspian Sea fields remain at far less than peak capacity, certainly not pumping the quantities of oil that could make a difference in worldwide supply and thus price. Other issues remain that contribute to the standstill. There is currently only partial agreement on boundaries in the Caspian Sea among the five littoral states, although the Azerbaijanis, Russians, and Kazakhs have announced an agreement between them on division of rights. Disagreements such as this are not, however, fundamental. What must occur is an agreement on a pipeline route and a guarantee that the route will be secured so that interruptions in supply do not occur.

What will have to happen to break the impasse? The probable answer involves extra-regional action. Regional powers cannot or will not act effectively. Russia has been unable to squelch the Chechens totally (despite the killing of Chechen leader Shamil Baseyev in July 2006), and Turkey is certainly in no political position to suppress Armenian interruptions, given the genocide by the Ottoman Turks against Armenia early in the twentieth century. Turkey and Armenia have met to explore ways to resolve their historical and ongoing differences, but the talks have not been conclusive. That means the impasse will remain until those who have the most vested interest in access to Caspian Sea reserves decide to act. Direct Western involvement opens up so many unpleasant prospects that, for now, it is far easier to dream of the prospects of Caspian Sea oil than to bring it home.

CONCLUSION

Scarcity of natural resources is a continuing source of friction between states that results in geopolitical competition to attain these resources. In some cases, these conflicts can lead to violence, in some instances they can be amicably resolved, and in others, they remain simmering sources of disagreement.

The problem of petroleum scarcity dramatically illustrates the general problem caused by limited natural resources. Petroleum is scarce today, and the situation will get worse as peak oil production is passed, and the vitality of petroleum to the current worldwide energy system makes its solution compelling. That solution requires accelerating the transition from a petroleum-based energy system to an interim solution within the energy cycle at this point. All four of the possible forms a solution can take—increasing supply, reducing demand, substitution, and conflict—are likely to be part of this process. At the end, however, petroleum *is* a finite, nonrenewable resource that will eventually run out. The world thus faces the potential for having to answer the Shah of Iran's question of whether the countries of the world will end up fighting over the last drop.

Petroleum is not only scarce, the energy derived from it is vital to the world, from economic activity to transportation to heating and cooling that makes life commodious. This vitality is what makes access to petroleum (along with water) such an important matter for states in their domestic and international relations. The link between burning petroleum and environmental degradation (global warming) only adds another facet to the urgency of the petroleum issue.

Currently, the struggle for access to and control over petroleum played out in places like Iraq and the Caspian Sea littoral is divisive and filled with conflict. Petroleum is indeed the lubricant that corrodes international relations.

But need it remain that way? The optimal use of remaining global oil reserves and the transition to an energy based in renewable resources like sea water used in fusion could be a global exercise in cooperation toward a more sustainable future for all of mankind rather than a source of friction between peoples gathered in national units. But how does one (or can one) induce this kind of change? And how might this transformation come about?

STUDY/DISCUSSION QUESTIONS

1. Resource scarcity and its geopolitical implications have not been a prominent topic in international relations to this point. What is the actual and potential problem that scarce resources can have? How might this be a bigger problem in the future?
2. What are the major dynamics of the international competition for petroleum? How do countries like China and India contribute to these problems?
3. The possession of a scarce resource may give particular leverage and power to its possessor. Using petroleum as an example, show how this leverage can work.
4. What are the possible means of resolving resource scarcities? Discuss each, using the petroleum scarcity problem as an example.
5. Discuss the importance and value of oil as a scarce resource. What is peak oil? Why is it so important in the discussion of petroleum?
6. What are energy cycles? Discuss the history of those cycles, including where the world is now and where it is headed. What is the major problem of the current transition?
7. What is the outlook for global oil futures? Toward what conclusions does this outlook lead?
8. What are the three examples of political impacts discussed in the chapter? Discuss each.
9. Why is access to Caspian Sea oil and natural gas such a large international priority? What political factors are interfering with the ability to bring this resource to market? What can be done to break the impasse?
10. Discuss the Iraq War in terms of petroleum scarcity. Do you find the argument that control or access to Iraqi oil may have been the principal motivation for the invasion convincing? Is oil sufficiently important to justify going to war? Why or why not?

READING/RESEARCH MATERIALS

Azerbaijan. *Microsoft Encarta Online Encyclopedia 2000.* Microsoft Corporation, 2000.

Azerbaijan. *CIA World Factbook 2008.* Washington, DC: Central Intelligence Agency, 2008.

BBC News. "Q & A: Why Does Nagorno-Karabakh Matter?" London, UK: BBC News, March 31, 1998.

Ferraro, Vincent. "Another Motive for Iraq War: Stabilizing Oil Market." *Hartford Courant* (online), August 12, 2003.

Fleischman, Stephen E. "Too Valuable to Burn." *Common Dreams Newscenter* (online), November 29, 2005.

Friedman, Thomas L. "The First Law of Petropolitics." *Foreign Policy*, May/June 2006, 36–44.

Hirsch, Robert L. *Peaking of World Oil Production: Recent Forecasts.* Washington, DC: National Energy Technology Laboratory, February 5, 2007 (www.netl.doe.gov)

Holt, Jim. "It's the Oil." *London Review of Books* (online edition), October 18, 2006 (http://www.truthout.org/docs_2006/101207.html)

Homer-Dixon, Thomas. "Environmental Scarcities and Violent Conflict: Evidence from Cases." In Sean Lynn-Jones and Stephen Miller (eds.), *Global Dangers: Changing Dimensions of International Security.* Cambridge, MA: MIT Press, 1995, 144–179.

International Energy Agency. "Oil Market Report" (online). February 11, 2010.

Kumins, Lawrence. "Iraqi Oil: Reserves, Production, and Potential Resources." *CRS Report to Congress*. Washington, DC: Congressional Research Service, April 13, 2005.

Kurlantzik, Joshua. "Put a Tyrant in Your Tank." *Mother Jones* 33, 3 (May/June 2008), 38–42.

Lewis, Charles and Mark Reading-Smith. *False Pretenses: Iraq: The War Card.* Washington, DC: Center for Public Integrity, 2008.

Maugeri, Leonardo. "Two Cheers for Expensive Oil." *Foreign Affairs* 85, 2 (March/April 2006), 149–160.

Morgan, Daniel and David B. Ottaway. "In Iraq Scenario, Oil Is Key Issue." *Washington Post,* September 15, 2002, A01.

"Oil and Corruption in Iraq Part III: Kurdistan's Gushing Crude Spawns Conflict." *Environmental News Service* (online), September 12, 2007.

Pope, Carl and Bjorn Lomborg. "The State of Nature: The *Foreign Policy* Debate." *Foreign Policy,* July/August 2005, 66–74.

Record, Jeffrey. *Dark Victory: America's Second War against Iraq.* Annapolis, MD: Naval Institute Press, 2004.

Roberts, Paul. "The Seven Myths of Energy Independence." *Mother Jones* 33, 3 (May/June 2008), 31–37.

Rohter, Larry. "Shipping Costs Start to Crimp Globalization." *New York Times* (online), August 3, 2008.

———. *What After Iraq?* New York: Pearson Longman, 2009.

Snow, Donald M. *National Security for a New Era: Globalization and Geopolitics after Iraq.* 3rd ed. New York: Pearson Longman, 2008.

Yergin, Daniel. "Ensuring Energy Security." *Foreign Affairs* 85, 2 (March/April 2006), 69–82.

———. *The Prize: The Epic Quest for Oil, Money, and Power.* New York: Simon and Schuster, 1991.

Zweig, David and Bi Jianhai. "China's Global Hunt for Energy." *Foreign Affairs* 84, 5 (September/October 2005), 18–24.

Limits on International Cooperation: War Crimes, the International Criminal Court, and Torture

PRÉCIS

Although events in the 1990s in places like Bosnia and Rwanda and more recently Iraq made the idea of war crimes and their prosecution a widely recognized part of international relations, the notion is a relatively recent concept. There have always been more or less well-accepted and enforced rules for conducting war, the violation of which was deemed criminal, but the ideas of crimes against peace and, especially, crimes against humanity are largely the result of the prosecution of German and Japanese officials after World War II. The 1990s revived this interest, which had receded during the Cold War.

While there is near-universal condemnation of war crimes as a general rule, efforts at international cooperation in regulating and prosecuting violations of war crimes norms have been less successful. The case examines why such limits on cooperation exist. It begins by looking at the content and evolution of the war crimes concept as background, then moves to its central thrust, which is an examination of the primary efforts to regulate war crimes, including torture, and why international cooperation has been limited in this important international area.

The idea that war crimes are reprehensible, that their commission should be outlawed, and that those who commit war crimes should be punished seems noncontroversial on its face. War is horrible enough, involving the violent taking of human life (if within certain boundaries or rules for its conduct), and criminal behavior is universally condemnable and generally unacceptable. When crime is committed in the violent context of war, the result is particularly horrific, and one would assume that the area of war crimes would offer fertile grounds for international cooperation aimed at eliminating their occurrence. And yet, international cooperation in the area of war crimes has lagged behind international solutions to other, often less compelling, areas.

Efforts to address the subject of war crimes have been attempted. The most obvious case was the war crimes trials against German and Japanese defendants at the end of World War II, which are discussed later in the chapter. The subject lay largely fallow between the end of those efforts and the early 1990s, when outrageous instances of war crimes occurred in places like Bosnia and Rwanda and reinvigorated interest in the war crimes issue. The major result of that emphasis was the negotiation of the International Criminal Court (ICC) through the Rome Treaty of 1998; accusations of U.S. abuses in Iraq added the question of torture, formally outlawed by the United Nations Convention on Torture (UNCAT) in 1987, to the mix.

The evolution of these efforts demonstrates, in important ways and for reasons worth noting, the limits of international cooperation in the war crimes/torture area. As of July 31, 2009, only 110 of the 190 or so countries of the world had ratified the ICC statute and become parties to the treaty. Of those countries that have not joined are five of the six most populous states in the world (China, India, the United States, Indonesia, and Pakistan), which between them have a population of 3.21 billion of a world population estimated at 6.83 billion, according to 2009 UN estimates. Of the six largest states, only Brazil has ratified the ICC treaty. When other nonsignatories' populations are added to the total, over half the people living in the world are not covered by the international regime forbidding war crimes. The situation is slightly better for the UNCAT: among the six most populous states, for instance, only India and Pakistan are nonsignatories.

The purpose of this case is to study the problem of war crimes and why finding concrete ways to discourage or eliminate their occurrence demonstrates the limits, rather than the positive possibilities, of international cooperation. At a commonsensical level, the idea that war crimes should be condemned and perpetrators punished seems obvious—a "no-brainer." Yet, within the more byzantine workings of international relations, other concerns, such as the protection of state sovereignty introduced as a bedrock principle in Chapter 1, may come into conflict with apparently consensual concerns that would seem to militate toward cooperation between states. War crimes are not the only place where this anomaly appears, but they are one of the most dramatic.

As noted, the phenomenon of war crimes reentered the international dialogue during the 1990s. The immediate precipitant had been a rash of so-called humanitarian disasters, in which intolerable acts against groups within states, often grouped under the name "ethnic cleansing," occurred during the decade. The worst of these occurred in Bosnia during the early 1990s and in Rwanda in 1994. A somewhat more limited case occurred in

Kosovo in 1998–1999. The result, according to one source, was a paradox: "Humanitarian law and international human rights has never been more developed, yet never before have human rights been violated more frequently. This state of affairs will not improve absent a mechanism to enforce those laws and the norms they embody." The ongoing tragedy in Darfur, Sudan, discussed in detail in Chapter 8, accentuates these concerns.

This quote suggests that the contemporary concern with war crimes stems from two parallel developments. One is the assertion that there are universal human rights to which people and groups are entitled and that, when they are violated, are subject to penalty. The second is an interest in some form of *international* mechanism for dealing with violators of these norms.

While the ideas of defining criminal behavior and enforcement of laws in international, universal terms may not seem extraordinary, both are in fact of recent origin in international affairs. The idea of universal human rights transcending state boundaries is really a phenomenon of the post–World War II period; the primary crime that has been identified in war crimes, genocide, was not identified until the word was coined by Richard Lemkin in 1944, and the United Nations Convention on Genocide, which bans the commission of genocide, was not passed until 1948. Torture is as old as mankind, but the UNCAT was only negotiated in 1987 (and ratified by the United States in 1994). Similarly, the term *war crimes,* which now refers to a broad range of activities associated with war, was basically linked with violations of the so-called laws of war (actions permissible and impermissible during wartime) until war crimes trials were convened in Nuremberg and Tokyo to prosecute accused Nazi and Japanese violators after World War II.

The subject of war crimes is unlikely to disappear from international discourse, for at least four reasons. First, acts now defined as war crimes continue to be committed in many places. Exclusionary nationalism (when national groups persecute nonmembers) in some developing-world states may actually increase the number of savage acts that are now considered war crimes. Second, the war crimes trials involving Bosnia and Rwanda that were empanelled in the early 1990s have only begun their work, and the international legal community fully recognizes that the outcomes of those trials will influence the subject in the future. Third, definitions are rapidly evolving. Rape, for instance, has only recently been added to the list of punishable crimes against humanity. Terrorist mass murders almost certainly qualify as well. The trial of Saddam Hussein gave wide publicity to these phenomena. Fourth, one outcome of the concern for war crimes has been the establishment of a controversial permanent International Criminal Court with mandatory jurisdiction over war crimes.

This statement of the problem suggests the direction this case study will take. It will begin with a brief historical overview of war crimes, emphasizing the major point that whereas the idea of crimes of war has long been part of international concerns, war crimes as they are now defined are of recent vintage. The case will then look at the various categories of war crimes that arose from the experience of the war crimes trials at the end of World War II, and how the existence of well-documented atrocities in places like Bosnia and

Rwanda rekindled interest in the subject. With the principles surrounding war crimes and enforcement of prohibitions established, the case will be applied to controversies surrounding the ICC and to the special case of torture as a crime to illustrate the core concern with war crimes as a prime example of the limits of international cooperation.

THE PROBLEM OF WAR CRIMES

The idea of war crimes is both very old and very new. Throughout most of history, the term has been associated with conformity to the so-called laws of war. This usage can be traced back as far as 200 B.C., when a code of the permissible behavior in war was formulated in the Hindu Code of Manu. Enumerated codes of warfare were part of Roman law and were later practiced throughout Europe. These rules began to be codified into international law following the Thirty Years' War (1618–1648), when most of Europe was swept up in very brutal religiously based warfare. The first definitive international law text, Hugo Grotius's *Concerning the Law of War and Peace,* was published in 1625 and included the admonition that "war ought not to be undertaken except for the enforcement of rights; when once undertaken, it should be carried on only within the bounds of law and good faith." Definitions of the laws of war, and hence violations of those laws, developed gradually during the eighteenth and nineteenth centuries, culminating in the Geneva and Hague Conventions of 1899 and 1907.

The concerns expressed in the laws of war continue to be an important part of international law, but the idea of war crimes has been expanded to cover other areas of conduct in war in the twentieth century. The precipitant for this expansion was World War II and wartime atrocities committed by the Axis powers (notably Germany and Japan). Some of the crimes fit traditional definitions of war crimes—the mistreatment of American and other prisoners of war (POWs) by the Japanese during the infamous Bataan death march, for instance. Many actions, however, went well beyond the conduct of war per se, as in the systematic extermination of Jews, Gypsies, and other groups in the Holocaust by Germany and the so-called Rape of Nanking, in which Japanese soldiers went on a rampage and reportedly slaughtered nearly 300,000 citizens of that Chinese city (some Japanese sources dispute the numbers) on the pretext that some of them were soldiers hiding among the civilians.

Contemporary Evolution of War Crimes

World War II thus provided the impetus for change. It was a truly global and brutal war, and one of its major "innovations" was to extend to civilian population what the American general William Tecumseh Sherman called the "hard hand of war" during the Civil War. The Allies discussed the problem throughout the war. The first formal statement on the subject was the Moscow declaration of 1943, which stated that Nazi officials guilty of "atrocities, massacres, and executions" would be sent to the countries in which they committed their crimes for trial and appropriate punishment after the war ended.

The London Agreement. The document that defined modern war crimes precedent was the London Agreement of August 8, 1945. It did two major things. First, it established the International Military Tribunal as the court that would try alleged war crimes and thereby set the precedent for a formal, permanent body later on. At the time, it specifically set the groundwork for the Nuremberg and Tokyo tribunals. Second, the agreement established the boundaries of its jurisdiction, which have become the standard means for defining war crimes.

The London Agreement defined three kinds of war crimes. The first is *crimes against peace,* "namely, planning, preparation, initiation, or waging of a war of aggression, or a war in violation of international treaties, agreements or assurances, or participation in a common plan or conspiracy for the accomplishment of any of the foregoing." This admonition was reinforced by the United Nations Charter that same year, in which the signatories relinquished the "right" to initiate war. Under this definition, the North Korean invasion of South Korea in 1950 or the invasion and conquest of Kuwait by Saddam Hussein's Iraq in 1990 both qualify as crimes against peace. What should be clearly noted is that this definition applies most obviously and directly to wars between independent states because of its emphasis on territorial aggression. The U.S. invasion of Iraq arguably also qualifies as a crime against peace.

The second category reiterates the traditional usage of the concept. *War crimes* are defined as "violations of the laws or customs of war. Such violations shall include, but not be limited to, murder, ill-treatment or deportation to slave labor or for any other purpose of civilian population of or in occupied territory, murder or ill-treatment of prisoners of war or persons on the seas, killing of hostages, plunder of public or private property, wanton destruction of cities, towns or villages, or devastation not justified by military necessity." This enumeration, of course, was a virtual laundry list of accusations against the Germans and the Japanese (although the Allies arguably committed some of the same acts). Although acts against civilians are mentioned in the listing, the crimes enumerated are limited to mistreatment of general civilian populations rather than their systematic extension to individuals and segments of the population.

The third category was the most innovative and controversial. It is also the type of war crimes with which the concept is now most closely associated. *Crimes against humanity* are defined as "murder, extermination, enslavement, deportation, and other inhumane acts committed against any civilian population, before or during the war; or persecutions on political, racial or religious grounds in execution of or in connection with any crime . . . whether or not in violation of the domestic law where perpetrated." The statute goes further, establishing the basis of responsibility and thus vulnerability to prosecution. "Leaders, organizers, instigators, or accomplices participating in the formulation or execution of a common plan or conspiracy to commit any of the foregoing crimes are responsible for all acts performed by any persons in execution of such plan." This latter enumeration of responsibility justified the indictment of former Yugoslav president Slobodan Milosevic, who was never accused of personally carrying out acts qualifying as war crimes, and also against Saddam Hussein.

To someone whose experience is limited to the latter part of the twentieth century, this notion of crimes against humanity may not seem radical, or possibly even unusual. At the time, however, the concept clearly was, for several reasons. First, wars against humanity criminalized actions by states (or groups within states) that, while not exactly common in human history, were certainly not historically unknown but had previously not been thought of as criminal. Imagine, for instance, Genghis Khan and the leaders of the Golden Horde being placed in the docket for their brutal actions while conquering much of Eurasia in the thirteenth century. The same applies to the Ottoman Turk executors of the genocidal campaign against the Armenians early in the twentieth century. Or, for that matter, the post–Civil War campaigns by the U.S. government against the Western Indian tribes (e.g., Wounded Knee) probably qualifies as well.

The second radical idea contained in the definition is that of jurisdiction. By stating that crimes against humanity are enforceable "whether or not in violation of the domestic law" of the places they occur, the definition adds a universality to its delineation that seems to transcend the sovereign rights of states to order events as they choose within their territory. That assertion remains at the base of controversy about the institutionalization of war crimes, because it entwines war criminal behavior (the reprehensibility of which is agreed upon) with the controversy over sovereignty (about which there is considerable disagreement). Third, the statute seeks to remove the defense that crimes against humanity can be justified on the basis they were committed on orders from a superior. Thus, anyone with any part in crimes against humanity is equally vulnerable under the law, and this provision allows the tribunal to delve as deeply as it wishes into the offenders' hierarchy.

The statute does not address one element about war crimes prosecution that is almost always raised. It is the problem of the so-called victors' law: the charge that war crimes are always defined by the winning side in a war, and those tried are always those from the losing side. The Nuremberg and Tokyo tribunals labored hard and long to make the proceedings as judicially fair as they could; it is nonetheless true that it was Germans and Japanese in the dock, not Americans or Britons. It is possible, but not very likely, that no one on the Allied side ever committed a war crime or a crime against humanity during World War II. It is arguable, however, that the officials who ordered and carried out the firebombing of Tokyo or the leveling of Dresden, in which many innocent civilians were killed, were guilty of crimes against humanity. None of these officials came before the war crimes tribunal. The recognition of the potential charge that any trial applies victors' law has been an ongoing concern in the further development of the concept of war crime and is reflected in the jurisdiction of the International Criminal Court.

This concern carried over into the postwar world. In 1948, the General Assembly of the United Nations passed the International Convention on the

Prevention and Punishment of the Crime of Genocide, known more compactly as the Convention on Genocide. Building on the assertion of crimes against humanity, the Convention on Genocide provided clarification and codification of what constituted acts of genocide. According to the convention, any of the following actions, when committed with the intent of eliminating a particular national, ethnic, racial, or religious group, constitute genocide: (1) killing members of the group; (2) causing serious bodily or mental harm to members of the group; (3) deliberately inflicting on the group conditions of life calculated to kill; (4) imposing measures intended to prevent births within a group; and (5) forcibly transferring children out of a group.

In important ways, enunciating the Convention on Genocide (and the parallel UN Declaration on Human Rights) was a form of international atonement for Axis excesses, and especially for the Holocaust. Most countries signed and ratified the Convention, which took force—without, one might quickly add, any real form of enforcement. A few countries, notably the United States, refused to ratify the document for reasons based in infringement of sovereignty discussed later.

Reemergence of the Problem

With the completion of the war crimes tribunals after World War II and the flurry of activity that produced the Convention on Genocide, the subject of war crimes dropped from the public eye, not to reemerge publicly until the 1990s. Well beneath the surface of public concern, attempts were made to create some sort of enforcement mechanism for dealing with these issues, but they never received much public attention, nor did they generate enough political support to gain serious international consideration.

Why was this the case? It is not because crimes against humanity became less unacceptable; those kinds of acts and traditional war crimes certainly continued to occur, at least on a smaller scale than had happened during World War II. Rather, the more likely explanation is that the subject matter became a victim of the Cold War, as did other phenomena such as the aggressive promotion of human rights.

It is almost certainly not a coincidence that the emergence of a broad international interest in war crimes emerged at a time of U.S.-Soviet cooperation right after World War II, that concern and progress ground to an effective halt during the ideological and geopolitical confrontation between them, and that the subject has resurfaced and been revitalized since the cessation of that competition.

Why would the Cold War competition hamstring progress on a subject that would, on the face of it, seem noncontroversial? No one, after all, officially condones war crimes, and yet, in the Cold War context, neither was their clarification or codification aggressively pursued internationally.

The problem was similar to, and had the same roots as, the advocacy of human rights, which also lay fallow on the international agenda through most of the Cold War period. In a sense, war crimes are a flip side of human rights:

The crimes against humanity clearly violate the most basic of human rights, and traditional war crimes violate those rights in times of combat.

In the Cold War context, issues like human rights tended to get caught up in the propaganda war between the superpowers. The Soviets would assume that American advocacy of certain principles (for instance, free speech) was championed to embarrass the Soviet Union, where such rights were certainly not inviolate. Had the Soviets decided to push for greater progress on war crimes during the American participation in the Vietnam War between 1965 and 1973, the United States would have assumed the purpose was to embarrass American servicemen and discredit the American military effort. The My Lai incident during the Vietnam War (in which a platoon of U.S. servicemen destroyed a Vietnamese village and slaughtered its residents) illustrates the extension of this dynamic to war crimes. Innocent civilians were slaughtered at My Lai in what was a clear crime against humanity, but dispassionate consideration was drowned out by wartime propaganda duels over Cold War issues. In such circumstances, little if any progress could be expected on issues with a Cold War veneer; by and large, there was little attempt to pursue agreements in areas where one side or the other might impose a formal veto in the United Nations Security Council or an informal veto by convincing its friends and allies not to take part.

There was a second problem with extending the idea of war crimes, and especially the codification of the idea into some enforcement regime, that has been a particular sticking point for the United States government: the issue of sovereignty. As noted in Chapter 1, the United States (as well as nondemocratic states like China) has been among the staunchest supporters of the doctrine of state sovereignty, the idea that supreme authority to act (in other words, sovereignty) resides exclusively with states and that any dilution of that status is unacceptable.

Because the Convention on Genocide is universally applicable to all states that have signed and ratified it and thus have acceded to its provisions, it can be viewed, and was by powerful political elements in the United States, as an infringement of the authority of the United States government to regulate its own affairs. This argument may seem strained in the area of genocide: One way of looking at the objection is that it preserves the right of the United States to commit genocide without breaking agreements of which it is part. Nonetheless, the argument against diluting American national sovereignty was sufficient politically to prevent the United States Senate from ratifying the convention until 1993, when it was submitted to the Senate by President Clinton and approved by the necessary two-thirds majority.

Two other things had changed between the 1970s and the revived international concern about crimes against humanity in the 1990s that help explain earlier international indifference and international activism in the 1990s. The first change was the emergence of much more aggressive global electronic media with the physical capability to expose and publicize apparent violations. During most of the Cold War, there was no such thing as global television; Cable News Network (CNN), with which many people associate the globalization of world news, was not launched until 1980 and did not become a prominent force for some time thereafter. Moreover, media tools such as handheld camcorders and satellite uplinks were theoretical ideas, not the everyday equipment of reporters. In this atmosphere, governments could and did obscure some of their most atrocious behavior, a practice that has become much more difficult, as governments from countries like Sudan (see Chapter 8) and Iran (see Chapter 7) have learned in recent years.

The other change has been the growing *de facto* (in practice) if not *de jure* (in law) acceptance of the permissibility of international intervention in the internal affairs of states or factions within states that grossly abuse other people or groups—in other words, commit crimes against humanity and especially genocide. Without an elaborate statement of the principle of *humanitarian intervention,* this is what the United Nations authorized when it sent UN forces into Somalia in 1992. This action was widely touted by then UN Secretary-General Boutros Boutros-Ghali as a precedent-setting exercise for the future—the establishment of international enforcement of universal codes of behavior.

By the early 1990s, the dynamics affecting international politics had changed sufficiently to raise the prospects of dealing with war crimes onto the international agenda. The end of the Cold War meant atrocities would not be hidden or accusations about them suppressed on ideological or propagandistic grounds. A more aggressive and technologically empowered electronic media with global reach was available to report and publicize atrocities wherever they were found. At the same time, the UN operation in Somalia had established something like a precedent about the notion of humanitarian intervention. Two particularly egregious cases during the 1990s, in Bosnia and Rwanda, drew particular focus on the problem and its solution.

The two cases were different but both contributed to the rising concern both with war crimes and their prosecution. The factional fighting in Bosnia involved military and paramilitary groups from each of the three major ethnic groups in the area (Serbs, Croats, and Bosnian Muslims or Bosniacs) attacking and seeking to displace the others to gain power in the new Bosnian state. Many of the operations undertaken were against defenseless civilians and thus involved crimes against humanity. In Rwanda in 1994, the Hutu majority engaged in a systematic attempt to eliminate the Tutsi minority in a genocidal campaign that trampled human rights and constituted clear crimes against humanity.

Individually and in combination, Bosnia and Rwanda thrust two unavoidable imperatives before the international community. First, they made the subject and horror of war crimes so public that it could no longer be ignored. Second, it created the need for some mechanism to prosecute those accused of committing war crimes, and the result was the formation of ad hoc war crimes tribunals to deal with each case. A major outgrowth of this process was a growing belief that there should be a permanent international institution both to deter potential future war criminals and to try future undeterred perpetrators.

WAR CRIMES APPLIED AND COOPERATION APPLIED: THE INTERNATIONAL CRIMINAL COURT AND TORTURE

The precedent of the Bosnian and Rwandan special war crimes tribunals inevitably created momentum for a permanent court. There was very little objection in principle to the idea of a war crimes court to deal with these two instances. Moreover, it was increasingly clear from atrocities being committed in other countries that there would be no shortage of situations in which allegations of crimes against humanity would emerge. Internal conflicts in places as widely separated as Sierra Leone in Africa, Kosovo nearby the Bosnian border, and East Timor on the Indonesian archipelago provided evidence of both geographic diversity and numerous opportunities to enforce sanctions against a new breed of war criminals, who perpetrated gross crimes against humanity—their fellow citizens. Beyond the anticipated amount of demand there would be for a permanent structure was the hope that the existence of such a court and the knowledge that it could bring criminals to justice might deter some future crimes against humanity. But how should the international community react?

Two aspects of the evolving debate over war crimes stand out in the contemporary international scene, and each is a matter of special interest to the United States. One is the desirability of a permanent institution (the ICC) with mandatory jurisdiction both to determine instances of war crimes and their prosecution. The second, and more recent, concern has been with the special problem of torture, which is a war crime when committed during war. Sovereignty-based concerns have made the United States the world's most vocal and prominent opponent of efforts to foster international cooperation in both areas. An examination of the ICC and the question of torture thus illustrate the limits of international cooperation in this area.

Proposals for a Permanent War Crimes Tribunal

The initial advocacy of a permanent court to adjudicate war crimes accompanied the flurry of activity surrounding Nuremberg and Tokyo and the adoption of the Convention on Genocide. In 1948, the UN General Assembly commissioned the International Law Commission (a private body) to study the possibility of establishing an ICC. The commission examined this problem until 1954 and produced a draft statute for the ICC. Unfortunately, it appeared during the darkest days of the Cold War; there were objections from both sides of the Iron Curtain, and the United Nations dropped the proposal.

The idea of an ICC lay dormant until 1989, when the tiny Caribbean island country of Trinidad and Tobago revived the proposal within the United Nations. Their motive, oddly enough, was to provide an instrument in their struggle against drug traffickers from South America. Nonetheless, the events in Bosnia and Rwanda revived broader interest that suggested the wisdom of a permanent body to provide a more effective, timely response to war crimes.

The idea of a permanent war crimes tribunal illustrated dramatically the clash between order and disorder inherent in a world order, the conceptual core of which is the sovereignty of its units. No country, to repeat, endorses the right to commit war crimes or to practice torture, but some states and groups or individuals within states from time to time violate the moral and legal norms that constitute war crimes. In some cases (some terrorist groups, for instance), the validity of these norms may be rejected, but this does not mean the mainstream does not accept the idea that war crimes are punishable acts.

The idea that these include crimes against *humanity* suggests universality in the condemnation of war crimes and enforcement of norms coterminous with that universality. Since virtually every country joins in the condemnation, the international institution of war crimes mechanisms would seem a ripe place for international cooperation. Such impulses, however, collide with other system values and come to a head in concrete instances like the ICC.

The proposal for an ICC has been controversial, especially surrounding the matter of jurisdiction. Champions contend that the court must have mandatory jurisdiction over all accused instances of war crimes and that its jurisdiction must supersede national sovereignty to be effective. Opponents object that this infringement on national sovereignty is unwarranted and could form the basis for future abuses of sovereignty. The ICC statute contains provisions for mandatory jurisdiction.

The Case for the ICC

The idea of an ICC flowed from renewed interest in dealing with war crimes and the perception that a permanent war crimes institution had several advantages over impaneling ad hoc tribunals. First, a permanent body would avoid having to start essentially from scratch each time suspected war crimes are uncovered. A permanent ICC would have, among other things, a permanent staff of investigators and prosecutors, and its staff would have the authority and jurisdiction to ascertain when crimes against humanity have indeed occurred.

Second, and related to the first point, a permanent ICC could be much more responsive to the occurrence—or even perhaps the possibility—of war crimes in the future. Not only would a permanent staff have or develop the expertise for efficient identification of war crimes situations, they could be rapidly mobilized and applied to the problem.

Third, it was hoped that a permanent ICC would act as a deterrent to future potential war criminals. Would, for instance, the Bosnian Serb leaders indicted (mostly in absentia) for authorizing ethnic cleansing in Bosnia have been dissuaded from doing so if they knew there was an international criminal authority to bring them to justice for their deeds? What influence would a permanent ICC have had on the planners and implementers of the slaughter in Rwanda? Although no one can know the answers to these questions, the existence of the ICC might have made a difference.

Fourth, the idea emerged in a time period when international cooperation was being instituted on a broad range of vexing issues, from human and women's rights to free trade (see Chapter 9). The end of the Cold War seemed to usher in an atmosphere where the narrow, conflict-driven paradigm of world politics was being replaced by a more open and cooperative atmosphere. The time for an ICC seemed ripe.

As a result, pressure to negotiate a treaty to create an ICC grew during the 1990s. As early as 1995, the Clinton administration became an activist in the movement in support of the idea. The movement culminated with the Rome Conference of 1998 (technically the United Nations Diplomatic Conference on the Establishment of a Permanent International Criminal Court). The conference produced a draft treaty to establish the ICC as a permanent court for trying individuals accused of committing genocide, war crimes, or crimes against humanity and gave the court jurisdiction over individuals accused of these crimes. When the draft was put to vote, it passed by a vote of 120 states in favor, 7 opposed, and 21 abstentions. In order for the treaty to come into force, at least 60 states had to ratify the treaty. It reached that level in 2002 and came into official existence on July 1, 2002. As of July 21, 2009, the number of states that had ratified and become part of the ICC stood at 110.

In what would prove a harbinger of future difficulties, the U.S. government was one of the seven states to vote against the treaty in Rome and has neither signed nor ratified the document, despite the Clinton administration's involvement in promoting and drafting its statute. In one of his final acts in office, President Clinton signed the statute in December 2000. In February 2001, Secretary of State Colin S. Powell announced that President George W. Bush had no intention of submitting it to the Senate for ratification; the Bush administration subsequently announced it was "unsigning" the treaty, an ambiguous international legal act punctuating its high level of opposition.

Objections to the ICC

That the United States advocated and then opposed the ICC statute may seem anomalous, but it is not entirely unusual. The apparent schizophrenia represents different views of America's place in the world, the American attitude toward the world, and especially the question of sovereignty. The Clinton administration saw the ICC statute as a way both to demonstrate responsible U.S. leadership and to improve the quality of the international environment, and thus became a champion of a war crimes court with "teeth." Other powerful political forces, however, summoned the specter of the loss of sovereignty that joining the treaty might entail. The problem came to focus on the potential loss of control of the U.S. government over its own forces in the field. More recently, being a nonsignatory has protected the United States from potential actions regarding the convention against torture.

David Sheffer, head of the American delegation, delivered the heart of the United States' objection at the end of the Rome Conference. He began by pointing out that the ICC would have jurisdiction only in countries that were parties to the treaty, and he noted that a number of countries that were producing accusations of war crimes could and would evade prosecution by simply not joining the treaty. Iraq was an example. The qualifying point of this objection was that a UN Security Council Resolution (UNSCR) can extend that jurisdiction in a given case. Helena Cobban argues this extension of jurisdiction is itself objectionable, since it extends authority over countries to which the court has only "an indirect line of accountability."

The heart of the objection was that the treaty forces countries to relinquish their sovereign jurisdiction over their forces and leaves those forces vulnerable to international prosecution with no U.S. ability to come to their aid when the United States participates in UN-sponsored peacekeeping operations, such as those in Bosnia and Kosovo or even torture in Iraq. As Sheffer put it, "Thus, the treaty purports to establish an arrangement whereby U.S. armed forces operating overseas could be conceivably prosecuted by the international court even if the U.S. has not agreed to be bound by the treaty. Not only is this contrary to the most fundamental principles of treaty law, it could inhibit the ability of the U.S. to use its military to meet alliance obligations and participate in multinational operations, including humanitarian interventions to save civilian lives." Jennifer Elsea summarized U.S. objections in a 2006 Congressional Research Service study, the gist of which remains American policy. "The ICC purports to its jurisdiction citizens of non-member nations," she wrote. Moreover, lack of adequate due process "will not offer accused Americans the due process guaranteed them under the U.S. constitution." The sovereign control of American forces potentially accused of war crimes thus stands at the base of the United States' refusal to sign off on the ICC statute.

In order to get around the problem of sovereignty forfeiture, the United States has dredged up a tactic it used after World War II to ensure Senate ratification of the statute of the International Court of Justice (ICJ or World Court), to which the ICC is affiliated. In the case of the ICJ, the United States insisted that the statute include the provision that the court would only have jurisdiction in individual cases if *both* (or all) parties granted jurisdiction for that action alone. In other words, countries, including the United States, can only be sued and have judgments made against them in situations in which they have given their permission: Sovereign control is only abrogated by explicit consent.

The same argument is incorporated in the American approach to the question of the jurisdiction of the ICC. The proposed "supplement" to the Rome Treaty read: "The United Nations and the International Criminal Court agree that the Court may seek the surrender or accept custody of a national who acts within the overall direction of a U.N. Member State, and such directing State has so acknowledged *only in the event (a) the directing State is a State Party to the Statute or the Court obtains the consent of the directing State, or (b) measures have been authorized pursuant to Chapter VII of the U.N. Charter against the directing State in relation to the situation or actions giving rise to alleged crime or crimes.*" (emphasis added). Parties to the statute have consistently rejected this American position.

Why does the United States object to this cooperation-inducing regime? The U.S. government, and especially the military, argues the United States, as the remaining superpower, is uniquely vulnerable to international harassment in the absence of this kind of protection. More specifically, there are usually American forces involved in major peacekeeping missions globally, where accusations of war crimes are commonplace. The military fears that unfounded accusations (what the Elsea study refers to as "trumped-up charges") against Americans can become a means of harassment of the United States against which they should guard and which the American amendment seeks to protect.

The U.S. position, which was formulated by the Bush administration but has been neither modified nor renounced by its successor as of mid-2010, goes on to add other objections based in the expansion of international authority contained in the ICC statute. Elsea cited two: an "unacceptable prosecutor" who would have "unchecked discretion to initiate cases," and the "usurpation of the role of the UN Security Council" in regulating ICC initiatives. Both find their base in the sovereignty issue: checks would presumably be exercised by states through the effective veto of prosecution of particular cases, and the Security Council's authority is based in the veto power of the permanent members, including the United States.

An extension of this concern that has arisen from the American "war on terror" and occupation of Iraq has been the accusation that the United States has engaged in acts of torture to obtain information from suspected terrorists and other opponents in Iraq and Afghanistan. Torture is an international crime in itself, but it is also a war crime within the jurisdiction of the ICC, making it the most contemporary example of controversy surrounding both war crimes and the tribunal.

The Specific Case of Torture

The practice of torture, akin to war crimes, is an ancient practice that has been used for many purposes, notably as a means of execution, to extract information from its victims, even as a means of religious exorcism or conversion. The methods that torturers have devised have been numerous, hideous, and often excruciating, and while many people find torture morally reprehensible, barbaric, and unacceptable in any circumstance, specific acts and purposes for torture have received at least tacit support among members of many societies across time.

The contemporary attempt to eradicate the practice of torture is a product of the post–World War II world and has paralleled the expansion of notions of both sovereignty and war crimes. The UN Universal Declaration of Human Rights, for instance, specifically states in Article 5, "No one shall be subject to torture or to cruel, inhuman, and degrading treatment or punishment." This 1948 statement requires an accompanying belief that individual rights can be enforced when they are violated by sovereign states. The Fourth Geneva Convention on War further specifies that torture is a war crime—a crime against humanity, including the torture or inhumane treatment of prisoners of war. As a war crime, torture falls under the purview of the ICC as well.

The most specific statement of international norms regarding torture is the UN Convention Against Torture (UNCAT), which came into force in 1987. The United States ratified the UNCAT in 1994 and in the process informed the United Nations that "Each act of torture within the meaning of the Convention is illegal under existing federal and state law."

The UNCAT begins by defining torture as "any act by which severe pain or suffering, whether physical or mental, is intentionally inflicted on a person for such purposes as obtaining from him or a third person information or a confession, punishing him for an act he or a third person has committed or is suspected of having committed, or for any reason based on discrimination of any kind, when such pain or suffering is inflicted by or at the instigation of or with the consent or acquiescence of a public official or other person acting in an official capacity." Article 2 excludes the existence of states of war as a justification or excuse for committing torture: "No exceptional circumstances whatsoever, whether a state of war or a threat of war, internal political instability or any other public emergency, may be invoked as a justification for torture." Article 3 (1) specifically prohibits so-called "extreme rendition": "No state shall expel, return ('refouler') or extradite a person to another state where there are substantial grounds for believing that he would be in danger of being subjected to torture."

These prohibitions are sweeping. They are based on various judgments about the use of torture: that it is immoral, that it is unreliable as a means to extract accurate information, and that it invites retribution by others against states that practice torture. Those countries that have joined the UNCAT (and not all countries have) have explicitly renounced the sovereign right to torture, just as they have renounced war crimes more generally.

The issue of torture has arisen from accusations that the Bush administration has condoned, even authorized, the use of torture against "detainees" captured in Iraq and Afghanistan and suspected of being terrorists in possession of information useful to authorities conducting the war on terror. The Bush administration has denied these allegations on two basic grounds crafted in 2002 by Assistant Attorney General John Yoo and White House Counselor (and later Attorney General) Alberto Gonzalez. The grounds are that those detained are not the representatives of states and thus do not enjoy prisoner-of-war status under the Geneva Conventions and the UNCAT, and that specific "extreme methods of interrogation" employed do not constitute acts of torture. Both explanations are contentious, and the 2008 Supreme Court ruling that detainees have certain legal rights previously denied them may lead to proceedings that further clarify the situation. The Bush argument, principally articulated by former Vice President Richard Cheney, further contends that exceptional practices it refuses to label as torture are justifiable because of the government's obligation to provide maximum protection for its citizenry by extracting crucial information by extraordinary means. Its mandate as the sovereign protector of its citizens' safety, in other words, overrides efforts at international cooperation in the same way that defying the ICC may defend citizens from frivolous or arbitrary prosecution.

Accusations of torture provide potentially specific war crimes charges that could conceivably be brought against American officials at the highest levels. Presumably, the venue for exploring those accusations would be the ICC, but the United States has insulated itself from that possibility by refusing to ratify the ICC statute and thus subject itself to its jurisdiction. The other possibility would be to try Americans in U.S. courts where the principles of the UNCAT have been incorporated.

CONCLUSION AND DILEMMAS

Now that it has been raised and publicly entered the international agenda, the question of war crimes—including torture—is not likely to go away. In a gradually democratizing world in which authoritarianism is still practiced but rarely extolled, there is no longer any organized, principled objection to the notion that there are limits on both the conduct of war and how individuals and groups can be treated. Although the development of something like a consensus on this matter is really quite recent in historical terms (particularly the idea of crimes against peace and humanity), it nonetheless seems well on its way to being established as an international norm.

The major remaining question is institutionalization of war crimes enforcement. As noted in a quote at the beginning of this study, the emergence of a consensus has coincided with a spate of war crimes, principally in the bloody, brutal internal wars in a number of developing-world states. Darfur is the current symbol of man's inhumanity to his fellow man. Detention facilities at Guantanamo Bay in Cuba are a symbol regarding torture. The practical implication of this situation is that there are almost certainly going to be places where war crimes tribunals will need to be formed if there is not a permanent court.

Is the ICC the answer? Clearly, it would solve some problems and have some advantages, as already noted. It would certainly be more responsive when problems arise; it would maximize whatever deterrent value a potential violator would experience knowing the court was waiting for him or her; and it would insulate the system from accusations of victor's law in future cases. Moreover, it would contribute to the general promotion of lawfulness in the international system and, in specific cases, might help defuse public passions by removing trials from the places in which alleged crimes took place. To its proponents, these are powerful and compelling justifications for the ICC.

Then there is the American position. The U.S. objection to the ICC is not a defense of war crimes or torture or an explicit defense of international disorder. Rather, it stems from a long-standing American fixation with state sovereignty and the need for the American government to have sole jurisdiction over its citizens. In practice, this policy puts the United States at cross-purposes with most of the international community, including most of its closest allies, and on the same side as some rogue states on this and similar issues. Within the United States, there is division on the position to take: The Clinton administration did, after all, both champion and subsequently back down into opposition about the ICC and it led the ratification of the UNCAT. The Bush administration has redoubled opposition to the ICC and remained mute on the UNCAT. The Obama administration has remained officially mute on the subject. Given the American status as the remaining superpower, the American decision on ratifying the ICC statute or an amended version is probably critical.

In the end, the international debate pitting the United States against most of the rest of the world (and especially its principal allies) is not about war crimes or the establishment of a court. No one is *for* war crimes or *against* a tribunal to prosecute offenders, and no one publicly defends torture. The debate is over the nature of the court's jurisdiction and possible justifications of what some contend constitute illegal acts of torture.

The result is a clash between advocacies of war crimes and torture regulation and punishment and defenders of sovereignty. Which is more important? At one level, international cooperation against crimes against humanity (including torture) is clearly virtuous and praiseworthy, but what if such cooperation is detrimental to the ability of the state to protect itself from evils being committed against the state, including evil committed using those very acts the cooperation attempts to but cannot prevent? More concretely, if acts of torture against terrorists will result in thwarting terrorism, what is the higher virtue?

At another level, the dilemma is over the rule of law versus the primal right of self-protection. International cooperation in adjudicating war crimes or outlawing torture, after all, is self-interest. One reason that crimes against humanity are outlawed is based in reciprocity: if I do not commit these acts, you cannot justify using them either, so it is in both our interests to obey them.

But there will always be exceptions. Some people will always break the law, and in the case of war crimes, doing so can endanger the people of sovereign states. What should the state do in these circumstances? It is easy to delineate the extremes: the cooperative rule of law should triumph regardless of the human consequences, or states should do whatever they feel they must to defend themselves, regardless of the impact on law and even civilization. But most cases in the real world lie between the extremes, where the choices are neither so stark nor clear cut.

STUDY/DISCUSSION QUESTIONS

1. The commission of war crimes, including torture, is universally condemned, and international cooperation to end and punish these acts seem the obvious solution, but this has not always been the case. Why?

2. Discuss the evolution of the war crimes concept. What was the impact of the end of the Cold War and the tragedies of Bosnia and Rwanda on that evolution? How is the International Criminal Court the product of that evolution?

3. What are the various categories of war crimes? Discuss them historically and in terms of their current importance. How does torture fit into this discussion?

4. Are the arguments in favor of the International Criminal Court compelling? How much of the American objection to the question of automatic, overriding jurisdiction should be accommodated?

5. Is the participation of the United States necessary for the success of the permanent war crimes tribunal? Assess the American objection. Is it reasonable, arrogant, or possibly both? If you were the representative of another government, how would you feel about the American position?

6. Most situations in which allegations of war crimes are likely to occur are internal wars in the developing world; how does this affect the value of having a permanent court rather than ad hoc tribunals, as we have done up to now? Would a permanent ICC be more effective in deterring violators or investigating and bringing them to justice?

7. Should some measure of national sovereignty be surrendered to make the ICC effective? Which value is more important: national control over a country's citizens or justice for the victims and perpetrators of war crimes when those two values come into conflict?

8. Define torture. What is the UNCAT, and what does it do? Place torture in the context of war crimes.

9. Do you believe there are circumstances in which torture should be permissible? Why or why not?

10. The dilemma of war crimes and torture is that they are both universally condemned, but half the world's population lives outside the regime intended to regulate war crimes and a significant part of the world rejects official condemnation of torture. Can this dilemma be resolved?

READING/RESEARCH MATERIAL

Cobban, Helena. "Think Again: International Courts." *Foreign Policy*, March/April 2006, 22–28.

Convention against Torture and Other Cruel, Inhuman, or Degrading Treatment or Punishment. New York: United Nations, December 10, 1984.

Dempsey, Gary. *Reasonable Doubt: The Case against the Proposed International Criminal Court.* Cato Policy Analysis No. 311. Washington, DC: Cato Institute, 1998.

Elsea, Jennifer K. *U.S. Policy Regarding the International Criminal Court.* Washington, DC: Congressional Research Service, August 29, 2006.

Greenberg, Karen Joy. *The Torture Debate in America.* Cambridge, MA: MIT Press, 2005.

Gutman, Roy and David Rieff, eds. *Crimes of War.* New York: W.W. Norton, 1999.

Hersh, Seymour. *Chain of Command: The Road from 9/11 to Abu Ghraib.* New York: HarperCollins, 2004.

Kahn, Leo. *Nuremberg Trials.* New York: Ballantine Books, 1972.

Neier, Aryeh. *War Crimes: Brutality, Genocide, Terror, and the Struggle for Justice.* New York: Random House, 1998.

Savage, Charlie. "Monitors of Torture Treaty Rebuke U.S." *Boston Globe* (online), May 20, 2006.

Schmid, Alex P. and Ronald D. Crelinsten. *The Politics of Pain: Torturers and Their Masters.* Boulder, CO: Westview Press, 1994.

Tusa, Ann and John Tusa. *The Nuremberg Trial.* New York: Atheneum, 1983.

WEB SITES

Collaboration of journalists, lawyers, and scholars on laws of war and war crimes
    Crimes of War Project at http://www.crimesofwar.org
Overview of documents and events leading to Rome Statute
    Rome Statute at http://www.un.org/law/icc/index.html

Arguments about ICC and U.S. security interests
"A Summary of United Nations Agreements on Human Rights."
http://www.hrweb. org/legal/undocs.html

"Sheffer on Why U.S. Opposed International Criminal Court." http://www.usembassy.
org/uk/

Human Rights Watch: http://www.hrw.org/english/docs/2003,12/19/ira_6770.htm and
http://hrw.org.europe/083104milo.htm

Summary of "U.S. and International Law Prohibiting Torture and Other Ill-Treatment of
Persons in Custody." Human Rights Watch, May 25, 2004.
http://hrw.org/english/docs/2004/05/24/Usint8614_txt.htm.

Irresolvable Conflicts: The Israeli–Palestinian Impasse

PRÉCIS

A difficult problem facing the international system that largely arises from sovereignty is the existence of irresolvable conflicts, disputes so difficult that they defy successful attempts at resolution. The most extreme example of such conflicts in the contemporary international system is the conflict between the Israelis and the Palestinians, which is the subject of this case study.

The case will begin with a description of irresolvable conflicts, including their common characteristics and the basic methods that are available to try to resolve them. With that framework established, the dynamics of irresolvable conflicts will be applied to the conflict between Israelis and the Palestinians arising from the partition of the "holy lands" that began in 1948 and has evolved since. Following a brief description of the issues involved, the discussion looks at the American-brokered peace process that has been ongoing for over a quarter century, both in terms of its successes and ultimate failures. It then looks at the difficult and intractable differences between the two sides that have come to center and be symbolized by the growing presence of Israeli settlements on the West Bank, and will conclude with the prospects of moving this conflict to one or another form of resolution—resolving the irresolvable.

In a world composed of sovereign states and marked by a scarcity of resources pursued by those states—two issues examined in previous chapters—conflict is an unavoidable, ubiquitous aspect of international relations. In most cases, the conflicts are not so basic and fundamental that the states cannot find means to resolve those differences. Ideally, outcomes can be found that are mutually acceptable and thus satisfactorily resolve the differences in ways with which both sides can live. In other cases, differences cannot so easily be resolved and, at least some of the time, armed force in some guise becomes the way in which attempts are made—not always successfully—to resolve these differences. It is in these circumstances of deep, even irreconcilable, conflict that some of the most difficult problems reside.

IRRESOLVABLE CONFLICTS

Thoroughly vexing conflicts that present irreconcilable, irresolvable differences between the parties represent an important genre of international reality. In these kinds of conflicts, the issues that divide the two (or more) sides are so deep and fundamental that they cannot be resolved peaceably through diplomatic methods, either because the positions are so far apart or because the animosities between the parties are so great (or both) that they cannot find a basis on which to reach accord. Moreover, in these situations a military resolution wherein one side imposes its will on the other is either impossible or unacceptable to the international community as a whole—or some part of it that influences the parties involved—so that a coerced solution cannot be implemented.

These kinds of situations, fortunately enough, are comparatively infrequent, but they do occur and are particularly intractable and difficult for the system to deal with. Within the contemporary international system, the ongoing differences between Taiwan and mainland China about the status of the island Republic of China and the Indo-Pakistani conflict over Kashmir stand out, but the most difficult example is the division between Israel and the Palestinian people over the political future of the piece of real estate known as Israel or Palestine, depending on the person to whom one is talking. The Israeli–Palestinian conflict is such a textbook example of irresolvable conflict that it is the subject of this chapter.

Irresolvable conflicts share at least seven common characteristics. The first, which flows from the introductory discussion, is that the scarce resource normally involved is territory, the scarceness of which arises from the fact that there are multiples claimants to sovereign control over a piece of territory over which only one side can exercise sovereignty. In the case of China and Taiwan, for instance, both sides agree that Taiwan is rightly a part of China (some native Taiwanese disagree), and the question is over which political groups should exercise that sovereignty. The Kashmir question similarly revolves around whether India or Pakistan should exercise sovereignty over the mountainous formerly princely state of Jammu and Kashmir. The centerpiece of the Israeli–Palestinian feud is over who should rule all or different parts of the pre-partition territory once known as Palestine and has come to be centered on the Israeli-occupied West Bank of the Jordan River.

The second characteristic is that these territorial conflicts tend to be extremely emotional, deep, and fundamental. The emotion and depth arises from the fact that the territory is generally viewed as the rightful homeland of one or both sides, or the claims are rooted in some deep and fundamental division such as religion or ethnicity. Often (in the case of Palestine, for instance) individual plots of land in the disputed territories are viewed as the rightful home sites of individuals on both sides of the conflict, making their emotional attachment all the deeper than it might be otherwise. This emotional element can be—and often is—politically manipulated by those either seeking to avoid resolution of the conflict or wanting to subvert outcomes that do not work to their advantage. The fundamental source of division also makes compromise solutions extremely difficult to discover: It is, for instance, daunting to try to figure out how to divide a single dwelling between two hostile families that claim it.

Third, this emotional, fundamental base creates positions that become mutually exclusive and that consequently require mutually exclusive outcomes. Irresolvable conflicts tend to be viewed by both or all parties as strictly zero-sum exercises, in which one side's success is the other side's loss; there is little effort made or point in trying to find an accommodation in which both sides can benefit (a positive-sum exercise) or in which losses are equitably and acceptably apportioned (negative-sum games). In irresolvable conflicts, both sides will only accept outcomes in which they succeed and the other side does not.

Fourth, this intractability resonates throughout the populations affected in such a way as to reinforce the unwillingness and unacceptability of compromise. The position of each side often becomes viewed as "righteous" by the antagonists to the point that the simple idea of compromise becomes virtually a sacrilege and those who promote compromise become suspect. Such depth of emotion may be limited to the extremists on both sides of the conflict, but their influence may be disproportionate to their numbers. One way this can occur is by the extremists succeeding in establishing the rhetorical high ground and thus being able to relegate the compromisers to the status of infidels or traitors. Another way is to resort to violence to pump up the emotions of followers against any movement toward resolution by peaceful means. Both these methods have been prominently evident in the Israeli–Palestinian conflict.

A fifth shared characteristic is often the failure of outside mediation to move the dispute toward resolution. When disputes become heated to the point of combustibility, as irresolvable conflicts often do, it is only natural for outsiders with interests on one or both sides of the conflict to want to aid a process that will help defuse the situation, either by resolving it or by at least reducing its intensity so that it loses the ability or likelihood of bubbling over and disturbing international tranquility.

In some sense, the degree to which the particular conflict could endanger the situation affects the degree to which outsiders become interested. Conflicts between the government of Indonesia and East Timorese seeking independence did not attract much notice until reports of large-scale killings focused attention on the island of Timor; the isolation of the region from the global system meant that intervention was effectively regionalized with the lead involvement of Australia (which was mostly motivated by the fear of a stream of East Timorese refugees crossing the 600-mile straits to its shores). Similarly, the conflict over Kashmir attracted less outside interest until both India and Pakistan tested nuclear weapons in 1998. The more volatile Middle East, on the other hand, has ensured a high level of interest by the outside world in making sure their conflict does not spread to a general conflagration.

The sixth characteristic is the inability of the parties to find acceptable outcomes to the conflict, thereby guaranteeing its continuation. Conflicts over exclusive possession of scarce territorial resources are, of course, inherently difficult to resolve in an amicable manner, meaning that normal methods of conflict resolution have generally failed (that failure is what defines irresolvable conflicts). In this case, the only way to reach a conclusion may be through the imposition of a settlement favoring one side at the expense of the other, which may be impossible for one of two reasons.

One reason may be that neither side has the resources available to force a settlement on the other, at least within acceptable bounds of resource expenditure. The reason Kashmir remains in a state of uncertain sovereignty is that neither India nor Pakistan has the required military might to impose a settlement on the entire territory. The only way either country could conceivably do so would be to escalate the conflict to the point that it might become nuclear, an alternative the international community would find unacceptable (as would the affected populations, presumably). The failure of Israel to eliminate Hezbollah in Lebanon in 2006 suggests the possibility that there is no military solution to the Israeli–Palestinian problem as well.

In other cases, the imposition of force may be physically possible but geopolitically unacceptable. Israel, after all, has maintained authority over a good bit of land jointly claimed by it and the Palestinians since at least 1967, and militarily it is certainly conceivable—although more questionable since the Lebanon invasion—that Israel could reassert its sway over all the contested territories. Doing so, however, would likely broaden the conflict within the region, with uncertain outcomes—the worst of which could be catastrophic; and doing so would strain Israeli resources and relations with the rest of the world. As a result, any instincts the Israelis may have toward an imposed solution are effectively stifled by the consequences such an imposition might bring.

A seventh characteristic is that the longer an irresolvable conflict remains unresolved, the more the status quo may harden into a de facto solution that is unattractive to both but which becomes the least unacceptable outcome by default. The situations in Kashmir and Palestine (especially the West Bank) are exemplary. Both conflicts have their roots in 1948 (the partition of the Indian subcontinent and the independence of Israel), and neither has moved toward resolution in the intervening sixty-plus years. The issues—Muslim claims on Kashmir and Palestine—remain unresolved, and an unhappy de facto status quo (division of Kashmir along the "Line of Control" and Israeli occupation of the West Bank) has evolved an uneasy permanence. In the Palestinian case, this position has hardened, possibly irredeemably, due to continued and growing Israeli settlement in the disputed territory.

THE ISRAELI–PALESTINIAN CONFLICT

The ongoing conflict between Israel and Palestine meets all the criteria for an irresolvable conflict. It is quintessentially about sovereign control of territory that is coveted with great passion by both sides. The positions that both the Israelis and the Palestinians take toward their claims to the land are fundamental, deep, and emotional, profoundly shrouded in historical tenure and even religious claims and bases. Because "God" has empowered both sides in their own minds, the claims each has are deeply held by their supporting populations and make it essentially impossible for leaders on either side to propose major concessions or compromises, which can be (and are) viewed as heresy by those at the extremes on both sides. The positions are thus intractable, and outside attempts to mediate (in this case led mostly by the United States) have not succeeded in reducing the issues dividing the sides, despite strong and concerted efforts at trying to act as the midwife of settlement. Moreover, no imposed settlement in which one side is forced to accept great sacrifices is acceptable to that side, and even if it could physically be imposed by one side on the other, such a settlement would be internationally unacceptable, particularly in a region as volatile and important as the Middle East. The longer the dispute remains at an impasse, the more permanent the current outcome, which is basically unacceptable to both sides, appears the de facto outcome.

In order to understand this conflict as irresolvable, it is necessary to examine it and how it has evolved. This examination begins by looking at the structure of the problem, how it has evolved, and what the basic unresolved obstacles to resolution are. One factor that distinguishes this conflict from other irresolvable conflicts is the extraordinary efforts and prestige a major power—the United States—has ultimately unsuccessfully invested in trying to overcome the conflict, and so the record of attempted solutions, beginning with the efforts of Jimmy Carter at Camp David in 1978 and going forward through George W. Bush's "road map" for peace, will be reviewed. This background will form the backdrop for examining the contemporary conflict and its current most vexing manifestations—the continuing growth of Israeli settlements on the Palestinian territories (the West Bank), the Palestinian election of a majority of members of Hamas to the Palestinian Legislative Council in January 2006, and the Israeli attack on Lebanon in 2006. The study will conclude with an assessment of what, if any, prospects exist for resolving the irresolvable.

The Israeli–Palestinian Problem

The heart and soul of the disagreement between Israel and the Palestinians is a real estate dispute over the rightful ownership and sovereign control of the territory known to Muslims as Palestine and now largely controlled by Israel.

The contemporary basis of this dispute has its roots in the late 1800s, when the Zionist movement in Europe promoted the migration of increasing numbers of Jews to Palestine to avoid religious persecution and to fulfill what they viewed as a biblical admonition to return to the "promised land." The movement gained momentum after World War II and the Holocaust stimulated a surge of Jewish immigration to what they called Israel. It crested and became a problem with the establishment of the state of Israel in 1948.

The piece of territory over which the conflict alternately simmers and rages has been the subject of contention and violence for far longer than is reflected in the current impasse, which is in some ways just the most recent chapter in the saga over the "holy land." The roots of this disagreement date back to biblical times and have been the subject of innumerable treatises and arguments regarding rightful ownership over centuries and millennia that need not be repeated here, other than to note both that these claims exist and that they form underlying arguments to which both (or all) sides make reference to buttress their claims. For present purposes, suffice it to say that all parties have impressive, if contradictory, historical and scriptural arguments that buttress the cases they wish to make.

The current dispute has its origins in the immediate post–World War II period, although the movement to return much of the largely European Jewish population to the area goes back to the Zionist movement. This movement was essentially peaceful and the Jewish influx was absorbed by the Muslim Palestinians before World War II, when the two peoples, Israeli and Palestinian, essentially lived side-by-side in peace. Only when the post–World War II flood of Holocaust survivors found its way to Israel did the question of land become critical.

Israeli Independence, War, and Displacement

The movement of a large number of Jews into Palestine (at the time a part of Transjordan) stimulated the desire to create a Jewish state of Israel that had been central to the Zionist appeal and that many Jews believed had been promised them by God. This movement obviously disquieted many of the Muslim Palestinians, who found this possibility inimical to their centuries-long possession of the territory (which had, until the end of World War I, been part of the Ottoman Empire). When the Israelis declared their independence in 1948, after a declaration supported by the United States and the Soviet Union in the United Nations in favor of Israel's statehood, the result was violence.

There were two basic reactions to Israel's declaration as a sovereign state. One was the exodus of a large part of the Palestinian Muslim population, which feared retribution and repression under the new Israeli government. (There had been numerous instances of intercommunal violence on both sides in the months and years leading to the creation of the new state, thereby enlivening the fears of the Palestinians.) Most Palestinians fled with little more than the shirts on their backs and a few possessions, so that they became an instant refugee problem in the territories—especially the West Bank of the Jordan River—to which they went. The second reaction was for most of the surrounding Muslim states to declare war on the new Israeli state and to launch attacks designed to destroy Israel. These attacks were ineptly carried out and absolutely uncoordinated, so that military and paramilitary forces within the new Jewish state (which had been part of the resistance to postwar British administration of the area) easily repulsed the attacks. In the process, the original territorial boundaries of the Israeli state were actually enlarged by the outcome.

The 1948 war established the basic conditions that exist today, although the details have changed over time. There were two major effects. The first, most profound and most relevant, was the effect on the Palestinian Muslims. Most of the Palestinian population fled their homes in Israel and became refugees, and collectively the Palestinians constituted a *stateless nation* (a distinct people with no home state that they could claim). Such statelessness had been part of the burden of the Jewish population for nearly a millennium; the status was now transferred to the Palestinians. Because the surrounding territories into which the Palestinians fled were generally poor and incapable of absorbing the new residents, the status of most refugees was wretched, powerless, and, as time went by, increasingly hopeless. This set of circumstances forms the basic rationale for a demand for the creation of an independent Palestinian state. Such a state could be of two natures, which divides the current debate. One possibility is that the Palestinian state could be carved out of part of the original Palestine (leaving both an Israeli and a Palestinian state as the outcome—an arrangement that was part of the original Zionist plan for the area). The other possibility is to return Palestinian domain over the entirety of the area, thereby eliminating Israel. The nature of the resulting Palestinian state remains the most basic division between the two sides, the resolution of which is necessary if the conflict is to be resolved. A particularly vexing part of the territorial puzzle is the final disposition of Jerusalem, the site of religious symbols basic to Islam, Judaism, and Christianity.

The other outcome was to endow the new state of Israel with a kind of special status. On the surface, the Israelis were severely disadvantaged when they were attacked by forces from the surrounding states, including Egypt, Jordan, Syria, Iraq, and Saudi Arabia. Post-conflict analysis has shown that the forces arrayed against the Israelis were nowhere near as formidable as a cursory examination would suggest and that the Israelis actually had their attackers significantly outgunned and were better organized militarily than their assailants. Nonetheless, the Israelis emerged from the conflict as the heroes of a David-and-Goliath struggle in which they had prevailed. That aura would gradually fade, but it was a worthwhile adjunct for a period of time.

Two other wars were of greater consequence, if in different ways, one rewriting the map of the region and the other creating the geopolitical incentive to move concertedly toward resolution of the difficulties between Israel and its Muslim opponents. Each is thus important to view at least briefly.

The Six Days War of 1967

Slightly less than 11 years after the Suez conflict of 1956, war broke out again between Israel and its neighbors. The precipitant of the fighting was the removal of a UN force (the United Nations Emergency Force, or UNEF) from the Egyptian-Israeli border, where it had acted as a peacekeeping tripwire to prevent either country from attacking the other. When it left, Egypt launched an attack on Israel and was joined by the armies of Jordan and Syria. The result was an utter disaster for the Muslim states. The Israelis managed to decimate their opponents in the remarkably short period of six days, changing fundamentally the power balance in the region and setting the groundwork for the current conflict.

When the dust had settled at the end of the war, Israel not only had defeated the armed forces of each of its opponents but had also occupied significant territories belonging to each. From Egypt, the Israelis gained the Sinai Peninsula and the Gaza Strip, a small appendix of Sinai along the Mediterranean coast adjacent to Israel.

This territorial exchange greatly enhanced the physical security of Israel, because any future Egyptian attack against them would first have to fight its way across Sinai, which the Israelis fortified against such an incursion. At the same time, Egypt was badly embarrassed by having such a large part of its territory taken from it, and the occupation also meant that the east bank of the Suez Canal was now in Israeli hands (although the canal was closed for a time because of ships sunk in its waters during the war). The Israelis seized the West Bank of the Jordan River from Jordan, thereby further increasing its physical security by making it much more difficult for a future enemy to dash across the narrowest parts of Israel and effectively cut the country in two. Jordan, however, lost its most economically productive region. The Israelis completed the occupation by seizing the Golan Heights, a mountainous region bordering northern Israel that the Syrians had used to launch artillery attacks against Israeli *kibbutzes* before the war.

These outcomes both altered the geopolitical balance in the region and created the physical basis for the peace process that would follow. Egyptian humiliation at the loss of Sinai and Gaza and the consequent desire to regain those lost territories helped form the basis for negotiations with Israel a decade later that would begin the peace process at Camp David. At the same time, Jordan's loss of the West Bank changed greatly the Palestinian situation. Part of the change was that many Palestinian refugees had settled on the West Bank after 1948, and they were again displaced by the events of 1967, as more fled into Jordan and also Lebanon, where they added to political problems in those countries. Many Palestinians, however, remained in the occupied West Bank, where they were subjected to Israeli rule over what they considered part of their own historic lands. Some of the fuel for the *intifadas* (uprisings) in the 1990s and 2000s was sown in this change of control. At the same time, the seizure effectively ended the Jordanian claim on the West Bank and allowed negotiators to think of a solution to the Palestinian real estate dispute in terms encompassing both Israel and the occupied West Bank and Gaza. This transformation is especially important in so-called two-state proposals (proposals to create a Palestinian state alongside Israel). Little noticed at the time, the occupation of the West Bank and Gaza created the necessary precondition for Israeli settlements in both areas, a process that began as a trickle and has grown to a possible peace process drowning deluge in recent years.

Yom Kippur War of 1973

The Six Days War created the conditions with which the peace process would have to deal, and the Yom Kippur War created the perceived necessity and impetus to begin that process. The reasons had to do with the conduct and outcome of the war, and more important, what almost—but did not—occur during its conduct.

Two things stand out about the 1973 war. The first is that it was the first time the Israelis suffered significant military defeats against their Muslim rivals. As a result, the Israelis reportedly authorized the arming of their clandestine nuclear

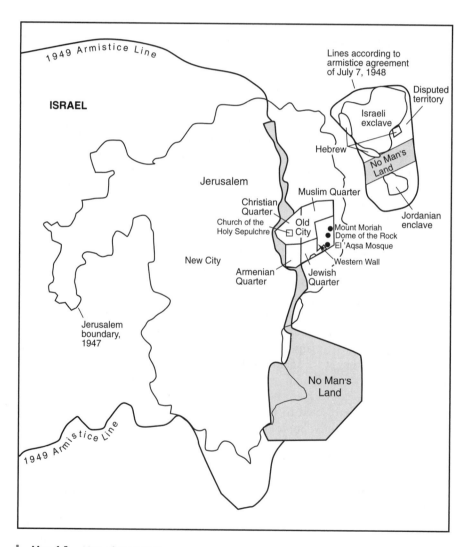

Map 4.1   Map of Jerusalem

arsenal for possible use against neighboring capitals to reverse their fortunes on the battlefield (the Israelis neither confirm nor deny that they either possess such weapons or that they activated them). This prospect greatly increased the likelihood that a Middle East conflict might escalate into a superpower nuclear confrontation, as the United States backed Israel and the Soviet Union backed the Islamic states in the conflict. Second, after the Israelis reversed the tide of military events and routed their opponents, the Soviets threatened to airlift troops to the front to save an Egyptian army from possible extinction, thereby further increasing the possibility of a superpower showdown. Like the nuclear arming by Israel, this possibility was also averted by diplomatic means.

The outcome changed the calculation of Middle East conflict in two ways. The very real prospect that the war could have somehow reluctantly drawn the United States into a confrontation that could have led to World War III convinced both sides, but especially the United States, that such a possibility had to be avoided in the future: The Arab-Israeli conflict was simply not worth a nuclear war that could destroy the United States. This recognition created the determination that finding a peaceful settlement (or at least averting future war) was absolutely necessary. The change made this outcome possible to pursue. The Soviets did not resupply their allies in the war—notably the Egyptians—as fast or as well as they would have liked, and Egypt broke its ties with the Soviet Union. The United States leaped into the power vacuum created by the Soviet departure and quickly established leverage with the Egyptians, in addition to its previous relationship with Israel. The possibility of a peace process was thus added to its perceived necessity.

THE PEACE PROCESS

The process of attempting to end the territorial imbroglio over Palestine was both the result of an outside determination by the United States that such an effort was necessary and an initiative by the parties involved. Some outside pressure was almost certainly necessary, because there had been no formal—or significant informal—relations between Israel and the surrounding Islamic states since the creation of Israel in 1948. Thus, it was necessary for some outsider to create a forum in which to pursue a settlement. Because the United States had supplanted Great Britain as the major outside influence in the area (a position enhanced by the forced withdrawal of the Soviets) and saw the necessity of ending the possibility that the region could ignite a global war, it became a logical candidate for that role.

The process began with the convening of Egypt and Israel for peace negotiations in the United States by U.S. President Jimmy Carter in 1978 at the presidential retreat at Camp David, and President William J. Clinton reprised that process in 2000. Between those events, Israel and Jordan independently negotiated an agreement, leaving only Syria and the Palestinians with unsettled differences with Israel. George W. Bush reactivated outside assistance in the process in 2003 when he presented his "road map" for solving the differences between the two. That initiative did not bear fruit, nor have attempts by the Obama administration broken the impasse.

The result has been some progress toward a peace agreement but a comprehensive settlement of this intractable conflict remains elusive. As is normally the case in complex negotiations, the parties settled what in retrospect appeared to have been the easier differences first, and as they peeled away the onion skin of differences, what remains are the most difficult issues. At the very core is the irresolvable conflict between Israel and Palestine, and notably the issue of territorial control and sovereignty centering on the West Bank.

Camp David I

That there even was a first meeting at Camp David is one of the miracles of twentieth-century diplomacy. Prior to the events that led to the meeting, Israel had never held official meetings of any kind with its neighbors (or the Palestinians), and all the Muslim states in the region were committed, to one degree or another, not only to denying the legitimate existence of Israel but also to destroying the Israeli state and hence to restoring Palestine to Muslim rule.

The process leading to Camp David began with the Yom Kippur War, as noted. When Jimmy Carter came to the White House in 1977, a peace in the region was at the top of his list of foreign policy priorities, and one of his first acts was to issue his plan for peace. The governments on both sides rejected the plan Carter proposed, but it became at least a beginning point for future discussions.

Egyptian president Anwar Sadat jump-started the process. In 1977, Sadat flew to Jerusalem, where he pointedly visited the Dome of the Rock and Al Aqsa mosque (the second-holiest sites in Islam, Muslim access to which had been denied since 1967) and met with Israeli Prime Minister Menachem Begin. The move was extremely bold because going to Jerusalem implicitly recognized the existence of Israel and thus broke ranks with his Islamic brethren in the region. Egypt and Sadat were roundly condemned in the region because of this contact, and, after the Camp David accords, were diplomatically and economically isolated. Begin took a chance because there was considerable Israeli opposition to the potential return of Sinai and Gaza to the Egyptians.

Sadat's visit to Jerusalem proved the stepping-stone for the meeting at Camp David in 1978. At the time, the very idea of accommodation between Israel and its enemies seemed a long shot at best. The meetings succeeded partly because Begin and Sadat showed extraordinary leadership in the face of tremendous opposition to the enterprise, and partly because they both needed something from the other that only the negotiations could provide. At the same time, what they could agree on was less than the entirety of the issues dividing Israel from the other states and from the Palestinians; on those issues that could not be resolved, the result was to defer the matter to future efforts.

There were three basic issues between the two negotiators. The first was Israel's desire to be recognized by its neighbors, including an admission of Israel's right to exist. Movement on this issue was sufficiently important to Begin that he was willing to compromise on other issues to realize it. Egypt represented the second and third interests. Egypt had been enormously humiliated by the forced cessation of Sinai and Gaza and badly wanted both back as a matter of national prestige and pride. At the same time, Egypt hoped that opposition to its discussions with the hated Israelis would be moderated in the Muslim world if it also managed to get the Israelis to move toward a Palestinian state.

Two of the three issues could be and were included in a quid pro quo, while the third was too difficult to settle in detail and was deferred for future consideration. As a result, the Camp David Accord (as it was known) consisted of three agreements:

1. The withdrawal of Israel from the Sinai Peninsula;
2. A peace treaty between Israel and Egypt that included recognition of Israel;
3. A promise to resolve the Palestinian question in the form of autonomy for the West Bank and Gaza Strip, which were to become the basis for a Palestinian state.

The first two provisions were implemented routinely. The Israelis withdrew from Sinai in two steps in 1979 and 1982, returning control (including control of an oil-producing capability developed by Israel during its occupation) to the Egyptians. The peace treaty between the two countries was signed in 1979, beginning the process leading to normal relations between them. Egypt got back the territory it wanted, and Israel got the recognition it desired.

The agreement foundered on the Palestinian question. The fate of the Palestinian state was much more complex and contentious than the other two issues, and thus it was deferred. The disposition of Jerusalem, a question that was and remains contentious, symbolizes this dispute. The problem is that both sides claimed (and continue to claim) the Old City (East) Jerusalem as their capitals, and there are numerous religious shrines that neither religious group is willing to entrust control over to the other side. The issue was thus intractable and effectively too difficult to resolve, so it was left unresolved for future negotiators. Carter explained the situation in a *New York Times* op-ed piece shortly after the conclusion of the negotiations: "We knew that Israel had declared sovereignty over the entire city but that the international community considered East Jerusalem to be legally part of the occupied West Bank. We realized that no Israeli leader could renounce Israel's position, and that it would be politically suicidal for Sadat or any other Arab leader to surrender any of their peoples' claims regarding the Islamic and Christian holy places." The fate of Jerusalem has remained a major sticking point in the process. At Camp David I, it was deferred for the future.

Camp David II

Between 1978 and the second Camp David summit in 2000 the peace process evolved. The most prominent example was the peace accord between Israel and Jordan signed in 1994. There was progress on some aspects of the relationship between Israel and its neighbors, but reaching a mutually satisfactory understanding and progress on the question of the Palestinians remained elusive.

The first Camp David Accord had promised a movement toward Palestinian "autonomy," but there was disagreement about exactly what autonomy implied. In the eyes of most of the Muslim world and among Palestinians themselves, autonomy over specific parts of the occupied territory was part of a process leading to full Palestinian control and sovereignty over the West Bank and Gaza and, eventually, to the establishment of a Palestinian state. To many in Israel, autonomy certainly meant turning over various local governmental functions to the Palestinian Authority (PA), but not necessarily total authority and not necessarily entailing a commitment to a sovereign Palestinian state. Most Muslim states saw this Israeli interpretation of Camp David I as simply further evidence of Israeli duplicity and intransigence.

A major breakthrough appeared to occur in 1993, when representatives of Palestine and Israel met secretly in Oslo, Norway, at the invitation of the Norwegian government. At those meetings, the parties agreed to what became known as the Oslo framework as a way to move talks forward. The Palestinian Liberation Organization (PLO) represented the Palestinians and agreed to end its call for the destruction of Israel and to renounce terrorism. In return, the Israelis agreed to withdraw their authority from Gaza and the West Bank city of Jericho and turn that authority over to the Palestinians. A deadline was also set for a final agreement to all issues by September 12, 2000.

Like Camp David I, progress toward fulfilling the promises of the Oslo accord lagged behind expectations. Violence continued on both sides, in the form of the first *intifada* by Palestinians and in isolated acts such as the assassination of Israeli Prime Minister Yitzhak Rabin by an Israeli extremist in 1995 and an attack against a Jerusalem mosque that left over 25 dead. At the same time, both sides accused the other of not living up to its side of the Oslo accords. The Israelis accused the PLO of failing to renounce violence and terrorism and used Palestinian suicide terrorist attacks as evidence. The Palestinians countered that the Israelis were not living up the agreements they had made for turning over jurisdiction to the PA.

With the September 2000 deadline looming and the end of his second term impending, American president William J. Clinton sought to revive the peace process in July 2000 by inviting Yasser Arafat, head of the PA, and Israeli prime minister Ehud Barak for a reprise of the 1978 meeting at Camp David. His hope was to achieve a comprehensive peace agreement that would simultaneously end the world's most intractable conflict and provide a pinnacle to his own term in office. Because of what proved to be irresolvable differences, the process ultimately failed.

By the time Clinton convened the parties at Camp David II, there were four major outstanding issues facing the conferees. They are presented from easiest to most difficult to resolve.

The largest and most public issue was the pace and extent of transfer of the West Bank and Gaza from Israel to the PA. Both sides had their own, very different timetables and formulas; as might be guessed, the Palestinians consistently insisted that more territory be transferred more quickly than Israel proposed. Israeli settlements in both Gaza and the West Bank exacerbated and continue to exacerbate the problem. These housing areas had been built after the 1967 occupation to accommodate the immigration of more settlers to Israel and were permanent enough in appearance to suggest that Israel would not turn them over to the Palestinians, although they were on land claimed as part of Palestine. Moreover, the Israelis placed the settlements on prime territory (for instance, where there was access to water, a scarce commodity), and the settlers stubbornly insisted that these settlements were permanent. These settlers, who feared being abandoned by Israel to what they assumed would be the not-so-tender care of the PA, became a highly emotional, vocal factor in Israeli politics; to many Israelis, abandoning the settlements and the settlers became equated with capitulating to the Palestinians. For some Israelis, permanent possession of the settlements and thus the West Bank is part of their plan for a "Greater Israel." The settlement problem now occupied center stage in the ongoing process.

The size and location of the settlements adds to the problem. Jeffrey Goldberg, for instance, reports that the settlers now number about 400,000, a little less than 10 percent of Israel's population, and are concentrated in more or less equal numbers on the West Bank and in the eastern suburbs of Jerusalem. Tiebel, for instance, asserts that "today, nearly 200,000 Israelis live in Jewish neighborhoods in East Jerusalem" that are claimed by Palestinians. Their continued existence, Goldberg maintains, is toxic: "These settlements have undermined Israel's international legitimacy and demoralized moderate Palestinians. The settlements exist far outside the Israeli political consensus, and their presence will likely incite a third *intifada*. Yet the country seems unable to confront the settlements."

Harry Siegman, former executive director of the American Jewish Council and of the Synagogue Council of America, agrees about the corrosive effects of the settlements: "No government serious about a two-state solution to the conflict would have pursued, without letup, the theft and fragmentation of Palestinian lands, which even a child understands makes Palestinian statehood impossible." Regarding apparent international indifference to the growth of these settlements, he adds, "What is astounding is that the international community, pretending to believe Israel's claim that it is the victim and its occupied subjects the aggressors, has allowed this devastating dispossession to continue." Kodmani reinforces this view: "Settlements and bypass roads amount to daily aggression, daily confidence-destroying measures, inflicted on Palestinians."

The settlement issue remains a central barrier to progress today. In November 2009, the Netanyahu government announced a freeze on new construction on the West Bank—largely at the insistence of the Obama administration—but in January 2010, Eldar reported that "dozens of settlements are experiencing a building boom" in apparent defiance of the Israeli self-proclaimed moratorium.

The second issue was the timing of the declaration of Palestinian sovereignty and total independence. The issue was, of course, related to land transfer by the question of sovereignty over what territory would become part of Palestine. This issue thus could be divided into two questions, on neither of which was there agreement: (1) *when* the transfer of authority would take place, and (2) *the physical extent* of the territory that would be ceded.

To Arafat, the answer to the first question was the deadline set under the Oslo accords, and he proposed that the declaration of the Palestinian state should occur on September 12, 2000, as set at Oslo, and he threatened to do so unilaterally if the conference at Camp David failed to reach an agreement. Barak, reflecting Israeli popular sentiment, believed the date should be deferred to when the PA had clearly put an end to terrorism against Israel by Palestinians (a position supported by Israelis who opposed any Palestinian independence).

The other question was the physical extent of the Palestinian state that would be created. At the time of Camp David II, the PA administered about 40 percent of the West Bank, and the question was, how much more territory (in addition to Gaza) would be added. As one would expect, the two sides were also divided on this issue, with Israel proposing less expansion than the Palestinians, who wanted the whole West Bank (the entire occupied territory). Such a division would deprive the Israelis of all the settlements they had built and was thus politically unacceptable in Israel. In the end, the two sides agreed that 95 percent of the West Bank would be ceded to Palestine, leaving the Israelis in control only of a few settlements basically contiguous to Israeli territory. Arafat eventually rejected this concession as part of rejecting the entire peace settlement.

Something like a compromise was possible in principle on the first two issues, but the same was not true of the third and fourth issues. The third was the question of East Jerusalem. As Jimmy Carter had noted over two decades earlier, the problem of who would control Jerusalem (or specific parts of it) had been a deal stopper that had been simply shelved in 1978, and no progress toward accommodation had ensued in the interim. The only difference now was that the eventual status of Jerusalem became an open matter of contention, and without a resolution to its status, an overall peace settlement could not be reached in 2000.

The issue itself had not changed. Both Israel and Palestine claim the city as their own, and Israel claims the entire city as its capital, whereas the Palestinians claim the Old City (East Jerusalem) as their capital. The positions are mutually exclusive, which means an agreement can be reached only if one or both sides agree to compromise.

Compromise, of course, is made all the more difficult because of the religious significance of Jerusalem to adherents both of Judaism and Islam (as well as Christianity). Access to the holiest sites (the Wailing Wall and the Little Wall to Jews and the Temple Mount to Muslims) is a *sine qua non* to both, but the physical contiguity of the sites makes the division of jurisdiction difficult or impossible. Because both Muslims and Jews have been denied access when the area has been controlled by the other, there is an understandable reluctance to cede control in any manner.

In the end, the impasse could not be overcome. The status of Jerusalem was not resolved, because the positions of each side is absolute (both sides claim sovereignty) and a history of animosity and treachery does not allow them to reach compromise solutions in which trust must inevitably play a part. This intractability is also built into the fourth and most irresolvable issue, repatriation.

The issue underlying repatriation (or what Palestinians call the "right to return") is conceptually simple, if extremely difficult to resolve. Palestinians who fled their homes in what is now Israel or were otherwise displaced from such home sites have never given up their belief that they are entitled to return and reclaim those pieces of real estate. Thus, they cling tenaciously to their supposed right to return to their homes. Israelis, who have since resettled and developed the land claimed by the Palestinians, equally believe they now hold clear legal title and that the Palestinian "right" to repatriation is not a right at all.

The issue is both geopolitical and political. The number of Palestinian expatriates who claim territory in Israel, when combined with the million or so Palestinian Muslims who reside in Israel (about one-fifth of Israel's population) and consider themselves "Palestinian citizens of Israel, not Israelis," according to Gorenberg, would exceed the Jewish population of the country. Thus, allowing the immigration of the Palestinians back to Israel/Palestine would effectively mean Israel would no longer be a Jewish state. Even though there are many Israelis who oppose the idea of a sectarian Jewish state, very few believe Jews should not be the majority in Israel. In addition, the return of the Palestinians would essentially double the population of the country, and it is not clear how such an influx could be physically accommodated. The same demographics result if a binational state (one state housing Israelis and Palestinians) is the final outcome of the dispute.

These geopolitical facts frame the political dilemma: The question of repatriation is fundamental, absolute, and nonnegotiable on both sides. No Israeli government could even consider repatriation because of the effects on the Jewish state and on individual Israelis who would suddenly find themselves in legal battles over their homes from former Palestinian occupants. Equally, no Palestinian politician can possibly renounce or negotiate away the right of the Palestinian refugees to return to what they view as their homes. The immediate prospects of return may be exceedingly dim, but the long-term goal is so strongly held as to be nonnegotiable.

Beyond Camp David: The Road Map

After the Camp David II talks collapsed without a final resolution, Palestinian violence returned in late 2000 in the form of the second *intifada* that has included Palestinian suicide/martyr bombings and reprisals by the Israeli Defense Forces (IDF). In February 2001, the Israelis elected a government that made Ariel Sharon prime minister, and he quickly visited the Wailing Wall, sparking predictable violence by the Palestinians. In addition, his government renounced the Camp David II proposals, a spokesman declaring "everything in Camp David is null and void unless it was signed, and nothing was signed." The government also took a hard line on remaining issues. Sharon backed away from Barak's offer of a Palestinian state composed of 95 percent of the West Bank, saying such a state would be based on the 42 percent of the territory administered at the time by the PA. In secret negotiating sessions held in 2007–2008, Yaari reports that the then Israeli prime minister, Ehud Olmert, reversed Sharon's course and "offered (PA President Mohammad) Abbas more territory than Ehud Barak had offered Arafat in 2000," but the offer was declined. On Jerusalem, Sharon declared the Old City is "the united and indivisible capital of Israel—with the Temple Mount as its center—for all eternity." On repatriation, he announced the renewal of the Zionist goal of Jewish immigration to Israel, which physically precludes the return of the Palestinians. None of these positions, of course, was or is acceptable to the Palestinians. At a tree-planting ceremony in early 2010, Kersner quotes Netanyahu as reiterating the hard-line Israeli position on these issues: "Our message is clear. We are planting here, we will stay here, this place is an inseparable part of the state of Israel for eternity."

The Bush administration made its contribution to the peace process in 2003, when it announced its "road map" for achieving peace, a set of guidelines to measure progress toward settlement. The road map proposed three sequential steps toward peace. In step one (2003), the Palestinians were to put an end to terrorism by Palestinians operating from Palestinian soil, and the Israelis were to suspend the building of new settlements on the West Bank and Gaza. In step two (2004), a provisional Palestinian government was to be established. In step three (2005), all "remaining differences" were to be settled and a Palestinian state was to be established.

THE CURRENT IMPASSE

The road map has failed to move the parties on any of the major issues. Between 2000 and 2004 there were no major changes in the conflict, but four sequential factors have coalesced that could influence the future. The first was the beginning of the erection of a fence dividing Israel from the West Bank, which began in 2004 and continues to the present. Depending on how it is completed, it could seal off the West Bank, both physically and psychologically, from pre-1967 Israel. Second, in 2005, the government of Ariel Sharon agreed to and carried out the end of the occupation of Gaza, thereby moving the territorial possibilities forward. In 2006, the dynamics changed as governments changed on both sides. Most dramatically in January, the Palestinians elected a majority of members of Hamas to the Palestinian Legislative Council. When Ariel Sharon was forced to resign his position as prime minister after a massive stroke left him incapable of remaining in office, new Israeli elections in April resulted in the election of Olmert as his successor. Olmert was succeeded in 2009 by Netanyahu after alleged scandals essentially drove him from office. Fourth, the outcome of the Israeli invasion of Lebanon in summer 2006 clouds the military balance in the region. Do these changes make a difference?

"The Fence," as it is simply known in the region, is a physical barrier gradually separating all of the West Bank from Israel proper. The Israelis erected a similar fence between its territory and Gaza in 1994. As David Makovsky explains, "since early 2001, not a single Palestinian suicide bomber has infiltrated Israel from Gaza." The Gaza fence thus serves as a precedent for building the similar structure dividing the West Bank from Israel proper. Moreover, Makovsky adds, the fence serves the Israeli interests "to reduce terrorism and to find a way out of the settlement morass that lets Israel keep a Jewish majority within its borders." In addition, Yaari argues the fence creates a psychological barrier that allows Israelis to avoid thinking about the personal impact of the occupation on Palestinians.

The fence has been loudly, and occasionally violently, opposed by the Palestinians on grounds as diverse as cutting through Palestinian territory to preventing (or making exceedingly difficult) Palestinian commuting to jobs in Israel. At the same time, an effective fence is bound to assuage Israeli fears of continued terrorism and thus relieve that barrier to creating a Palestinian state. By now, the fact of the fence is well enough established that its existence is not so much the issue as *where* it is placed, as it may form a boundary between Israel and a Palestinian state. If the fence minimizes Israeli settlements and thus maximizes the territory available to Palestine, it may turn into a blessing rather than a curse in the peace process. In an interview published in the April 17, 2006, edition of *Newsweek*, Olmert suggested that the final shape of the fence will reflect changing realities, saying, "The fence will have to be adjusted to the makeup of these blocs of settlements," which include the consolidation and elimination of some existing settlements. As Israelis point out, there have been no suicide bombings in Israel from Gaza or the West Bank since the fence was built.

The most fundamental change has occurred in Palestine, where the January 2006 elections swept Arafat's Fatah party from control of the Palestinian Legislative Council, replacing it with a militant government led by Hamas. Hamas has a dual image as both a scrupulously honest political movement (in contrast to the notoriously corrupt Fatah) as well as a continuing commitment to violence (including terrorism) and the destruction of the Israeli state. Its election resulted in international isolation (especially from outside assistance) for Palestine as a means to try to force Hamas to moderate its stance, especially on terrorism and the future existence of Israel. Its earliest statements have not spoken directly to either of these points (which Israel considers "deal breakers" on future progress), instead arguing that the initiative on future peace discussions lies with Israel. The ascension of Hamas does, however, create "a momentous experiment—the results of which will have a major impact on the future of Palestine, Israel, and the Middle East at large," according to Michael Hertzog (the son of Israeli military hero Chaim Hertzog). Having Hamas in control of Gaza and Fatah in control of the West Bank does not, however, create an opportunity for Israel to split the two apart in negotiations, because, as Kodmani asserts, "Gaza cannot be dealt with separately from the West Bank, just as a peace agreement cannot be reached with the West Bank alone."

The impact of Israel's failed attempt to destroy Hezbollah in Lebanon is related. It changes the military factor in two ways. First, as Salem argues, it punctures "the aura of invincibility long projected by the Israeli defence forces." Second, it makes the prospect of a forced resolution less plausible. As Djerejian argues, the "confrontation has further proved what should have been painfully clear to all: there is no viable military solution to the Arab-Israeli conflicts."

The Israeli situation has changed as well. Before his second stroke, Sharon orchestrated the turnover of Gaza (the stronghold of Hamas) to the Palestinians, despite enormous resistance from settlers and their supporters in Israel. The emergence of the Kadima Party (which Sharon created) as the leader of a new coalition after his stroke accentuates the winds of change. Prime minister Olmert took the bold position of favoring removing most Israeli settlements from the West Bank under a policy he called "convergence." This policy means "most of the settlements that would have to be removed . . . will be converged into the blocs of settlements that will remain under Israeli control," he said in his *Newsweek* interview. Netanyahu has backed away from these positions, and the recent growth of settlements potentially derails the peace process.

Consequently, the sincerity or likelihood of Israeli abandonment of the settlements seems increasingly suspect. The number of settlements and settlers continues to grow to over 270,000 settlers in 140 settlements in 2007, and others make higher estimates (a major variable is whether parts of east Jerusalem are included). Moreover, the spread of the settlements is rapidly changing the geography of the West Bank in ways unfavorable to the Palestinians. Friedman describes the conditions in June 2008: "The West Bank today is an ugly quilt of high walls, Israeli checkpoints, 'legal' and 'illegal' Jewish settlements, Arab villages, Jewish roads that only Jewish settlers use, Arab roads and roadblocks."

CONCLUSION

The Israeli–Palestinian dispute has remained irresolvable despite nearly 30 years of negotiations in which the United States has taken an active lead. Some progress has been made along the way, including the narrowing of the dispute to its current status as an Israeli–Palestinian conflict and the narrowing of the unresolved—and to this point unresolvable—issues of the size and shape of Palestine (of which Israeli settlements on the West Bank are the clearest manifestation); Jerusalem; and the right of return. The most notable prospect for progress has been the territorial issue of Palestinian statehood. A negotiation of the location of the fence could produce a Palestinian state on the West Bank and Gaza on which both sides can agree, but the timing and growth of Israeli settlements in occupied territories the Palestinians argue must be part of a Palestinian state muddies the prospects. Such an agreement will not, however, alter the intractability of the remaining issues, Jerusalem and repatriation.

The central issue about a Palestinian state is what kind of state it will be (or if it will come into existence). There are three possibilities. None of the possibilities is acceptable to all parties, and all parties arguably suffer from whichever of the three ultimately adheres. The failure to solve the underlying source of disagreement, notably the continued population of the West Bank by Israelis, prejudices the process and its outcomes.

The first possibility outcome is a continuation of the status quo of Israeli occupation of the West Bank. Many Israelis, and especially Netanyahu and his supporters, endorse this outcome, at least implicitly. From their viewpoint, a continued occupation allows further settlement and thus the pursuit of the Greater Israel goal of bringing a maximum part of Jewry to Israel by providing a place for these immigrants to live (a large portion of the current settlers are immigrants). Further, this policy, especially combined with the fence's forceful separation of the Palestinians from access to Israel, is popular with a not insignificant part of the Israeli electorate—notably the right. The disadvantages, of course, are that this outcome is totally unacceptable to the Palestinians, thereby ensuring their continued militant opposition, and brands Israel as an international "criminal," since settlement of occupied territory is a violation of international law.

The second solution is the two-state settlement, wherein an independent state of Palestine is established on the current occupied land on the West Bank (or at least most of it) and in Gaza. This solution has been the historic preference of the outside world, is favored by the Obama administration, and has support of the Israeli left. Hard-line Israelis have always opposed a fully sovereign Palestinian state on the grounds it would be a legally protected source of terrorist violence against Israel. There are, in addition, indications that the Palestinians may not really support this outcome either. As Yaari explains, "Many Palestinians now feel that by denying Israel an 'end of conflict, end of claims' deal, they are increasing their chances of gaining a state for which they would not be required to make political concessions." The reasoning is that the two-state solution offers only a partial recovery of Arab lands seized by the Israelis, when the real desire is for a return of *all* Palestinian lands.

The third possibility is a single Israeli/Palestinian state encompassing both pre-1967 Israel and the West Bank and Gaza, which might fulfill the Palestinian dream. Demographically, such a state would have a majority of Palestinian Muslims, meaning it could remain a Jewish state (or Jewish-dominated state) only by becoming what former U.S. President Jimmy Carter referred to as an "apartheid" state wherein the Israeli minority had full political rights that would be denied to the Palestinian majority. A democratic (one-man one-vote) state would be dominated by the Palestinians, which is the ultimate Israeli nightmare.

The ongoing impasse prejudices these options as realistic alternatives. The most notable example is the continuation (and especially expansion) of the settlements on the West Bank and the two-state solution. Given the sheer volume of Israelis now living in the occupied territories, it may already be impossible to implement a two-state outcome simply because of their presence: no Israeli government is likely to try to remove all of them (where they would put them is a virtually insurmountable problem), and such an action would ignite a domestic firestorm against any Israeli government that attempted it. At the same time, the continued presence of the settlers relieves the Palestinians of any need to push for a West Bank/Gaza state that many apparently privately oppose, because a continued Israeli presence would be intolerable in such an entity. Effectively, this may mean the two-state solution is already effectively off the table, leaving the unpalatable options of the status quo or a unified state.

The settlements issue remains the most prominent face of continued intractability in the peace process. In late 2009, the Israelis instituted a moratorium on new construction in the disputed territories (while allowing continued construction of dwellings already begun) for 10 months, and the result was a flurry of peace negotiations in September 2010, notably a Washington meeting between Palestinian leader Mohammed Abbas and Netanyahu sponsored by President Obama that temporarily rekindled hope for progress. The moratorium expired on October 1, 2010, however, and building resumed on the West Bank, effectively dampening hopes for peace again.

The Jerusalem and repatriation issues are both either/or propositions with little leeway for compromise, but an outcome on each is necessary for any overall settlement. Both also meet the criteria for irresolvable conflicts: They are territorial; they are based on mutually exclusive perceptions of outcomes; they are deeply held and emotional; the positions held on both sides do not facilitate compromise; outside efforts at mediation have failed to remove the issues; and unilateral solutions are unacceptable internationally.

Of the two issues, Jerusalem is—at least in principle—resolvable. A formula for dividing physical sovereignty over parts of Jerusalem is conceptually possible, if both sides find ways to lower the emotional trappings of devotion to their religious shrines and the question of what parts of the city might be the capital of each state. Some resolution is critical, because as Palestinian negotiator Ahmed Qurei put it in June 2008, "If there is no Jerusalem there is no agreement," as quoted in Kershner.

Repatriation, the right of return, is another matter. Palestinians either have or do not have a right to return to their former homes, and Israelis either do or do not have a legal or moral imperative to accommodate the Palestinians. The only possible forms of compromise are possible to state, but not to implement. One solution is deferment of the problem, which is the de facto current nonsolution. Under this arrangement, neither side must compromise, but the implementation of the outcome is put off to a future time. This solution simply puts off the problem. The other solution is to allow *some*, but not all Palestinians to return. Such a solution eliminates the outcome of a non-Jewish state of Israel, but leaves for future resolution *who* gets to return and *which* Israelis have to forfeit their property. It is hard to imagine how that can be done, but until it is, the Israeli–Palestinian conflict remains a classic example of an irresolvable conflict.

STUDY/DISCUSSION QUESTIONS

1. What is an irresolvable conflict? What distinguishes such a conflict from differences that can be resolved?
2. What are the characteristics of an irresolvable conflict? How do they build on and reinforce one another?
3. In terms of the six characteristics of an irresolvable conflict, assess the Israeli–Palestinian conflict.
4. Discuss the basic dynamics of the Israeli–Palestinian conflict. How did it come about? How did it evolve between 1948 and the beginning of the peace process in 1978? Why are the Six Days and Yom Kippur Wars so important in that evolution?
5. What have been the steps in the peace process between the Israelis and Palestinians? Discuss each step in terms of accomplishments and failures.
6. What basic issues continue to divide the two parties? Rate and discuss each in terms of intractability and thus its contribution to the inability to resolve the conflict.
7. What is the current status of the conflict? What recent events have occurred that might affect the dynamics? Will they?
8. Is there realistic hope for a resolution of the Israeli–Palestinian conflict? What forms could such a resolution take? Assess each.

READING/RESEARCH MATERIAL

Bronner, Ethan. "Carter Says Hamas and Syria Are Open to Peace." *New York Times* (online), April 22, 2008.

Carter, Jimmy. "A Jerusalem Settlement Everyone Can Live With." *New York Times* (online), August 6, 2000.

———. *Palestine: Peace Not Apartheid.* New York: Simon and Schuster, 2006.

———. "Palestine: Peace Not Apartheid. Jimmy Carter in His Own Words." *Democracy Now* (online), November 30, 2006.

Djerejian, Edward P. "From Conflict Management to Conflict Resolution." *Foreign Affairs* 85, 6 (November/December 2006), 41–48.

Eldar, Akiva. "Construction in West Bank Settlements Booming Despite Declared Freeze." *Haaretz.com* (online). January 1, 2010.

Friedman, Thomas L. "U.S. Must Shake Up Peace Process to Have Any Hope of Success." *Island Packet*, June 8, 2008, A16 (reprinted from *New York Times*, June 7, 2008).

Goldberg, Jeffrey. "Unforgiven." *The Atlantic* 208, 4 (May/June 2008), 32–52.

Gorenberg, Gershom. "Think Again: Israel." *Foreign Policy*, May/June 2008, 26–32.

———. *The Accidental Empire: Israel and the Birth of the Settlements: 1967–1977.* New York: Times Books, 2006.

Haas, Richard N. "The New Middle East." *Foreign Affairs* 85, 6 (November/December 2006), 2–11.

Hertzog, Michael. "Can Hamas Be Tamed?" *Foreign Affairs* 85, 2 (March/April 2006), 83–94.

Kershner, Isabel. "Netanyahu Says Some Settlements to Stay in Israel." *New York Times* (online), January 25, 2010.

Khalidi, Rashid. "Palestine: Liberation Deferred." *The Nation* 286, 20 (March 20, 2008), 16–20.

Kodmani, Bassma. "Clearing the Air in the Middle East." *Current History* 107, 709 (May 2008), 201–206.

Makovsky, David. "How to Build a Fence." *Foreign Affairs* 85, 2 (March/April 2006), 50–64.

Ottaway, Marina S. "Promoting Democracy after Hamas' Victory." Washington, DC: Carnegie Endowment for International Peace, March 2006.

Robinson, Glenn E. "The Fragmentation of Palestine." *Current History* 106, 704 (December 2007), 421–426.

Rubin, Barry. "Israel's New Strategy." *Foreign Affairs* 85, 4 (July/August 2006), 111–125.

Sadat, Anwar. *In Search of an Identity: An Autobiography.* New York: Harper and Row, 1978.

Salem, Paul. "The Future of Lebanon." *Foreign Affairs* 85, 6 (November/December 2006), 13–22.

Shlaim, Avi. "A Somber Anniversary." *The Nation* 286, 20 (March 20, 2008), 11–16.

Siegman, Henry. "Tough Love for Israel." *The Nation* 286, 27 (May 5, 2008), 7–8.

Tiebel, Amy. "Netanyahu Stakes Claim to West Bank Settlement." *My Way* (online), January 24, 2010.

Waxman, Dov. "Between Victory and Defeat: Israel after the War with Hizballah." *Washington Quarterly* 30, 1 (Winter 2006–2007), 27–42.

Weymouth, Lally. "We Are Ready for Change." *Newsweek*, April 17, 2006, 34.

Witte, Griff. "Carter: Hamas Ready to Live Beside Israel." *Washington Post*, April 22, 2008, A10.

Yaari, Ehud. "Armistice Now." *Foreign Affairs* 89, 2 (March/April 2010), 50–62.

WEB SITES

The Middle East Peace Summit, 2000: http://www.mfa.gov.il/go.asp/MFA
UN documents on Palestine question: http://www.un.org/Depts/dpa/qpal
U.S. policy: http://www.state.gov/p/nea
Israeli positions on conflict: http://www.mfa.gov.il
Palestinian positions: http://minfo.gov.ps.

National and International Security

Arguably the most important function that states provide their citizens is physical security against harm from other states or groups (national security), and the security of the entire world (international security) is at least an implied goal of those promoting national security. Security, like any other element of international politics, is a complex and multifaceted problem, and the chapters in Part II attempt to look at four important aspects of that question: the evolution of warfare to a contemporary emphasis on asymmetrical war; the proliferation of weapons of mass destruction, principally nuclear weapons; the problems created by important regional states whose interests come into conflict with those of the leading powers; and the international practice of peacekeeping as a response to humanitarian disasters. Each problem is viewed through the lens of a contemporary example.

Chapter 5, "Asymmetrical Warfare," looks explicitly at the direction that physical warfare is taking and will likely take in the future. In a world where conventional military power (symmetrical force) is concentrated in the largest countries (notably the United States) but where the disagreements that lead to violence often pit weaker powers against the strongest, the result has been the increasing recourse to unconventional, asymmetrical measures that allow weaker powers to compete with their stronger adversaries. The current best example of asymmetrical warfare is the ongoing war in Afghanistan, which is the subject of Chapter 5.

Chapter 6, "Proliferation," addresses the highly politically explosive problem of the spread of weapons of mass destruction, notably nuclear weapons, to countries that do not currently possess them. The problem of proliferation has been a major concern for nearly a half-century, and the chapter discusses the dynamics of why states seek to gain weapons others do not want them to have and what those who seek to limit proliferation can do to prevent the spread of those weapons. The case of the Democratic People's Republic of Korea (DPRK or North Korea) is a particularly vivid example of this problem, with major implications for the future.

Chapter 7, "Pivotal States," looks at the impact of prominent regional powers, what are called pivotal states, on regional and international power balances. Pivotal states are countries that are important within their regions of the world, and their interests often clash with the global interests of the largest powers. The problem for the great power is how to gain support for its interests among pivotal states, and the results are not always positive. The case of Iran in the Persian Gulf region is a particularly poignant contemporary instance of the role pivotal states play.

Chapter 8, "Peacekeeping," deals with the use of internationally created and sanctioned military force to bring peace to war-stricken areas where great human suffering (humanitarian disasters) is occurring. Peacekeeping, as this phenomenon is generally known, has been associated with the United Nations, but it covers a range of activities that go well beyond the traditional roles of UN peacekeepers. The chapter examines the various aspects of peacekeeping, and then applies them to the most publicized contemporary instance, the peacekeeping mission to the Darfur province of Sudan.

Asymmetrical Warfare: The Case of Afghanistan

PRÉCIS

Anticipating the nature of future conflict and preparing for that form of combat has always been a primary responsibility for those charged with national and international security. Doing so is always a difficult process involving extrapolation of the past into the future.

Warfare in the twenty-first century, at least as manifested in its first decade, differs significantly from how and why warfare was conducted in the prior century, and those differences extend to the outcomes and expectations that come from war. The dominant characteristic of contemporary warfare is its asymmetrical, or unconventional, nature, and this description is unlikely to change in the near future. This case examines the nature of modern, asymmetrical warfare, applies those observations to the war in Afghanistan, and extrapolates those observations into thinking about war in the future.

War is one of humankind's oldest institutions, involving the attempts by groups of people to impose their will on other groups of people by the use of coercive force. Humans have organized in different ways to conduct wars—as ethnic tribes in Biblical times, Greek city-states, the Roman Empire against tribal armies to the enormous clashes between coalitions of states locked in the world wars that made the twentieth century humanity's bloodiest epoch. Exulted or decried, warfare has been one of history's constants.

The early twenty-first century is no apparent exception to this historical continuity. In some ways, warfare has changed in the new millennium, but the preparation for and the conduct of war remains an apparently inexorable part of human existence. As a result, thinking about and planning for war always has been, and continues to be, an important endeavor. As will be argued in this chapter, warfare in the new century has taken on different characteristics than those that dominated the past 100 years, but it is still war, and it still must be understood.

It is, and always has been, a difficult problem. War planning, by definition, is a projection into a future that does not yet exist and which, by definition, cannot be known entirely in advance. Will the same kinds of weapons be available in the future as there were in the past? If there are new weapons, what will they be like, how will they be used, and what will be their effect? Who will have the new weapons, and who will not? How will weapon balances affect patterns of war? For that matter, who will the enemy be? Where will I have to fight the next adversary? How likely am I to succeed?

Because the answers to any of these questions cannot be known precisely in advance, uncertainty has always been a major part of the operational universe of the military planner. Uncertainties produce an environment laced as well by an aura of conservatism and seriousness. It is conservative because reckless innovation and lack of preparedness can lead to devastating vulnerabilities. It is serious because the wrong decisions—the failure to prepare properly or adequately—can literally endanger national existence. Because of these potential consequences, there is a built-in propensity to overprepare—to anticipate more threats than realistically exist. Conservatism and the seriousness of mistakes also predispose planners to emphasize ways of doing things that have worked in the past—to stay "inside the box"—rather than to embrace change and its uncertainties. The result is a tendency to prepare "to fight the last (most recently concluded) war."

The problem of gauging the future of war is especially acute today. Since the end of the Cold War, much of the preparation that states have undertaken in planning for war has been an attempt to adapt military planning and practice from its roots in conventional war between large powers to new realities of which the movement toward asymmetrical warfare is the prime example. Will this effort succeed?

It depends. One of the most important aspects of preparing for future war is anticipating against whom one is likely to have to fight. Although many Americans sought to ignore the warning signs during the 1930s, it was pretty clear that World War II would find the United States on one side and countries like Germany and Japan on the other (at least retrospect suggests that structure of the conflict). During the Cold War, it was absolutely clear that the enemy was the Soviet Union and its communist allies. The structure of the situation dictated the content of the planning process.

Not all planning has such a clear focus. In August 1990, Iraq invaded and quickly conquered Kuwait. This act of aggression would ultimately activate a coalition of over 25 states, none of whom had given much if any thought to the possibility of war with Iraq as little as a few months before the invasion occurred. The lesson was that some problems can be easily anticipated; others cannot. The largely unanticipated terrorist attacks of September 11, 2001, redouble the point.

The answer begins by examining how, or if, war is changing. Most of the past century or more was dominated by a style and philosophy of warfare that was heavily Western and which culminated in the way World War II was fought, what is now called symmetrical warfare (both sides fight in the same manner and basically by the same rules). Since early in the post–Cold War world, that has changed. Arguably, warfare is changing fundamentally from the confrontation and clash of mass armies to a more asymmetrical form in which weaker foes seek to negate Western styles with non-Western variants on war in which the two sides are dissimilar in organization and purpose and do not fight honoring the same rules and conventions. September 11, 2001, may be remembered as the harbinger of this change in the nature of warfare. The American and NATO effort in Afghanistan may be the precedent for the future.

The problem of preparing for future war boils down to four basic considerations. The first is the conflict environment, and the main factor in that environment is the nature of the adversaries one may encounter in the future, including why and how one may have or want to fight them. In the past, war was between the organized armed forces of states. Contemporary conflicts often pit traditional armed forces against so-called nonstate actors, forces with neither territorial base nor governmental affiliation. The second consideration is the physical structure of warfare, which encompasses the means available for adversaries to fight one another and the degree to which the means available are appropriately adapted to achieve military ends. In the contemporary era, the means are widely disparate for different foes, creating the basis for asymmetrical approaches for the disadvantaged. The third concern is determining against whom one might have to fight in an environment that has not witnessed a major war in over 65 years—and where possible enemies are difficult to anticipate in conventional ways. The fourth, and often incompletely considered, factor is the postwar peace: What conditions will be created in the so-called "postconflict environment"? Failure to consider this aspect adequately can result in the so-called "winning the war and losing the peace."

Planning for the wars of the twenty-first century requires applying these criteria to contemporary conflicts and extrapolating into an uncertain future that is unlike the past experience of the twentieth century in several important ways. For one thing, there are no obvious major, conventional adversaries in the system, due in large measure to the ideological harmony among the major powers in the current international system. The answer to the question, "preparing to fight whom?" is especially fraught with uncertainty regarding who to prepare to fight and how to prepare to fight them. The long gap between major wars has allowed the accumulation of many militarily relevant technologies that have greatly enhanced the conventional capabilities of those who possess them. Some of the electronically based innovations have been employed in "shooting galleries" like the Persian Gulf War and Operation Iraqi Freedom in 2003, and the primary lesson these victims seemed to have learned is not to fight the West (especially the United States) on its terms. The imbalance in symmetrical capabilities has in effect done two things: It has made the development of asymmetrical, technology-negating methods the primary dynamic of the present, and it has arguably rendered symmetrical warfare archaic because no one will fight that way. Finally, fighting against unconventional opponents complicates the task of planning and executing stable postconflict peace arrangements. This is true in part because these wars rarely have decisive "end games" where one side or the other capitulates. The calculation is further muddied by the fact that the real outcome—whose purposes were and were not served by war—is often unknown for some time, often years, after the fighting stops.

The remaining pages of this chapter are devoted to understanding the challenge of asymmetrical warfare to thinking about war—its purposes, its conduct, and its outcomes. It will proceed in two sequential parts. First, it will examine the evolving, often amorphous nature of asymmetrical warfare, the conceptual core of the chapter. Second, it will apply those observations to the international system's most prominent current instance of asymmetrical warfare, the war in Afghanistan. The observations from the general description and Afghan application will then be extrapolated to the problem of war in the future.

ASYMMETRICAL WARFARE: NEW/OLD WAR

Warfare, particularly as it involves major powers like the United States, has changed enormously since the end of the Cold War, for essentially two obvious reasons. The first is the collapse of militarily based major power rivalry. Unlike the Cold War confrontation between the world's two most militarily powerful countries, such rivalry has receded to economic competition with very little potential to escalate to armed violence. The large, heavy conventional (symmetrical) armed forces and accompanying purposes for war have been made arguably obsolete in the process. Second, the remaining conflicts in the world are mostly in the so-called developing world, either pitting developing countries against one another or against major powers, or in the form of internal conflicts within countries in which the major powers may have an interest. Weaker countries or movements cannot compete against the major powers militarily on their own symmetrical terms and this must turn to other asymmetrical means of competition.

The result is the rising prominence of asymmetrical warfare in the pantheon of modern warfare. Before beginning to explore this phenomenon, however, two preliminary observations are necessary. On one hand, what some have called the "new" way of war is not new at all. Asymmetrical warfare, in its simplest description, features the adaptations an inferior force makes when it is faced with a more powerful force with which it cannot compete successfully on the terms preferred by the superior force. Thus, asymmetrical warfare is as old as war itself. Relatedly, asymmetrical warfare is an approach to warfare, not a form of war or combat. Put another way, it is a methodology, a way to organize the problem, not a method or set of battlefield of theater instructions.

For those reasons, all the elements of the planning process are different than they used to be. The conflict environment and the physical structure of warfare are no longer based on the European model of conflict featuring the clash of similarly organized and equipped mass armed forces. The composition of likely enemies to be deterred or, if necessary, fought, is more likely to be that of a developing world country, or even more likely, some subnational group such as insurgent or even terrorist organization. The nature of stable postconflict environments is much more fluid, indeterminant, and less distinct.

Conflict Environment

Traditional geopolitics has clearly taken a beating since the end of the Cold War. The traditional base—politico-military alliances facing one another—has evaporated. The first victim of the end of the Cold War has been the structure of adversarial relationships that provided concrete military problems against which to prepare. In some ways, this is a considerable improvement over the past. It means that for now, as noted, there is virtually no likelihood of major war between the most powerful countries of the world on the scale of the world wars. Certainly the tools for such a war are still available, but it is difficult to conjure the circumstances that would ignite such a conflagration. There are a few places in the world, for instance the Indian subcontinent, where adversaries might become involved in a war of fairly large proportions, but none of those places would raise the distinct likelihood of drawing in other major actors on opposite sides and thus widening the conflict to anything like the scale of World War III (the major planning case of the Cold War).

The conflict environment is thus different in two distinct ways. First, the imbalance in conventional capability between the United States and the rest of the world means no one is likely to confront the United States in large-scale conventional warfare. Those who oppose the United States must devise new ways to do so. As Bruce Berkowitz puts it, "Our adversaries know they cannot match the United States in tanks, planes, and warships. They know they will most likely lose any war with us if they play according to the traditional rules." This innovation is the second new characteristic of the environment: the adoption and adaptation of asymmetrical ways to negate the advantages of overwhelming military capability and the emergence of new categories of opponents, such as nonstate actors. Asymmetrical approaches are intended, in Berkowitz's terms, "to change the rules to strategies and tactics that avoid our strength head-on and instead hit us where we are weak." This problem is progressive, because the core of asymmetrical warfare is constant adaptation, meaning the problem is never exactly the same from instance to instance. Moreover, traditional warfare is directed at state-based political opponents, and it is not clear how one subdues an opponent who lacks such a base.

Asymmetrical warfare is ancient. As Renee de Nevers points out, asymmetrical wars are "perhaps better understood as reversions to very old wars." The Thirty Years' War, for instance, featured marauding bands that would now be called nonstate actors, and the nineteenth-century resistance to colonialism certainly featured highly mismatched forces. It is different in terms of the problems for which it is conducted; how those who carry it out think and act; and in terms of the motives of the asymmetrical warrior. Asymmetrical warfare is not only militarily unconventional but it is also intellectually unconventional.

The United States' first major encounter with asymmetrical warfare was in Vietnam. (The country had previous limited experience in places like the

Philippines at the turn of the twentieth century, but on a much smaller scale.) Vietnam mixed symmetrical and asymmetrical characteristics. In terms of its purposes, it was quite conventional: The North Vietnamese and their Viet Cong allies sought to unify Vietnam as a communist country, and the South Vietnamese and the Americans sought to avoid that outcome. In terms of conduct, however, the war was unconventional. The North Vietnamese concluded early in the American phase of the war that they could not compete with the United States in symmetrical warfare because of visibly superior American firepower. Instead, they reverted to tactics of harassment, ambush, and attrition, the purpose of which was to produce sufficient American casualties to convince the American people that the cost of war was not worth the projected benefits. The North Vietnamese could not have succeeded fighting by the American rules. Their only hope was to change the rules and fight in a way that minimized American advantage and gave them a chance. It worked.

The heart of asymmetrical warfare is not a set of tactics or strategies, but instead is a mindset, as already noted. The potential asymmetrical warrior always begins from a position of military inferiority, and the problem, as Berkowitz points out, is how to negate that disadvantage. Adaptability is at the heart of asymmetrical approaches to warfare. If one asymmetrical tactic does not work, try another. Vietnam was a primer for those who may want to confront American power, but an organization like Al Qaeda or the Iraqi resistance to the American occupation could not succeed simply by adopting Vietnamese methods (for one thing, there are no mountainous jungles into which to retreat after engagements). Instead, the asymmetrical warrior learns from what works and discards what does not. Iraq is a case in point.

In 1990–1991, Iraq attempted to confront the United States conventionally in Kuwait and was crushed for its effort. It apparently learned from this experience that a future conflict with the United States, the prospects of which Iraq faced after September 11, 2001, could not be conducted in the same manner as before without equally devastating results, which included the decimation of Iraqi armed forces.

What to do? The answer, largely unanticipated by the United States, was to offer only enough resistance to American symmetrical force application to make the Americans think they were prevailing, while regrouping with important parts of the military structure to resist an occupation that they were powerless to prevent. Thus, the limited form of irregular warfare (ambushes, car bombings, and suicide terror attacks) became the primary method of resisting the Americans, aimed, apparently, at the same goal the Vietnamese attained 30 years earlier—convincing the Americans that the costs of occupation were not worth the costs in lives lost and treasure expended.

Whether this was some carefully modulated plan formulated in advance of the invasion by the Iraqis or not is not the point (and it is a point for which adequate evidence is not available anyway). What is hardly arguable is that the United States underestimated the likelihood of such an asymmetrical response in planning the invasion in the first place. In postinvasion analysis, the argument is frequently made that American planning was flawed in, among other ways, its failure to allocate sufficient troops to the effort. The criticism is valid but somewhat misses the point. The troop numbers were clearly adequate for a symmetrical invasion and conquest, which is all that was anticipated. The troop levels were (and remained) inadequate for a protracted resistance to occupation, which was an asymmetrical response that was not anticipated. If asymmetrical actions are likely in the future (and the success of the Iraqi resistance has to be encouraging to potential asymmetrical warriors), it is necessary to look at the physical dynamics of these kinds of situations.

Physical Structure of Warfare

What is absolutely clear about the future of warfare involving asymmetrical methods is that its face is uncertain. Part of the reason is the changing nature of the face of war. A primary characteristic of future conflict is that it is itself changing. Vietnam was a prototype, but the experience in Vietnam became the baseline from which others would adapt, changing the problem the next time it was applied. Similarly, the next asymmetrical challenge will incorporate elements of Iraq, but it will not be identical. Preparing for the next war has become very perilous. Past experience provides the baseline for new asymmetrical applications, and the side that prevails is likely to be the one that correctly determines the necessary adaptations and prepares either to apply or to counter them.

The problem is finding a conceptual frame for organizing considering the permutation of future asymmetrical situations. Writing in 1995, the then U.S. Army Chief of Staff Gordon Sullivan and Anthony M. Coroalles analogized the problem to "seeing the elephant," a phrase borrowed from the American Civil War (the idea of deriving what the initial exposure to combat was like from descriptions by others—like having an elephant described). They wrote, "Our elephant is the complexity, ambiguity, and uncertainty of tomorrow's battlefield. We are trying to see the elephant of the future. But trying to draw that metaphorical elephant is infinitely harder than drawing a real one. We don't know what we don't know; none of us has a clear view of what the elephant will look like this time around."

Modern asymmetrical warfare is today's elephant. As an American Marine officer in Iraq has been quoted as saying: "The enemy has gone asymmetric on us. There's treachery. There are ambushes. It's not straight-up conventional fighting." In other words, it does not conform to the accepted rules of symmetrical warfare for which the Marines had prepared themselves.

In trying to determine the changing shape of the new elephant of asymmetrical warfare, one can begin by looking at predictable problems that the asymmetrical warrior will present in the future. With no pretense of being exhaustive, at least five stand out.

First, political and military aspects of these conflicts will continue to merge, and distinctions between military and civilian targets and assets will continue to dissolve. The asymmetrical warrior will continue to muddy the distinction for two reasons. One is that he is likely to see conflicts as pitting societies against societies, so there is no meaningful distinction between combatants and noncombatants, whereas traditional symmetrical warfare draws sharp distinctions between combatants and noncombatants, including prohibitions against attacking noncombatants. The other reason is that imbedding conflict within the fabric of society removes some of the advantage of the symmetrical warrior. Urban warfare, for instance, can only be waged symmetrically by concentrating firepower intensity on areas where civilians and opponents are intermingled, where traditional rules of war prohibit actions aimed at civilians, thereby inhibiting some actions. The asymmetrical warrior likely rejects these distinctions, leaving him free either to attack or fight among civilians.

Second, the opposition in these kinds of conflicts will increasingly consist of nonstate actors often acting out of nonstate motivations and without state bases of operation. International terrorist organizations, for instance, often carry out operations that cannot be tied to any state, and are not clearly based in any state. This creates a problem of response for the symmetrical warrior. Who does he go after? Who does he attack and punish? If the asymmetrical warrior remains in the shadows (or mountains or desert) and the government plausibly denies affiliation or association, then the lever of using force against the opponent's base is weakened. This is a major problem the United States has faced in dealing with Al Qaeda in Pakistan.

Third, the opposition posed by asymmetrical warriors will almost certainly be protracted, even if the tempo and intensity of opposition varies greatly from situation to situation. The reason for protraction flows from the weakness of the asymmetrical warrior compared to his symmetrical foe. Since direct confrontation is suicidal, the alternative is patient, measured application of force not designed to destroy the enemy, but instead to drag out the conflict, testing the will and patience of the opponent. The United States first saw this dynamic in Vietnam, saw it reprised in Iraq, and is currently encountering it in Afghanistan. The antidote is recognition of the tactic and a considerable degree of patience, generally not the long suit of the United States or political democracies.

Fourth, these conflicts will often occur in the most fractured, failed states, a dynamic explored in Chapter 15, where conditions are ripe for people to engage in acts of desperation that include actions like suicide bombing. In situations of high desperation and deprivation, the systemic obstacles will be extraordinarily difficult to address and solve. The problem is recognizing the multifaceted nature of the wants and needs of the people. The difficulty in rectifying these situations is having the patience and level of physical (including financial) commitment to remove the festering problems that give rise to violence in the first place. As of 2010, the United States, according to Haass, had invested about one trillion dollars in directly accountable costs in Iraq, and any development plan to stabilize that country will require years of patient action and the infusion of countless billions of additional dollars.

Fifth, asymmetrical warfare will change in the future. The problem of Iraq is more than overcoming the Iraqi resistance, it is a matter of defeating and discrediting its methods, so it will not form the basis for the opposition of others in the future. From the vantage point of potential asymmetrical warriors, the

Iraqi resistance has already been successful enough that parts of it will be imitated. Can anyone doubt the next asymmetrical warriors will come armed with improvised explosive devices (IEDs) to be detonated against symmetrical opponents?

This aspect of the problem, of course, flows from the observation that symmetrical warfare is more of an approach (or methodology) than a game plan or set of actions to be taken (a method). The trick is figuring what else will be learned from the experience to be countered and what new and unique elements will be added.

Determining Opponents

Virtually by definition, asymmetrical warfare will take on a variety of forms and be conducted by a variety of opponents in the future. Some variant will occur whenever a technologically inferior force confronts an opponent so superior that it cannot be confronted directly. Although the precise nature of future asymmetrical opponents is impossible to predict with great confidence, this section will look two current variants as examples of plausible futures. One is hybrid symmetrical–asymmetrical conflicts, of which Afghanistan is a prime example. The other example is internal wars involving factions within a state that are only partially military—or quasi-military—in nature. Each poses a different planning problem. Hybrids are likely to be confused as symmetrical wars, and quasi-military situations are likely to be overly militarized. Both provide harbingers for the post-Iraq experience.

Hybrid Symmetrical–Asymmetrical War   One of the most difficult aspects of dealing with asymmetrical war situations is recognizing them for what they are. The United States faced this recognition problem in Vietnam in the 1960s and concluded, after the first major encounter between American and North Vietnamese regulars in the Ia Drang Valley, that the war was conventional, a symmetrical conflict between two similar foes that could be prosecuted in a conventional manner.

The problem was that the strategy of the Vietnamese contained both symmetrical and asymmetrical elements. After the battle of Ia Drang, the North Vietnamese concluded they could not match American firepower and switched their method to guerrilla-style warfare, one of the classic forms of asymmetrical warfare. Their purpose was to harass and drain the Americans sufficiently to cause them to give up the fight as unwinnable at acceptable cost. After the United States abandoned the war, they returned to conventional, symmetrical warfare against a South Vietnamese opponent that they could defeat conventionally. Afghanistan and Iraq are contemporary hybrid symmetrical–asymmetrical examples.

In 2001, the United States entered an altogether symmetrical civil war between the Taliban government of Afghanistan and a coalition of opposition clans collectively known as the Northern Alliance. Both sides relied heavily on guerrilla warfare tactics, but because both sides used the same rules, the situation was symmetrical. The role of the United States was to aid in the overthrow of the Taliban government that was providing sanctuary to Al Qaeda—an extension of the war on terrorism. The American military role was to provide strategic airpower against the Taliban forces facing the Northern Alliance. The tactic was successful in the short run. Taliban forces were decimated, their government was forced to flee, and victory was proclaimed. The problem was that crushing the extant armed forces of the opposition did not destroy their will to resist, and the Taliban returned in 2003, and they became the de facto primary opponent of the United States there.

The effort in Iraq was in some ways similar. In the conquest phase of the war, the American effort was almost entirely symmetrical, with U.S. forces quickly brushing aside those Iraqi conventional forces that offered any resistance. The problem was that doing so only solved part of the problem. The remnants of the disbanded Iraqi armed forces and disgruntled Iraqi tribesmen organized a spider web of asymmetrical forces that bedeviled the American occupiers through much of the occupation phase of the war, as well as engaging in ethnic cleansing that has effectively partitioned large parts of the country into essentially Sunni, Shiite, or Kurdish enclaves. The American surge beginning in 2007 coincided with and contributed to a decrease in violence, but the underlying dynamic of a restive population remains. Elections in early 2010 and the scheduled withdrawal of all U.S. forces in 2011 will place the overall success of the effort in the spotlight. The success (or failure) of the effort will ultimately be decided by the Iraqis themselves, and whether a peaceful, stable Iraqi state will evolve, which was a large reason for the American involvement, will ultimately be outside American hands to dictate.

Quasi-Military Situations   A second set of circumstances in which military force may be employed in the future is in quasi-military unconventional roles and missions. Some of these are outgrowths of the struggles between the haves and the have-nots within developing countries and are manifested in things like terrorist acts either within the society or against outsiders, with the objects normally being the major powers (the African embassy bombings against the United States in 1998, and most dramatically, the attacks against New York and Washington, D.C. in 2001). Others are extensions of the general decay of some of the failed states and often are exemplified in activities such as criminality. Attempts to deal with the prospects of potential WMD attacks also fit into this category. What these phenomena share is that they are only semimilitary, even quasi-military, in content.

The Western, and specifically American, problem with Usama bin Laden illustrates the phenomenon. For a variety of reasons that he has publicly stated, bin Laden blames the United States for a large number of the problems afflicting the Middle East and is consequently devoted to inflicting as much pain and suffering on the United States and Americans as he can through acts of terror committed by his followers and associates. The campaign to eradicate Al Qaeda since 2001 has in fact decimated much of the ranks and leadership of the original organization, but it has also spawned a series of spin-off, copycat, and affiliated organizations that make the terrorist threat much more hydra-headed than it was before. Al Qaeda in Mesopotamia (Iraq) and that in the Arabian Peninsula (Yemen) are two often cited examples. These successful actions have, by and large, been the result of intelligence and law enforcement efforts, as in the June 2006 assassination of Abu Musab al-Zarqawi, the leader of Al Qaeda in Iraq.

The Iraq Precedent   The situations faced by the United States and cooperating states in Iraq and Afghanistan (and in associated states like Pakistan) offer a possible portent of the future of asymmetrical warfare for the United States. All are extremely complicated situations: intercommunal and intertribal warfare in Iraq, deep clan divisions and traditions of autonomy in Afghanistan, and endemic instability in Pakistan. All have occurred in countries with which the United States has limited historical experience, and where, as a result, American understanding of the situation and how (or whether) to assuage it has been suspect. In the most prominent cases, those who have opposed American (Iraq) or American-led (Afghanistan) forces have reverted to asymmetrical warfare to blunt American efforts, and they have done so with some success.

The latter point is critical in assessing the future of asymmetrical warfare. Even if (and it is a big *if*) the United States eventually subdues the opposition in either (or both) countries, the fact that comparatively undermanned and underarmed irregular units have competed successfully with the world's most powerful military offers a shimmer of hope to others in the world who contemplate a similar situation but who might despair of their chances. The lesson is not that the American juggernaut can be smashed; that is too much to ask. Rather, the lesson is that a patient, persistent resistance can neutralize and frustrate the Americans, cause them to question the worth of their efforts, and eventually cause them to conclude their mission is not worth the effort and leave (exceed American cost-tolerance, in terms used in Snow and Drew). Moreover, the costs of active efforts in places like Iraq are, in Haass' opinion, "clearly too great to be replicated."

This strategy worked in Vietnam, it may well work in Iraq and Afghanistan, and it will almost certainly be repeated in the future. It will almost certainly be the model for America's future opponents. The United States does not possess a clearly effective antiasymmetrical warfare doctrine (General Petraeus' Field Manual 3-24 on counterinsurgency notwithstanding). Even if it did, it would be of limited utility, since the heart of asymmetrical warfare is adaptability and innovation to the situation at hand: doctrine based on past experience will almost certainly be incomplete for the future.

Postconflict Peace

Planning for the peace that follows these highly fluid asymmetrical conflicts is generally as difficult as their prosecution and, partly as a result, tends to be underemphasized in the planning process. Nevertheless, no durable peace is likely to ensue unless there are concrete plans to alleviate the conditions that gave rise to the violence in the first place or that were created by the violence. Iraq is the dramatic case in point.

This means wartime planning must work backward, in Clark's terms. Most asymmetrical conflicts begin with prominent internal bases that must be addressed after the fighting in what Clark calls the "four-step minuet" of planning (development, deployment, decisive [military] operations, and post-conflict operations). Describing Afghanistan, former minister of the interior Ali A. Jalili argues the need for "human security, which assumes the sustainability of the peaceful environment . . . . Freedom from fear and freedom from want lead to human security, and they require more than building the state's security forces." He cites good governance, social security, economic development, and protection of human and political rights as additional needs. This realization leads backward to military operations, as Gray points out: "The primary objective in counterinsurgency is protection of the people, not military defeat of the terrorists-insurgents." It is not clear that adequate attention to these kinds of concerns was present in American prewar planning for Afghanistan or Iraq.

CASE: THE AFGHANISTAN WAR

Unless one counts long occupations such as the U.S. Marines' two decades in Haiti between 1915 and 1934, the American military effort in Afghanistan now represents America's longest war, and it is one where any definitive outcome seems no more imminent than it did at the beginning. Those who committed the first American forces to Afghanistan did not plan for nor envision such an outcome when the first Americans were dispatched there in October 2001. Spurred by the 9/11 attacks by an Al Qaeda whose principal sanctuary was in Afghanistan and protected by the Taliban government, the overt purpose was to attack, capture, and destroy the terrorist organization and its leader Usama bin Laden. The American action, however, also enmeshed the United States in a conventional civil war between the Taliban and insurgents under the banner of the Northern Alliance.

The campaign against bin Laden and Al Qaeda, of course, failed, as the terrorist leader and his followers managed to elude their pursuers and to slip across the border into areas of Pakistan not under effective control of the Pakistani government (see Chapter 15), where they remain and from which they continue to operate. Despite this inability to accomplish the primary—and universally supported—goal of destroying Al Qaeda, the United States remained engaged in Afghanistan. After the 2003 return of the Taliban in their attempt to reassert their lost domain, this meant the United States became part of the Afghan civil war, which was not part of the original overt purpose but which became justified as necessary to prevent an Al Qaeda return. The American effort was subdued and limited because of heavy American commitment in Iraq, but as that mission has wound down, American resources have been increasingly deployed in Afghanistan.

The result is a classic asymmetrical war. On one side is the Afghan government, aided by a NATO-based coalition and the United States, acting both as a member of the coalition and independently of it. Thanks to outside assistance, this side possesses clearly superior conventional force which, if applied effectively, could be militarily decisive. On the other side is the insurgent Taliban, whose forces are clearly inferior to those of the United States and its allies (NATO and the Afghan government). As a result, the Taliban had no choice but to adopt the methodology of asymmetrical force.

Conflict Environment

By virtually any measure and for virtually any purpose, Afghanistan is one of the most forbidding, unforgiving, and difficult countries in the world. It is an ancient land with a discernible history that dates back to three and four millennia; it has always been a harsh and contentious place whose history is punctuated by occasions in which it has united to repel foreign invaders and then fallen back into fractious disunity and violent rivalry once any particular outsider has been repulsed. Rudyard Kipling's nineteenth-century admonition—"Don't let your sons die on Afghanistan's plain"—has been sound advice for a long time.

Historic interest in Afghanistan has largely geographic bases. Although the country has few natural resources to exploit or physical bases for development, it has a strategic location in the heart of Asia that has made it a junction point, what the U.S. government has called a "land bridge," for travelers and traders throughout history. East–West commerce from the Orient to the Middle East and Europe traversed the country, and the north–south axis from Central Asia to the Asian subcontinent has modern Afghanistan in its path as well.

This strategic location has placed Afghanistan on the transit route or made it the object of some of history's greatest conquerors. Alexander the Great passed through what is now Afghanistan in both directions as he sought to subdue India, and Genghis Khan's Golden Hordes swept through and for a time occupied this rugged land of barren mountains and high mountain valleys. More recently, independent Afghanistan (it originally achieved its independence in 1747) was occupied and partially subdued by Great Britain, which fought three wars there in the nineteenth and early twentieth centuries. In the nineteenth century, indeed, Afghanistan was the object of the "Great Game" between the British and the Russians, as the Russians sought to extend their influence southward toward the British Raj in India and the British wanted to retain influence over Afghanistan and part of what is now Pakistan as a buffer area protecting British domain in the area. Most recently, prior to the current war, the Soviet Union invaded Afghanistan in December 1979 in a feckless attempt to shore up a communist regime in Kabul. Like virtually all the conquerors that had come before them, the Soviets retreated ignominiously in 1988, having failed utterly in their quest and having weakened themselves to the point of facilitating the downfall of Soviet communism that began in 1989.

The Afghan experience has been enigmatic. For most of its history, Afghanistan has been a deeply divided society, with loyalty being toward tribal affiliations rather than the state. Afghanistan has never evolved a strong, stable central government, and its attempts to create one have been fleeting and ultimately unsuccessful. What passes for unity and peacefulness normally has occurred when geographically based, ethnic tribal groups have had substantial autonomy and where such central regulation as existed was the result of *loya jirgas,* extensive meetings of tribal elders from around the country. Whenever a central government in Kabul has attempted to assert its authority outside the tribal council system, it has been actively resisted, often violently. The exception has generally been when Afghanistan has been invaded by outsiders, at which time the various Afghan tribes have temporarily set aside their differences long enough to expel the foreigners. Once that goal has been achieved, the traditional practice has been to return to rivalry and suspicion.

The result is an Afghan society that is dominated by its tribal parts and which has a xenophobic dislike and suspicion of outsiders. Within the tribal structure of the country, however, one tribal entity has traditionally been most prominent. The Pashtuns are the largest ethnic group in the country. Through most of Afghan history, they were a majority, and for a time the terms "Afghan" and "Pashtun" were used synonymously. Forced migration—largely to Pakistan—has cost the Pashtuns their majority status, but they retain a plurality (currently estimated as about 42 percent). Traditional Pashtun lands are concentrated in the southern and eastern parts of the country adjacent to and overlapping the Duran Line (the legal boundary between Afghanistan and Pakistan but not accepted as valid by many Pashtuns). The Pashtuns are also the second largest ethnic group in Pakistan (behind the Punjabis), and the territory dominated by the Pashtuns on both sides of the border is also known as Pashtunistan, and a sovereign state by that name remains the goal of some tribal members.

The Pashtuns are important in the current context for three reasons. First, is that virtually all Afghan governments have been headed by a Pashtun and have had the active support of the Pashtuns. Hamid Karzai, the president of Afghanistan since 2002, is a Pashtun, but his support within the Pashtun rank-and-file is suspect. Karzai is a Western-educated, urbanized member of the Durrani sect of Pashtuns (the other major sect of the tribe, to which most rural members belong, is the Ghilzai), and he has cooperated with other Afghan tribes distrusted by most Pashtuns (notably the Tajiks, who are prominently represented in the current government). Second, the support base of the Taliban comes almost exclusively from rural-based Pashtuns, and most of the hotbeds of Taliban activity and control are in traditional Pashtun lands. All Pashtuns are by no means Taliban, but virtually all Taliban are Pashtuns. Third, much of the very strong identity and values of Pashtuns derive from Pashtunwali, a code of morals and proper behavior. Among the central tenets of this code is hospitality and protection of honored guests. Arising from their collaboration in the anti-Soviet resistance, one of the recipients of this protection is Al Qaeda.

Physical Structure of War

The structure and issues underlying the current war in Afghanistan are the direct result of the Afghan resistance to the Soviet occupation during 1979–1988 and its aftermath. In predictable fashion, the invasion produced a fierce resistance by the various Afghan tribes, aided by, among others, the Americans and the Pakistanis. The mujahidin, as the resisters were collectively known, had two distinct elements: native Afghan tribesmen who, in typical Afghan fashion, formed a loose coalition to repel the Soviets that dissolved when the Soviets departed; and foreign fighters, mostly from other Islamic countries. The native Afghans formed the basis for both sides in the later civil war, the Taliban and the Northern Alliance. The foreign fighters, some of whom had been recruited by a then obscure Saudi activist named Usama bin Laden, became members of Al Qaeda.

The expulsion of the Soviets ended communist rule in Afghanistan. Between 1988 and 1996, a number of governments came and went in Kabul, but they were equally inept, corrupt, and unpopular. In reaction, a new movement primarily comprising students (talibs) from religious schools (madrassas) largely in Pakistan formed and swept across Afghanistan. In 1996, the Taliban became the government of the country. That same year, Al Qaeda was expelled from Sudan, partly because of pressure from the U.S. government. Looking for a new sanctuary, bin Laden and his followers appealed to their old allies in the new Afghan government, who welcomed them and, under the tenets of Pashtunwali, provided them with protection.

The Taliban government's rule—or misrule—is well documented (e.g., tyrannical fundamentalist excesses, including the draconian suppression of women) and this perhaps inevitably spawned its own opposition, and gradually a coalition of primarily non-Pashtun tribes formed under the banner of the Northern Alliance. By 9/11, the Northern Alliance and the Taliban were locked in a full-scale civil war, the outcome of which was very much in doubt. Meanwhile, Al Qaeda continued to operate training facilities in Afghanistan, planning, among other things, the 9/11 attacks.

While decrying the Taliban's policies and providing some small amount of assistance to the opposition, the United States stayed on the sidelines of this conflict until 9/11. The public face of the American decision to intervene physically in Afghanistan was the "war on terror," with Al Qaeda as its centerpiece. When U.S. forces entered the country, they in effect created a second conflict with its own objectives and conduct separate from and independent of the ongoing civil war. Although bin Laden's flight from the country effectively ended the military effort against Al Qaeda in Afghanistan (since the terrorists were now in Pakistan), that did not end the Western (including NATO and

U.S.) military involvement. Rather, outside assistance had helped drive the Taliban out of power and into Pakistani exile, and the result was the formation of the new Karzai government as the representative of the victorious Northern Alliance, with American blessing. When the Taliban left, the outsiders remained to mop up residual Al Qaeda and Taliban resistance and to insure they did not return.

The Taliban did, of course, begin to infiltrate back into the country and to launch a new phase of the civil war with the pre-9/11 roles reversed: the Karzai-led Northern Alliance was the government and the Taliban were the insurgents. Now reconfigured as the Afghan national force, the Northern Alliance was no more capable of defeating the Taliban than they had been before. As the returning Taliban gradually reasserted its authority over increasing parts of Afghanistan (especially traditional Pashtun territories), opposition to them gradually fell to NATO. The current civil war was thus engaged.

It has become a classic asymmetrical war. The Taliban are almost certainly more powerful than the government forces on their own, but they are far less powerful than and incapable of defeating the NATO/American forces in symmetrical warfare. They have thus adopted an unconventional, asymmetrical approach to the war, aiming most clearly at overcoming American cost-tolerance by prolonging the conflict sufficiently that American public opinion will turn against the effort and force a withdrawal. This is, of course, a classic insurgent strategic approach against an outside occupier and is consistent with the historical Afghan treatment of outsiders. The American response has been that of counterinsurgency (COIN) as outlined in the Petraeus-inspired FM 3-24, which seeks to liberate Taliban territory and engage in a successful campaign for the "hearts and minds" of the Afghan people to turn their loyalty away from the Taliban and toward the government. At the same time, the strategy calls for expanding the size and quality of Afghan government forces to the point that they can defeat the insurgency on their own eventually.

Determining Opponents

The dual nature of the Afghanistan war has complicated the specification of the opposition. This difficulty is particularly acute for the United States, which has become the de facto major opponent of the Taliban in the fight. The two possible opponents, of course, are the Taliban and Al Qaeda, and they are by no means the same. The Taliban, for instance, are almost all Afghan Pashtuns, whereas members of Al Qaeda are almost all non-Afghans. Thus, the two opponents are distinct. The problem for the United States is that there is widespread, virtually universal public support for opposing Al Qaeda, but since Al Qaeda is now physically in Pakistan, it is not the opponent the Americans are fighting. Rather, the physical foe is the Taliban, who are American enemies only in the sense that they might invite an Al Qaeda return to Afghanistan if they win.

The purposes of these two opponents, and thus how they must be opposed, differ substantially as well. Both problems are difficult. Al Qaeda, of course, is a terrorist organization that has goals that are murky to Americans but which include inflicting as much pain and suffering on Americans and others as they can, presumably in order to extract some political concessions—noninterference in Middle Eastern countries and abandonment of Israel are the goals most often articulated. The Al Qaeda opponent is physically small—probably no more than a few thousand operatives worldwide—but elusive and difficult to destroy, which is the obvious goal against them. The problem, of course, is that the members of Al Qaeda in the region enjoy protection under Pashtunwali, and they are not present in any numbers in Afghanistan. Assuming their locations can be established, the only way to attack them has been through pilotless Predator air strikes, which the Pakistanis oppose and which often result in civilian casualties which simply create new Al Qaeda recruits (see Chapter 16). Moreover, it is not clear that effective action will not simply cause Al Qaeda to pack up and relocate in sanctuaries elsewhere, such as in Somalia.

Opposing the Taliban insurgency is a different, and in many ways more familiar, problem. The Taliban are conducting an asymmetrical campaign using largely guerrilla tactics and insurgent goals, to which the symmetrical warriors have responded with the American COIN strategy. This effort, however, is plagued by at least two difficulties. One is that the Taliban have proven to be tough, adept, and adaptive fighters defending harsh territory with which they are more familiar and comfortable than their opponents: the going is very difficult. The other problem is that the outsiders—who are, to repeat, currently doing most of the fighting—find themselves aligned with what many Afghans view as an anti-Pashtun coalition, Karzai's ethnicity notwithstanding. Afghan history has been remarkably consistent in the sense that no government that is opposed by the Pashtun plurality has much chance of succeeding. Recasting the war as one where the Pashtuns are not the implicit enemies is a necessary (if not necessarily sufficient) condition for success against the Taliban.

Postconflict Peace

The war in Afghanistan became an asymmetrical war and continues to be one because of the outside intervention of the United States and its NATO allies following 9/11. Prior to that involvement, there had been a fairly conventional civil war going on against the Taliban (a not unusual circumstance) that would likely have continued with some internal resolution. Interfering in that internal affair was not a prominent part of the rationale for intervention. Destroying Al Qaeda was the purpose, and the Taliban were in the way. Operationally, the anti-Al Qaeda mission in Afghanistan ended when Al Qaeda fled. The outside mission remained, it became the shield behind which the anti-Taliban government of Karzai was formed, and by staying, it became the protector and sponsor of the new regime. When the Taliban returned, they came back as asymmetrical warriors, the only way they had a chance of prevailing.

How the Afghanistan War will end is a matter of speculation. Its evolution has been conceptually contorted, but it does provide some potential precedent for the future. The international environment is not favorable to symmetrical applications of conventional, Western-style warfare: the developed countries that could wage such wars against one another have scant reason to do so, and the developing countries cannot compete with the symmetrical warriors on their own terms. Regardless of which Afghan faction eventually wins or retains control of the country (which is what the actual conflict and fighting are about), the more general and enduring lesson will be about whether asymmetrical warfare in developing countries is how the major powers wish to expend their armed might and treasure. The content of that lesson remains to be decided; whoever masters that lesson will be the real victor in the Afghanistan War and beyond.

CONCLUSION

Warfare is both an ever-changing and never-changing human endeavor. The opponents change, the purposes for which wars are fought change, and the methods and tools of war change. At the same time, the fact that groups of humans find reasons to fight and kill other groups of humans seems ubiquitous, one of history's true constants.

What is now called asymmetrical warfare is part of this larger march of history. As noted, the idea, and even some of the methods, underlying this kind of war is as old as warfare itself and has been a recurring part of the historic pattern. What is arguably different is that differential fighting capabilities among and between countries and groups have widened to the point that symmetrical warfare has become much more prominent than it was in the past. The ongoing war in Afghanistan is only the latest and most currently obvious example of this form of warfare. How it ends will, in turn, have some effect on this form of warfare.

STUDY/DISCUSSION QUESTIONS

1. The military planning problem has changed markedly since the end of the Cold War. What is the nature, and what are the causes, of that change? Discuss.
2. What is asymmetrical warfare? Contrast it with symmetrical warfare. Why has it arisen as the major military problem of the twenty-first century? Is it likely to continue to be the dominant problem?
3. Discuss the problem posed by asymmetrical warfare in terms of the conflict environment, physical structure of war, opposition, and postconflict peace.
4. Discuss the background and evolution of the Afghanistan War, beginning with its roots in the Afghan resistance to the Soviet occupation and leading to the 9/11 attacks. Why does the war have two distinct facets? What are they? Explain.
5. Building on the dual nature of the war, describe the Afghanistan War in terms of conflict environment, physical structure, opposition, and postconflict peace.
6. Should it be a major priority of the most advanced countries to involve themselves in trying to ameliorate internal violence in the developing world? If so, what kind of criteria should be adopted to guide involvements? If not, what should we prepare for?
7. Predict where and in what kind of conflict the United States is most likely to be fighting 10 years from today? Try to devise the basic principles for a counter asymmetrical warfare strategy to deal with that future.

READING/RESEARCH MATERIAL

Berkowitz, Bruce. *The New Face of War: How War Will Be Fought in the 21st Century.* New York: Free Press, 2003.

Brodie, Bernard and Fawn M. Brodie. *From Crossbow to H-Bomb: The Evolution of Weapons and Tactics in Warfare.* Bloomington, IN: Indiana University Press, 1965.

Clark, Wesley. *Winning Modern Wars: Iraq, Terrorism, and the American Empire.* New York: PublicAffairs, 2003.

Coll, Steve. *Ghost Wars: The Secret History of the CIA, Afghanistan, and bin Laden from the Soviet Invasion to September 10, 2001.* New York: Books, 2004.

Crews, Robert D. and Amin Tarzi, eds. *The Taliban and the Crisis of Afghanistan.* Cambridge, MA: Harvard University Press, 2008.

Ewans, Martin. *Afghanistan: A Short History of Its People and Politics.* New York: HarperCollins Perennial, 2002.

Gannon, Cathy. "Afghanistan Unbound." *Foreign Affairs* 83, 3 (May/June 2004), 35–46.

Goulding, Victor J. Jr. "Back to the Future with Asymmetrical Warfare." *Parameters* XXX, 4 (Winter 2000–2001), 21–30.

Gray, Colin S. "Stability Operations in Strategic Perspective: A Skeptical View." *Parameters* XXXVI, 2 (Summer 2006), 4–14.

Haass, Richard N. War of Necessity, War of Choice: A Memoir of Two Iraq Wars. New York: Simon and Schuster, 2009.

———. "The Weakest Link." *Newsweek*, March 8, 2010, 36–37.

Jalali, Ali A. "The Future of Afghanistan." *Parameters* XXXVI, 1 (Spring 2006), 4–19.

Kaplan, Robert D. "Man Versus Afghanistan." *The Atlantic* 305, 3 (April 2010), 60–71.

Lind, William S. et al. "The Changing Face of War: Into the Fourth Generation." *Marine Corps Gazette*, October 1989, 22–26.

Lowther, Adam B. *Americans and Asymmetrical Warfare: Lebanon, Somalia, and Afghanistan.* Westport, CT: Praeger Security International, 2007.

Nevile, Leigh. *Special Operations Forces in Afghanistan.* New York: Osprey Publishing, 2008.

Rubin, Barnett E. "Saving Afghanistan." *Foreign Affairs* 86, 1 (January/February 2007), 57–78.

Scales, Maj. General Robert H. Jr. *Future War: Anthology.* Carlisle Barracks, PA: Strategic Studies Institute, 1999.

Snow, Donald M. *When America Fights: The Uses of U.S. Military Force.* Washington, DC: CQ Press, 2000.

———. *What after Iraq?* New York: Pearson Longman, 2009.

———. and Dennis M. Drew. *From Lexington to Baghdad and Beyond: War and Politics in the American Experience.* 3rd ed. Armonk, NY: M. E. Sharpe, 2009.

Stoessinger, John. *Why Nations Go to War.* 9th ed. New York: St. Martin's Press, 2003.

Sullivan, General Gordon R. and Anthony M. Coroalles. *Seeing the Elephant: Leading America's Army into the Twenty-First Century.* Boston, MA: Institute for Foreign Policy Analysis, 1995.

United States Army and U.S. Marine Corps. Counterinsurgency Field Manual (U.S. Army Field Manual No. 3-24, Marine Corps Warfighting Publication No. 3-33.5). Chicago, IL: University of Chicago Press, 2007.

Van Creveld, Martin. *The Transformation of War.* New York: Free Press, 1991.

WEB SITES

Research projects on national security issues conducted by the RAND Corporation for
the U.S. defense establishment
National Security: Research and Analysis at http://www.ran.org/natsec_area
Leading organization studying military matters
The International Institute for Strategic Studies at http://www.iiss.org
Alternate visions of defense issues
Stockholm International Peace Research Institute at http://www.sipri.se.

Proliferation: The Case of North Korea

PRÉCIS

Nuclear proliferation, a subject of concern since the dawn of the nuclear age, returned to the world agenda with a vengeance in late June 2006. Two states, Iran and North Korea, occupied the spotlight because of actions they had taken or were contemplating taking with strong overtones for the world's nuclear balance. Iran and much of the West were engaged in negotiations regarding the potential of that country's nuclear power industry being upgraded to include the possibility of producing nuclear weapons, a subject discussed in detail in Chapter 7. North Korea, which almost certainly already has a small number of nuclear arms, threatened to test a ballistic missile delivery system possibly capable of delivering payloads to parts of the continental United States, among other places, and did test a nuclear bomb. While the problem was reduced by an agreement between North Korea and the West, the general problem of proliferation remains a lively international security concern.

The spread of different categories of weapons to states that do not possess them and whose possession concerns other states is not a new phenomenon. Trying to place limits on the numbers and types of weapons that states possess goes back to the period between the world wars in modern times; the Washington Conference on naval fleet sizes and the Kellogg–Briand Pact, both of which were negotiated in the 1920s, were early prototypes of the concern that is now called proliferation. Dealing with the spread of nuclear weapons has been a concern since the early 1950s.

The post–World War II concern with the spread of nuclear weapons reached a crescendo with the negotiation of the Nuclear Non-Proliferation Treaty (NPT) of 1968. The NPT prohibited additional states who did not already have nuclear weapons from acquiring (or trying to acquire) them. It also required current possessors not to aid in the spread of nuclear weapons and made them promise to reduce and eliminate their own arsenals. The NPT has enjoyed a mixed level of success.

Concern about proliferation has ebbed and flowed across time. When the membership in the nuclear "club" (the counties that possessed the weapons) was very small during the 1950s and 1960s, there was great concern about additional countries acquiring the weapons, and the body of nuclear proliferation thought was developed to deal with that contingency. During the 1970s and 1980s, that level of concern became more muted, both because the number of nuclear states did not grow perceptibly despite the dire warnings of proliferation theorists whose entreaties increasingly had a kind of "cry wolf" quality, and because of concern with other matters, including the demise of the Cold War and the need to adapt to that change in the international environment.

Interest in proliferation has returned since the turn of the millennium. The revived interest has been tied closely to the problem of international terrorism, because of the fear that terrorists might acquire and use nuclear or other deadly weapons (so-called weapons of mass destruction or WMDs), a concern important enough that the 2006 National Security Strategy of the United States intoned, "There are few greater threats than a terrorist attack with WMD."

The current emphasis on WMD has two basic sources that culminate in the possibility of terrorist acquisition and use of proscribed weapons. The first has to do with the countries that might acquire such weapons, and it focuses currently on countries such as the Democratic People's Republic of Korea (DPRK or North Korea). The second source of concern is the various types of WMD that might be acquired. Ultimately, the WMD that most matter are nuclear weapons because of their enormous destructive capacity, but other forms are of importance as well.

This case study seeks to clarify and apply the problem of proliferation. It begins with a discussion of the general problem as it has evolved through scholarly and policy concerns, including the nature of the problem and how the international system has attempted to deal with it. Proliferation is a real and vital current problem, and the case then applies the general principles to one of the most important current potential nuclear proliferators, the DPRK, looking at both attempts to prevent North Korea from joining the nuclear club and the dynamics that have made such conformance difficult to achieve. Some references to the same dynamics are introduced as additional examples of and as a foundation for the discussion in Chapter 7.

THE PROLIFERATION PROBLEM

Proliferation is a delicate international problem, in large measure because its underlying aim is both discriminatory and condescending to those at whom it is aimed. In the modern context, the desire to limit possession of nuclear and other proscribed weapons has come from countries that already possess those weapons and is aimed at those who do not possess them. Thus, current efforts to prevent countries like North Korea from obtaining nuclear weapons are made most loudly by countries like the United States, Britain, and even China, which already have them.

The delicacy of the situation comes from rationalizing why it is all right for some states to have nuclear weapons whereas other states should not. Such assertions and arguments are, of course, inherently discriminatory, and the question that must be answered is, why some but not others? Invariably, the answer to that question comes back to an assumption regarding responsibility: Those who have the weapons, it is argued (usually by those countries that have them) can be trusted to act responsibly with the weapons (which basically means they will not use them). Others, however, are not necessarily so trustworthy and, by definition, have no track record of responsible possession. This logic is convincing to the countries already possessing the weapons but not necessarily to those who do not, who feel that the assertion is inherently, and from their vantage point, unjustifiably condescending. This dynamic is a major conceptual barrier to enforcing proliferation policies.

The proliferation problem is also complex. To understand and be able to analyze current cases such as the DPRK, one must look at the structure of the problem. This will be done by raising and trying to answer three questions: What is the nature of the problem? Why is it a problem? And what can be done about the problem? The answers collectively form the context for analyzing the case application to North Korea.

What Is the Nature of the Proliferation Problem?

The roots of the contemporary proliferation problem lie in the Cold War. The major purposes were to prevent the spread of nuclear weapons to states that did not have them, and also to limit the size and destructiveness of the arsenals of possessing states. These two intents were related to one another. In addition, there was concern about the destabilizing impact of burgeoning nuclear possession, which in turn spawned two additional concerns. One was about the kind of capability that countries were attempting to proliferate (what forms of WMD), and the other was the mechanics of how proliferation could occur (and thus what steps had to be taken to prevent it from happening).

Two basic forms of proliferation were identified and targeted during the Cold War: vertical and horizontal. Vertical proliferation refers to incremental additions of a particular weapons system by a state (or states) that already has the weapon. It is a concern both because additional increments of weapons add to the potential deadliness of confrontations and because those increments can spawn arms races in which additions by one side cause the other to build more, resulting in an arms spiral that was potentially destabilizing. Efforts to control vertical proliferation generally aim at curbing or reducing levels of particular arms and are the traditional object of arms control. Most of the nuclear arms treaties negotiated by the United States and the Soviet Union during the Cold War (the Strategic Arms Limitations Talks—SALT—and the Strategic Arms Reduction Talks—START—are examples) were attempts to limit vertical proliferation.

Contemporary proliferation efforts center on horizontal proliferation: the spread of nuclear or other weapons to states that currently do not possess them; generally, when the term proliferation is used in contemporary discussions, it is shorthand for horizontal proliferation. The two forms are linked because many of the calls for limiting horizontal proliferation have come from states (like the United States and the former Soviet Union) who have been engaged in vertical proliferation (nuclear arms races) that made their entreaties to others to self-abnegate attempts to gain the weapons seem disingenuous and created demands to link the two (see discussion of the NPT below).

The kinds of capabilities being proliferated was also a concern that led to independent efforts to curb each kind of capability. The kinds of weapons that may be proliferated are (and were) WMDs, which generally are categorized into three groups captured by the acronym NBC: nuclear, biological, and chemical weapons. Though all are of concern, the dangers they pose are different. Nuclear weapons are arguably the only unambiguous weapons of mass destruction, because of the size and destructiveness of nuclear explosions. Biological (or agents of biological origin, ABO) and chemical weapons can cause large numbers of deaths that are often particularly hideous, but their extensiveness of destruction is more limited. On the other hand, biological and especially chemical weapons are much easier to construct than nuclear weapons. In an era when terrorist possession and use is a major concern, chemical and biological weapons take on added importance because they are the kinds of weapons that terrorists are more likely to be able to obtain (or make) and use than nuclear weapons. Efforts to contain proliferation have centered on nuclear weapons, although they have been extended to other forms of WMD. In addition, there is also concern about how WMD might be delivered to target. The most dramatic form of WMD (and especially nuclear) delivery is by ballistic missiles, because at present there are no reliable means of engaging in highly effective defenses against ballistic missiles.

The mechanics of producing (and avoiding the production) these capabilities have also been a matter of major concern, centering particularly on nuclear weapons and ways to get them to target. The problem of nuclear weapons production is straightforward and has two components. The first is the knowledge of how to fabricate a nuclear device. Nuclear physics has been taught openly for over 60 years now in the world's (and notably American) universities, so that knowledge is widely available both to most governments and undoubtedly to many private groups. The knowledge genie is clearly out of the bottle. The other requirement for building nuclear weapons is possession of adequate supplies of weapons-grade (i.e., highly enriched) isotopes of uranium/plutonium, which generally are by-products of nuclear reactions in certain types of power generators and the like (which is why many concerns are raised about the kinds of nuclear reactors potential proliferators have or propose to build). Access to such materials is highly guarded and restricted, and aspirants to nuclear weapons either have to come into possession of nuclear reactors that produce weapons-grade materials or they must purchase or steal such material from those who possess it. Nonproliferation efforts have been concentrated on denying access to weapons-grade material to potential proliferators.

The other, somewhat less publicized, aspect of nuclear proliferation surrounds the ability of proliferating states to deliver those weapons to targets—specifically to targets in the United States and other Western countries. Terrorist horror scenarios center on clandestine shipment of assembled bombs via cargo ship and the like to places like New York or the dispatch of so-called suitcase bombs (small nuclear devices contained in luggage or other parcels) or dirty bombs (conventional explosives coated with radioactive materials dispersed with detonation of the bomb). More conventional analyses deal with the ability of nuclear pretenders to build or buy ballistic missiles to deliver these weapons, because a country that can deliver weapons over only a short distance creates much less of a problem than a country that can deliver the same weapon over intercontinental ranges. The question of ballistic delivery systems has been a particular problem in dealing with the DPRK.

Why Is Proliferation a Problem?

The short answer to this question is that one has much less to fear from a weapons capability that one's actual or potential adversaries do not possess than from a capability that they do possess. In the classic, Cold War seedbed of thinking about nuclear proliferation, the problem was conceptualized as the difficulty of keeping additional sovereign states from achieving nuclear capability. The more such additional countries obtained the weapons, the more "fingers" there would be on the nuclear "button," and thus as a matter of probability, the more likely nuclear war would be. That problem remains central to the contemporary problem, but is augmented by the fear that some of the potential proliferating states might share their capabilities with terrorist non-state actors, who would allegedly be more difficult to dissuade from using those weapons than would state actors.

In classic terms, the problem of the spread of nuclear (or other) weapons to nonpossessing states is known as the $N+1$ problem. The idea is straightforward. In the formulation, N stands for the number of states that currently possess nuclear weapons and refers to the dynamics among them. *Plus 1*, on the other hand, refers to the added problems that would be created for the international system (notably the states that form N) by the addition of new $(+1)$ states to the nuclear club.

The problem is that the current members (N) and potential proliferators $(+1)$ see the problem essentially from opposite ends of the conceptual spectrum. The current members generally believe that the current "club" represents a stable, reliable membership (even if earlier members opposed the addition of some current members before they "joined"). Viewed this way, the emphasis of the club is on the problems that will be created by new members, and the criterion for concern is the likelihood of destabilization of the system created by new members. Looking from this perspective, it is not surprising that members of N tend to look for and find sources of destabilization that should be opposed and want to restrict membership to existing levels.

Members of +1, however, see the problem differently. The nonmember does not see his own acquisition of nuclear weapons as destabilizing and is righteously indignant at the notion that his acquisition would have a detrimental effect on the stability of the system. The accusation of destabilization is a backhanded way of suggesting that the new member would be a less responsible possessor than those who already have the weapons. Put more bluntly, the imputation that a new state would destabilize amounts to accusing such a state of a greater likelihood of using the weapons than those who already have them and have refrained from doing so. If you are a member of the government of North Korea, for instance, you would like an explanation of exactly why the United States, which maintains over 30,000 troops on the soil of your next-door neighbor (South Korea), should be treated as more responsible with weapons of mass destruction than you are. It is not an easy sell.

Indeed, in the current context, nonpossessors are more likely to make the argument that their membership in the nuclear club will actually stabilize their situations, because it is a fact (even if the causality is arguable) that no state that possesses nuclear weapons has ever been the victim of an aggression against it. Indeed, one of the arguments that both the Iranians and North Koreans (among others) have made in recent years is that gaining nuclear weapons capability is a useful—even necessary—means to avoid being attacked by an aggressive United States. Would, for instance, the United States have attacked Iraq if Iraq actually had, rather than being accused of trying to get, nuclear weapons? Some nonpossessing countries argue the American attack would have been less likely and that Saddam Hussein's major error was in not getting the kinds of capability that would deter the United States. Some even argue that had he not abandoned his nuclear weapons program, he might still be alive and in power.

There is a further irony that attaches to the N+1 a problem—it is generally only viewed as such by the current nuclear club. A country that aspires to become a member (a +1 country) may be viewed as a problem before it gets the capability, but once it has and has demonstrated its "responsible possession" of the capability, it ceases to be a part of the problem and instead views other aspirants as part of the problem. Thus, for instance, when only the United States and the Soviet Union had nuclear weapons, they viewed the addition of the third member (Britain) as a potential problem. When Britain obtained the weapons, it ceased to be a problem, but viewed the addition of other countries (France, China) as destabilizing prospects. When those countries joined the club, they became part of N and thus looked at other prospective members as part of the problem.

The proliferation problem is obviously worse when there are more nuclear powers, but one obstacle to sustaining international momentum behind proliferation control has been that proliferation has not occurred at the pace that those who most fear the prospects have projected. The nuclear club was pretty well established by 1964, when China obtained nuclear weapons and pushed the number to five—in order of acquisition: the United States, the Soviet Union, Great Britain, France, and China. At the time, there were fears that the number, unless constrained, might jump to 20 or 30 or even more nuclear states, but that simply has not happened. Since the 1960s, only four states have gained nuclear capability. One state (Israel) does not formally admit it has the weapons (it also does not deny it), one state obtained and then renounced and destroyed its weapons (South Africa), and two countries openly joined the club in 1998 (India and Pakistan). The total number of currently acknowledged nuclear states thus stands at eight, which is far less than the doomsayers predicted. In the current debate, four states have been mentioned with varying levels of likelihood of attempting to join the club: Iran, Iraq, North Korea, and Syria. The American invasion of Iraq precluded that country's membership for the foreseeable future, and international pressures effectively curb any Syrian ambitions. That leaves Iran and North Korea as the most likely new members.

What activates the level of contemporary concern is thus clearly not the quantity of states that may join, but rather it is the quality of new aspirants. The DPRK's reclusive regime is regularly accused of being unstable and bellicose and raises fears on those grounds. Because it is so desperately poor and in perpetual need of foreign capital, the fear that the DPRK will simply sell nuclear capability to some undesirable buyer is a continuing nightmare. The question thus arises of what can and should be done to try to keep proliferation from occurring, thus avoiding the possibility that nuclear weapons might be shared with terrorists.

What to Do About the Problem?

Once again, because the roots of thinking about the control of nuclear weapons have their origins in the Cold War, so too does thinking about how to prevent proliferation. The key concept in dealing with nuclear weapons in the Cold War context was the idea of deterrence, and that concept dominates historic and contemporary discussions of proliferation as well.

The problem of deterrence has changed with the end of the Cold War system. In the past, nuclear deterrence existed among states with very large arsenals of nuclear weapons—principally the United States and the Soviet Union—and the dynamic of deterrence, captured in the idea of assured destruction, was that any nuclear attack against a nuclear-armed superpower would be suicidal, because the attacked state would retain such devastating capabilities even after absorbing an attack as to be able to retaliate against the attacker and destroy it, making any "victory" decidedly Pyrrhic (costing far more than it was worth). Because potential attackers were presumably rational (or at least not suicidal), the prospects of a counterattack that would certainly immolate them was enough to dissuade (or deter) an attack in the first place. The same logic applies to the continuing viability of the NPT, the major international regime on proliferation.

Deterring Proliferation in a Changed World   That situation has changed in two important respects. First, the possession of such large amounts of nuclear power is now unilateral: Only the United States has the unquestioned ability to launch a devastating nuclear attack against anyone in the world, and because of recent improvements in American capability and degrading of the capabilities of historic possible opponents, Kier Lieber and Daryl Press argued in 2006 that "it will probably be possible for the United States to destroy the long-range arsenals of Russia or China with a first strike." This means that the old system of mutual deterrence (i.e., the United States and the Soviet Union deterring one another) has disappeared or been seriously compromised. More important in the current context, the threats in the contemporary environment come from states that will, at best, have a small number of nuclear weapons at their disposal but may not be dissuaded by the same threats that deterred the Soviets during the Cold War. Thus, as Joseph Pilat puts it, "There are real questions about whether old, Cold War–vintage concepts . . . really address the needs of today."

What was the structure of deterrent threats that were available both to dissuade states from acquiring nuclear weapons and to convince states that had those weapons not to use them during the Cold War? Answering that question is logically a precondition to assessing whether such mechanisms will work in the current context.

In a text published originally in 1996, Eugene Brown and I laid out a reasonably comprehensive framework for categorizing types of mechanisms that could be used to deter unwanted nuclear behavior. Within this framework, arms proliferation can be dealt with in two ways, acquisition (or front-end) and employment (or back-end) deterrence. Acquisition deterrence, as the name implies, consists of efforts to keep states from obtaining nuclear weapons in the first place. The effort consists of two related and, for many purposes, sequential activities. Persuasion, or convincing states that gaining nuclear weapons is not in their best interests (often accompanied by the promise of related rewards for nonproliferation or punitive threats if compliance does not occur), seeks to cajole possible proliferating states into not doing so. In contemporary terms, efforts through the United Nations and the European Union to dissuade Iran from making a positive nuclear weapons decision fall into this category. If persuasion does not work, then coercion (threatening or taking punitive—including military—action to prevent proliferation) may occur. The attacks by Israel against an Iraqi nuclear reactor in 1981 and more recently against Syria are extreme examples of coercive options.

The success of acquisition deterrence has been mixed. These efforts were most successful during the Cold War, when the potential negative consequences of proliferation—the possibility of a general, civilization-destroying war—were greatest. In that circumstance, the leaders of the opposing coalitions could and did bring pressure on the states within their orbits to refrain from gaining nuclear weapons. The leading supporting members of the coalitions on both sides—Great Britain in the West and China in the East—did proceed with nuclear weapons programs, but they were the exceptions.

The current focus on proliferation has become the spread of nuclear weapons to countries—and especially unstable countries—in the developing world. The stalking horses of this concern were Israel and South Africa, both of which conducted highly clandestine weapons development programs that led to their acquisition of nuclear capability. Both countries developed their programs outside the Cold War context: Israel because of its fear its Islamic neighbors might destroy it; South Africa because of the alleged threat posed by neighboring black states (the so-called "frontline" states). When South Africa dismantled its apartheid system, it also destroyed its nuclear weapons. Israel continues to maintain, without publicly admitting it, its nuclear arsenal.

Israel and South Africa form a bridge of sorts to the present concern because both are instances where the attempt to restrain proliferation by the major powers was unsuccessful. Developing world states have proven less prone to geopolitical constraint than were Cold War allies, and thus India and Pakistan ignored rejoinders and joined the nuclear "club" in 1998. One of the major commonalities of George Bush's 2002 Axis of Evil designation of Iraq, Iran, and North Korea was their aspiration to nuclear status.

The other form of dissuasion is employment deterrence. If efforts to keep states from gaining nuclear weapons fail, then one must turn to efforts to keep them from using the weapons they do acquire. Once again, there are two mechanisms that can be employed. One is the threat of retaliation against any nuclear possessor who may choose to use its weapons against another state (and particularly the United States). The threat is to retaliate with such devastating—including assured destruction—force that it would not only be suicidal for an attacking state to use its weapons (there is an argument that this deterrence could also apply to attacks with other forms of WMD) but the suicide would also occur without having inflicted comparable damage to the retaliating state. Thus, a possible North Korean attack against the United States would consist of lobbing a handful of weapons against American targets and inflicting severe but not fatal damage; North Korea would be destroyed in the U.S. retaliation. The question that is raised about the extension of this form of deterrence in the current context is whether potential proliferating states' leadership are sufficiently rational (i.e., nonsuicidal) that this form of threat will be effective against them. The other form of employment deterrence threat is denial, the promise that if an attack is launched, it will fail because the potential attacked state has the capability to defend itself from an attack. The question here is whether the claim to be able to deny an attack is credible given the wide variety of means by which someone could attack, say, the United States with nuclear weapons.

Employment deterrence efforts have, to this point, been 100 percent effective, in that no state has used nuclear weapons in anger since 1945. While one cannot state with certainty that deterrence threats have been the reason for this, nonetheless the record remains perfect. From a proliferation perspective, of course, keeping the number of states who could "break" this record as small as possible is the most compelling concern.

The mechanism by which nonproliferation has been enforced is the NPT. The NPT was negotiated in 1968 and went into effect in 1970. Most countries of the world are or have been members of the regime—Iran and North Korea, for instance—and the question is whether the treaty will remain a viable means to avoid more proliferation in the future.

The Role of the NPT. The NPT was, and still is, the most dramatic, open international attempt to prevent and reverse the spread of weapons of mass destruction around the world. Conventions exist banning the production, use, and sale of chemical and biological weapons and their components, and the Missile Technology Control Regime represents an effort by the major powers (it was initiated by the G-7 powers) to control the spread of missile delivery technology, and all have been reasonable successes. The crown jewel of proliferation control, however, has been the effort to prevent the spread of nuclear weapons in the world, and the instrument has been the NPT.

The NPT was not the first international agreement that addressed horizontal proliferation, but it was the first treaty to have proliferation as its sole purpose. In 1963, the United States, the Soviet Union, and Great Britain negotiated the Limited Test Ban Treaty (LTBT), which prohibited the atmospheric testing of nuclear devices, and this was supposed to have a secondary proliferation effect, because the technology at the time virtually required nuclear weapons aspirants to explode a nuclear device in the atmosphere to achieve adequate confidence such a device would work. As a proliferation action, accession to the LTBT effectively eliminated contracting parties' ability to acquire reliable nuclear weapon capability.

The same three states cosponsored the NPT. Its major purpose was to create a nuclear caste system on the basis of nuclear weapons possession. Nuclear weapons-possessing states party to the NPT are allowed to keep their nuclear weapons, but agree not to share nuclear technology with nonpossessing states and to work toward disarmament of their arsenals. These provisions, one should quickly note, require very little action on the part of possessors, and are thus generally innocuous and painless. Nonpossessing states, on the other hand, incur real obligations, because they agree, as long as they are members of the treaty (and there are provisions to renounce one's membership), not to build or seek to build nuclear weapons. Among the nonweapons states who have signed the NPT, this creates a varying obligation. Some states (Sweden, for instance) have never had any intentions to build nuclear weapons and so could join the treaty regime without noticeable effect. Other states (most of the states of sub-Saharan Africa, for instance) lack the wherewithal to even think of developing the weapons, and thus they sacrifice little by joining either.

There is, however, a third category of states: countries that do not have nuclear weapons but might want the ability to exercise the option sometime in the future. For these states, the NPT creates a real potential problem, because ratifying it means giving away the right to exercise the nuclear option as long as one is a member. Although states can withdraw and thus free themselves from NPT restrictions, doing so is traumatic and would brand whoever did so as a potential aggressor. As a result, only one state that has signed NPT has ever left it (North Korea in 2003), joining Israel, Cuba, India, and Pakistan as nonmembers among the world major countries.

States desiring to retain the nuclear option have two ways to deal with the NPT. One is not to sign it, thereby avoiding its restrictions. The most prominent states not to do so have included Israel, India, and Pakistan. Other states with potential nuclear aspirations have signed the agreement and either complied fully with it or have engaged in activities that come close to noncompliance but stop short of that level. Iran and North Korea fall into this category.

Suspicion that some countries are not living up their NPT obligations has led to additional steps to try to enforce the goal of acquisitions deterrence. The Bush administration, for instance, created something it called the Proliferation Security Initiative (PSI) among like-minded states to, in Andrew Winner's words, "aggressively interdict weapons of mass destruction (WMD), their components, and their delivery systems." The PSI originally consisted of 11 members (Australia, France, Germany, Italy, Japan, the Netherlands, Poland, Portugal, Spain, the United Kingdom, and the United States) and has, according to the 2006 National Security Strategy (NSS) of the United States, attracted the interest of over 70 countries.

The nonproliferation enterprise remains a work in progress. Since the NPT was launched over a third of a century ago, there has been little overt nuclear weapons proliferation (India and Pakistan have been added, South Africa subtracted from the list). Yet, proliferation has emerged in the post–September 11 world as a major concern, fueled by the fear some rogue state—some member of the "axis of evil"—might acquire such weapons and either use them personally or through some terrorist surrogate. Whether this fear is real or fanciful is not the point; that this perception fuels international concern is the point. States like North Korea and Iran, however, retain interest in possibly gaining nuclear weapons status for different reasons that make the problem of proliferation an ongoing concern.

THE PROLIFERATION PROBLEM APPLIED: THE CASE OF NORTH KOREA

The general problem of proliferation gains meaning in the specific context as of individual states that might or that are suspected of attempting to exercise the nuclear weapons option. The distinction of North Korea is that it has actually gone several steps through the proliferation process. It is, for instance, the only country physically to withdraw from the NPT, an action it undertook and completed in 2003. It is also the only potential new member of the nuclear club that has attempted to conduct actual nuclear weapons tests: in 2003, it attempted a small underground test, the success of which is disputed, and in 2009 seismic readings monitored in Japan indicated a seismic event consistent with a low-kiloton underground explosion in the DPRK. North Korea has also conducted medium-range ballistic missile tests with varying success, but has not demonstrated the ability to wed nuclear weapons and ballistic missile delivery capabilities by testing a missile capable of delivering the weight payload of a nuclear weapon.

The other states that have been mentioned prominently in proliferation concerns are Iran and Iraq, the two countries that joined the DPRK as members of George W. Bush's 2002 "Axis of Evil." All share several characteristics.

First, they have or have had significant foreign policy differences with the United States (although of different natures and for different reasons) and have been categorized among America's adversaries. Second, all three possess or have possessed the technology and expertise to produce nuclear weapons and either have or reasonably easily could have access to the weapons-grade plutonium necessary for bomb construction (this commonality separates them from other worrisome states). Third, all deny any interest or desire to build, and especially to use, nuclear weapons, claims that are widely disbelieved in policy circles, especially in the United States. Fourth, although they are or have been members of NPT, they are or have been deemed to be untrustworthy, rogue regimes whose word cannot be trusted at face value.

They are also different in an important respect already identified. Iran and Iraq are not currently nuclear powers, although Iran has active aspirations, as discussed in Chapter 7. There has never been verification that either has fabricated a nuclear weapon, and their regimes deny any interest in doing so. As such, they pose a problem of acquisition (or front-end) deterrence. North Korea is different. According to former assistant secretary of defense Ashton Carter and former secretary of defense William J. Perry (both under President Clinton) in a June 22, 2006, column in the *Washington Post*, the DPRK "openly boasts of its nuclear deterrent, has obtained six to eight bombs' worth of plutonium since 2003 and is plunging ahead to make more." A 2003 article in the *Bulletin of the Atomic Scientists* went so far as to state that "North Korea has apparently become the world's ninth nuclear power." Thus, the problem posed by North Korea is one of employment (or back-end) deterrence.

Background of the Problem

Although other ties between Iran, Iraq, and North Korea were tenuous (especially between the DPRK and the others), they all shared a place on the proliferation agenda—especially the extent to which that agenda is affected, even dominated, by the United States. Each was an adversary of the United States, thereby creating the interest a country has in its opponents, although the sources and nature of opposition varied. America's adversarial relationship with the DPRK was longest standing, dating back to the Korean War of 1950–1953, and its nuclear weapons program is normally dated back to the 1950s, when a nuclear-armed United States remained the occupying power in South Korea, a circumstance some argue helps explain the DPRK's perceived need for weapons of their own.

A common thread that runs through the North Korean and other cases is that the chief protagonist in the process has been the United States, which, of course, is the original N state, and it has consistently opposed almost all other attempts at proliferation. Great Britain's attainment of membership is the exception, and the United States has generally not been an overt opponent of the presumed Israeli program. Nuclear aspiration is one of the common attributes of the Axis of Evil state, and the long-standing animosity between the DPRK and the United States and the advanced status of the DPRK program give it especially poignant status for the United States. The location of the DPRK in East Asia, of course, makes the context different, a part of the east Asian power balance rather than the extreme volatility of the Middle East.

The East Asian context influences the perceptions of the relevant states in different ways than in the case of Iran and Iraq. Compared, for instance, to Iran, the DPRK is a relatively minor player in a region dominated by China, Japan, South Korea, and even Russia, and it is the nuclear weapons program that gives North Korea what little power and leverage it has in regional affairs. Whether it is motivated by a simple desire to be noticed and recognized, by the perceived need to have some kind of bargaining chip to ensure outside assistance, or for some geopolitical reasons, nuclear weapons have a unique place in the North Korean calculation of their place in the world.

The proliferation problem posed by North Korea has ebbed and flowed. In the early 1990s it seemed to be settled. In 1994, the Clinton administration made a deal with the DPRK (the Framework Agreement), under which the United States would furnish the North Koreans food, fuel oil, and light (nonweapons grade) nuclear fuel in return for the DPRK abandoning its nuclear weapons program. That agreement held until the Bush administration, deeply suspicious and arguably ignorant of the North Koreans, threatened to renege on the deal. Cumings states the case regarding the Bush administration dramatically: "Bush combined utter ignorance with a visceral hatred for his counterpart in Pyongyang." This action led the North Koreans to remove themselves from the NPT in 2003 and to resume their nuclear program, the most recent chapter of which began in 2006.

The Continuing Problem

The proliferation problem regarding the DPRK is thus distinctive. North Korea, of course, poses a more advanced problem than the other pretenders, because of its presumed possession of a small number of nuclear weapons and its development of long-range missile systems. This means antiproliferation efforts must be based in employment deterrence or convincing the DPRK to disarm its arsenal, an unlikely prospect.

The North Korean case is also distinctive in that it has been, at various times, in the process of being resolved through negotiation. After several years of off-again, on-again negotiations between the DPRK and the other countries involved in the so-called six-nations talks (the United States, Russia, China, Japan, and North and South Korea), a breakthrough occurred in summer 2008 that will, if fully implemented, result in North Korean disassembly of nuclear facilities capable of producing bomb-grade plutonium, destruction of nuclear bomb materials, and re-accession to the NPT. In return, the DPRK has already been removed from the U.S. State Department's list of terrorist states and the Axis of Evil, and some provisions of the American Trading with the Enemy Act pertinent to the DPRK have been lifted. Full implementation was interrupted in late 2008 by the apparent serious illness suffered by Kim Jong II, leaving DPRK leadership in limbo. Still, implementation of DPRK nuclear disarmament lags.

The rift between Pyongyang and Washington is far longer and deeper than it is between Tehran or Baghdad and Washington. The DPRK is the only country to withdraw from the NPT, and it has been much more recalcitrant about its weapons programs, including both nuclear weapons and ballistic delivery systems. Moreover, the Korean peninsula's location in the heart of East Asia gives it a great deal of geopolitical importance. On the other hand, North Korea has no oil and is one of the most destitute countries on the globe and relies heavily on outside assistance to maintain its meager standard of living.

The DPRK's unique situation cuts both ways in terms of trying to deal with them. Their extreme poverty and lack of developmental prospects makes them receptive to outside assistance, as was part of the 1994 agreement. The regime is anxious to avoid letting the population know just how miserable their condition is and prospects are, particularly to the circumstances of surrounding countries, but this is an ever-increasingly difficult condition to maintain, according to Lankov. Moreover, as Lankov notes, the nuclear program serves to ameliorate some of the country's woes: "Pyongyang cannot do away with these programs. That would mean losing a powerful military deterrent and a time-tested tool of extortion. It would also relegate North Korea to being a third-rate country, on a par with Mozambique or Uganda."

The history of the North Korean nuclear program—and concerns about it—is long-standing and, as noted, is largely framed in terms of U.S.–North Korean relations. The United States and the DPRK have, of course, been antagonists since the Korean War (1950–1953) in which they were primary opponents. Aside from the general antagonism this confrontation created, it may have provided the impetus for North Korean nuclear pretensions. As Robert Norris put it in his 2003 *Bulletin of the Atomic Scientists* article, "The fact that North Korea was threatened with nuclear weapons during the Korean War, and that for decades thereafter U.S. weapons were deployed in the South, may have helped motivate former President Kim Il Sung to launch a nuclear weapons program of his own." Regardless of whether one accepts this explanation at face value, the North Koreans have been consistent over time that they need to maintain the option to develop nuclear weapons.

The genesis of the current crisis goes back to the Clinton administration. A May 1992 inspection of North Korean nuclear facilities by IAEA inspectors headed by Hans Blix concluded the North Koreans might be engaged in weapons activity (converting spent nuclear fuel into weapons-grade plutonium). This precipitated a crisis in which the North Koreans threatened the until-then unprecedented step of withdrawing from the NPT in March 1993 (they had joined the treaty in 1984). At this point the Clinton administration intervened, entering into direct talks and that produced a negotiated settlement to the problem, the Framework Agreement. Under its provisions (reference to the complete document is found in the suggested readings), the North Koreans agreed to freeze and eventually to dismantle its nuclear weapons program under IAEA supervision. In turn, it would accept light water nuclear reactors to replace those capable of producing weapons-grade materials and would receive heavy fuel oil for electricity and heating purposes. In addition,

Norris adds, "political and economic relations would be normalized, and both countries would work toward a nuclear weapons-free Korean peninsula and strengthen the nuclear proliferation regime."

How well this arrangement worked was primarily a partisan political question in the United States. Republican critics—notably neoconservatives like John Bolton—of the Clinton policy underlying the Agreed Framework argued that the North Koreans were cheating on the letter and spirit of the agreement in terms of their handling of materials from their light water reactors, a claim vigorously denied by Selig Harrison in a 2005 *Foreign Affairs* article, who equates the intelligence reports of violations in North Korea to distortions similar to those coming out of Iraq in 2002.

At any rate, the current, ongoing crisis was precipitated when the Bush administration cut off the flow of heating oil to North Korea and terminated the Framework Agreement in December 2002. The DPRK responded by announcing on January 10, 2003, that it was withdrawing from the NPT, which it did after the mandatory 90-day waiting period following the announcement of intent. Following saber rattling on both sides in the ensuing months, six-party negotiations between the DPRK, South Korea, Japan, Russia, China, and the United States opened on August 28, 2003, at which point North Korea announced it was prepared "to declare itself formally as a nuclear weapons state" (which it did in December 2006) and added that it possessed the capability to deliver these weapons to target by ballistic means.

The North Koreans have always viewed the six-party format for negotiations (an American construct) as undesirable, preferring bilateral negotiations that the Bush administration refused to accept. On September 9, 2004, an explosion occurred at a nuclear site (Ryanggang) in North Korea that may have been a nuclear test, although the North Koreans denied that the test was of a nuclear device. The North Koreans announced on February 10, 2005, that they had developed nuclear weapons for self-defense purposes and suspended participation in the six-party talks. In a direct reversal that illustrates some of the flavor of the ongoing relationship, the six-party talks resumed in September 2005 and produced an agreement whereby the DPRK agreed to dismantle its nuclear weapons program in return for economic assistance. In June 2006, as the Taepodong crisis (tests of North Korean Taepodong missiles, some of which flew over Japanese territory) unfolded, critics Carter and Perry declared that "the six-party talks . . . have collapsed."

The summer 2006 brouhaha over North Korean missile tests emerged from this context. North Korea has for some years had a missile development program, and its potential ability to deliver WMD by ballistic means distinguishes the DPRK from other proliferators, as noted. The last missile crisis occurred in 1998, when the DPRK tested a Taepodong 1 missile that passed over Japan and created an international incident. The Clinton administration had exacted a moratorium on missile testing from the North Koreans in 1998, which, according to a June 21, 2006, *Los Angeles Times* report by Barbara Demick, it renewed in 2002. The North Koreans, in keeping with their nuclear tradition of denying they are engaged in WMD activities while asserting their right to do so if they choose, maintain the current Taepodong 2 test is intended to see whether North Korea can insert a satellite into space, while arguing they retain the right to develop military missiles.

Was the missile dispute just another round of U.S.–North Korean bickering or something more serious? Carter and Perry, who were officials during the 1990s when agreements were reached with the DPRK, believed the crisis was real and that the United States should consider a preemptive strike against the missile launch site if the North Koreans fail to decommission the missile. Alarm was raised because the Taepodong 2, especially if equipped with a third boost stage—which the purported test did not include and which the North Koreans have never done successfully—could reach targets in the United States (purportedly the current version could hit Hawaii, Alaska, and possibly parts of the West Coast of the United States). On the other hand, the Taepodong series of missiles are old technology, very vulnerable liquid-fuel rockets that take literally days to fuel at above-ground launchers and could hardly be used for a sneak attack against the United States or anywhere else. They are also very vulnerable to being attacked and destroyed during the fueling process, as Carter and Perry admit. "The multi-story, thin skinned missile filled with high-energy fuel is itself explosive—the U.S. airstrike would puncture the missile and probably cause it to explode." There is no reliable public information available on the accuracy of such missiles; presumably, they are fairly inaccurate.

One is left with what to make of the North Korean nuclear "threat." If, as they imply, they are nuclear-capable, the question is what would keep them from using their weapons? It is difficult to conjure reasons why North Korea would launch an offensive, preemptive nuclear strike against anyone, given the certain response would be its own utter and certain destruction. Using the nuclear weapons most observers say they have—and that the North Koreans do not strongly deny—may make little sense, but possessing such weapons may make sense if North Korea believes they help deter the United States from attacking them. The idea that the United States needs to be deterred may seem outlandish to most Americans, but not to the North Koreans. As Cumings puts it, "it seems irrational for Pyongyang to give up its handful of nukes when the United States still threatens to attack." In February 2007, both sides in effect "blinked." The DPRK agreed in the six-party talks to suspend its nuclear weapons program in return for the same kinds of incentives offered in 1994 by the United States.

The resumption of six-party talks (this time under Chinese chairmanship) resulted in the agreement announced in June 2008. It was an agreement from which both sides benefited. Those concerned with proliferation saw North Korea join South Africa as countries that have joined then quit the nuclear club, although some issues remained (whether the DPRK had actually constructed bombs and provided nuclear aid to Syria, for instance). In return, the DPRK succeeded in removing international sanctions against it that have prevented badly needed assistance from flowing to it (food and fuel, for instance). As President Bush said on June 27, 2008, "if, it [the DPRK] continues to make the right choices it can repair its relationship with the international community."

Mutual distrust and American concentration on Iraq and Afghanistan left the details of implementing these agreements uncompleted when Barack Obama became president in 2009. At one level, the prospects for agreement seemed improved; Obama lacked the Bush administration's intense hatred of the DPRK, and Obama had suggested his willingness to negotiate with adversaries, including the North Koreans. At the same time, the DPRK leadership clearly believes maintaining the nuclear option is in their best interest as their main sources of international stature and leverage. As a result, Cumings concludes that "it seems unlikely that the North can be coaxed into negotiating another nuclear agreement." Moreover, Lamkov contends, "the United States and its allies have no efficient methods of coercion at their disposal." The DPRK proliferation problem is not, in other words, going to go away anytime soon.

CONCLUSION

The North Korean case study stands as a potential harbinger for other proliferation cases. The DPRK defied the proliferation regime and paid a price in terms of international sanctions, but international knowledge of its nuclear program and its nuclear weapons provided it with leverage that allowed it to maintain control of its nuclear fate and thereby to preserve the advantages they believe nuclear weapons provide them. Iraq lacked such leverage and it was flattened; Iran faces the international community exposed but weaponless, and its fate is uncertain. Is there a lesson here for future proliferators?

No one, except potential proliferating countries that are part of +1, argue that the spread of nuclear and other weapons of mass destruction to nonpossessing states is in principle a good idea that should be encouraged. On the other hand, the empirical evidence of the impact of individual proliferations (when individual countries joined the nuclear weapons "club") hardly provides incontrovertible proof of the most dire perils that have been predicted. What is the evidence, for instance, that the world is a less stable place because Israel, India, or Pakistan possess the bomb? One can contend it would be better if they did not, but the peril remains theoretical, not demonstrated.

How should future proliferators view the scene? Should they conclude that their attempts to attain nuclear weapons status will be viewed as internationally dangerous and destabilizing, prompting an international response that will reduce their security if they do not eschew proliferation? Or will they decide a positive nuclear weapons decision will protect them—provide them a deterrent—from attacks by predators, thereby increasing their security?

Nuclear-possessing states have one answer to that question, but recent experience may offer a different interpretation. When they ask themselves (as the North Koreans apparently have) if Saddam Hussein would have been immune from an American invasion had he not stopped pursuing nuclear weapons, many believe he made the wrong choice. At the same time, its nuclear weapons may have won the DPRK a ticket off the Axis of Evil by presenting the world (and especially the United States) with a threat that harsh rhetoric alone could not solve. At a minimum, recent experience does not unambiguously tell potential proliferators not to pursue the nuclear option.

There is one distinctly American irony in the ongoing conflict over proliferation. The United States—the original nuclear power (the first N)—has been the most vocal advocate of others' nuclear abstention. In the contemporary context, however, the most prominent candidates as the next proliferators (the DPRK, Iran, Iraq) are also rivals of the United States and are countries which, rightly or wrongly, contend that maintaining the nuclear option is a way to deter the United States. American discussions of proliferation tend to ignore or downplay this dynamic, but should they? Is it possible, indeed, for a state to provide the solution to a problem of which it may be a significant—in some cases the most significant—part?

STUDY/DISCUSSION QUESTIONS

1. What is the basis of the current international concern for nuclear proliferation? How does the DPRK exemplify this problem?
2. Why is proliferation a "delicate" problem? Distinguish between types of proliferation, including what kinds of materials and capabilities are being proliferated and what difference each makes.
3. What is the N11 problem? Define it and why it suggests the delicacy of the proliferation problem. Why is it so difficult to resolve?
4. What means are available to deal with proliferation? Distinguish between acquisition and employment deterrence. How does each work? How does the Proliferation Security Initiative contribute?
5. What is the Nuclear Non-Proliferation Treaty (NPT)? How does it work? What categories of states are there in regard to the treaty? How are they different?
6. Define the DPRK in proliferation terms. What is its status? How has it evolved to where it is? How serious is it to international stability, and what can be done about it?
7. How has the success of the six-party talks changed the proliferation situation regarding the DPRK? Who gets what from the agreement?
8. Put yourself in the position of a country contemplating nuclear proliferation. Does recent experience suggest that pursuit of the nuclear option will enhance or detract from your security? Why?
9. If you were representing a country contemplating gaining nuclear weapons but in an adversarial relationship with the United States, how would that fact influence your decision process? Elaborate.

READING/RESEARCH MATERIAL

Arnoldy, Ben. "How Serious Is North Korea's Nuclear Threat?" *Christian Science Monitor* (online), August 27, 2003.

Carter, Ashton B. and William J. Perry. "If Necessary, Strike and Destroy." *Washington Post*, June 22, 2006, A29.

Cumings, Bruce. "The North Korea Problem: Dealing with Irrationality." *Current History* 108, 719 (September 2009), 284–290.

Demich Barbara. "Few Moves Left with N. Korea." *Los Angeles Times* (online), June 21, 2006.

Harrison, Selig S. "Did North Korea Cheat?" *Foreign Affairs* 84, 1 (January/February 2005), 99–110.

Lankov, Andrei. "Changing North Korea." *Foreign Affairs* 88, 6 (November–December 2009), 95–105.

Lieber, Kier A. and David G. Press. "The Rise of U.S. Nuclear Supremacy." *Foreign Affairs* 85, 2 (March/April 2006), 42–54.

Mendelsohn, Jack. "The New Threats: Nuclear Amnesia, Nuclear Legitimacy." *Current History* 105, 694 (November 2006), 385–390.

The National Security Strategy of the United States of America. Washington, DC: The White House, March 2006.

Norris, Robert S. "North Korea's Nuclear Program, 2003." *Bulletin of the Atomic Scientists* 59, 2 (March/April 2003), 74–77.

Onishi, Norimitsu and Edward Wong. "U.S. to Take North Korea Off Terrorist List." *New York Times* (online), June 27, 2008.

Perkowich, George. "The End of the Proliferation Regime." *Current History* 105, 694 (November 2006), 355–362.

Pilat, Joseph F. "Reassessing Security Assurances in a Unipolar World." *Washington Quarterly* 28, 2 (Spring 2005), 59–70.

Sigal, Leon V. "The Lessons of North Korea's Test." *Current History* 105, 694 (November 2006), 364–365.

Snow, Donald M. and Eugene Brown. *The Contours of Power: An Introduction to Contemporary International Relations.* New York: St. Marin's Press, 1996.

Specter, Arlen and Christopher Walsh. "Dialogue with Adversaries." *Washington Quarterly* 30, 1 (Winter 2006/2007), 9–26.

Winner, Andrew C. "The Proliferation Security Initiative: The New Face of Interdiction." *Washington Quarterly* 28, 2 (Spring 2005), 129–143.

WEB SITES

North Korean Weapons Program Summary (Wikipedia) http://en.wikipedia.org

Text of U.S.-DPRK Agreed Framework of 1994
http://www.carnegieendowment.org/static/npp/agreed_framework.cfm.

Pivotal States: Confronting and Accommodating Iran

PRÉCIS

Although the theory of sovereign equality makes all states equal, their influence within the international system is variable. At one extreme are the most powerful states, the great powers or superpowers, and at the other end are more minor states, whose power is less. Between them are a number of regional powers which, by virtue of history, size, and a number of other measures, are powers whose interests must be taken into account within their parts of the world. In this case study, these states are referred to as pivotal states. In the contemporary international system, one of the most important pivotal states is Iran, making it the subject of this case. Pivotal states become important when their interests and those of the major powers come into conflict, and this aspect of the pivotal state phenomenon is explored through an examination of U.S.-Iranian contemporary relations.

There is a category of states in the international system that falls somewhere below the most important powers (what used to be called major powers and since the Cold War superpowers) but above the "rank and file" of states in the system. Major states, especially the most powerful superpowers, wield predominant influence on the international scene and are its most influential members. Generally, their reach goes beyond the physical region in which they are located and has an impact on other countries around the world. At the other extreme are the mass of states that are comparatively weak, have some limited regional influence at best, and generally can be influenced by the major powers and more important regional states.

The category in between these extremes is composed of a limited number of states. They lack the comprehensive power and influence to play a major role globally, but are substantially powerful enough that they cannot be manipulated easily by the major powers and generally can influence the

126

behavior of other states and thus events in their regions. Moreover, even though the power such states possess may compare unfavorably with that of the major powers on a broad array of measures (military might or economic size, for instance), they may be capable of frustrating the designs of more powerful states, at least within their particular regions. While their ability to influence global politics may not compare favorably to the capabilities of the most powerful countries, they are nonetheless consequential within the range of their influence. One way to think about states in this category is as regional powers; another is as *pivotal states.*

The effects of pivotal states can be benign or problematical, depending on circumstances and who is affected by their actions. Brazil, for instance, is clearly a pivotal state in the Western Hemisphere (with arguable aspirations to major power or even superpower status) that, most of the time, is not a negative factor in the politics of its region and lacks the global reach to make it a major world power despite its aspirations. It does, however, provide an occasional obstacle to the interests of its hemispheric superpower, the United States, in areas such as the expansion of a free trade association within the region (the Free Trade Area of the Americas proposal). At the same time, Brazil is the largest country in Latin America in size and population, making it the predominant regional actor south of the American-Mexican border. In, for instance, Asian affairs, the impact of Brazil is not generally critical; within the Western Hemisphere, its interests cannot be ignored.

It is when pivotal states come into conflict with the major powers that their influence becomes problematical and their presence and status become controversial. Particularly to the largest powers like the United States, each region of the world is but one theater of its global interests, and it prefers an order in the region congruent with its worldview. The American foreign policies of globalization in the 1990s and democratization in the 2000s are examples. In each case, the United States has seen the success of its foreign policy in the success or failure to bring countries in different regions either into Clinton's circle of market democracies or Bush's expanding circle of democracies. When that vision comes into conflict with the regional interests of the most important state or states in a particular region, then the prospect for conflict emerges. The superpower may have greater global resources to apply to achieving its ends worldwide, but since those resources must be parsed across the globe, this does not necessarily translate into resources with which to confront successfully the contrary interest of the pivotal state in a given place. In addition, the regional pivotal state's interests are likely to be more important to it within a region than the major power's interests in that region are to it, and although the major state may have greater power than the pivotal state, the pivotal state's power is more proximate and may be easier to apply than that of the major power.

In the contemporary international system, no state better exemplifies the roles of a pivotal state than does Iran, which Nasr and Takeyh identify as the aspiring pivotal state in the Middle East in a January/February 2008 *Foreign Affairs* article that was an inspiration for the theme of this case study. Iran is arguably the pivotal state in the Middle East as a whole and certainly in its oil-rich section, the Persian Gulf. The world's second oldest existing state (after China), Iran—or Persia, or the Persian Empire—has been a major power in the Middle East for centuries, dating back at least to 1500 B.C. When that part of the world was at the center of the world system, it was one of the world's major powers, a superpower of its time. The inheritors of the Peacock Empire are well aware of their heritage and their place in the global politics of the oil-rich Middle East, and it is a past status to which many Iranians cast a wistful eye. Iran views itself as *the* most consequential state in the region, and on the basis of that perception, it believes its interests are of paramount importance in the region and even beyond.

Iran and the United States have been engaged in a superpower–pivotal state struggle since 1979, when the pro-American Iranian government of Shah Reza Pahlevi was overthrown and replaced by a stridently anti-American, theocratic Islamic Republic of Iran. As a result, the existence and actions of the pivotal state of Iran became particularly vexing for the United States, as American interests and those of the regional pivotal state came into conflict across a range of issues affecting the region to the point that a U.S. Secretary of State quoted in Nasr and Takeyh has declared that "Iran constitutes the single most important single-state challenge to the United States and the kind of Middle East we seek." Major powers are used to getting their own way most of the time and are particularly frustrated when the actions of supposedly lesser powers—and notably the pivotal powers—provide an effective obstacle to achieving those interests. In the Persian Gulf region, Iran poses the primary barrier to outside influence, and its challenge is increasing. As Milani puts it, "Iran now rightly considers itself as an indispensable regional player." The United States' relationship with Iran is an absolutely classical example of the clash between a superpower and a regional pivotal state.

This case study serves two purposes. The first is to explore the nature of the pivotal state, using Iran as the primary example. The second is to examine the problems that pivotal states can create for the international system. This in turn requires looking at what makes pivotal states important and thus provides them with power and leverage and also at the frustrations that major powers have both understanding and coping with recalcitrant pivotal states. The enormous frustration of American foreign policy makers in their attempts to control the behavior of Iran serves as the prime example of superpower–pivotal state relations problem.

IRAN: A PIVOTAL STATE

Iran occupies a unique place in the world. It has been a major part of world civilization through most of recorded history, and it has been a central actor whenever its region has been the focus of the international system. As a result, it has seen its place in the international sun wax and wane, and it clearly aspires and is actively working to seeing it rise again. Part of the basis for this ambition is its physical presence, including, most prominently in the contemporary setting, energy resources over which there is a growing global competition (see Chapter 2). At the same time, Iran has a unique history and historical legacy that is both a part of and simultaneously apart from the rest of the region. Its unique attributes help explain its contemporary evolution and Iran's place in the contemporary international system.

The Physical Setting

Iran is a large country. It has a land area of 631,659 square miles (slightly larger than Alaska and about three times the size of Arizona), which makes it the largest physical state in the Middle East and the world's second largest state in area (after Indonesia) with a Muslim majority. With a population of 66,429,284 (2009 estimate based on *World Almanac and Book of Facts* figures), it is the third most populous Muslim state (following Indonesia and Egypt) in the world. Its economy ranks 20th among world countries, the highest of any Islamic country, and its per capita gross domestic product is at $12,300, making it globally a middle-range economy.

It is also a resource-rich country. It is one of the world's leading exporters of oil, selling 2.52 million barrels per day internationally out of a total daily production of 4.15 million barrels in 2006. Its proven reserves of oil are the world's third largest at 132.5 billion barrels (after Saudi Arabia and Canada, although nearly all of Canada's reserves are in hard-to-extract Albertan oil tar beds). Its natural gas reserves are among the largest in the world, at an estimated 26.37 *trillion* cubic meters. Taxes on oil revenues currently account for over 80 percent of governmental revenues.

Iran's renaissance as a world power is directly related to the growing importance of petroleum energy in the last century, an importance that continues to exist. Due to its central location, Iran is a pivot in the burgeoning global oil competition of which neighboring China and India, as well as Russia, will be growing players in upcoming years. As Baktiari puts it, "China and Russia . . . are wrapped up in Iran's energy sector. China is aggressively pinning down future sources around the world, and Russia is assisting Iran in the construction of a civilian nuclear reactor in Bushehr." Aside from Iran (Iraq is a partial exception), the oil-rich states of the region happen also to be relatively small, under populated, and possessed of limited military resources with which to protect themselves. Iran is *the* major power, in potential and reality, in this part of the world, and it will hold that position as long as the world appetite for fossil fuel energy remains unrequited. Dependence on oil is, however, a double-edged sword for the Iranians, as it is for all the countries whose economies depend on oil revenues. As long as demand and price remain high, the fact that, according to Vaki, "the oil sector is vital for the government's export earnings, 80 percent of which are oil-related," is tolerable. Should oil revenue become less stable, the Iranian economy will become vulnerable unless the economy is diversified. Indeed, some analysts like Chadar argue that economic factors may become the pivot of potential economic stability and demands for political change.

In several ways, Iran's physical location also contributes to its pretension as a pivotal power. It sits astride the vital Persian (or Arabian) Gulf, through which most of the region's petroleum moves to the marketplace, and its coastline on the Gulf includes one of the world's major maritime choke points, the Straits of Hormuz. The mere possibility that Iran might, at some time, menace the flow of oil to the West is the basic reason for a large (and physically vulnerable) American naval presence in the Persian Gulf region. At the same time, Iran is located strategically beside the oil-rich Arab states of the Persian Gulf littoral (Saudi Arabia, Kuwait, and Iraq) and the potential oil producing giants of Central Asia and the Caspian littoral, which will likely be a major exploitable source of world energy (oil and natural gas) in the near future. Iran also is not far from both Russia and China, as the accompanying map shows. The result is that good relations with the regime in Tehran are important for both countries.

Iran as a Unique State

Iran stands at odds with the other states of its region. It is not "just another" Middle Eastern country that can be lumped conveniently with others in the region. Two ways in which Iran differs from most Western associations with the Middle East region conflicts within it—are worth mentioning: its historical significance and its ethno-religious status. Each contributes to the uniqueness of Iran and why it is misleading and potentially distorting to consider Iran within the context of other regional states.

Iran, as the second oldest continuous state in the world, was known for most of its history as Persia; the name changed in 1935 to Iran. Its history dates back at least to 549 B.C. when Cyrus the Great declared the Persian Empire and, among other things, restored Jerusalem to Jewish rule. Through its history, the central location of Persia/Iran made it attractive to foreigners, and the result has been a history marked both by independence and greatness and also by occupation. Persia was conquered by Alexander the Great in 333 B.C. and the Turks and Mongols in turn ruled Persia from the eleventh into the sixteenth centuries. In more modern history, the Russian and British empires competed for influence in Iran in the nineteenth century, and in 1941, the British and Soviets forced the abdication of the first Shah of Iran (Reza Khan, the father of Shah Muhammad Reza Pahlevi) because of his suspected Nazi sympathies and the likelihood he might deliver Iranian oil to the fascist powers in World War II. Iranian independence was restored with the ascension of Muhammad Reza Pahlevi as Shah of the Iranian (Peacock) Empire in 1941, and it has remained independent ever since. Persian/Iranian civilization is among the oldest in the world, creating a sense of nationalism and identification that is much stronger than in other states in the region.

Iran also stands out from its neighbors in ethno-religious terms in ways that have become familiar to many Americans because of connections made between the Iranians and Iraqis during the American-instigated war and occupation of Iraq. Of the major (and especially oil-producing) states of the Middle East, Iran is both the only non-Arab major oil producer and the largest Shiite

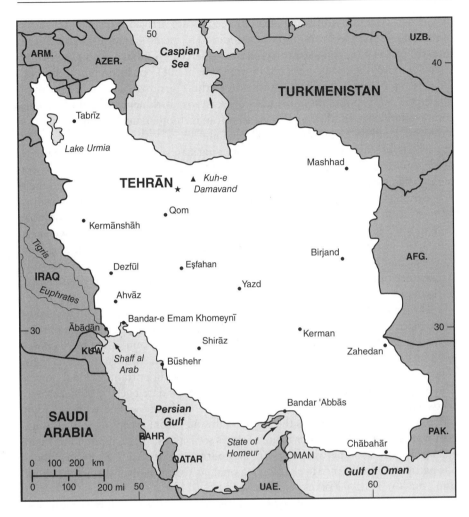

Map 7.1   Map of Iran

state in the region. Both characteristics create major distinctions between Iran and its neighbors. Without understanding these differences, it is impossible to appreciate the nature and extent of Iranian participation as the region's pivotal state and why that status is opposed not only by the United States but also by other regional powers.

Although Iran is a multiethnic state, its core population is Persian. Persians make up just over half of the Iranian population. Ethnically, they are Aryan as opposed to Arab, the ethnic designation of most of Iran's neighbors, especially to the west and south. The Kurds of Iran, Iraq, and Syria share Aryan lineage, as do several other minor ethnic groups in the region. Historically, the relationship between the Persians and the Arabs has been antagonistic, including mutual histories of conquest and occupation. Indeed, Islam arrived in Persia as a result of its conquest by the Arab Empire. In addition to the dominant Persians, Azeris (mostly in the northwestern province of Azerbaijan adjacent to the former Soviet Republic and current state by the same name) constitute an additional 24 percent of the population, and other ethnic groups each with less than 10 percent of the population include Kurds, Arabs, Turkmen, and Baluchis. This composition leads Bradley to suggest that Iran is "not so much a nation-state as a multinational empire dominated by Persians."

Iran is also distinguished from surrounding states because almost 90 percent of its population belongs to the Shiite sect of Islam. Shia Islam is a minority sect within Islam overall (only about 15 percent of Muslims are Shiite, although their proportion is growing). Sunni Islam is the sect to which the majority of Muslims in most neighboring states (Iraq, with a 60 percent Shiite majority, is a notable exception) belong. Sunnis and Shiites have been in conflict since the two sects split apart in the aftermath of the death of the Prophet Mohammad, and they view one another as political rivals within Islamic countries and internationally. Acceptance of Iran as the region's pivotal state, for instance, is denied or decried in the region both because the Iranians are Persian and because they are Shiite.

The result of these distinctions is to complicate the Middle East and to muddy Iran's place in it. With a population of over 65 million people, Iran dwarfs the rest of the Persian Gulf states and is, on purely geopolitical grounds, the most consequential and thus pivotal state in the region. Were Iran an Arab, Sunni state, there is little question that it would be accepted as the most important regional power. The fact that animosities between Persians and Arabs date back to Biblical times (between Persia and Mesopotamia, for instance) and are overlaid with sectarian differences within Islam keeps the Sunni Arab states from accepting Iranian leadership and, indeed, most other regional states see Iran as a rival, if not an outright enemy. This division between Persian, Shiite Iran, and its Arab, Sunni neighbors has particular significance in shaping regional, as well as global, suspicions about Iran's nuclear weapons plans, as discussed below.

This wariness is especially evident in Iranian relations with two countries, Iraq and Israel. The Iraqi connection is most obvious: Iraq and Iran share a long common border that includes, at its southern reaches leading to the Persian Gulf, the oil-producing regions of the Iraqi Basra and Persian Khuzestan oil fields and the refining capacities along the Shatt al-Arab, the waterway created by the confluence of the Tigris and Euphrates rivers that flows into the gulf. The two counties are, in important respects, the successors of Persia and Mesopotamia, and they have had a turbulent past, most recently demonstrated in the Iran–Iraq War between 1980 and 1988.

The current role of Iran in the politics of Iraq has become particularly problematical as Iraq moves back toward full sovereign independence. Common Shiite roots give Iran an automatic interest in how Iraq emerges from the American occupation. Iran has involved itself in Iraqi politics, providing support for virtually all the Shiite movements both inside and outside the al-Maliki government, and the American command in the country accuses the Iranians, principally through its Quds force, of providing military hardware that is used against both American and Iraqi forces. Vaki describes Iranian policy in Iraq as "controlled chaos, in essence a stealth strategy designed to undermine American initiatives while strengthening Iran's regional position." At a minimum, the Iranians hope to have influence in a likely Shiite-dominated post-American government in Iraq; how much more they desire is problematical. The major factor limiting the extent of Iranian influence is the fact that the Iranians are not Arabs.

Iran has also had a unique relationship with Israel. Through its creation and support of Hezbollah, which is dedicated to the elimination of the Israeli state, the Iranian position appears to be one of total antipathy toward Israel, a useful position among Muslim states in the region. Over time, however, the relationship has been more complicated. As already noted, Cyrus the Great did return Jerusalem to the Jews, and under the rule of the Shah of Iran from the end of World War II until 1979, Iran was a major supplier of oil to Israel in the face of the antipathy of its neighbors. The militant revolutionary regime that succeeded the Shah after the Iranian Revolution has been steadfastly anti-Israeli, making western countries like the United States that support Israel even more leery of the Iranians.

The Evolution of Contemporary Iranian Politics

Modern Iranian politics has been schizophrenic, and part of its changeability has been a result of the relationship that Iran has had with the United States. In essence, the political history of contemporary Iran can be divided into two polar opposite periods: the period of rule by Muhammed Reza Pahlevi, the Shah of Iran, and the period since his overthrow, the Iranian revolutionary period. The first period is marked by close collaboration and relations between the United States and Iran; the latter has been distinguished by sometimes bitter enmity between the two countries.

As noted, the Shah of Iran came to power originally in 1941 as the successor of his father, Reza Khan; he was briefly removed from office in 1953 by the democratically elected government of Dr. Mohammad Mossadeqh over a dispute about the nationalization of Iranian oil, but the Shah was returned to power with the aid of the Central Intelligence Agency late in that year (an American action that remains a source of anti-Americanism to this day). The Shah remained in power until 1979, when he was forced into exile by the Iranian Revolution.

Reign of the Shah. The major theme and goal of the Shah's rule was the restoration of Iran—the Peacock Empire—to its former glory among the countries of the world. It was a highly nationalistic appeal to a people who had spent 200 years under foreign domination before the rise of his father and had been heavily influenced by the European powers in the years surrounding World War II. To restore Iran to its historic place among the world's powers, the Shah tied Iran's oil wealth to an ambitious program of economic and social modernization and westernization that sought to create a modern Iranian state that would be a worthy successor to the Persian Empire. To help him accomplish that goal, the Shah found a ready ally in the United States. In return for American assistance in modernizing Iran's economy and society (and, not coincidentally, its military), Iran served as the guarantor of oil supplies flowing from the Persian Gulf, thereby obviating the need for a direct American military presence in the region to ensure the supply of petroleum to the United States and its allies.

The principal vehicle of this transformation was the *White Revolution,* a series of economic and political reforms that underpinned Iran's transformation. Among other things, the reforms created a modern industrial society including the creation of a technocratic middle class and military officer corps largely educated and trained in the West (especially the United States) that became a major vehicle for social westernization. In addition, the Shah introduced reforms that led to a massive movement of people from the countryside to urban centers like Tehran that were unequipped to absorb the influx and undercut much of the traditional power of the religious community—nationalizing land holdings and reforming the judicial system to exclude the clergy from its historic role in areas commonly thought of as civil law in the West.

This transformation came with costs that gradually accumulated. For one thing, the supporters of the shah became a highly visible, affluent, and westernized elite that flaunted its status through conspicuous consumption (alcoholic usage, gambling, western dress, for instance) that offended the sensibilities of the extremely conservative Shiite majority. The society became highly stratified, and the westernized middle class came to realize that they lived under a glass ceiling limiting their upward status mobility. At the same time, the vast majority of Shiite peasants lived in poverty, even squalor, in the urban slums created by forced urbanization or in the countryside. The religious hierarchy, stripped of much of its power but forming the natural leadership of the peasants, seethed at their displacement and vowed holy revenge.

The contradictions of the White Revolution began to boil to the surface in the early 1970s. The lightning rod of discontent was a Shiite religious figure, the Ayatollah Ruhollah Khomeini. The recognized leader of Iran's Shiites, Khomeini was forced into exile first in Iraq (where most of the holiest shrines of Shia Islam are located) and later, after the Shah brought pressure on the Iraqi regime, to Paris. From his Parisian exile, the Ayatollah advocated the overthrow of the Shah's regime, a cudgel taken up by the mullahs (religious teachers) who opposed the Shah.

The movement against the Shah grew as the 1970s progressed. Initially, the Shah employed his hated and feared secret police, SAVAK, to suppress dissidence, but by the middle of the 1970s, anti-Shah protests grew, aided by two unrelated phenomena. First, the United States elected Jimmy Carter president in 1976, and one of his principal themes was the promotion of global human rights enforcement. Iran was one of the worst offenders in the human rights area, and the administration came down especially hard on the Shah's government to improve its record. The Iranians complied by restraining SAVAK, and the result was largely to decrease its coercive ability and thus to loosen control on the dissidents. Second, the Shah was diagnosed with the cancer that eventually killed him, and when critical decisions had to be made about how to deal with the dissenters in the late 1970s, the Shah was apparently so physically debilitated that he was unable to reach critical decisions about how to confront the growing unrest.

Matters reached a head on January 16, 1979, when the Shah and his family left the country on what was officially a foreign visit but which everyone recognized was an abdication. Within two weeks, Khomeini and his entourage returned from exile, and the process of revolutionary change was begun. Leaders of the middle class and the religious hierarchy vied initially for power, but it became increasingly clear that the religious majority would consolidate power to itself. The country's name was changed to the Islamic Republic of Iran as symbol of the change. On November 4, 1979, Iranian "students" overwhelmed the American embassy in Tehran and took its occupants hostage. The resulting crisis lasted until January 20, 1981, when the hostages were released in an atmosphere where newly inaugurated U.S. President Ronald W. Reagan threatened dire military action if they were not. The era of U.S.-Iranian collaboration was ended.

Revolutionary Iran.   Since 1979, a highly antagonistic, theocratic Iran has emerged, that is, a highly disruptive and bedeviling force in the region and particularly toward the United States. The details of the operation of Iranian politics since the overthrow of the Shah are byzantine and beyond capture in the limited space available here. The essence of that evolution can nonetheless be described.

The Iranian Revolution was both a religious and a political event. At one level, it was a revolt against the policies and person of the Shah and his entourage and particularly against the repression that had been part of the Shah's way of dealing with dissidents from the White Revolution. This opposition was based both in the vast under class of Iran and also in the middle class adversely affected by limits on their upward mobility. The other level of the revolution was religious, the revolt of the Shiite majority, led by the religious hierarchy that is a feature of Shia but not Sunni Islam. This aspect of the revolution was both revivalist and fundamentalist in the classic Muslim tradition of religious purification and return to Quranic purity, a strand also present in Sunni Islam (the Wahhabi sect of Sunnism that dominates Saudi Arabia arose originally as a revivalist movement opposing dilution of Islamic purity, for instance). These two strands coalesce and blend together in the theocratic framework that is particularly strong among Iranian Shiites and their religious leadership.

These two strands of the revolution are not and have not been totally in agreement with one another in terms either of the revolution or the Iran the revolution has created. In the months after the departure of the Shah, there was, indeed, a competition between those who supported one or the other emphasis. The middle class, by and large, saw the revolution as a vehicle to remove the tyranny of the Shah and his instruments of repression with some more participatory, democratic political system. In this desire, they owed a common heritage with the Mossadeqh tradition. As a well-educated and sophisticated segment of the population, they viewed themselves as the logical inheritors of political power and assumed that the lower classes and their religious leaders could be brought to heel in support of their claim to leadership. Iranians from this tradition form much of the core of the potential dissonance that periodically resurfaces, as in the case of demonstrations protesting the outcomes of the 2009 presidential election.

The religious elements, whose appeal was based in Shiite fundamentalism, had different visions, and they prevailed. The vast mass of discontented peasants saw westernization and modernization as both the vehicle of their repression and as an abomination before Allah, and they supported the religious hierarchy that promised a return to Quranic virtue. With Ayatollah Khomeini acting as their spiritual symbol (Khomeini never held any political office, even though he was the de facto political leader of the country), the religious conservatives successfully overwhelmed the middle class and rapidly took over and consolidated control of the country. Their principal vehicle for seizing and consolidating their power was through the actions of the Revolutionary Guards and Courts, originally vigilante bodies who identified opponents of religious revivalism and suppressed both these heretics and anyone else associated with the Shah's regime. Gradually, this element has been incorporated as a major part of the government.

The result has been a militantly religious Islamic Republic of Iran that has been an increasingly important element in the politics of the Middle East. Its political system operates at two different levels. The real seat of power remains in the firm control of the religious hierarchy. The Supreme Leader of the country is Ayatollah Ali Khamenei, who operates the system of revolutionary guards and courts through something known as the Guardian Council (which, among other things, selects candidates for formal political office). Parallel to this structure is the democratically elected government, consisting of a parliament (the Majlis) and an executive branch, the top elected official of which is the president. The first president was Mohammed Khatami, described as a "moderate" cleric, who gained office in 1997 and was viewed in the West as someone who would lead Iran back to a more conventional place in the hierarchy of countries.

Khatami was replaced in 2005 by Mahmoud Ahmadinejad, who has become a well-known figure in the West and the lightning rod for American concern about the direction of Iranian international politics. Ahmedinejad, the former mayor of Tehran, was initially elected in 2005 and reelected in 2009. He had been one of the six candidates allowed to run for office by the Guardian Council in 2005 and is known as a conservative, savvy politician. He has been particularly anti-American because, as Takeyh explains, the president "understands that the carnage in Iraq, the stalled Israeli–Palestinian peace process, and the inability of Arab rulers to stand up to Washington have created an intense anti-Americanism throughout the Middle East" that he hopes he can exploit to his own and Iran's advantage.

The United States serves as a useful foil in Iranian politics. As Milani describes it, "For decades, the Iranian regime has used anti-Americanism to crush its opponents and expand its power abroad." The association of the "Great Satan" with the Shah and the White Revolution makes the United

States a useful displacement object to arouse scorn and to obscure the very real weaknesses of the current regime's performance. The great hope that the United States has for inducing change in Iran derives from the nascent desire for political freedom that is most strongly voiced by Iranian students, and it is associated with the middle class and the Mossadeqh days. The middle class is less anti-American than are the supporters of the revolution, and many of the ideas and demands they have are for reformed conditions not dissimilar to the goals of the White Revolution. Despite some common ground, anti-Americanism remains a strong influence-limiting factor in Iranian politics.

DEALING WITH IRAN

Iran is an important and pivotal state with its own unique place in the world, and it is a prominent member of the Middle Eastern equation that cannot be ignored. The current Iranian government sees its interests very differently than did the Shah of Iran, and almost all of the changes from pre- to postrevolutionary Iran have caused increasing antagonism between the United States and Iran. Iran sees itself as the logically dominant state in the Persian Gulf region—the pivotal state, a status it covets and which has important regional ramifications. As Ehteshami puts it, "Given Iran's significant weight and influence in the broader Middle East, developments in that country will cast a shadow over everything else."

U.S.–Iranian relations have become a textbook example of the sometimes fractious relations between a major power (the United States) and a pivotal regional power (Iran) in the pivotal state's region. Based upon a comparison of gross power along virtually any dimension of power, the United States is clearly the more powerful state, and the comparison would suggest that the United States should prevail in a struggle over those interests. That, however, has not been the case, and the result is an Iran that both frustrates the United States by not conforming to its wishes and continues to pursue policies the United States opposes. The interaction demonstrates the importance of pivotal states in the international order.

The most visible source of U.S.–Iranian disagreement focuses on Iran's nuclear program. The main reason that former Secretary of State Condoleezza Rice deemed Iran such a menace is the prospect that Iran might use what it says is a peaceful nuclear power program to produce nuclear weapons, a prospect that multiple American politicians have said is absolutely unacceptable and about which there have been dire warnings issued. This issue is closely entwined with disagreement over Iranian policy toward Israel—the connection being Israel's unadmitted but universally accepted possession of nuclear weapons. The conflict extends to the regional power balance in the Persian Gulf region, in turn focusing on Iranian actions and intentions toward Iraq. McFaul, Milani, and Diamond summarize these areas of disagreement, adding American interests in Iranian domestic politics: "limit Iran's assertiveness in the region; halt Tehran's support for terrorism, promote Iranian democracy and human rights; and stop Iran from obtaining nuclear weapons."

The Nuclear Weapons Issue

The Iranian nuclear program has been the lightning rod of U.S.-Iranian enmity. The United States maintains that Iran's nuclear program is intended to result in nuclear weapons possession, an outcome it opposes in principle and because it fears the radical Iranian regime might use any weapons it obtains irresponsibly, including possibly sharing them with terrorists or attacking Israel. The Bush administration had deemed the avoidance of this outcome so important that it had even hinted at the use of military force to prevent it. The 2006 *National Security Strategy of the United States* puts the implications most dramatically: "We face no greater challenge from a single country than from Iran." The Obama administration has not contravened that emphasis. The Iranians, on the other hand, deny any intention to develop and possess nuclear weapons and argue that their program is fully in compliance with international atomic guidelines.

Why would Iran want to obtain nuclear weapons? There are at least three possible reasons. The first is as a demonstration of Iran's place of prominence in the world, a matter of prestige. Although the designation has a Cold War aura about it, one way to distinguish the most powerful countries in the world from one another is through nuclear weapons possession. As Baktiari explains, "Iranians tend to support the nuclear program as a matter of national pride. The conservatives in Iran's government are successfully using the nuclear issue as a means to cement their own power through nationalist fervor." He adds a touch of irony: "In this, they have been unwittingly assisted by President Bush," whose objection to the program simply makes it more popular in Iran. Moreover, as Chadar adds, "Tehran has effectively turned U.S. opposition to its program into a nationalistic cause," as well as "an effective bargaining chip."

There are two other motivations for the Iranians. One, which Pollack argues is their primary motivation, is to deter an American attack on them. "From an Iranian perspective," he asserts, "possession of nuclear weapons makes sense for purely defensive reasons. If you have nuclear weapons, the United States will not dare use force against you, but if you do not, you are vulnerable." This motivation reflects a perception that many people in the Middle East share that the primary mistake Saddam Hussein made in the years leading to his overthrow was in abandoning his nuclear weapons program under international pressure, as noted in Chapter 6. In the eyes of McFaul, Milani, and Diamond, this motivates the Iranian program: "In large measure, Iran's leaders seek nuclear weapons to deter a U.S. attack." Even if one questions this motive (which seems anomalous from an American viewpoint), there is a more practical motivation, according to Maloney: "No regime is likely to bargain away its deterrent capability as long as it believes that the other side's ultimate objective is its own eradication." The nuclear weapons possibility thus provides a basic part of its foreign policy, as stated by Milani: "Tehran has responded to Washington's policy of containment with a strategy of deterrence."

This argument is based, in other words, on Iran's sense of insecurity in the face of what it views as capricious U.S. policy and actions in the Persian Gulf region. It does not matter that the American public overwhelmingly opposes military action against Iran; the invasion of Iraq and American intransigence toward Tehran create an atmosphere where the nuclear program serves as a useful hedge against the "crazy" Americans. As Bowman puts it, "To the degree that the Iranian nuclear program is motivated by insecurity, the consistent American unwillingness to engage in ongoing, unconditional talks with Iran on issues beyond Iraq, as well as excessive U.S. saber-rattling and regime-change rhetoric and a suffocating military posture, may only serve to validate the perceived necessity of Iran's long-term quest for nuclear weapons."

The other part of the nuclear equation in Iran's eyes is Israel. If one discounts Pakistan as regionally marginal, the only state in the Middle East that has nuclear weapons is Israel, and since 1979, relations between Iran and Israel could hardly be worse. One major aspect of this antagonism is Iranian creation of and continuing support for Hezbollah, which has the destruction of the Israeli state as one its major goals. Anti-Israeli and anti-Semitic rhetoric by Ahmadinejad (questioning whether the Holocaust really occurred, for instance) have only fanned the fire of Israeli–Iranian antipathy.

This antagonism is reciprocal. Israel has been among the loudest doomsayers about Iranian intent and especially the nuclear program. The Israelis have the precedent of having attacked an Iraqi nuclear reactor to destroy its weapons program in 1981, and took similar actions against Syria in 2006. Part of the reason the Iranians have greatly dispersed and hardened elements of their nuclear capacity underground is to discourage a reprisal against them. Because of Israeli antipathy, Donovan argued in 2002 that "the Israeli nuclear arsenal will continue to drive Iranian . . . WMD acquisition efforts in the foreseeable future."

Israeli–Iranian antagonism may prove to be the most combustible aspect of the Iranian nuclear program. Israel clearly feels more threatened by Iranian nuclear weapons than anyone else (given its small size and population concentration, as well as proximity, Israel is quite vulnerable to attack) and has threatened to take preemptive action to prevent the Iranian program from reaching fruition. The fear of a possible Israeli preemptive decision may, in turn, push Tehran toward a nuclear decision to gain a capability to deter such an attack. Iran's Sunni Arab neighbors are also suspicious of the Iranian program, however, and Iran's attainment could spur some of them such as Saudi Arabia to similar action. As Ehteshami argues, "Israel's nuclear monopoly could end in rapid proliferation."

For the time being, the standoff between the United States and Iran over the latter's nuclear weapons program remains a stalemate. Iran denies any intentions to convert its program to nuclear weapons acquisition, but it could do so in the future. For now, it argues that the development of a peaceful nuclear power capability is the purpose of its nuclear efforts, and that those efforts are clearly allowed under international norms. Thus, the Iranian nuclear program is perfectly legitimate in its eyes, and there is little international disagreement. Moreover, Iranians believe they have every right, as a pivotal state, to pursue nuclear technology. As Kodmani puts it, "Iranians are almost unanimous in believing that their country has a sovereign right to enrich uranium. They want international acknowledgement of their country's importance in the region." The United States, reflecting both its own and Israeli concerns, worries more about the ability of Iran to "break out" and redirect its program toward weapons capability, a situation it deems entirely unacceptable. At this point, the two sides are at loggerheads, and the United States, the great power, has been unable to force compliance with its wishes from the regional pivotal power. Why not?

The Limits of Power

The current impasse between the United States and Iran is frustrating, occasionally even infuriating, to American leaders, because of their inability to bring the Iranians to heel on a number of issues. The nuclear issue, including its Israeli component, heads the list of complaints, vying with the Iranian role in Iraq for primacy as an irritant. If the United States is to find an acceptable way to exit its Iraqi imbroglio, it must gain the support of regional actors, and Iran is the single most important actor with which it must deal. And yet, any semblance of movement toward accord has remained noticeably elusive.

Iran remains obdurate in the face of American opposition, because it feels it operates from a position of strength. It is, after all, by far the largest state in the region and cannot be bullied like the smaller, weaker states (including Iraq). Since it exports roughly 2.5 million barrels of oil a day, it gains leverage as well both from those it supplies and those whom it might supply (China, for instance) when sanctions are threatened against its export of energy. As Baktiari explains, "as long as oil prices stay high, Iranian leaders know that they will face little danger of an international oil embargo." Moreover, Iran does business with other powers (Russia, for instance, which is assisting its nuclear energy program), and the result is that it does not suffer from any kind of isolation in the world. As a result, Takeyh maintains, "The guardians of the theocratic regime do not fear the United States; they do not relate to the international community from a position of strategic vulnerability. Tehran now seeks not assurances against American military strikes but an acknowledgement of its status and influence."

What options does the United States have for dealing with Iran? Basically, these options come in two categories, military and diplomatic. The problem is that one option (military force) is not meaningfully available to the United States, and although the Obama administration has sought to reverse the Bush policy of isolating and ignoring Iran, that policy change has yet to bear fruit, thereby reducing the potency of diplomatic tools. The result is that the Americans scowl at and curse the Iranians, who return the favor.

The possibility of using military force against Iran is tied principally to two issues, the Iranian nuclear program and Iranian support for and supply of Iraqi Shiite forces operating against the American occupation of Iraq.

The Bush administration had issued veiled threats suggesting the United States would not rule out "any option" in the face either of convincing evidence of Iranian nuclear weapons progress or of continued Iranian support for Shiite militias operating in Iraq. Particularly this latter source of tension highlights the interplay between the pivotal power and the great power in the region.

As the two largest countries in the region, Iran and Iraq have been the chief rivals in the Persian Gulf area for decades, and the inconclusive Iran–Iraq War of 1980–1988 demonstrated, among other things, that neither was clearly dominant. Iran, however, would clearly like to have dominant influence in Iraq for both geopolitical and religious sectarian reasons, and the American war in Iraq has increased Iranian influence. As Nasr and Takeyh explain, "For close to half a century, the Arab world saw Iraq's military as its bulwark in the Persian Gulf." One result of the invasion was to disband the Iraqi military, and, according to Norton, "By crushing the regime led by Saddam Hussein, the Americans gave a geopolitical gift to Iran, which is now the most powerful opponent of U.S. hegemony in the Gulf." The gift, of course, was the destruction of the Iraqi military counterweight to Iran. As a result, Baktiari contends, "It is Bush's policies that have put the Iranian regime in its present strong position. No one has benefited more from American blunders in the Middle East than the conservatives in Iran."

What can the United States do (or threaten to do) militarily to get Iran to abandon its nuclear program or to quit interfering in Iraq? To some, the answer is not much. Takeyh puts it bluntly: "the United States has no military option in Iran." That assessment probably needs qualification. As long as the bulk of American ground forces are tied down in Iraq and Afghanistan, it is no doubt true that the United States could not launch any large, meaningful ground action against Iran, and certainly not a ground action that would obviously overwhelm the half-million man Iranian armed forces. The option it does have available is American air power, but to what end?

The ability of the United States to deal politically with Iran was certainly compromised by the Bush administration's unwillingness to interact politically with the Iranians—at least in public. When Ahmadinejad visited UN headquarters in 2007, he had no meetings with American officials, and when, in April 2008, Secretary of State Condoleezza Rice visited Amman, Jordan, for a regional meeting on Iraq, she pointedly prefaced her attendance with the assurance she would have no discussions with the Iranians. It is, of course, difficult to make diplomatic progress with someone to whom you will not speak. Barack Obama has repeatedly indicated a willingness to talk to Iran, a sign of possible change from the previous administration that has not been reciprocated in any public manner.

The 2009 presidential elections in Iran have created some glimmer of hope in the West about future relations, although those hopes may be exaggerated. The elections, and especially their outcome, created an outpouring of public resentment both internally and internationally about vote rigging that was widely interpreted in the West as evidence of an underlying, suppressed desire for democratization. Chadar, however, disputes that interpretation, suggesting instead that "the protests in the streets . . . had as much to do with economic mismanagement as with election improprieties."

The demonstrations, nonetheless, have been seen as evidence of a crisis of legitimacy regarding theocratic rule. Such sentiment has historically been primarily the province of the middle-class inheritors of the Mossadeqh tradition, but it could spread more widely and result in some moderation of Iranian politics. At the same time, Milani contends, "For decades, the regime has used anti-Americanism to crush its opponents and expand its power abroad."

The short-run barometer of U.S.–Iranian relation is likely to center on Iraq (in addition to the nuclear weapons question). It seems unlikely that the United States can keep Iran from having some influence on a postoccupation Iraqi government unless that government excludes the majority Shiites, which is highly unlikely. Iran and Iraq are two of the few Shiite-majority countries in the world. Vaki summarizes the deep connection between the two: "most of the elements of [Iran's] power base are allied with the U.S.-backed Iraqi government. Indeed, the largest party in the ruling coalition is the Supreme Islamic Council. Its leader spent years in exile in Iran, and it was recognized by Iran's clerics as a government-in-exile when Hussein was still in power." As the struggle for power in Iraq continues, the only thing the United States might do to limit Iranian influence would be to downgrade the power of those Iraqi elements it supports, but that is unlikely given Iran's penetration of the majority Shiites.

The other U.S. diplomatic objective may be to limit outside, including Iranian, influence on postoccupation Iraq. The United States remains publicly wedded to the idea of a democratic Iraq, and by extension, Iran. It is not at all clear that the Iraqis can decide among themselves the form such a democracy would take (see Snow, *What After Iraq?* for a detailed discussion). Unless the outcome is a form of majoritarian rule that would guarantee the primacy of their fellow Shiites, it is an outcome that Iran disfavors as well, partly because its geopolitical aspirations in the region are best served by a friendly Shiite state and partly because they fear American success would embolden their calls for a more pluralistically democratic Iran. Of the latter concern, Vaki observes that "Washington's democracy promotion program . . . is received in Tehran as an unmistakable attempt at regime change" (i.e., the overthrow of the current regime).

The postoccupation Iraqi-Iranian relationship represents the dynamics of pivotal state—great power relations in its purest form. The United States and Iran are far apart on the kind of Iraq the United States leaves behind. Despite policies that have had the effect of promoting Shiite rule in Iraq, the United States does not want a militantly Shiite regime to take hold after it leaves, whereas Iran is committed to helping the Shiites reign. Who will prevail?

Regionally, Iran has the advantage over the United States. American will to remain in Iraq is waning, and the Americans will leave, at which point their ability to influence Iraqi developments will shrink rapidly. The Iranians know this, and they do not suffer the same debility: Iran is a permanent part of the neighborhood. If Iranian influence over Iraq and the extent of Shiite dominance in Iraq are to be controlled, it will have to be because of the actions of regional forces who oppose such dominance (essentially the Sunni states of the region). The power of Saudi Arabia, Jordan, Syria, and the Gulf states are not as great as those of the United States, but they are more relevant. The shape of postoccupation Iraq and the extent of its ties to Tehran are simply more important to, say, Kuwait, than they are to the United States, and thus the role the United States must support that reality. In this case, it means that the United States cannot dictate the terms of settlement, but, rather, can only seek to broker the interaction between the other regional actors and pivotal power Iran.

CONCLUSION

The role of pivotal states, and especially Iran in contemporary international relations, provides a limiting factor on the exercise of power within the international system and particularly for major powers like the United States. In one sense, the emergence of pivotal states as important, *independent* actors whose interests cannot readily be subjugated by the power of larger states is just another sign of the greater pluralization of the post–Cold War order. During most of the Cold War, after all, Iran was a loyal ally of the United States against Soviet communism, and even after the revolution of 1979, Iran did not make common cause with its Soviet neighbors. In an international order that is much less hierarchical than the Cold War order, there is greater independence for—or less restraint on— the actions of uncommitted states. Iran's actions in the Persian Gulf are but one prominent example of this freedom.

Iran also demonstrates the frustration that pivotal states provide for the great powers like the United States. American power is, for the most part, quite irrelevant to ordering its relations with the government in Tehran. The religious conservatives who rule Iran can—and do—snub the United States, and the United States resents that treatment and is frustrated by it. One can argue that this frustration caused the Bush administration to treat Iran with more pique than sound reason and has, in the process, made the relations worse than they otherwise would have been. It is now up to the Obama administration in Washington to try to improve that relationship, and it will have an incentive to do so as it tries to extricate itself from Iraq in a way that insures the final outcome in that country will be minimally embarrassing. If it is to do so, it will have to come more fully to grips with the problems posed by the pivotal states.

STUDY/DISCUSSION QUESTIONS

1. What is a pivotal state? How do pivotal states fit into the hierarchy of states in the international order? Why are they important and sometimes problematical?
2. Why does Iran qualify as a pivotal state? In general terms, discuss those attributes of Iran that contribute to this designation.
3. What is it about Iran that makes it a "unique" state? Discuss this uniqueness in both physical and historical terms.
4. Discuss the ethnic and religious demographics of Iran. How do they contribute to its special status in the Middle East region and the world?
5. Describe contemporary Iranian politics since the revolution of 1979. Who controls the country? How? Why is understanding this evolution critical to understanding the contemporary place of Iran in the international order?

6. How are U.S.–Iranian relations a "textbook case" of the relations between pivotal states and great powers? Elaborate.

7. What are the major foci of U.S.–Iranian political differences? Describe each. Why does the inability of the United States to compel Iran to change its policies on each issue demonstrate the limits of its power?

8. Is the Iranian position on the nuclear weapons option reasonable or outlandish? Depending on your answer, what should the United States attempt to do about that program? Why?

9. What is the Iranian position on postoccupation Iraq? Do you find it reasonable for Iran to try to influence Iraqi politics given its place in the region? Or is the Iranian position outrageous? Based on your assessment, what should the United States do about Iranian policy toward Iraq?

10. What must the new American administration do to repair relations with Iran? How important is Iran's status as a pivotal power to determining the direction of that policy?

READING/RESEARCH MATERIAL

Baktiari, Bahman. "Iran's Conservative Revival." *Current History* 106, 696 (January 2007), 11–16.

Bradley, John R. "Iran's Ethnic Tinderbox." *Washington Quarterly* 30, 1 (Winter 2006–2007), 181–190.

Chadar, Fariborz. "Behind Iran's Crackdown, an Economic Gap." *Current History* 108, 722 (December 2009), 424–428.

De Bellaigue, Christopher. "Think Again: Iran." *Foreign Policy*, May/June 2005, 18–26.

Donovan, Michael. "Iran, Israel, and Nuclear Weapons in the Middle East." *CDI Terrorism Project* (online), February 14, 2002.

Dreyfuss, Robert. "Is Iran Winning the Iraq War? *Nation* 286, 9 (March 10, 2008), 22–28.

Ehteshami, Anoushiravan. "The Middle East's New Power Dynamic." *Current History* 108, 722 (December 2009), 395–401.

Elliot, Hen-Tov. "Understanding Iran's New Authoritarianism." *Washington Quarterly* 30, 1 (Winter 2006–2007), 163–180.

Fuller, Graham E. "The Hizbollah-Iranian Connection: Model for Sunni Resistance." *Washington Quarterly* 30, 1 (Winter 2006–2007), 139–150.

Goldberg, Jeffrey. "How Iran Could Save the Middle East." *The Atlantic* 304, 1 (July/August 2009), 66–68.

Gonzalez, Nathan. *Engaging Iran: The Rise of a Middle East Power and America's Strategic Choice*. Westport, CT: Praeger Security International, 2007.

Kodmani, Bassma. "Clearing the Air in the Middle East." *Current History* 107, 709 (May 2008), 21–26.

Maloney, Suzanne. "The US and Iran: Back to Containment?" *Current History* 106, 704 (December 2007), 440–442.

McFaul, Michael, Abbas Milani, and Larry Diamond. "A Win-Win Strategy for Dealing with Iran." *Washington Quarterly* 30, 1 (Winter 2006–2007), 121–135.

McInnis, Kathleen J. "Extended Deterrence: The U.S. Credibility Gap in the Middle East." *Washington Quarterly* 28, 3 (Summer 2005), 169–186.

Milani, Abbas. "U.S. Foreign Policy and the Future of Democracy in Iran." *Washington Quarterly* 28, 3 (Summer 2005), 41–56.

Milani, Mohsen M. "Tehran's Take: Understanding Iran's U.S. Policy." *Foreign Affairs* 88, 4 (July/August 2009), 46–62.

Nasr, Vali, and Ray Takeyh. "The Costs of Containing Iran." *Foreign Affairs* 87, 1 (January/February 2008), 85–94.

The National Security Strategy of the United States. Washington, DC: The White House, March 2006.

Norton, Augustus Richard. "The Shiite 'Threat' Revisited." *Current History* 106, 704 (December 2007), 434–439.

Pollack, Kenneth M. "Bringing Iran to the Bargaining Table." *Current History* 105, 694 (November 2006), 365–370.

Ritter, Scott. "Notes from Iran: The Case for Engagement." *Nation* 283, 17 (November 20, 2006), 13–18.

Snow, Donald M. *What after Iraq?* New York: Pearson Longman, 2008.

Takeyh, Ray. "Time for Détente with Iran." *Foreign Affairs* 86, 2 (March/April 2007), 17–32.

Trenin, Dmitri. "Travel to Tehran." *Foreign Policy*, January/February 2008, 72–73.

Vaki, Sanam. "Iran: Balancing East Against West." *Washington Quarterly* 29, 4 (Autumn 2006), 57–66.

———. "Tehran Gambles to Survive." *Current History* 106, 704 (December 2007), 414–420.

Wood, Graeme. "Iran: Among the Mullahs." *The Atlantic* 305, 1 (January 2010), 15–16.

Zaborski, Jason. "Deterring a Nuclear Iran." *Washington Quarterly* 28, 3 (Summer 2005), 153–168.

WEB SITES

Status of Iranian Nuclear Program (Global Security): (http://globalsecurity.org/WMD/world/Iran/nuke.htm)

Peacekeeping: Humanitarian Disaster and International Responses in Darfur

PRÉCIS

A recurring security problem is the phenomenon of governments and other groups inflicting great harm and suffering on individuals and groups and international responses to these actions. During the 1990s, instances of such behavior became more frequent than before and were identified as humanitarian disasters that were an appropriate concern for international response. International responses have tended to be associated with the United Nations, which has, for better or worse, conceptualized those responses as peace-keeping. Darfur, a rebellious province of Sudan, has been the most recent example of both a humanitarian disaster and a peacekeeping response, and it reveals the real limits and weaknesses of employing the peacekeeping approach in these situations.

Humanitarian disasters—manmade conditions of individuals and groups that are so wretched that the entire international community has an obligation to alleviate them—and ways to respond to them became iconic symbols on international relations in the 1990s. While instances of and interest in these kinds of situation has waned in the 2000s, the problem of humanitarian disasters remains a troubling and embarrassing undercurrent in the contemporary system. Darfur is the most persistent, public manifestation of that concern.

In the international relations literature, the term *humanitarian disaster* is sometimes used in a broader sense than that employed in this chapter. In addition to suffering directly and purposely inflicted against individuals and groups by others, the broader usage encompasses a second category of causes of suffering, namely, natural disasters, their human consequences, and how to deal with them. The present concern, however, is restricted to those humanitarian disasters caused by "man's inhumanity to his fellow man."

The phenomenon of enormous human suffering inflicted by groups or individuals on other groups or individuals is certainly nothing new or unique in human history. What has changed, however, are at least three surrounding factors. The first is the *increasingly public nature of human atrocity*. Due to advances in electronic technology, the world has become enormously more transparent than it has ever been before, and this transparency extends to human depravity and the ability to obscure or deny it. The case of the Darfur region of Sudan illustrates this dynamic. A civil war that has raged periodically in southern Sudan since 1962 has received very little publicity, because it is and has been a largely internal matter where the government has blocked outside observers from seeing and reporting its atrocities. When civil war broke out in Darfur in 2003, on the other hand, refugees quickly began to flow into neighboring Chad, where they shared their tales of woe with the outside world.

The second factor has been the *growing unacceptability of atrocities by government and others committing humanitarian atrocities*. This is also a relatively recent change, because the principle of sovereignty has historically included the notion that sovereign states exercise total control over those who reside within their borders. The Holocaust and post–World War II instances of humanitarian disasters have eroded support for this absolutist interpretation of sovereign control and stimulated the contrary assertion that individual rights supersede state sovereignty and those individual rights can and should be enforced internationally. This revisionism is controversial among defenders, including, not surprisingly, the government of Sudan.

The assertion of rights superseding state governmental authority has been extended to the idea of an *international obligation to try to alleviate manmade disasters*. This notion is controversial. It poses a direct challenge to the principle of state-based sovereignty, which is fiercely defended by those states who want to protect the discretion and independence to act on their own behalf. Reconciling the contradictory implications of protecting human right and sovereignty will likely remain an issue for sometime.

The assertion of an international obligation also raises the question of who will decide upon and enforce international actions. It is not coincidental that these questions arose with clarity in the 1990s coinciding with and reflecting the enhanced post–Cold War status of the United Nations. Although it was a somewhat inconsistent contributor to the management of world peace during the Cold War, the United Nation's lead role in the international effort to evict Saddam Hussein from Kuwait in 1990–1991 created the precedent for utilizing the United Nations in a variety of situations, including humanitarian disasters. Chapter VII of the UN Charter authorizes the world body to act in these kinds of situations, and the United Nations has become the "legitimizer of choice" for international responses to humanitarian disasters. The method the United Nations has evolved as threats to and breaches of the peace is peacekeeping.

The discussion follows from this brief introduction. It will begin with a brief description of the humanitarian disaster phenomenon and how it and responses to it have changed over time. Because peacekeeping has been the primary international form of response, peacekeeping and its appropriateness will be examined. These distinctions will be applied to the ongoing situation in Darfur.

HUMANITARIAN DISASTERS

The concept of humanitarian disaster is perspectival. Acts that cause violence and suffering are certainly "disasters" from the vantage point of those on whom they are inflicted and by outside observers who view their existence and find them unjust. The language, even acceptance, of humanitarian disasters is generally denied by perpetrators of the infliction of wrongdoing, who normally will deny or attempt to obscure the commission of such acts and will offer justifications for their actions. Although much of the rest of the world may disagree, for instance, the government of Sudan steadfastly denies there have been actions on its part (or on the part of agents working on its behalf) constituting humanitarian disaster in Darfur. To Sudan, the situation is strictly a civil disturbance within the jurisdiction of and being dealt with by the government of Sudan.

Some other phenomena are sometimes linked with the humanitarian concept. A term that often arises in describing these situations, for instance, is *genocide*. The Bush administration used this term to decry the Darfur situation, and there are some clearly genocidal aspects to what has gone on there. Whether one described Darfur or other situations as genocide or humanitarian disasters is not as important as is recognition of the pernicious behavior it represents and the need to respond to instances of it.

The term *humanitarian disaster* entered the language of international relations largely in the 1990s. During the Cold War, there had been isolated instances of activities that could have been described in these terms but were not. The most flagrant case was in Cambodia, where the murderous Khmer Rouge exterminated as many as 1.7 million people in the "killing fields" between 1975 and 1979 in order to "purify" the community, in their views. The rampage was essentially ended by the invasion and conquest of Cambodia by the Democratic Republic of Vietnam. World outrage and demands for responses were, however, muted, at least partly because the slaughter was viewed largely as an internal problem of the communist world, with the Khmer Rouge supported by China and the Vietnamese by the Soviet Union. The United States, recently removed from the area by the end of the Vietnam War, was not about to involve itself, and criticism was seen as little more than Cold War propaganda.

Three things changed in the 1990s to create an international mood in which humanitarian disasters were identified as problems requiring international mediation. First, the end of the Cold War meant that the international system had the communist–anticommunist mantra removed, meaning events and responses no longer had to pass through a Cold War filter and could be examined on their own merits. Moreover, resources (including military) were now available for other than Cold War purposes. Thus, the end of the Cold War allowed countries to consider problems they had formerly ignored, including humanitarian disasters. Second, as the Cold War thawed, new ideas entered international discourse. Of direct relevance was the idea of humanitarian interests, the notion that humankind as a whole had an interest in promoting and protecting individuals and groups that superseded the right of governments to treat people however they might choose.

If the first two changes cleared the way for activism, there was also a third, pernicious change that made such actions compelling. In many Third World countries, internal conflicts during the Cold War had their potential viciousness attenuated by the superpowers, which acted as sponsors of factions within some of these countries and restrained their clients because of the fear of being criticized should those clients act in especially barbaric ways. When the Cold War ended so did superpower involvement and constraint. The result in some places was to unleash the very worst behavior of people against other people.

The litany of humanitarian disasters in the 1990s is familiar and formed the major face of violent conflict for that decade. Somalia was the first instance, reaching levels of suffering in 1992 that could not be ignored, and it was followed by outbreaks in the Balkans (Bosnia beginning in 1992 and Kosovo in 1997) and in Haiti in 1994. Its most extreme manifestation came in Rwanda in 1994. The question was what should be done to halt these atrocities?

Flush from its anointment as the peacemaker of international choice in the Persian Gulf War of 1990–1991, the answer was the United Nations. During the Cold War, the United Nations' role had been limited to involvement in situations without Cold War overtones, which meant situations where the United States and the Soviet Union (each with a Security Council veto) did not support contending sides. Such situations were, however, limited. For those situations where UN involvement was possible, the response was in the form of peacekeeping.

THE PEACEKEEPING RESPONSE

The concept of peacekeeping is dynamic and has evolved across time and experience. During most of the Cold War, there was relatively little peacekeeping activity, because the authorization of such missions by the United Nations required the concurrence (or at least lack of opposition) of all the five permanent members of the UN Security Council. Since the United States and the Soviet Union were both permanent members and were often on opposite sides of conflicts into which such missions might be contemplated, the result was that they could not agree on the mandates of such potential missions and they were not formed. Since the end of the Cold War, that inhibition has disappeared, and UN peacekeeping missions have become more numerous and well publicized.

Peacekeeping practices have evolved as well. The earliest Cold War peacekeeping missions were generally limited to the insertion of lightly armed forces between former combatants to insure that they did not revert to armed violence. Typically, these missions were placed between independent states to separate them. The first large-scale UN mission, the United Nations Emergency Force (UNEF) that was inserted along the Egyptian-Israeli border in 1956 to keep those countries apart is the popular prototype, and it succeeded until 1967, when the parties (specifically Egypt) demanded the removal of UNEF from its territory, and the result was war. The UNEF represented the conceptual prototype and commonsensical meaning for peacekeeping: the maintenance of a state of peace between two former combatants. In some cases, traditional peacekeeping missions occurred within the sovereign territory of states, as on Cyprus, where the United Nations Forces in Cyprus (UNFICYP) was put in place in 1967 to separate Greek and Turkish Cypriots, each of which sought the annexation of the island to their native country. That mission remains active to this day.

The Cold War also witnessed the expansion of the concept of peacekeeping in one troubling way that has contributed to the confusion that surrounds the peacekeeping concept today. In 1960, the former Belgian Congo declared its independence, which an exasperated Belgian monarch (the colony was technically solely owned by the King) granted in haste, and the result was a rapid spiral into a chaotic civil war with Cold War overtones (factions aligned with both the West and the Soviet bloc). The United Nations was drawn into this imbroglio when a peacekeeping force, the United Nations Operation in Congo (ONUC), was authorized and inserted into the fray. Although its mission was neutral—restoring peace and order—it was inevitably drawn into the contest, especially when one major Congolese state, Katanga (now Shaba), tried to secede. The Congolese operation is generally viewed as the least successful application of UN force under the peacekeeping label, but it unfortunately has been a precedent that has been revisited in other situations, especially since the end of the Cold War.

The end of the Cold War moved the United Nations onto the center stage of world affairs. In less than a year after the Berlin Wall fell, the United Nations became the vehicle for organizing the world's resistance to and reversal of Saddam Hussein's invasion and attempted annexation of Kuwait to Iraq in 1990. Although the physical mission was largely an American operation (well over half the forces involved were American), the United Nations was the legitimizing agent for the effort, and the world body received much credit and appreciation. In addition, the United Nations became—as its Charter had envisioned but the Cold War had prevented it from doing—the world's policeman for international breaches of the peace.

The peacekeeping sobriquet became the umbrella concept for UN efforts, because peacekeeping was already a UN role. The problem was, and is, that few of the threats to the peace in the contemporary world meet the description of what UN peacekeeping was initially designed to accomplish—the separation of formerly warring parties so that they can move toward an enduring peace without the threat of reversion to war. At the same time, the peacekeeping model called for a specific kind of UN force wearing the powder blue helmets and berets—lightly armed, defensive forces incapable of engagement in real combat. When such forces have been inserted into inhospitable situations, their performance has not always been as effective as it might be.

The current crucible for this form of activity is the Sudan, and more specifically, the civil war that has been raging in the Sudanese province of Darfur since 2003 and which has caused hundreds of thousands of deaths and millions of displaced Sudanese who fled from the violence into Chad, among other places. Early international efforts to rein in Sudanese government support for the so-called *janjaweed* "rebels" responsible for the carnage have been unsuccessful, and the result was the authorization of a UN 26,000 strong peacekeeping force in 2007 to augment 6,000 African Union forces already in place. That force has yet to achieve anything like its authorized troop level and has been less than totally successful in pacifying the situation.

Peacekeeping in Theory and Practice

What exactly is peacekeeping? It is a term so commonly used (which is part of the problem) that one would assume there was some generally agreed notion about what does and does not constitute peacekeeping. Such a distinction would seem particularly appropriate for the United Nations, which has been the primary instrument for forming and administering peacekeeping operations (PKOs). In fact, the United Nations had sponsored 63 PKOs as of July 1, 2008, seventeen of which are currently ongoing: eight in Africa, one in the Americas, two in Asia and the Pacific, and three each in Europe and the Middle East. Yet the UN's own homepage admits that the concept "simply defies definition." Instead, the UN Department of Peacekeeping Operations (UNDPKO) often uses the term *peace operations* instead, explaining that while "originally developed as a means of dealing with inter-state conflict, UN peacekeeping has been increasingly applied to intra-state conflicts and civil wars." In these instances, the situation confronting UN forces is often not one of peace to be kept, but rather of either simmering or actual violence that must first be suppressed before there can be a peace to keep.

Why is there ambiguity about what constitutes UN peacekeeping? At least two reasons stand out, both of which have their roots in the UN Charter. The first is that the Charter itself makes no mention or provision for anything like peacekeeping. The Charter speaks of peaceful means to resolve disputes between countries (Chapter VI) and deadly means—up to and including the use of force—the organization may undertake (Chapter VII), but nowhere does it specifically anticipate or mention the possibility of inserting passive military forces into conflict situations as a method of separating combatants or of bringing about peace. This omission led former UN Secretary General Dag Hammarskjold to typify PKOs as "Chapter Six and a Half" operations.

The second problem is that contemporary world problems are unlike those envisaged by the framers of the Charter, as the Charter did not, in particular, envisage two salient characteristics of the system as it evolved after World War II. On one hand, it presumed that world problems would involve mature states in the developed world, whereas most problems are in the developing world. This situation is reflected in the distribution of current PKOs in the world already mentioned (13 of 17 are in Africa and Asia, and the 3 in Europe are in the Balkans, that continent's least developed and most newly independent region). On the other hand, a UN relevant to peace and stability must contribute to the creation or enforcement of order where disorder exists, and that is often within the boundaries of sovereign states. As pointed out in Chapter 1, the maintenance of sovereignty is a core value of the Charter, and attempts to intervene in civil disputes or violence (which is the nature of many developing world problems) involves violating the very sovereignty the Charter is committed to protect. This is a particular problem in Darfur, as will be shown later in the case.

The end of the Cold War reenergized the United Nations as a major player in international security. The event that caused this change was, of course, UN leadership in the Persian Gulf War's expulsion of Iraq from Kuwait. Because the organization served such a useful role in coordinating and legitimating international efforts in that case, it was thrust into a variety of situations in the 1990s for which it was arguably not well equipped, especially in the Balkans (Bosnia, Kosovo, even Macedonia). These involvements have created a mixed assessment of the utility of the United Nations for contributing to a more peaceful world that is relevant to understanding the UN role in Darfur. Much of the ambivalence about UN operations, however, is the direct result of ambiguities about what exactly it is that the United Nations, or anyone else, can do under the rubric of peacekeeping. This ambiguity is reflected in differing international attitudes toward peacekeeping as a reaction to, among other things, humanitarian disasters.

Peacekeeping and Peace Operations

Much of how the members of the UN view its peacekeeping role is an extension of the original conception of what a peacekeeping force was and what it did. As noted, the original concept was that peacekeepers would be used to reinforce situations where peace had succeeded states of armed conflict between formerly warring parties, and that the function of the peacekeepers would be as a symbol of international resolve that the peace should be honored.

That basic view helped form the parameters of future operations. They had several characteristics. Because they were intended to *keep* formerly warring parties separate rather than to pry them apart, their role was essentially passive. Their mission was not to force or enforce peace, but rather to monitor and observe whether a condition of peace was intact. Because of this orientation, the peacekeepers were lightly armed with just enough firepower to allow them to defend themselves against unexpected attacks. Peacekeeping forces neither had nor were supposed to need heavy, complicated, or offensive armaments to carry out their missions, and as a result, they were relatively inexpensive to equip and to maintain. This latter characteristic was (and is) particularly attractive to a perpetually poor organization like the United Nations, which must rely on supplemental assessments of its members to pay for PKOs. Peacekeeping using the traditional model also reinforced a built-in bias among many UN officials against the warlike activities associated with more active employments of force.

Beyond observation and monitoring, the role of traditional UN peacekeepers was to provide a physical barrier between formerly warring parties. The idea was that if one or more of the former antagonists wanted to start fighting again, they would first have to encounter and cross UN lines serving as the symbol of international opposition to their resumption of war, which could prove difficult, particularly if UN casualties occurred during such a breach.

The problem is that relatively few contemporary international situations conform to the characteristics for which peacekeeping was originally developed, and as a result, PKOs based on the traditional model are likely to be inadequate for accomplishing the goals for which they are designed. Very rarely is the United Nations asked to enter a conflict where peace has been restored and simply needs mending. Rather, most real situations involve some kind of civil disorder that has turned violent and that violence is either ongoing or, at best, has been calmed but remains a combustible prospect. That means a passive, monitoring role is inapplicable: there is little, if any peace, to monitor and observe. Instead, the confrontation is likely to be more volatile and dangerous, where peacekeepers may well find themselves in combat zones for which the defensive, light armament prescribed by the traditional model may leave them ineffective, even endangered. When there is no peace to be kept, PKOs are transformed into peace operations, yet another euphemism.

These changed circumstances in the peacekeeping environment have not gone unnoticed by the UNDPKO or the international community generally, of course. There is an initial temptation to apply the traditional model at the outset of conflicts because, if it happens to hold, it will likely be successful at acceptable costs to the international community and the United Nations as its representative. If the situation requires a peace operation, both the base of events into which peacekeepers may be thrust and what they must do to be successful is broadened. To understand this transformation and its relevance to places like Darfur, it is helpful to look at the contemporary environment through two conceptual lenses: conflicts that peacekeepers may be called upon to attend and tasks and measures that are appropriate and effective for different circumstances.

Situations. As already discussed, there are a greater variety of circumstances for which UN PKOs may be contemplated than were originally envisioned by those who first evolved the model for Chapter Six and a Half endeavors. In retrospect, the original tasks of monitoring conflicts where the parties have agreed to end hostilities, prefer that hostilities remain suspended, and thus welcome the role of the peacekeepers seems simple and straightforward. In those instances, peacekeepers are a *welcome addition* to the political landscape.

Most contemporary cases, however, are more complex and hostile. They can be thought of as existing on a continuum depicted in Figure 8.1: PKO Situations.

War ---------------------------------- Unstable Peace ---------------------------- Stable Peace

FIGURE 8.1 PKO Situations

The figure posits three conditions. The first is *war*. In these situations, a state of war means that there is physical violence among armed groups at the potential target location, and that there is no clear indication either that the violence is likely to cease or that all parties wish it to cease, probably because one or all groups have goals they want to accomplish through continued fighting. Regarding the prospects of peacekeepers, the salient characteristic is the combatants' will to continue fighting, meaning they are likely to resist attempts to curtail their violence, unless they are forced upon them effectively. At the other extreme is *stable peace*. In conditions of stable peace, fighting has been stopped, both (or all) sides prefer peace to renewed violence and are willing to work to ensure the continuation of peace. In this circumstance, outsiders who reinforce this situation are likely to be viewed as a positive reinforcement to the desired state of affairs, unless their actions belie their intent (e.g., they upset the peace that exists).

The broad range between these extremes is *unstable peace*. Generically, unstable peace refers to the condition where peace (at least the absence of war) has been established, but where it is uncertain whether the peace would hold in the absence of outside involvement. The continuum between the two end points represents a changing likelihood that peace is self-sustainable. The nearer the situation is to war, the less likely it is that all parties agree that they prefer peace to continued violence and the more likely it is that peace depends on the outside imposition of that condition. The closer the situation is to the stable peace end of the continuum, the more support there is for peace and the more likely it is to be self-sustaining.

The kinds of situations for which peacekeeping operations are those at the stable peace end of the continuum. The problem is that most current situations where peacekeeping is contemplated are not at or near the stable peace end of the continuum, which is the realm in which peace operations become more relevant. Such kinds of situations involve either states of war or states of unstable peace that are closer to the war than the stable peace end of the continuum. In that circumstance, it is not clear that peacekeeping is the appropriate response or that the kinds of forces that are suited for peacekeeping are applicable.

Tasks and Forces. The kinds of situations that invite outside involvement can be elaborated by adding an additional dimension to Figure 8.2: the tasks that are demanded in different situations and the kinds of forces necessary and appropriate for those different tasks. They are depicted in Figure 8.2.

The distinctions are straightforward and commonsensical. *Peace imposition (PI)* refers to actions, normally military in nature, that are taken to stop

Situation	War	Unstable Peace	Stable Peace
Task	Peace Imposition	Peace Enforcement	Peacekeeping
Forces	War-fighters	War-fighters/ police/observers	Police/observers

FIGURE 8.2 PKO Situations, Tasks and Forces

the violence in a war zone. To be effective, whoever imposing peace must have sufficient forces to make the combatants (who presumably do not want to) cease military operations via the use or credible threat of force. This in turn requires that the peace imposers understand thoroughly what and who the source of violence is and both know and are capable of taking the actions necessary to cause violence to cease. Unless the peace enforcers possess such overwhelming force that they can intimidate the opposition into compliance, this may be difficult, because the opponents prefer the continuation of violence to its ceasing (or they would have stopped it themselves). Moreover, it is usually true that whenever peace is imposed, it will, purposely or inadvertently, favor one side over the other(s), depending on the situation at hand. Since Third World conflict situations tend to be fluid and complex, determining exactly who should have peace imposed upon them and affecting it in a manner that makes things better rather than worse is not as easy as it may seem and may entail unforeseen and undesirable consequences.

Operation in a war zone requires forces capable of war-fighting actions. The peace imposers must have adequate numbers and weaponry to convince combatants to lay down their arms, and this may require military actions against combatants. If the forces sent to impose the peace are inadequate in numbers or lacking in sufficient force, they may be ineffective, or even worse, they may become victims of the fighting itself. Peace imposition missions, however, are more expensive than traditional PKOs, and a financially strapped organization like the United Nations may be reluctant to categorize situations as war zones in need of peace imposers because of the potential costs involved.

In the middle of the continuum is *peace enforcement*. As the term suggests, peace enforcement is the appropriate response when a peace has been put in place (possibly as the result of peace imposition operations) but where the peace might not hold on its own (unstable peace). In these situations, more or less active measures must be undertaken to keep those parts of the population that have not accepted the peace in line—enforce peace against them. Clearly, the efforts of peace enforcers serve to modify a situation so that those who prefer war come to prefer peace, thus moving the conflict progressively closer to stable peace.

Peace enforcement contains elements of peace imposition and peacekeeping. Toward those who resist peace, the requirement may be akin to peace imposition, until recalcitrant elements can be convinced, forcibly or otherwise, to embrace the peace rather than work toward violent change. Thus, it is necessary to possess war-fighters, who hopefully will deter reversion to war by their simple presence or who can, if the need arises, take active military actions to *re*impose peace on those who need it. Unstable peace also means that some elements of the population have embraced the peace and require only monitoring and nurturing rather than the physical coercion that is the stock and trade of the peace imposers.

Because peace enforcement encompasses situations from near war to near stable peace, the composition of peace enforcement forces will vary: the closer to a state of war the situation is, the greater the proportion of war fighters necessary, and the closer to stable peace, the greater the proportion of monitors and observers (or police officers). In many cases, peacekeeping operations employ the same forces in both roles, but it is not always clear that good war fighters make good monitors or policemen, or vice versa.

The stable peace end of the continuum represents the condition where traditional peacekeeping is appropriate. In a situation of truly stable peace, all major parties prefer peace to war, and the task of the peacekeeper is to maintain that condition. The task, as already described, is to monitor a situation that the parties prefer and thus are not predisposed to violate. In this circumstance, the task of peacekeeping can be entrusted to the lightly armed, small forces that have been the mainstay of UN operations, without unduly exposing those forces to terrible personal risks.

These distinctions seem self-evident: ending states of war requires imposing peace, keeping peace alive in a situation of some opposition means enforcing the peace, and where peace has taken root and is embraced by virtually all parties, all that is needed is peacekeeping. Yet, in application, the distinctions get blurred. From an international, and particularly a UN, vantage point, all PKOs tend to be conceptualized in terms of the traditional peacekeeping model that evolved from the institution's history. Why? Partly, it is a matter of conceptual comfort: the UNDPKO, after all, has peace *keeping* in its title. At the same time, peacekeeping is something that seems to fit within the UN framework: the so-called Chapter Six and a Half operations. A mission that requires the United Nations to go into a country, pry apart warring parties, and impose an order that not all may accept reminds many within the organization of the Congo fiasco of a half century ago. Finally, of course, there is the matter of cost. The United Nations perpetually lives on the brink of financial insolvency, dependent for its fiscal survival on an international community of states that can be quite niggardly, particularly if the organization seems intent on getting involved in new and uncharted (and more expensive) enterprises. The result may be to cloak operations in inappropriate conceptual dressing that ensures they do not succeed. The degree of danger of untoward outcomes, however, also depends on what outcomes are intended in these operations.

The purpose of this discussion is to point out two very important characteristics that undergird PKOs. The first is that a PKO almost always entails more than peacekeeping, because the real situations for which these missions are formed are rarely ones of stable peace that must simply be monitored and observed. Almost always, they contain some element of war, in the sense that not all parties desire a cessation of hostilities or accept a cessation of fighting that may have been imposed. This means that actual missions will almost always require more force than is expected of a true peacekeeping mission, and that the task at hand will be more strenuous and stressful than the basically passive act of peacekeeping implies.

The second observation is that the initial designation of these operations as peacekeeping distorts both the nature of the problem and the likelihood that the task will be more arduous and difficult than a peacekeeping designation may imply. The false expectation that initial conceptualization of PI and PE situations as PK creates the illusion that PK-style and -sized operations will suffice, when generally they will not. The most salient problems come in terms of forces and financing of PKOs. A number of countries (Canada and Norway, to cite two prominent examples) designate forces for PK duty as part of what they consider their international obligations and others (Ghana and a number of other African countries) designate troops for PK for basically mercenary reasons (to collect the fees that UN assessments provide for deployed peace-keepers). In all these cases, however, the forces are not regular combat units, but units with noncombat roles (military police or signal corpsmen, for example). Real world situations require some level of combat forces. The matter of financing reinforces the tendency to send inadequate (in a combat sense) forces: as noted, the requirements for sustaining combat forces in the field are uniformly higher than those for traditional peacekeepers.

Because of the operational needs for forces appropriate for real situations and the reluctance of the international community to provide combat forces, it is simply easier to call all operations peacekeeping and allow UN members to accept the fiction that they do not perform more arduous PI and PE functions. At the same time, designating operations as peacekeeping in nature seems less potentially offensive to the sovereignty of countries in which the operations are imposed. Particularly when an operation is proposed in a country that is reluctant to accept a UN presence (usually because the government has some role in the violence the United Nations seeks to interrupt), it may be important to the world body to avoid the charge of violating sovereignty.

Changing Assessments. The international community has shown considerable ambivalence on the subject of peacekeeping, especially when the more stressful implications and dictates of succeeding in the peacekeeping mission are included. Because the United States is both the largest contributor to UN finances and thus peacekeeping (contributions to finance the United Nations are done on a weighted basis roughly reflecting a country's economic position in the world) and because of the United States' position of political and military leadership in the world, its role is particularly important. As is the case with many international issues (such as the International Criminal Court or torture, discussed in Chapter 3, or global warming, discussed in Chapter 13), the American position has vacillated wildly on the subject.

Attitudes toward UN peacekeeping in humanitarian disasters have been a barometer of feelings about UN activism generally. Since PKOs are one of the most active forms that the world body employs in the arena of international security, this stands to reason. Thus, when deep political division paralyzed the United Nations during the Cold War, UN PKOs were limited to passive monitoring missions between countries that were outside the Cold War competition. When the Cold War ended and those divisions dissolved, the United Nations was thrust into the middle of international attempts to moderate conflict in the world. During the 1990s, when this activism was greatest, the United Nations sponsored humanitarian interventions under the peacekeeping banner in the Balkans (Bosnia and Kosovo), in Africa (Somalia), and in Asia (East Timor, although the mission there was primarily Australian).

Peacekeeping receded with the turn of the millennium. Partly this reflected the fact that the United Nations had become bogged down in several places, such as the former Yugoslavia, where peacekeeping mandates had proven less than effective for dealing with peace imposition/enforcement needs. The dramatic rise in international terrorism symbolized by the September 11, 2001, attacks on New York and Washington, DC, presented an overwhelming international security problem for which peacekeeping was clearly an inadequate response and for which the international body had no clearly apparent capability. The Bush administration in the United States rode to power in the 2000 election campaign partly on a very public derision for American participation in UN PKOs, with particularly harsh indictments of the Bosnia and Kosovo missions, and vowed to avoid future involvements in those kinds of operations. At the same time, the world's security focus moved to the Middle East, specifically to countries like Iraq and Afghanistan. Both these involvements have clearly been war zones where the language and logic of peacekeeping is inapplicable.

The early years of the 2000s thus witnessed a retreat from heavy international reliance on peacekeeping. In 2003, however, internal violence re-erupted in Africa's physically largest state, the Sudan, and that violence rapidly became an international humanitarian disaster centering on victims among the population of the western Sudanese province of Darfur. That tragic situation was for sometime overshadowed by events in the Middle East, but in 2006, it became so pressing that the peacekeeping concept was revived to come to the aid of the displaced people of Darfur.

PEACEKEEPING IN DARFUR

The humanitarian disaster known as Darfur began in the western Sudanese state that bears that name. Sudan is the largest country in Africa with a physical area of just less than a million square miles (a little more than one-quarter the size of the United States) and has a population of about 40 million. The province of Darfur covers much of the western part of the country, with a size slightly less than that of Texas and a population of about 7 million. The conflict known simply as Darfur has been going on since 2003, although it can be seen as a distinct part of broader upheavals in this Islamic country.

Sudan has a turbulent history. It was the first African state to attain its independence, but it has been wracked by religious violence between Muslims and others (Christians and animists) since 1968, when a bloody civil war erupted that has continued episodically to the present. In 1983, an Islamist government was formed, leading to instability that eventuated in the ascension of Sudan's current beleaguered President, Omar al-Bashir, in 1993. Darfur is the latest installment of Sudanese instability.

As described by Straus, Sudan suffers from two interlocking crises. One is a long-standing conflict between the "northern, Arab-dominated government and Christian and animist black southerners." This conflict has been ongoing since 1968 and has resulted in numerous accusations of humanitarian atrocities, particularly among Christians, that created some anti-Sudanese sentiment among conservative Christians that blends with appall at the conditions in Darfur. At the same time, "the region (Darfur) is split between two main groups: those who claim black 'African' descent and primarily practice sedentary agriculture, and those who claim 'Arab' descent and are mostly semi-nomadic livestock herders."

The Darfur crisis broke out originally in 2003 when Darfurian rebels openly opposed the Sudanese government over the extent to which Darfur received benefits from the central government. Two groups, which have since splintered, led the rebellion: the Sudanese Liberation Army/Movement (SLA/M) and the Justice and Equality Movement (JEM). The Sudanese government reacted by attempting to crush these outbreaks, and these efforts included attacks on Darfurian villages they alleged were sympathetic to SLA or JEM. As has been the case frequently in modern Sudanese politics, the government enlisted informal "militias" to aid in the suppression, and these militias became known as the *janjaweed*, a term that Straus says "translates roughly as 'evil men on horseback' " and was "chosen to inspire fear, and the *janjaweed*, who include convicted felons, quickly succeeded." Beyond thousands of deaths and countless accusations of atrocities, the result was the internal displacement of over 2 million residents of Darfur and the flight of another 200,000 into neighboring Chad, where they now live in highly publicized desperation more than eight years after the violence broke out.

Two additional aspects of the crisis stand out. One is the question of whether acts of genocide have occurred in Darfur. As the slaughter mounted, accusations of genocide were widely made, and even American Secretary of State Colin Powell declared the Darfur crisis an instance of genocide in September 2004, a position reiterated by President Bush in January 2005. The designation, which the Sudanese government of course denies, is important because the UN Convention on Genocide, of which most states (including the United States) are signatories, requires action against perpetrators of genocide. In July, 2008, the chief prosecutor of the International Criminal Court (which has jurisdiction in these matters) demanded an indictment of Sudanese president Omar Hassan al-Bashir on charges of genocide (see Simon and Polgreen and Lynch and Boustany). Bashir was indicted and an arrest warrant was issued for him in absentia in March 2009 for war crimes and crimes against humanity, but not for genocide.

The second aspect has been the international response to the Darfur tragedy. To date, it has not been especially successful, particularly in ending the armed aspect of the situation. A ceasefire was signed in April 2004, but it was "repeatedly violated by all sides to the conflict," according to Human Rights Watch. The Darfur Peace Agreement (DPA) followed in May 2006, but like the original ceasefire, it has been generally ignored by the parties. Meanwhile, the deaths and displacements have continued. The original international presence was the African Union Mission in Sudan (AMIS), but with less than 6,000 soldiers, it was unable to impact the situation. In July 2007, the UN Security Council authorized a "hybrid" African Union–UN Mission in Darfur (UNAMID) with an authorized troop strength of 26,000. As of October 2009, UNAMID's military and police personnel numbered less than 19,000.

The UNAMID response has been undertaken as a peacekeeping mission, which is why it is the case for this chapter. To this point, UNAMID has not only been unsuccessful but it is also arguably an abject failure. Much of the reason for this is that it has been conceptualized and formed as a classic, traditional peacekeeping operation that has been given the task of keeping peace where peace does not exist. Why this is the case and what prospects there are for the future occupies the pages that follow.

The Situation in Darfur

Conditions in Darfur have not improved. In October 2004, Straus reported that approximately 1.8 million residents of Darfur had been uprooted by the violence, including 1.6 million internal refugees and another 200,000 in Chad. According to Human Rights Watch, matters have not improved over time: "As of April 2008, some 2.5 million displaced people live in camps in Darfur and more than 200,000 people have fled to neighboring Chad, where they live in refugee camps. In addition...at least 2 million additional people are considered 'conflict-affected' by the United Nations, and many need some form of food assistance." While NGOs have attempted to aid in the relief of these people, their efforts are hampered by thefts of their supplies, attacks against humanitarian aid givers, and the murder of international aid workers by various factions. As Human Rights Watch summarizes it, "Between January and April 2008 four humanitarian workers were killed in Darfur, and 102 humanitarian vehicles were hijacked, while 29 drivers contracted by World Food Program to deliver food aid were missing." In addition, splinter rebel groups fight among themselves, usually to the detriment of local populations caught in the middle.

The situation within Darfur remains both fluid and chaotic. SLA/M and JEM are reported to have splintered into at least 12 separate groups often working at cross purposes. The Sudanese government has signed the DPA and officially condemns the *janjaweed,* although some of its members have reportedly been absorbed into positions within the government. Because of accusations of genocide, a number of *janjaweed* and Sudanese government officials were earlier indicted for crimes against humanity by the International Criminal Court (ICC), but the Sudanese government refuses to turn these individuals over to the ICC, saying they will investigate and prosecute offenders themselves, a promise met with cynicism within the international community (one of those indicted was subsequently named Minister of Humanitarian Affairs by President al-Bashir).

The situation, particularly when considered in tandem with the civil war in southern Sudan, clearly constitutes a humanitarian disaster. Although the violence in southern Sudan has been largely contained within Sudanese borders and thereby reliable statistics have been suppressed by the government, the carnage and atrocities are likely greater than those in Darfur, where the results have spilled past the boundaries of Sudan and the ability of the government to hide information. In toto or individually, however, the tragedies seem clearly tailor-made for a 1990s-style humanitarian intervention, but the response has been limited and tepid at best. Why?

Sudan has been able to turn aside and ignore international efforts to deal with the Darfur tragedy, largely on grounds that international attempts to intercede physically represent a violation of Sudanese sovereignty—which they do. They have been able to get away with this resistance because their actions have not been universally condemned, particularly in the UN Security Council. Both Russia and China have offered support to the Sudanese government on the grounds of noninterference in the internal affairs of a member state, and China has important economic dealings with Sudan, notably agreements on access to Sudanese oil. Sudan is a minor oil producer, currently exporting about 400,000 barrels per day, and with proven reserves of nearly 6.5 billion barrels. With a burgeoning demand for petroleum, China is aggressively seeking petroleum concessions globally, and Sudan is one of the objects of its efforts. Sudan has friends and leverage unavailable in the Balkans in the 1990s.

While there has been a great deal of publicity given to the plight of the Darfurians, this has not translated into effective protection from the hostilities surrounding and directed at them. Both care givers like the World Food Program and Care International have attempted to mount significant efforts to assist in the occurring malnutrition and starving, and *Medicins sans Frontieres* (Doctors without Borders) and others have been on the scene, but their efforts have been hampered by opposition from contending elements and the inability of the international community to act aggressively to protect the care givers (a problem reminiscent of the situation in Somalia in the early 1990s that led to a large American and UN intervention in that east African country that shares a long border with Sudan). Amnesty International and Human Rights Watch have led an international effort to publicize the plight of Darfur, but neither their efforts nor those of other private entities have led to effective action. Prunier states the outcome starkly: "In the end, none of them (the great powers) went beyond talk. The UN, the AU (African Union), and the humanitarians were left holding bloody babies."

Part of the reason for a lack of international effort is a focus on other problems, notably terrorism. A prime example is the United States, which has been prominent among those decrying but not acting forcefully in this crisis. As already noted, the United States condemned the situation in genocidal terms over six years ago, and it has supported UN declarations aimed at Sudan for its unwillingness to end the suffering. It has not, however, taken or proposed direct action of its own. Partly, this was the result of the Bush administration's wariness with involvement in peacekeeping operations that goes back to the PKOs it inherited in the Balkans, but it also reflects that there is little it can do as long as American forces and resources are tied down in Afghanistan and Iraq. An American direct commitment of forces (even logistics) to the situation would possibly energize international efforts, but, as Lynch put it in a late June 2008 article in the *Washington Post,* "the United States struggles to press countries to commit more troops to the U.N. force in Darfur." Those efforts, and the efforts of others, have not yielded significant results.

UN Peacekeeping in Darfur: UNAMID

On July 31, 2007, the United Nations Security Council Resolution (UNSCR) 1769 authorized augmenting the existing 6,000 troop African Union (AMIS) force with a so-called hybrid force of 26,000 soldiers plus, 6,000 civilians and other support forces. As noted, that contingent remains undermanned, and there are no immediate prospects that forces can be found to move it toward its authorized limits. The existing force has itself been the subject of controversy (one of its military leaders, General Emmanuel Karake Karenzi, has been accused of genocide during the Rwandan massacre of 1994), and its future is uncertain. UNAMID's prospects of success are dim indeed. Why?

The largest problem with UNAMID is conceptual: in an almost classic mission-force mismatch, UNAMID is a peacekeeping force being asked to go into a situation which can hardly be described as one even closely resembling or approaching a stable peace. Rather, Darfur (and the regions of eastern Chad where external refugees are located) is a war zone, and the efforts to date to ameliorate the situation cannot possibly move it to a condition much better than the most unstable form of peace.

The other problem with UNAMID is its physical size. Darfur is, as noted, a very large place, and it has a very primitive infrastructure. There is no developed road system around which to move UNAMID troops to particular crises, and as of mid-2008, UNAMID had at its disposal a grand total of seven helicopters as an alternative means to move about the region (it has requested, but not received, 24 helicopters to aid in its monitoring mission). For an area the size of France, a total of 26,000 troops have been authorized to keep a peace that does not exist; certainly the 19,000 or so forces that have actually been dedicated to the mission cannot adequately patrol the entire Darfur region (by way of contrast, the United States has had upwards of 160,000 troops in occupation of Iraq, a country of similar size and geographic nature, and there has been widespread criticism of the adequacy of those forces in the face of the various aspects of Iraqi resistance to the occupation). Moreover, the UN-authorized budget for 2009–2010 was $1.6 billion, a drop in the bucket given the situation.

One way to judge the UNAMID peacekeeping response is to measure it against the criteria laid out earlier in the chapter. By any measure, Darfur (as well as southern Sudan) qualifies as a humanitarian disaster for which precedents set in the 1990s clearly apply. What kind of ongoing situation exists? Is it a state of war, a stable peace, or something in between? Clearly, Darfur has been a war zone, replete with widespread fighting and killing, and while SLA/M and JEM form part of the pattern, janjaweed and related actions form most of the basis for atrocity. The DPA has arguably reduced the situation from open warfare to some kind of unstable peace—unstable because there continue to be sporadic attacks by various elements on one another and on civilians. No one would argue that a state of stable peace is in existence.

What tasks need to be performed under these circumstances? The size of UNAMID suggests that they are a peacekeeping force, but in size and orientation, the situation of unstable peace (at best) would seem to dictate a larger and heavier force that includes a war-fighting as well as a monitoring and observation function. Just where along the continuum between war and stable peace Darfur exists is a matter of debate, but it is clearly a situation of unstable peace that requires a peace enforcement force to ensure that any peace agreement is honored—with force when necessary.

UNAMID falls short of being this kind of force. It does not meet even the meager size of its mandate because, as Finian points out, "there is a problem finding forces to carry out peacekeeping." Part of that problem arises from Sudan's insistence that the bulk of UNAMID troops be from African countries, because they say they fear the use of Europeans would make UNAMID a potential outside occupying, even neocolonial force. There are simply not enough African forces available (witness the size of the AMIS force), particularly troops that can serve as war-fighters. American absence adds to the problem.

The result is a force that cannot fulfill the peace imposition or peace enforcement mission. As Grignon and Kruslak put it, "UNAMID is unlikely to provide much relief to Darfurian civilians under attack from the janjaweed militia, Khartoum's bombardments, or rebels." The British Broadcasting Company, in its assessment of the situation, agrees: "Even after all 26,000 troops and police are deployed, they will not be able to stop the rebels, army, and pro-government militias fighting if they really want to. *There must be a peace for them to keep.*" (Emphasis added)

The international community, to the extent that it views the tragedy in Darfur in any detail, has not been enormously critical of its own response to the situation. At the moment, there is a desire to end the genocide, but not much will to confront and deal with the actual situation on the ground. Grignon and Kruslak put it bluntly: "Sadly, in Darfur and beyond, the world seems more willing to contribute money to humanitarian efforts than to tackle the causes of conflicts. Peacekeeping missions are often used as Band-Aids for complex conflicts, and are rarely equipped to do the political work that is vital to addressing the causes." In the case of UNAMID, the Band-Aid analogy might be expanded to add that it is a very small dressing for a very large wound.

The Dafurian situation is currently the most prominent example of a humanitarian disaster, and beyond its stark imperatives per se in terms of the human suffering of the afflicted, how it is handled—or mishandled—will be the precedent this decade will send forward for handling similar situations in the future. The precedent is, at this point, bleak. The military dimension of ending the situation has certainly been unimpressive, but what happens if and when the killings end? Very little public attention has been given to what is supposed to happen once the fighting ends. It was, after all, political grievances that caused the SLA and JEM to begin the actions that caused government counteractions and thus start the fighting and killing in the first place, and eventually these will have to be addressed. At the same time, one of the reasons why so many Darfurians have fled their homes is because the places they live have been destroyed, and these must be rebuilt before the end of the crisis can even be glimpsed. The issue of rebuilding Darfur, in other words, has not been addressed at all, beyond some assurances that the parties would settle their differences in the DPA.

It is hard to escape the conclusion that the international community is not seriously committed to ending the tragedy in Darfur. By forming a response within the intellectual and physical confines of peacekeeping, it has not shown that it understands the situation on the ground, nor is it admitting that it lacks the resources, will, or both to make a more effective attempt to end the suffering of the residents of Darfur. Peacekeeping, after all, is a minimal and inexpensive form of international involvement in world crises. When situations are appropriate for a peacekeeping solution (a stable peace between warring parties who prefer the maintenance of peace to a return to war), it is a satisfactory response. Darfur, however, is not such a situation, and the world is only kidding itself if it believes that a peacekeeping response will transform the suffering into some better condition for the beleaguered Darfurians.

CONCLUSION

Peacekeeping began as a specific form of response to particular traumas in the international system, situations that fall short of the great human suffering that mark and make prompt and decisive actions in humanitarian disaster areas. When the problem centered on keeping apart formerly warring parties who remained contentious and distrusting but who nonetheless realized peace was preferable to war, the concept worked. The "blue berets" of the United Nations could interpose themselves, and the parties, unwilling to risk the global ire they assumed would result from crossing UN lines (and possibly killing UN forces in the process), would cease hostilities. That kind of peacekeeping worked.

It is the widening of the term to encompass situations like humanitarian disasters that renders its relevance questionable. To repeat, peacekeeping presumes peace as the initial condition, and where peace is not present, peacekeeping—taken literally—cannot be applied. The problem is that peacekeeping is one of the few UN activities that most observers agree works. Because of this perception of success, there has been a tendency to label all situations for which a UN response is requested as peacekeeping and then to act as if the situations were indeed peacekeeping situations. Increasingly, however, situations like Darfur that exist are more violent and unsettled than peacekeepers are prepared to quell, and the result is that the peacekeeping response does not work.

The international effort to end the genocide and relieve the suffering in Darfur has been, to this point, ineffectual. UNAMID is the most visible symbol of that effort, and it is under-resourced, undermanned, and conceptually inappropriate for the task at hand. What does that say about the nature of the international response to the tragedy? More poignantly, what does it say about the fate of the Darfurians?

The inadequacy of the international response to Darfur may be as much a matter of timing as anything else. As mentioned earlier, international responses to crises, and especially the humanitarian disasters that have been so prominent since the end of the Cold War, have generally required some firm level of American leadership that has not been present at the governmental level. The U.S. government has acknowledged the crisis, as already noted, but when pressed about what its response would be, it has been quiescent. Why? As noted, the Bush administration had some philosophical reluctance to involve itself in violent humanitarian disasters, but more importantly, the United States has been so heavily invested in Iraq and Afghanistan as part of its response to terrorism that it has little energy, and even less resources, for other initiatives such as Darfur. One can charitably ask whether the response to Darfur would have been much more positive and decisive if America's armed forces were not so heavily committed in southwest Asia and if American financial resources were not under such siege—from expenditures on Iraq to the current economic crisis gripping the country. Would the world have responded differently to Darfur under different circumstances?

Regardless of how it *might* have responded differently, the world has not acted in such a way as to relieve the suffering that Darfurians are experiencing within Sudan or in external exile in Chad. Darfurian internal and external refugees continue to languish, suffer, and die while the world averts its gaze. Until, or unless, these circumstances change, the humanitarians will, to repeat Prunier's phrase, be left holding the "bloody babies" of Darfur.

STUDY/DISCUSSION QUESTIONS

1. What is a humanitarian disaster? What factors constitute such situations? How has international concern with these situations evolved?
2. Discuss the evolution of peacekeeping (PK). What was the original concept, and how has this concept changed over time? Use examples.
3. Define peacekeeping. How and why is the concept "ambiguous"? What is a Chapter Six and a Half operation? How does this relate to the ambiguity of the idea?
4. What tasks and forces follow from the different situations for which peacekeeping operations (PKOs) may be commissioned? Describe the different tasks and forces and how they relate to the different kinds of situations.
5. What are the goals for which PKOs may aim? Compare and contrast the two forms. How does the international community feel toward PKOs generally and toward different goals?
6. Describe Darfur and the basic sets of conflicts that beset it. What caused the current conflict to erupt?
7. What has the UN reaction to Darfur been? What are AMIS and UNAMID? What has the United States' role been?
8. Why is UNAMID, as currently conceived and authorized, bound to fail? Why has the world community allowed this to happen?
9. What do you think the United States and the United Nations should do about the tragedy in Darfur?

READING/RESEARCH MATERIAL

Boutros-Ghali, Boutros. *An Agenda for Peace: Preventive Diplomacy, Peacemaking, and Peacekeeping.* New York: United Nations, 1992.

Dagne, Ted. "Sudan: The Crisis in Darfur and the Status of the North-South Peace Agreement." Washington, DC: Congressional Research Service Report for Congress 7-5700. July 16, 2009.

Durch, William, ed. *The Evolution of UN Peacekeeping: Case Studies and Comparative Analysis.* New York: St. Martin's Press, 1993.

Feinstein, Lee. *Darfur and Beyond: What Is Needed to Prevent Mass Atrocities.* New York: Council on Foreign Relations Press, 2007.

Finian, William W. Jr. "Darfur and the Politics of Altruism." *Current History* 106, 700 (May 2007), 235–236.

Grignon, Francois and Daniela Kroslak. "The Problem with Peacekeeping." *Current History* 107, 708 (April 2008), 186–187.

Lefever, Ernest W. "Reining in the U.N." *Foreign Affairs* 72, 3 (Summer 1993), 17–21.

Lynch, Colum. "U.S. Backs U.N. Official in Darfur Indicted in Rwandan Deaths." *Washington Post*, June 29, 2008, A17.

——— and Nora Boustany. "Sudan Leader to Be Charged With Genocide." *Washington Post*, July 11, 2008, A01.

Mamdani, Mahmoud "The New Humanitarian Order." *The Nation* 287, 9 (September 29, 2008), 17–18.

Pickering, Thomas R. "The U.N. Contribution to Future International Security." *Naval War College Review* 46, 1 (Winter 1993), 94–104.

Prunier, Gerard. *Darfur: The Ambiguous Genocide.* Ithaca, NY: Cornell University Press, 2007.

Simon, Marlise and Lydia Polgreen. "Sudanese President Accused of Genocide." *New York Times* (online), July 15, 2008.

Snow, Donald M. *National Security for a New Era: Globalization and Geopolitics.* New York: Longman, 2004.

———. *Peacekeeping, Peacemaking, and Peace Enforcement: The U.S. Role in the New International Order.* Carlisle Barracks, PA: Strategic Studies Institute, 1993.

———. *Uncivil Wars: International Security and the New Internal Conflicts.* Boulder, CO: Lynne Rienner Press, 1996.

———. *When America Fights: The Uses of U.S. Military Force.* Washington, DC: CQ Press, 2000.

Straus, Scott. "Darfur and the Genocide Debate." *Foreign Affairs* 84, 1 (January/February 2005), 123–133.

WEB SITES

Q&A: Crisis in Darfur. Washington, DC: Human Rights Watch, 2004 http://hrw.org/english/docs/2004/05/05.darfur8536-txt.htm

International Political Economy

One of the most dramatic and heralded characteristics of the contemporary international system has been the increasing rise of economic activity across national boundaries, a process often referred to as globalization. The increasing economic interdependence arising from globalization has been viewed by some as a tool for increased international peace and stability. Globalization became an international force in the 1990s, but it remains a very complex and uncertain work in progress. The chapters in this part portray a sequential view of the heart and evolution of globalization.

Chapter 9, "Free Trade," examines the post–World War II birth and evolution of the idea of free trade, the basic international dynamic of globalization. It traces the various efforts culminating in the creation of the World Trade Organization (WTO) in 1995. It also raises questions about the desirability and inevitability of free trade and its future as a key element in international relations.

The first post–World War II economic integration effort began in war-torn Europe and has evolved into the European Union (EU), globalization on a regional scale and in its most evolved manifestation. Chapter 10, "Regional Integration," explores the evolution of the EU from its beginnings as a limited-scope free trade arrangement to its present level of economic and political integration. It also explores future directions and problems of the union, principally through the debate between those who seek to maximize the size of its membership (wideners) and those who seek a more complete integration of its present members (deepeners).

Two of the most successful states in adapting to a globalizing world have been China and India, the subject of Chapter 11, "Rising Powers." The phenomenon of countries challenging the established world power structure (rising powers) is not a new aspect of international relations, but countries challenging the existing order primarily at the economic level is. How this challenge arose and how it is evolving are explored in this chapter.

Chapter 12, "Extending Globalization," brings the discussion full circle to the question of how the system of globalization can and is being spread to current nonparticipants. The chapter examines the dynamics of globalization and the different paths to globalization proposed by current participants and aspirants. The lens for focusing the process is the current institutional movement of the debate over extension from the G-7 to the G-20, a process in no small measure prompted by the economic rise of China and India.

Free Trade: From ITO to WTO and Beyond

PRÉCIS

Free trade is, and for a long time has been, a controversial concept, as has its institutionalization in the form of an intergovernmental organization. This case begins by looking at the question of promoting free trade historically, from before the early post–World War II advocacy of an International Trade Organization through the creation of the World Trade Organization (WTO) in 1995. As events like massive demonstrations against the WTO at Seattle in 1999 and more recently indicate, this institutionalization remains controversial.

Because of this controversy, one must ask the question of whether free trade is a good idea. This in turn leads to breaking the question into two aspects argued by advocates and opponents: the desirability of free trade as an idea and phenomenon, and what kind of institutional structure is most desirable for promoting and enforcing free trade. The case concludes by combining the two aspects and comparing them in the current economic climate.

Trading goods and services has been one of humankind's oldest forms of interchange with other peoples and communities, and it is at the heart of the contemporary emphasis on economic globalization. In ancient times, the purpose of trade was generally to acquire goods that either did not grow or could not be produced locally, such as the importation of exotic fabric like silk, or spices. As the ability of political communities to span greater distances in shorter periods of time increased, trade expanded both in extent and in terms of what was and was not traded. The modern issue of trade probably congealed over whether to import goods and services that were also produced domestically. That question is near the top of the agenda in contemporary discussions of trade and is manifested in most disagreements on the subject, from questions of barriers to trade to environmental impacts of importation versus domestic production. In the economic downturn of 2008, the contribution of trade to prosperity entities has been a particular point of concern, especially in the United States. Despite accusations that the trade practices of some countries provided them artificial, unfair advantages during the difficult economic times of the past few years, free trade has transcended the crisis.

The debate over the impact of trade is not new, either internationally or in the United States. The emergence of the capitalist system first in Europe and then worldwide pitted global traders against what are now called protectionists in the form of mercantilists seeking to protect new, infant industries from destructive outside competition. Historically in the United States, advocacy and opposition have been sectional and remain as part of the contemporary landscape. As Michael Lind explains, "From the eighteenth century on, the Southern plantation oligarchy was content for the United States to specialize in exporting agricultural goods and raw materials to more industrial nations, importing manufactured goods in return. Thanks to the dominance of the South and Southwest, what was once the foreign economic policy of the Confederate States of America has become the trade policy of the United States as a whole." In turn, he argues, this has caused the United States to lead "the campaign to reduce or eliminate tariffs worldwide."

Whether to allow the unfettered movement of goods and services internationally (free trade) or to place restrictions of one kind or another on that flow is a central element in contemporary international relations. The removal of barriers to trade emerged as the centerpiece of the economic globalization movement of the 1990s, one of the engines designed to draw countries into closer collaboration by entwining them in the global prosperity of that decade. The global economic downturn at the turn of the millennium and the rise of the global war on terror took some of the luster from the free trade issue and relegated it to a less prominent place on the international political agenda. Yet, while attention is diverted elsewhere, globalization continues, and proponents and opponents continue to fight over whether to expand or constrict free trade arrangements.

The basic poles in the free trade debate have been between those seeking to expand trade (free traders) and those seeking to restrict trade (protectionists). Nestled between the extremes are those who advocate freer, but not necessarily totally free, trade (who often portray themselves as fair traders). While the Industrial Revolution was raging in Europe and later North America, the need to buffer nascent industries from outside competition militated toward restriction, largely under the intellectual banner of mercantilism. During the period leading to World War II, protectionism ran rampant in a Great Depression–riddled Europe, and economic restrictions were partially blamed for the bloodiest war in human history. The "lessons" of interwar economics, in turn, helped frame the international political debate and its institutionalization, the topics of this case.

The economic aspect of this debate has been, and is, asymmetrical, and proponents on one side or the other tend to talk past one another, meaning interchange often devolves into monologues. The arguments for free trade tend to be mainly abstract, impersonal, and macroeconomic. Free trade is said to be beneficial because it unleashes basic economic principles like comparative advantage that make overall economies (national or international) stronger and economic conditions within and between countries more vital. Overall, advocates argue that arrangements promoting trade have had a net positive impact. Anti–free trade arguments, on the other hand, tend to be specific, personal, and microeconomic. Cries to restrict trade tend to be posed in terms of the adverse impact that opening up trade opportunities has on individuals. Trade is not about economic theories; rather, it is about peoples' jobs and livelihoods. Thus, opponents hone in on things like jobs lost by individuals in particular industries to make their points. Fair traders seek a compromise somewhere between the extremes, advocating selective trade reductions in conformance with the principle of free trade but seeking to minimize negative microeconomic impact. Frequently, fair traders emphasize the need for compensatory actions for those individuals adversely affected by what they basically see as the beneficial impacts from free trade.

The argument over textiles illustrates the asymmetry in this debate. To pro–free traders, moving clothing manufacturing overseas, where labor costs are lower, makes economic sense. As a result, clothes are cheaper, and the economies of new textile producers are stimulated, which allows them to buy things produced in the United States. Uncompetitive textile manufacturers can redirect their efforts to other production areas in which they can compete successfully (produce better products at lower costs). Moreover, all consumers benefit, because goods are produced at the lowest possible costs, and the savings are passed along to consumers. Moving the manufacture of clothing overseas means Americans can buy their clothes at cheaper prices than they could from domestic producers with higher labor costs in this labor-intensive industry. In the end, it is a macroeconomic win-win situation with the added benefit of drawing countries closer together, thus promoting greater cooperation and reduced international tension.

From the anti–free trade viewpoint, these abstractions are unconvincing, because moving textile manufacturing overseas costs American textile workers their jobs. It is a concern centered on the impact on individuals, not on abstract phenomena. Thus, when free traders extol the removal of barriers and anti–free traders deride that possibility, they are, in a very real sense, not talking about the same thing.

The debate is intensely political at both the domestic and international levels. At the level of American national politics, the asymmetry is reflected between branches of the federal government. Historically, the executive branch of government, more concerned with the overall health of the economy and somewhat more removed from the impact on specific individuals or groups (as opposed to the whole), tends to be more free trade–oriented and macroeconomic. Members of Congress, whose constituents are the people whose jobs are endangered when foreign goods and services are allowed to enter the country more freely, tend to be more microeconomic and opposed.

At the international level, the debate tends to get muddled with preferences for the general orientation toward political interactions with the world. Broadly speaking, two positions have dominated the American experience (and that of other countries as well, to some extent). *Internationalists* generally advocate a maximum involvement of the United States in the international system; in a world where the United States is the remaining superpower in the system, this means advocacy of the United States playing a prominent leadership role working with other countries. Advocacy of free trade and globalization are an extension of that political preference to the economic realm.

The other position, *isolationism,* advocates a much more restrained level of American involvement in the world. This position reached its institutionalized zenith between the world wars, when "splendid isolationism" sought to keep the United States entirely separated from world, and especially European, politics. The belief that the United States could remain aloof from world affairs was, of course, punctured permanently by Pearl Harbor, and its successor ideology, *neoisolationism,* advocates a restricted level of U.S. interaction from the world, but not total rejection of the world outside American boundaries. In its pure form, isolationists are also protectionist, because protectionism limits international economic interactions.

The terms of the debate are not purely economic. Pro-trade advocates of the 1990s, for instance, argued that the globalization process of which free trade is an underpinning produces political as well as economic benefits. As noted in Chapter 11, one of the major reasons for promoting trade with China is to draw that country more intimately into the global political system. At the same time, anti–free trade arguments have expanded to include strictly noneconomic concerns ranging from environmental degradation to compromises of sovereignty, as well as politico-economic arguments about the effects on different groups within societies.

This introduction frames the structure of the case, which has three purposes. The first, and major, purpose is historical, tracing the process whereby free trade has been institutionalized in the international system since the end of World War II. That process has crystallized the principal reasons for advocating and opposing free trade, a discussion of which supports that evolution and is the second purpose of the case. Finally, it will attempt to apply this institutional framework and the positions of the two sides to the current, ongoing debate on the issue.

INSTITUTIONALIZING TRADE

The genesis of the contemporary debate over free trade was the period leading to World War II, the traumatic impact of the world's bloodiest war, and the determination to attempt to do a better job than had been done at the end of World War I to restructure the international system so that those circumstances would not recur. One major reason for the war was economic conditions that had arisen during the Great Depression and had produced economic chaos that worsened conditions and made the descent into the maelstrom of global war more likely.

Economic nationalism and protectionism were deemed to be among the chief culprits for this situation. As the Great Depression took hold across Europe and North America, governments scrambled to minimize the effects on their own economies and peoples. One way to do this was to protect national industries from ruinous foreign competition, and the vehicle was the erection of prohibitively high trade barriers to keep foreign goods and services out and thus to keep domestic industries (and the jobs they created) alive. The erection of tariff and other barriers resulted in retaliation and counter-retaliation that brought European trade to a virtual standstill. At the same time, currency fluctuations and devaluations became commonplace as a means to prop up failing enterprises. The resulting destabilization was felt strongly especially in Germany, which faced stiff reparations requirements exacted at the Versailles Peace Conference that ended World War I. Unable to meet reparations schedules with foreign exchange from trade that had dried up, the German economy spun out of control as the depression hit that country harder than any other. Beyond the horrible economic privations that these practices created, they also fueled the animosities and hatreds that made the slide to war easier. In that atmosphere, Adolph Hitler arose, promising, among other things, to restore prosperity.

The process of rebuilding the world after World War II began early during the war itself, largely through British and American collaboration. The purpose was to ensure that the mistakes made in 1919 were not repeated and that the structure of postwar peace would prevent a recurrence of another global war. Politically, this collaboration produced thoroughly internationalist constructs such as the United Nations Charter and the North American Treaty Organization. Economically, it produced a series of agreements to restructure the global economy, a construct known as the Bretton Woods system.

The Bretton Woods System and Free Trade

Encouraged and cajoled by the governments of Great Britain and the United States, representatives of 44 countries met in the White Mountains resort town of Bretton Woods, New Hampshire, in July 1944 to plan for the postwar economic peace. The site, at the picturesque Washington Hotel at the foot of Mt. Washington, was chosen both for its splendor and its isolation (the site was accessible only by a single two-lane highway). At Bretton Woods, the conferees hammered out a series of agreements that produced international economic institutions that have endured into the twenty-first century and have become staple parts of the system of globalization.

The conferees agreed that the heart of the 1930s economic problem was protectionism, manifested in international financial and economic practices such as large fluctuation in exchange rates of currencies, chronic balance-of-payments difficulties experienced by some countries, and prohibitively high tariffs. All of these practices had contributed to restriction of international commerce, and the conferees agreed that a major antidote to these practices was the encouragement of much freer trade among countries. This explicitly free trade preference was held most strongly by the U.S. delegation to Bretton Woods (the British, seeking to protect the series of preferences for members of the Commonwealth through the Imperial Preference System, sought a more restrained form of trade restriction reduction). This preference, coming from the Roosevelt administration, had some opposition domestically from some conservative members of Congress and from private organizations like the U.S. Chamber of Commerce (a close ally of American businesses that benefited from protectionism).

The Bretton Woods process was more successful in confronting some of its priorities than others. Two international organizations were created, the International Monetary Fund (IMF) and the International Bank for Reconstruction and Development (IBRD or World Bank). The IMF was originally chartered to deal with the problem of currency fluctuations by authorizing the granting of credits to shore up weak currencies, thus contributing to economic stabilization. The IMF has gradually widened its purview to a variety of other economic matters. The World Bank, on the other hand, was to assist in economic stabilization by granting loans originally for reconstruction of war-torn countries, and later for the development of the emerging Third World.

The priority of freeing trade did not enjoy as successful a fate. Although Bretton Woods produced two organizations, it failed to see the third pillar of its vision institutionalized, an international organization devoted explicitly to the promotion of free trade. Instead, that process became gradual and convoluted, not reaching fruition until the 1990s. The length of time involved is, in important ways, a testimony to the endurance and strength of the anti–free trade position, especially in the United States.

The Road from Bretton Woods to the WTO

Although there was a clear sentiment for institutionalizing a free trade–promoting international organization at Bretton Woods, there was enough opposition to the idea both internationally (British misgivings about infringements on its Imperial Preference System relationship with the Commonwealth, for instance) and domestically to keep such an organization from being part of the Bretton Woods package. That did not mean, however, that there was no active enthusiasm for the creation of an International Trade Organization (ITO). The problem was that the proposal to create the ITO ran into the familiar ambivalence of American politics relating to foreign affairs. For nearly half a century, the United States found itself alternately championing and opposing the creation of an organization to promote free trade, depending on whether free trade or anti–free trade elements held sway in the domestic decision process.

During and shortly after the war, the idea of the ITO largely existed within the executive branch of the American government, and more specifically the U.S. Department of State. When Harry S. Truman succeeded Franklin Delano Roosevelt as president in 1945, he adopted the ITO as his own project. The Truman administration took the leadership role in proposing a United Nations Conference on Trade and Development (UNCTAD) in 1946, a major purpose of which was to draft a charter for the ITO. That proposal was, however, opposed by powerful elements in the U.S. Congress, and as a result, a meeting was held in Geneva, Switzerland, in 1947 to lay out the principles of a General Agreement on Tariffs and Trade (GATT), as an interim, partial solution to the free trade issue. The proposal for GATT was to be a temporary "fix," while the treaty to create the ITO was being honed and perfected. A meeting was scheduled for Havana, Cuba, in 1947 to formally propose the ITO.

Then American domestic politics got in the way. ITO, like other free trade institutions since, would have done two things of varying controversy. The first of these was to provide an institutional basis to promote the reduction of barriers to trade. Although there were objections to the proposal on this basis from protectionists and others, it was the less controversial aspect. The second, and more divisive, purpose was to create an instrument with jurisdiction and authority to enforce trade agreements, including the capability to levy enforceable penalties against sovereign governments. Opponents of ITO and its successors complained that this enforcement provision represented an unwise infringement on American sovereignty, a position that resonated with both opponents and some proponents of the principle of free trade.

The ITO proposal was undermined by political actions in the United States in 1948. A coalition of powerful elements in the Congress led the way. The major players in this array against the ITO included conservative Republicans backed by protectionist agricultural and manufacturing interests seeking to protect American goods from foreign competition, liberal Democrats who viewed the ITO document as too timid an approach to promoting free trade, and conservatives who feared the sovereignty infringement that ITO enforcement provisions represented.

This Congressional array faced a Truman administration that favored ratification of the ITO statute but that was unwilling to expend scarce political capital in the process. Competing in the foreign policy agenda was the North American Treaty Organization (NATO) proposal. As an initiative to create the first peacetime alliance in American history, NATO was also a controversial concept. The Truman administration reasoned that it could muster support for one or the other of the treaties, and that of the two, NATO was the more critical (the Cold War was heating up at the time). At the same time, 1948 was a presidential election year, and underdog incumbent Truman feared that spirited advocacy of a controversial idea like the ITO could become a negative campaign issue. Thus, the Truman administration backed away from its advocacy of the ITO, and the proposal died. The United States had, not uncharacteristically, both enthusiastically endorsed and helped develop the charter for the ITO and then destroyed it, further evidence of American ambivalence toward international involvements.

The demise of the ITO elevated GATT to a more prominent and permanent position than those who had originally proposed it had envisioned. GATT survived as the banner carrier for international free trade from 1948 until the WTO came into existence in 1995. Those who oppose free trade in principle or effect were unenthused by GATT, but felt less threatened by it than by the ITO.

The reason GATT was less objectionable than the ITO was that it lacked the second characteristic of the ITO, an enforcement capability. GATT, in effect, was not an organization at all, but rather a series of negotiating sessions (called "rounds" and normally named after wherever a given round's first session was held) among the sovereign members. The result of these sessions was to create international agreements on different free trade issues, but these were less threatening than the ITO. For one thing, GATT was not an organization and thus lacked more than a modest staff; therefore, it had no investigating capability. Moreover, GATT was never granted any enforcement authority, and all of the agreements reached during GATT negotiations had to be ratified by all participating countries before its provisions affected them. Thus, those who feared institutionalizing free trade on sovereignty grounds had little to fear from the GATT process.

Although it lacked the foundation of a permanent international organization, GATT was not useless. Indeed, the outcomes of the various rounds did produce a series of principles and practices that have been incorporated into the WTO. At heart, the principal thrust of GATT action was centered on the *most favored nation* (MFN) principle: the idea of providing to all trading partners the same customs and tariff treatment enjoyed by a country given the greatest trade privilege—the most favored country. Thus, if one country lowers its tariffs on a particular good to another country, it should extend that same tariff treatment to all GATT members. John Rothgeb argues that the GATT experience can be categorized around four distinct principles flowing from the MFN precedent. They are: *nondiscrimination* (the promotion of MFN status among all countries regardless of status); *transparency* (the unacceptability of secret trade restrictions and barriers); *consultation and dispute settlement* (resolution of disputes through direct negotiations); and *reciprocity* (the idea that all members should incur balanced obligations).

The last, or Uruguay, round of GATT included among its proposals the establishment of the WTO. In a very real sense, the WTO is the ITO reincarnated, because it combines the two basic elements of the ITO again within a permanent international organization: the promotion of free trade, *and* mechanisms to enforce trade agreements and the legal authority to penalize members of the organization who violate international trade agreements.

When the WTO was first proposed in 1993, it did not produce the same volume of objection that the ITO did in 1948. The same basic opposed interests, if with different representatives, were against the WTO. Protectionists disfavored the principle of free trade; in 1948, these were mostly business-related Republicans, but in 1993 they were mostly union-supporting Democrats. Some again objected on the grounds that the organization was too timid—in this case the objectors were principally environmentalists concerned the WTO would not aggressively protect the environment. Others raised objections on the grounds of infringements of national sovereignty. These problems are discussed in the next section.

The WTO statute was ratified by the U.S. Congress on December 1, 1994. It was not submitted as a treaty (requiring the advice and consent of two-thirds of the Senate), but instead as an economic agreement under the provisions of so-called *fast track* procedures (now known as trade promotion authority).

Treating the WTO as an economic agreement meant it had to pass both houses of Congress, but with only a simple, rather than a weighted, majority. Designating it under fast track (a provision to facilitate the passage of trade agreements) meant there were limits on congressional debate on the matter and that it could only be voted up or down in its entirety (the authority to amend it was removed). The date is important because it came after the November 1994 off-year elections but before the newly elected Congress was inaugurated (qualifying it as a lame duck session). Critics wailed at the timing and procedures (some maintained, for instance, that had WTO accession been presented as a treaty that it never would have gotten a two-thirds majority), but their cries of "foul" were in vain. Nearly 50 years after its principles were first proposed, institutionalized free trade became reality in 1995.

The WTO has now been in existence for over a decade and a half. Its membership has increased from approximately 70 in 1995 to 153 as of July 23, 2008 (according to its Web site). In addition, 30 nonmember countries participate in the organization (observers have five years to apply for full membership), including Russia, Iraq, Iran, and Afghanistan. According to the WTO home page, the membership does 97 percent of world trade. The headquarters, including the secretariat, are located in Lausanne, Switzerland. The WTO has established itself as a leading international economic organization in the process.

Its brief tenure has also been filled with controversy and a great deal more visibility than functional international organizations (those that deal with a specific policy area rather than generalist organizations like the United Nations) usually attract or desire. In some ways, the acceptance of or opposition to the WTO reflects the status of globalization, whose central principle of free trade it exemplifies. When the charter came into effect in 1995, globalization was at its apex and the new WTO only activated its most ardent opponents. By the end of the 1990s, on the other hand, globalization was less in vogue, and the WTO has become more controversial. This controversy became extremely public during widespread and highly destructive demonstrations at its 1999 convention in Seattle, Washington. As globalization has gradually become more universal, some of this controversy has receded.

IS INSTITUTIONALIZED FREE TRADE A GOOD IDEA?

This is really two separate but related questions, and there is disagreement on both of them. One question has to do with whether free trade itself is a worthy goal, and it has as a subtext the question whether free trade *as it is currently defined and being pursued* is a good idea. One can, for instance, believe that the general principle of removing barriers to trade is a good idea, but disagree that the overarching implementing principle of removing "barriers to trade" should override other principles, such as the promotion of human rights. The other question is whether free trade advocacy and implementation should be institutionalized, and that question has the subtext of whether the WTO *as it is currently organized and with the authority it has* is a good idea. Many who believe that free trade is a good principle and accept the idea that it needs some institutional base, for instance, disagree with the current structure of the WTO and advocate a more open, democratic structure for the organization. Clearly, those who oppose free trade (in principle or in its present guise) oppose the WTO as well.

The WTO has become a lightning rod on the free trade issue. Those who oppose free trade, generally on the basis that its effects are not as desirable for individuals or societies as its advocates suggest, clearly oppose an advocating institution, and especially one with mandatory authority to impose its values on individuals and countries. Proponents of free trade generally support the idea of an institutional base from which to promote their advocacy, but may or may not like the structure that exists. To make some reasonable personal assessment on the issue of free trade requires unraveling and analyzing each aspect.

Free Trade or Not Free Trade?

The generalized defense of free trade rests on the macroeconomic benefits it brings to countries and the microeconomic benefits it accords to individuals and groups. Both benefits are controversial. Free trade is the international application of the Ricardian principle of comparative advantage. The argument asserts that removing barriers to the movement of goods and services across national boundaries, the most efficient producers of goods and providers of services will come to dominate the markets in the areas of their advantage, to the benefit of consumers who will receive the best goods and services at the lowest prices from these providers. Presuming all countries can find products or services at which they have such advantages, all will find markets, and the result will be a general and growing specialization and prosperity. The application of free trade internationally is the handmaiden of the process of economic globalization, because the result should be the gradual widening of participation in the global economy, as more and more countries find and exploit areas in which they have or can develop a comparative advantage.

The petroleum-driven energy crisis of 2008 has added another variable to the Ricardian mix. To the extent that goods and services produced at remote locations meet the Ricardian dictate of being less expensive, the comparative advantage of remote producers must include both the cost of production and the cost of transporting goods and services to market. Increased energy and thus transportation costs thus can erode some comparative advantage.

Freeing trade has the added benefit of promoting a more cooperative, peaceful environment, according to its champions. The major conceptual vehicle for this dynamic is *complex interdependence*, the idea that as countries become increasingly reliant on one another for essential goods and services, their ability and desire to engage in conflict, and especially war, becomes more remote—either because the desire to fight is decreased by proximity and acquaintance, or because the intertwining of economies makes it impractical or impossible to fight.

This macroeconomic argument is abstract and intellectual, and its dynamics are not universally accepted. It argues that free trade improves the general lot of peoples, and thus increases the prosperity of individuals: "a rising tide lifts all boats," to borrow a phrase. As an abstract matter presented in this way, it is difficult to argue with the virtue of free trade, although some do. At a slightly less abstract level, proponents of free trade also point to largely macroeconomic indicators, especially from the mid-1990s, to demonstrate growth in the global economy and within individual countries, phenomena they attribute to free trade–driven globalization. Despite these arguments, when these statistics are applied at more specific levels—to those of individuals or even sectors of economies within countries—the case is not as clearly positive.

The major objections to free trade come not from these abstract principles, but from the way they are applied. In the current debate about free trade, many of the objections go back to the conjunction of free trade and the values of market economics in fact if not in theory. It is the effects of the kind of free trade that the advocates put forward that is the problem.

A key element in opposition arises from the presumption that all countries (or whatever entities are part of a free trading arrangement) will in fact find areas of production at which they have a comparative advantage. As mentioned later, this is not always the case. It also presumes that areas of uncompetitive production undercut by free trade can find compensatory equivalent areas of comparative advantage that will replace uncompetitive enterprises, and it is central to microeconomic objections to free trade that this is also not always the case.

This contrast in macro-level versus micro-level benefits helps explain why free trade is more popular among economic elites than the general population and why the issue becomes a flash point in economic debates during American political campaigns. The economic elites—investors, entrepreneurs, and the like—are all more likely to be insulated from negative micro-level but more affected by broader, more macro-level effects like the overall impact on the stock market. If globalization indeed produces benefits to the broader economy, then they are likely to benefit personally and be supportive. Negative micro-level effects have a direct impact on the jobs of individual voters, and candidates for public office are likely to reflect the suffering that displaced individuals and industries feel. Thus, it is not surprising to see opposition to globalization in areas where globalization has produced declines in noncompetitive industries, from the textile workers of the Carolinas to automobile workers in Michigan or steelworkers in Pennsylvania.

An international example of negative effects is the impact of institutionalized free trade on the economic development of poor countries. Because the basis of free trade is the MFN principle, opponents argue that poor countries are in a disadvantageous situation. Because they are at a comparative disadvantage at producing nearly everything (a major reason they are less developed), they are vulnerable to a flooding of goods and services across the range of economic activity if they are part of a free trade system. Their inability to protect nascent economic activities means that indigenous development will be systematically undercut by the free trade regime and domestic industry and thus development will be retarded. The net impact of being exposed to MFN has thus been, according to critics, to contribute to greater economic inequality between the rich and poor countries, the very opposite of what the proponents of free trade argue.

For the "turtles," as Thomas Friedman labels the countries that cannot compete in the free trade environment, there are two options, as the example suggests. One is to stay outside the WTO framework, since its principles and rules only apply to members. Notably, almost all the countries that have not joined WTO are extremely poor, and although the WTO has tried to develop outreach programs to these nonmembers, they have not been entirely successful at overcoming these objections. The other alternative is to join the WTO and suffer the consequences of assault on the domestic economy in the hopes that doing so will help "lift" the national boat.

The policies that implement free trade can have similar effects. Joining the free trade–driven globalizing economy requires adopting both macroeconomic and microeconomic policies that require individual privation and thus engender popular political opposition both to the policies and to the governments that advocate them. The result, seen most keenly in Latin America, has been a considerable backlash against globalization.

The WTO: Problem or Solution?

The WTO is the final fulfillment of the dreams of the Bretton Woods planners. Freeing trade was a central part of the remedy they saw for the international economic ills associated with protectionism and its contribution to the war. When the idea was first presented, American objections prevented the first institutional form, the ITO, from coming into being. In 1995, the proponents succeeded, but the controversy remains. Is the WTO the answer, or the problem?

Assessing whether the WTO helps or hinders the progression of free trade can be broken into three separate concerns. The first is the kind of free trade that the WTO advocates. To its opponents, the WTO is little more than a hand-maiden to the large multinational corporations (MNCs). Global Exchange, a Web-based research organization that is very critical of the WTO, calls it an "unaccountable, corporate-based government" that reflects the values of the MNCs at the expense of virtually everyone else. At least to some extent, this should come as little surprise. The globalization process of which free trade is an implementing device is based in the promotion of capitalist, free market economics, of which corporations are a prominent part. Moreover, much of the economic resources on which the spread of globalization is based is in the form of foreign direct investment (FDI) by private sources, and entities like international banks and multinational corporations provide most of the FDI. Because they do so out of a profit motive and not from a sense of philanthropy, it follows that these entities would have an interest in helping to shape the philosophies and policies the WTO promotes. As indirect evidence of the success of the MNCs in this regard, it might be remembered that corporations within the United States were major opponents of the ITO because of protectionist motives, but have by and large been equally strong supporters of the WTO.

The advocacy of free trade and the promotion of its implementation through the WTO thus contains two substantive judgments. One is whether there is an alternative economic philosophy that could be attached to free trade that would make it more palatable to those who oppose the idea or its consequences. Is there some alternative to a market-economy-based, free trade–driven globalized economy? The second judgment flows from the first: If there is no acceptable alternative underpinning, are the positive outcomes of institutionalized free trade better or worse than the absence of such a system? The analogy of the rising tide and the boat is sometimes used to frame this question. Pro–free traders admit that not everyone benefits equally from free trade, but that everyone does benefit to some extent and thus everyone is better off under a free trade regime (the tide lifts all boats). Opponents argue the benefits are so inequitably distributed that gaps are actually widened to the point that some are left relatively worse off (some boats get swamped).

The second disagreement concerns the structure of the WTO itself. To reiterate, the WTO has two basic functions: the promotion of free trade and the enforcement of free trade agreements. The enforcement mandate is and always has been the more controversial aspect of WTO. The mechanism for enforcement was agreed on during the Uruguay round of GATT in the form of the Dispute Settlement Understanding (DSU). Under the DSU, the WTO is authorized to establish and convene the Dispute Settlement Body (DSB). *The Geneva Briefing Book* describes the considerable authority of the DSB, "which has the sole authority to establish such panels to adjudicate disputes between members and to accept or reject the findings of panels and the Appellate Body, a standing appeals body of seven independent experts. The DSB also . . . has the power to authorize retaliation when a member does not comply with DSB recommendations and rulings."

These powers are not inconsiderable and include the power to identify alleged violations; to convene and prosecute those alleged violations; and then to issue binding rulings and penalties and to enforce those penalties, ostensibly without recourse to an outside, independent source of appeal (all appeals are internal to the process). The membership of these panels is chosen by the WTO itself, and, according to Global Exchange, "consist of three trade bureaucrats that are not screened for conflict of interest."

To critics that span the ITO–WTO debate, a chief objection to this arrangement is its effect on national sovereignty. The rulings of the DSU process have the effect of treaty law on the countries against which they are levied, which means that they cannot overturn the effect of those laws. This is particularly a concern in the United States where, as noted, there is particular sensitivity over intrusions on state sovereignty. In the specific case of WTO rulings, these have disproportionately affected the United States. According to the *Geneva Briefing Book*, "From the advent of the WTO, in January 1995, until October 1, 2003, the United States has been a party in 56 out of 93 WTO dispute settlement panel reports and 36 out of 56 Appellate Body reports." The source does not indicate how many of these involved judgments against the United States, but it is likely at least some of them did.

The third concern regards what unforeseen consequences the institutionalization of free trade has had, and whether those consequences are acceptable. As one might expect, most unforeseen outcomes that have been identified are negative and are expressed most vocally by opponents of the process and its outcomes. Two in particular stand out as examples: the alleged antilabor bias of the WTO, and its negative environmental impacts. Unsurprisingly, these two arguments have been raised by two of the most prominent and visible opponents of the WTO, neither of which was evident in the 1940s but are today. Both touch on the dual questions of whether free trade itself or the way it is institutionalized is the problem.

Objections to free trade on the basis of being antilabor contain both elements of objection. Free trade is, of course, the culprit among those people working in industries and services that do not enjoy comparative advantage and can only compete if protected by some form of trade barrier. The textile industry cited earlier is a prime example. Labor unions also contend that the way in which the WTO operates to remove barriers to trade provides incentives for corporations to move their businesses to places that engage in unfair labor practices (everything from low wages and benefits to child labor), thereby creating an unfair environment within which to compete. Moreover, they believe that the corporatist mentality they say reigns supreme within the WTO encourages foreign direct investors to nurture and create these unfair practices as ways to create and sustain comparative advantage. These allegations are parallel to older domestic arguments about union busting and scab labor practices. Because these are extremely emotional issues among trade unionists, it helps explain the depth of their animosity toward the WTO and the prevalence of trade unionists in anti–free trade, anti-WTO activities.

Environmentalists' objections to free trade and the WTO are parallel. The need to establish conditions of comparative advantage drives some countries to rescind environmental regulations that add to the cost of production (e.g., dumping hazardous chemicals used in processing materials into the environment rather than rendering these chemical's harmless before release), thereby making their industries more competitive than industries in the United States that must meet environmental standards that add to production costs. Critics cite cases in Latin America (especially Mexico) in which environmental standards have indeed been relaxed or done away with to attract industry.

The environmentalist objection is also applied directly to the WTO. Environmentalists contend that most corporations resist environmental restraints philosophically and only accede to environmental regulation reluctantly and unenthusiastically. Because the WTO is alleged to be largely controlled by corporate interests and reflects corporate values, they are thus predisposed to be suspicious of the organization on those grounds. Environmentalists are also generally conspicuous at demonstrations against the WTO.

CONCLUSION

Whether to advocate or oppose free trade and its institutionalization is not, nor has it ever been, an easy or straightforward proposition. At the abstract, theoretical level of international macroeconomics, the case for free trade is very convincing, and it is not surprising that many of the defenses of free trade spring from these theoretical arguments. At the applied level of the impact of free trade on individuals and groups (the microeconomic level), the proposition creates more ambivalence. Certainly, individuals as consumers benefit when comparative advantage produces goods and services at lower cost and higher quality through free trade rather than from less efficient, protected domestic industries. Imagine, for instance, the impact on Christmas gift spending if all goods made in China were eliminated. At the same time, removing protection can terminate employment for those in the less efficient industries. Although the theory of comparative advantage says that people so displaced should find alternative employment in more competitive fields, accomplishing that task is almost always easier said than done. When these dislocations affect large portions of a society, there may also be a negative political reaction both to the phenomenon of globalization (and hence free trade) and to those politicians who are supporters of free trade.

The question of institutionalizing free trade is related but not synonymous, because one can reasonably take one of three positions on the desirability of free trade per se: one can favor free trade unconditionally, one can oppose it equally unconditionally, or one can favor free trade with some restrictions, the fair trade position. For the "pure" positions, the answer to whether some organization should be established to promote and enforce free trade is fairly straightforward. If one believes free trade is comprehensively desirable, then a free trade–promoting institution is clearly a desirable instrument to that end (although the kind and extent of enforcement capability may be debatable). Conversely, if one opposes free trade across the board, then it would be nonsensical to support any instrumentality that promotes or enforces a rejected idea.

That leaves the "fair traders," who support expansions in trade through the reduction of barriers to trade, but who believe there should be exclusions or limitations on the extent and degree of trade promotion. Such an advocacy attempts to finesse the dichotomy between free trade and protectionism by advocating some of both, depending on the context. This position is generally politically tenable as well, because it allows support for free trade (which, in the abstract, most people favor) with restrictions to protect politically significant victims of free trade.

The advocacy of freer trade leads to three questions that can be applied to the dual thrusts of free trade and its institutionalization. The first is, "How free should trade be?" The general criterion for answering the question is how much of the benefits and costs of free trade is one willing to bear, and one's answer will, in turn, vary with the level of personal benefit one (or one's group, or country) derives from various levels of free trade.

The second question is, "What kinds of values should underlie a free trading system and, especially, the institution that supports and promotes it?" If the current free trade–based system of globalization is based on the values of market-based, capitalist economics, as it at least partly is, it leads to a form of organization based on pure economic competition in which the less government regulation exists, generally the better. If, as alleged, the WTO is dominated by people with these values and interests, then the *kind* of free trade system that evolves and is institutionalized will reflect those values. On the other hand, if one enters values such as equity (fair trade) and social consciousness (environmentalism) into the values underlying a free trade system, it probably looks different than the current system.

The third and final question is, "What kind of enforcement mechanism is most desirable?" The answer, of course, begins with the level of enthusiasm one has about free trade in the first place: The more enthusiastic one is, the more enforcement one is likely to favor or tolerate. But the answer also incorporates how one has answered the second question: One's enthusiasm for enforcement may depend on what kinds of values are being enforced and whether one supports those values. In a favorite example cited by critics of the current system, the American ban on tuna fishing using mile-long nets that also ensnare and kill dolphins was overruled in a judgment by the WTO. In an action brought by Mexico, the WTO said the law, when applied to American territorial waters, was a barrier to trade. Does a free trade regime need to lead to that kind of conclusion?

The free trade movement has apparently weathered the economic storm created by the worldwide economic crisis that emerged in 2008. Despite economic conditions that could give rise to protectionist efforts to shield individual countries from vagaries like high unemployment, such solutions were not seriously proposed. If anything, the crisis was viewed as an indication of the need for more, rather than less, globalization. As one of the crown jewels of globalization, that meant continuing, even growing, support for free trade as well. Naim summarizes the impact: "Globalization is such a diverse, broad-based, and potent force that not even today's massive economic crash will dramatically slow it down or reverse it. Love it or hate it, globalization is here to stay." If that bold assertion is true, then free trade, as a prime pillar of globalization, will be enduring as well.

STUDY/DISCUSSION QUESTIONS

1. What is free trade? Why is it an issue, both historically and in the contemporary context? What are the basic disagreements about the desirability of free trade? What basic positions do people take on the trade issue?

2. Describe the process of institutionalizing free trade from the Bretton Woods conference of 1944 to the ratification of the World Trade Organization in 1995. Why did the International Trade Organization fail to come into existence in 1948 but the WTO succeed in 1995? What was the role of the General Agreement on Trade and Tariffs in this evolution?

3. What are the principal arguments for and against free trade? How do the disputes over intellectual property rights and the impact of free trade on development of the poorest countries illustrate this debate?
4. What are the major controversies surrounding the WTO? What values does it promote? What powers does it have? How do labor and environmental objections illustrate this controversy?
5. Answer the three questions posed in the conclusion: How free should trade be? What kinds of values should it promote? What kind of enforcement mechanism is most desirable? After determining your personal answers to these questions, do you consider yourself a free trader, an anti–free trader, or somewhere in between (a fair trader)? Why?

READING/RESEARCH MATERIAL

Barshefsky, Charlene. "Trade Policy in a Networked World." *Foreign Affairs* 80, 2 (March/April 2001), 134–146.

Bauman, Zygmunt. *Globalization: The Human Consequences.* New York: Columbia University Press, 1998.

Dierks, Rosa Gomez. *Introduction to Globalization: Political and Economic Perspectives for a New Era.* Chicago, IL: Burnham, 2001.

Dregner, Daniel W. *U.S. Trade Strategy: Free versus Fair.* New York: Council on Foreign Relations Press, 2006.

Friedman, Thomas L. *The Lexus and the Olive Tree: Understanding Globalization.* New York: Farrar, Straus and Giroux, 1999.

———. *The World is Flat: A Brief History of the Twenty-First Century.* New York: Farrar, Straus, and Giroux, 2005.

Landau, Alice. *Redrawing the Global Economy: Elements of Integration and Fragmentation.* New York: Palgrave, 2001.

Lind, Michael. *Made in Texas: George W. Bush and the Southern Takeover of American Politics.* New York: New America Books, 2003.

McBride, Stephen and John Wiseman, eds. *Globalization and Its Discontents.* New York: St. Martin's Press, 2000.

"Measuring Globalization." *Foreign Policy*, March/April 2004, 46–53.

Naim, Moises. "Think Again: Globalization." *Foreign Policy*, March/April 2009, 28–34.

O'Connor, David E. *Demystifying the Global Economy: A Guide for Students.* Westport, CT: Greenwood Press, 2002.

Panagariya, Arvind. "Think Again: International Trade." *Foreign Policy*, November/December 2003, 20–29.

Park, Jacob. "Globalization after Seattle." *Washington Quarterly* 23, 2 (Spring 2000), 13–16.

Rothgeb, John M. J. *Trade Policy: Balancing Economic Dreams and Political Realities.* Washington, DC: CQ Press, 2001.

Schaeffer, Robert K. *Understanding Globalization: The Social Consequences of Political, Economic, and Environmental Change.* Lanham, MD: Rowman and Littlefield, 2003.

Shah, Anup. "Free Trade and Globalization." *Global Issues* (online), July 25, 2009.

"World Trade Organization." *The Geneva Briefing Book.* Lausanne, Switzerland: World Trade Organization, 2004.

WEB SITES

Critical views of the World Trade Organization

Global Exchange at http://www.globalexchange.org/campaigns/rulemakers/topTen Reasons.html

The home page of the World Trade Organization

http://www.wto.org.

Regional Integration: The European Union Faces the Future

PRÉCIS

The process of economic integration is both global and regional. Within the context of the post–World War II world, the process began in Europe shortly after the war through the establishment of a small group of institutions which have evolved into the European Union (EU). They represent a geographically limited (but physically expanding) area but have achieved a far greater degree of integration than global schemes and proposals. The EU has moved from being a limited-scale free trading arrangement to a true economic union with strong political implications, controversies, and problems. It is also, however, an extremely dynamic competitor in the world economic system. The evolution of the EU offers some reasonable precedents about at least one way in which the movement toward globalization may evolve. The case will concentrate on how the growing physical size of the EU and the extent of the degree of integration it seeks to affect have created the problems that currently affect the organization.

The European Union celebrated its fiftieth birthday at the beginning of 2008, marking the golden anniversary of an organization that came into being with the implementation of the Treaty of Rome in 1958. Regional economic integration of the nature and on a scale such as the European Common Market, as it was known then, was unprecedented, and it had both political and economic purposes. The frank underlying political goal was to create a Europe in which a repetition of the events leading to the century of warfare centering around Germany and France would be interrupted, even eliminated, and the precursor institutions that became the core of the EU had this purpose fully in mind as they sought an institutional setting in which war between the major European powers would become impossible. Economically, the process proposed to stimulate the economies of its members through an integration that would apply the principles of the theory of comparative advantage to the continent.

The EU has been an enormous success. A Europe devastated by World War II, in a state of economic doldrums after its conclusion, was rapidly transformed into an economic force in the world that could compete on a global scale with the United States and Japan and as a political equal to the Soviet Union. Moravcsik recently called it "the most ambitious and successful international organization of all time." The EU has grown over its 50 years physically and in its extent of integration from a free trading arrangement between six adjacent continental states to an evolving economic union of 27 states with more waiting in the queue for inclusion. At the same time, the attendant process of political integration and the extension of the EU to countries unlike the original membership have created a crisis of sorts within the EU that is a source of concern as the organization moves further into the twenty-first century.

Globalization represents the process of economic integration on its grandest scale, incorporating the entire world or at least those parts of it willing and able to participate into the globalization process. The purpose of this economic integration is to create greater economic efficiency by promoting Ricardian comparative advantage within the units undergoing the globalization process.

All economic integration schemes are not the same. Rather, they differ on at least two salient characteristics. One is the *physical dimensions* of the unit under consideration. In the evolving history of globalization, there have been two major geographical foci of economic integration: regional approaches and worldwide applications. In Chapter 9, the discussion centered primarily on the global level, as represented by the concept globalization and institutionalized through entities such as the World Trade Organization (WTO). The EU is the original and by far most advanced regional approach to economic integration.

The second dimension is the *extent* of integration being sought. While the averred purposes of economic integration schemes have the removal of economic barriers and the promotion of trade among participating units as their major purpose, there are inevitably political consequences and goals involved as well. The admixture of economic and political purposes tends to grow as the extent of the integrating unit expands, and in some cases, political integration may even be the coequal or overriding purpose of the economic integration effort.

Extent of integration goes beyond the incorporation of political integration, and indeed, most economists viewing the process tend to downplay the political implications and instead look at the extent of economic integration that is proposed. In rough terms, integration spans a range of ever closer association and commitment that begins with the establishment of free trade among the members and moves through stages such as a customs union, a common or single market, a monetary union, and a true economic union. Most of the global schemes have proposed no more than a free trade area–level of integration, as have some regional organizations (the North American Free Trade Agreement (NAFTA) and the Asia-Pacific Economic

Cooperation (APEC) are examples). The EU is unique in that it has traveled through all the steps of economic integration.

Because it has traversed more fully the path of economic integration than any other contemporary economic set of institutions, the EU provides the best available precedent for judging the desirability, opportunities, and pitfalls associated with regional attempts at integration that go beyond free trade arrangements to a much deeper and more pervasive form of integration. To understand the dynamics of the regional economic integration process, the discussion will begin with a general discussion of the dynamics and forms of regional integration and how the political and economic dynamics intertwine. These observations will then be applied to the evolving case of the EU.

THE REGIONAL INTEGRATION PROCESS

Regional integration—binding together the economies of physically proximate states within a geographical area—is simultaneously simpler and more difficult than global approaches to integration. It is simpler because of smaller geographical reach and jurisdiction and because regional groupings are likely to contain peoples of similar culture and history with some understanding and history of interaction among them. The Germans and the French, in other words, have known each other for a long time. This very familiarity can, however, breed contempt and animosity among regional actors that make their cooperation more rather than less difficult. One reason Germans and Frenchmen know each other so well is that they have been fighting so long. Within regions, there may be dissimilarities between potential members (the United States and Mexico within NAFTA, for instance) that create unique problems and circumstances.

While it may be difficult, even misleading, to try to generalize on the regional integration process, it is possible to describe it. The discussion will be centered on two major benchmarks surrounding integration, both of which are applicable to the global and regional levels but are particularly poignant when dealing with a highly integrated regional structure like the EU. One is the degree of integration involved in any particular proposed or existing scheme. A taxonomy of gradually increasing levels of integration will be laid out. The other concern is the degree of political and economic integration and controversy involved, and the relationship between existing or potential economic and political goals. As a general rule, the more complex and extensive an economic association is, the more political concerns either arise or underpin the effort.

Forms of Integration

The process of economic integration, whether pursued at global or regional levels, can produce greater or lesser degrees of interdependence and interpenetration among parties. In the general discussion of globalization, most goals are stated in terms of the pursuit of *free trade*, as introduced and discussed in

Chapter 9. Agreements like that creating the WTO or regional arrangements like the APEC have the promotion of free trade as their primary, even sole, focus. The principal objectives of free trading arrangements are to encourage greater trade among members by reducing barriers to trade—tariffs, quotas, and the like—among the members. Such arrangements represent the initial, and least binding or formal, means to approach greater economic—or political—integration.

There are a series of increasingly entangling forms of economic integration that go beyond free trade arrangements. These can be placed in a sort of hierarchical order of greater complexity and commitment to the form of integration. The ultimate expression is economic union, of which the EU is the sole example.

The next step beyond a free trade area is a *customs union*. In this form of arrangement, the members adopt a common external tariff toward all goods and services entering any of the members. In a free trade area that is not also a customs union, the various members all have their own external tariffs. The effect is that import duties are not uniform among members for different goods and services. If there is a free trade agreement in force, high duties on goods and services against which one member can be circumvented by importing that good or service into a country where there is a lower barrier, then moving that good or service through the free trade area into the country with the higher tariff, thereby avoiding the original high tariff through indirect importation. The old European Free Trade Area, composed of early nonmembers of the European Common Market (or European Economic Community), was of this nature, and it did not work terribly well.

When a free trade area and customs union are created for the same physical area, the result is the creation of a *single* or *common market*. The goal of a common market is to create the free circulation of goods, capital, people, and services within the geographic constraints of the common market region. This is done by reducing, preferably to zero, all trade barriers among the members (the basis of a free trade area) and by creating a common external barrier against goods and services imported anywhere within the region (a customs union). The result is to create an economic area that maximizes the flow of goods, services, capital, and people within the single market area while excluding or making more difficult the entry of items produced outside the area at lower costs. This was the original form that the European Economic Community assumed in the 1960s and beyond, and it was a huge success in stimulating the economies of the member states and in attracting the interest of other states which wanted to join the process. It is a form of association that goes far beyond most current conceptions of integration beyond Europe.

A common market's level of integration, however, is circumscribed if its members maintain their individual currencies, because this means that commerce is slowed by the necessity of establishing and enforcing exchange rates, and translating transactions from one currency to another. The solution to this barrier to further integration is the establishment of a *monetary union*, a financial institution which can issue a common currency and make monetary policy that is binding in all the political units. The EU has established a monetary union, but it is, as will be shown, one of the most controversial aspects of the EU, because a monetary union requires a common monetary policy among the members, and this requires a political body that has the authority to make such policy. This "power of the purse" comes at the expense of national legislatures and is, in some cases, a major source of political concern on sovereignty grounds. One way to attenuate the dilution of national sovereignty created by a monetary union is to leave the setting of fiscal policy (such as taxation) under national control, as is done in the EU. As Gros explains, "Monetary union was not intended to lead to a transfer of power in the fiscal field." The *euro* is the most visible manifestation of the monetary union, and resistance to adopting the *euro* in countries like Great Britain is a symbol of the controversy.

The ultimate form of economic integration is the *economic union*, an arrangement that combines a single or common market and a monetary union. This is the form of association that was created originally by the EU in 1993, and it remains one source of controversy surrounding the organization. At the purely economic level, the creation of an economic union is the culmination of the process of economic integration, because the formation of the monetary union removes the last barrier to economic activity across political boundaries created by the necessity of exchanging currencies when transactions occur. If economic integration is the goal, economic union is its zenith.

The movement toward an economic union, however, also has the strongest possible political reverberations. Economic and political unions are, in theory, separable, because one deals with what can be viewed as purely economic consequences and benefits, whereas political union implies an arrangement or rearrangement of political authority in the proposed unit. Economic associations at whatever level and form have tended to be less controversial, because their economic benefits tend to overwhelm political concerns and implications. Certainly that has been the case through most of the process of European economic integration; the current controversy over the political implications of the NAFTA in areas like immigrant flow is a contrary example. The movement to an economic union has stronger political implications for EU than previous steps short of the creation of an economic union per se.

Political and Economic Integration

Separating politics and economics in any real situation is always difficult. The realm of politics is authoritative (normally governmental) decision-making. I have elsewhere defined politics as "the process by which conflicts of interest over scarce resources are resolved." The definition is fairly conventional and suggests politics is both a process (a set of rules for making authoritative allocations of resources) and a substantive concern over those resources being allocated (the conflicts of interest over scarce resources). Although there are many scarce resources that may require allocation, one of the most common and prominent is economic resources, the subject of economic integration schemes.

Economic resources are so important that deciding how they should be divided may become a major concern in deciding who can make political decisions. One such concern, for instance, is what political authorities have the right to levy taxes and spend money, and who has what authority certainly influences which resources are allocated for what purposes (fiscal policy). In the case of the movement to an economic union, a major political question is what political authority will have the jurisdiction over matters such as monetary policy (including currency regulation). Because of the centrality of monetary policy to the overall operation of any political or economic unit, the adoption of political authorities for this function of government can have very serious political effects for countries party to these agreements. These effects indeed extend to issues of national identity and sovereignty and thus become matters of controversy.

The reasons for entering into economic associations have a more or less political underpinning as well. At the most obvious level, economic associations are supposed to stimulate economic activity and create prosperity, and those who propose and construct those associations expect political support for having done so. When the European Common Market was first instituted, for instance, it was wildly successful and overwhelmingly popular; part of the underlying purpose of forming the organization was indeed to strengthen governments as a way to discourage support for communism among populations in Western Europe.

Political and economic aspects of economic schemes may be so inextricable as to be impossible to disaggregate altogether, and the EU is a prime example. The roots of what has become the EU go back to World War II and the attempt to reconstruct the international system—and specifically Europe—after the end of the second European-based world conflagration in less than 40 years. For planners who were intent on producing a more peaceful world order, the UN system was the general solution for matters of war and peace. The more specific problem, however, was what most believed to have been the root cause of the world wars—Franco-German rivalry for control of Europe. World War II, in effect, was the fourth violent round in that competition that began with the Napoleonic wars and came forward through the Franco-Prussian War of 1870 and World War I. The first four rounds had proven inconclusive, and there was a strong desire to avoid the possibility of a fifth round. But how?

The answer, devised through allied consultation during the war in which the Frenchman Jean Monnet played a very prominent role, was to make future warfare between Germany and France functionally impossible. The planners began from the assumption that modern, symmetrical warfare of the kind practiced by Europeans rested on the ability to produce steel and thus the implements of war. If a country could not independently produce steel, it could not go to war. Thus, the planners sought to see if they could create an international political unit that would deprive France and Germany of the ability to produce the wherewithal of war independently of one another. The result was the European Coal and Steel Community (ECSC) of 1951, the first institution in what evolved into the EU.

For many planners during the war, the movement leading to the EU thus had both distinctly political and economic intents that have become impossible to disentangle over time. The great successes and support for the movement have been economic and seen in expanding economies and prosperity and the impatient demands of European countries outside the association to be included. At the same time, the political intents have never been far below the surface. Those who planned the progression of the EU recognized that economic integration would create increasing pressures for political unification as well, and this was the intention of the earliest planners of the regional economic integration that the EU represents. For Monnet and many others, a *real* underlying goal was political integration of the European continent into something like a United States of Europe (an American depiction, of course), with the fruits of economic integration providing the impetus and demand for that evolution.

This political goal was mixed with a more politically-tinged economic goal. As noted already in Chapter 9, most of the planners in the aftermath of World War II agreed that economic policies had played a large role in the form of economic nationalism that caused the breakdown of commerce among European states and fueled animosities leading to conflict. The Bretton Woods institutions were clearly intended to respond to this perceived problem, but so was the movement toward European economic integration. A Europe that was politically united could not be economically divided, and vice versa.

Much of the history of the EU thus has been an attempt to maximize the economic benefits that provide the popular base for integration while deferring or trying to soften political consequences that were viewed as being equally necessary but which might rouse political opposition. Most of the potential political opposition was based in the dilution of national sovereignty that an expanding integration movement created. Common policies inevitably require common political institutions that transcend national boundaries and encroach upon purely national political prerogatives, and that movement has always been controversial and thus a matter not to be confronted directly. An approach that emphasized economic benefits while downplaying political costs was possible until the fateful step was taken to create a full economic union; since that step was taken in 1993, the *politics* of European regional economic integration have largely been about how to deal with the political implications of union. The final ratification of the Lisbon Treaty in 2009 (discussed later) represents an important step in that process.

Because of these overt and important political implications, the EU stands apart from other efforts leading toward the general goal of globalization or economic integration. In the current debate over globalization, none of the proposed or actual forms have gone beyond proposals for free trade areas, which can be and are negotiated by national governments that retain control under them. If countries involved in globalization (or other regional approaches) seek to expand beyond a status as free trade areas to some more advanced form of economic integration, the experience of the EU as both an economic and a political institution may prove instructive.

THE EUROPEAN UNION EXPERIENCE

By any measure, the EU is by far the most successful experiment in cross-national economic integration. It began modestly in 1951 as an association of six continental states, France, Germany, Italy, and the Benelux countries (Belgium, the Netherlands, and Luxembourg), with a limited agenda and limited integration goals. From its very beginning, it was wildly successful and popular, consistently exceeding expectations in terms of the amount of growth and prosperity it created. The very success the process enjoyed in turn led to demands for expansion in two simultaneous directions: horizontally in terms of the accession of new members and vertically in terms of greater integration of the economies of the member states. These two directions have been reflected in the longest existing debate within and outside the organization, between so-called *wideners*, who believe the primary focus of regional integration should be to bring as much of Europe under the EU umbrella as possible (widening membership), and so-called *deepeners*, who believe that primary energy should be placed on maximum integration of the economic systems of the members (deepening relationships between existing members).

From its modest beginning, the EU has grown to a membership of 27 states that incorporates most of western and eastern Europe, except only most of the former republics of the old Soviet Union and a few, largely less economically developed states on the physical fringes of the continent. At that, most of the states in or contiguous to the EU seek membership because of the perceived economic boost such membership would bring. The result of that growth has been to make the EU a major competitive force in the world's economy with a size, economic strength, and market rivaling that of the United States. According to the *CIA World Factbook* for 2010, for instance, the population of the EU today stands at 491 million (July 2008 estimate), compared to about 307 million for the United States. The GDP per capita of EU members is $32,700 (2009 estimate); the comparable figure for the United States is $46,400. The physical area of the EU is a little less than half that of the United States.

The EU is a unique phenomenon. It is the most far-reaching of all the attempts at international economic integration. Moravcsik summarizes its achievements as of 2010: "The EU has enjoyed an astonishingly successful run: It has completed the single market; established a single currency; created a zone without internal boundaries ; launched common defense, foreign and internal security policies; promulgated a constitutional treaty; and most importantly, expanded from 12 to 27 members." The uniqueness of the EU goes back to its birth in the crucible of the immediate post–World War II world and the mandates for change the times created. The fact that the European continent was a more homogeneous cultural, historical, and developmental area than other parts of the world has undoubtedly contributed to a degree of success that would be much more difficult or impossible in more diverse, heterogeneous regions. If, however, the EU experience is ever to be translated on a parallel or larger scale, one must first assess its unique evolution.

Birth and Early Evolution

At the end of World War II, Europe, which had been the primary battlefield of the conflict, lay in tatters. It had been the center of world civilization for over 300 years, but the two great wars left the major European powers prostrate. To the east, the Soviet Union stood as a giant military and ideological opponent that had also been devastated economically by the war but retained a huge armed force with which it occupied most of Eastern Europe and menaced the rest. To the west, an ideologically compatible but upstart United States stood as the only country physically strengthened by the war. In between was Europe.

The question was how to revive Europe, to make it strong enough to withstand Soviet military power, and prosperous enough to rebuff the ideological blandishments of communism. Militarily, the North Atlantic Treaty Organization (NATO) formed in 1949 to provide an American-led bulwark against Soviet military expansion, and in that same year, the first political association of western European states—the Council of Europe—formed to link the countries culturally, socially, and economically.

The process leading to European economic integration began in 1950. At the suggestion of Monnet, French Foreign Minister Robert Schuman proposed the pooling of French and German coal and steel resources. This initiative, known as the Schuman Plan, formed the basis for negotiating the first European Union institution, ECSC, in 1951. With the six core members (France, Germany, Italy, and the Benelux countries), ECSC began operating in 1952, and it was so successful that it spawned interest in a wider form of association. The result was the negotiation of the Treaties of Rome in 1957, which created the European Atomic Energy Community (EURATOM) and, more importantly, the European Economic Community (EEC) among the six members of ECSC. The EEC expanded the previous degree of economic cooperation among the ECSC by creating both a common or single market and a customs union. Thus, the integration process was begun toward both the free circulation of goods, services, people, and capital among the states of the EEC area and a common external tariff for the rest of the world.

The Rome Treaty was the platform from which the EU evolved. It has followed two basic tracks already raised. One has concerned membership. The primary emphasis of the wideners (and their most ardent outside supporters, notably the United States) has been to expand EU membership to more countries than it originally represented. Its current membership is 27 countries, and there is a waiting list of aspirants. The other form has been deeper integration of the membership, through movement to the economic union that was created by the Treaty of Maastricht in 1992 and more deeply implemented by the

Lisbon Treaty. How much further the EU will progress toward a full political union has been a matter of considerable contention since the original days of the EEC and remains a source of major difference within the EU.

Ongoing Issues: Widening and Deepening

Although they are analytically distinct, these two questions are in fact closely related, because they suggest different directions for channeling the EU's primary energies. The wideners believe that the EU (and the rest of the world) is best served by extending membership, drawing as many of the formerly contentious states and regions of Europe under the common banner of the EU as possible and thereby reducing as much as possible the prospect of renewed conflict in Europe. In addition, many wideners have seen widening as an *alternative* to creating deeper institutional bonds that restrict national sovereignty and, for some, sacrifice aspects of national identity. As Rachman puts it, "the wideners believed that the larger the EU was, the more diverse it would become, and the more difficult it would be to achieve the deepeners' goal of a united Europe." Deepeners, on the other hand, see a more inextricably bound Europe as the best way to insure prosperity, to insulate and protect Europe from outside influence (especially from the United States), and, in some cases, as a way to slow spreading membership to states that are historically unlike those of the core EU and who may serve as an economic and political drag on the community.

The process of increasing the membership of the EU has occurred through a series of what the organization calls rounds. To date, there have been five identified rounds of membership accretion, taking the organization from its core of six members to its current complement of 27. This membership process is summarized in Table 10.1:

TABLE 10.1

Membership Growth in the EU

Round 1 1957	Round 2 1973	Round 3 1981	Round 4 1995	Round 5 2004	Round 5 2007
Belgium	Denmark	Greece	Austria	Cyprus	Bulgaria
France	Ireland	1986	Finland	Czech Republic	Romania
Germany	United Kingdom	Spain	Sweden	Estonia	
Italy		Portugal		Hungary	
Luxembourg				Latvia	
Netherlands				Lithuania	
				Malta	
				Poland	
				Slovakia	
				Slovenia	
6	3	3	3	10	2

The table requires a little explanation. Rounds 1, 2, and 4 consisted of single actions on membership in a single year (1957, 1973, and 1995). The other two rounds consisted of actions in more than one year. Thus, the first accession of Round 3 was Greece in 1981, followed by the addition of Portugal and Spain five years later. Round 5 also has consisted of actions in two different years, with ten states admitted in 2004 and two in 2007.

The pattern of membership growth reflects the debate about who should be members of the organization. Through the first two rounds, all the countries were essentially similar: market democracies of relatively long standing, western in their political and security orientations, with vibrant, similar levels of economic development (Ireland at the time was a partial exception). Thus, there was little economic or political controversy or much need for adjustment when adding the three new members in 1973.

Round 3 introduced more explicitly the question of who should be allowed into the union. Greece had a long tradition of political democracy that had been interrupted by authoritarian interludes, and it was not as developed as the other members, meaning there would have to be a development effort by the existing members to bring the Greeks up to the economic standards of the rest. Portugal and Spain represented this same problem even more starkly, since both had just begun the process of movement toward full political democracy. As a result, their membership applications were delayed.

The introduction of new kinds of states and the end of the Cold War caused the EU to formalize what it believed to be the bases for new membership. In 1993, the union adopted the so-called Copenhagen criteria (so named because they were agreed to in the Danish capital). There were four criteria established that are interesting, because it is neither clear how strictly they have been applied since adoption nor how they will be applied in the future. The four criteria for a new member are as follows:

1. It must be a stable democracy.
2. It must demonstrate respect for human rights and the rule of law.
3. It must possess a functioning, market economy.
4. It must be willing to accept all membership obligations.

The first accession under these rules occurred in 1995 and was relatively straightforward. The three new members (Austria, Finland, and Sweden) had all been, by virtue of history and geography, Cold War neutrals who, had they joined earlier, might have caused Cold War consternation because of their proximity to the Soviet Union.

The fifth round is in some ways the most interesting and most indicative of the problems the EU will face in the future. A total of 12 states have been added over two accessions in 2004 and 2007. Most are formerly communist states that were either members of the old Warsaw Pact (the Czech Republic, Hungary, Poland, and Slovakia in the first accession, Bulgaria and Romania in the second), former Soviet republics (Estonia, Latvia, and Lithuania) or parts of Yugoslavia (Slovenia), or Mediterranean island countries (Cyprus and Malta). None unambiguously meet the criterion of long-standing political democracies, and most have economies far less vibrant than the older, more traditional members. In most cases, their accession is difficult to justify in purely economic terms, suggesting that more political, even geopolitical, considerations have become more prominent in the membership process.

Not all states of Europe are members. Two states, Norway and Switzerland, have declined the invitation to join. Switzerland's reasons include its long tradition of neutrality (the Swiss have not been combatants in a foreign war since 1515) and the possibility that membership in the organization would subject the Swiss banking system to international regulation, thus undermining its unique and sometimes controversial place in the world. Norway voted down membership in 1994 because of the fear that its national identity would be compromised (Norway is a relatively young European state, having broken away from the Kingdom of Sweden in 1905), and many Norwegians were unwilling to forfeit their hard-won national independence. Three other countries have candidate status for membership: Croatia, Macedonia, and Turkey. In the past, all states who have been candidates have become full members; the application of Turkey has, however, been controversial for some time. In addition, a number of former republics of the Soviet Union (notably Ukraine) and western Balkans states (former parts of Yugoslavia—Serbia, Bosnia and Herzegovina, and Montenegro, for instance) are still in the queue for membership consideration.

The worldwide economic crisis that engulfed the global economy in 2008 did not spare the countries of the EU, and one impact has been to raise questions about the continuing pace and extent of membership expansion. As Cohen explains, because of the economic downturn, "EU elites and publics have been forced to revisit whether they can afford the costs of both EU enlargement and a more centralized and activist union." Still, the possibility of membership in EU remains, in Moravcsik's words, "the most powerful policy instrument Europe possesses" in its dealings with the region, and it is highly unlikely it will abandon it.

Further Integration

Although hardly anyone within the EU area opposes the economic impacts of the economic union, the political implications of increasing levels of integration do raise opposition. The problem is straightforward: the more deeply the economies of the members of the union become intertwined, the greater the need for common political decision-making bodies to make political decisions on economic issues. Policies regarding common monetary policy may be economic in content, but they are political decisions derived through political processes. For a common policy to be arrived at and enforced in the most efficient and effective possible way, the political body that makes that decision must be coequal in authority to the physical area for which it is making policy. A union-wide set of policies thus requires a union-wide political set of institutions with union-wide authority. Since policies made by such a body would override, even replace, the same kinds of decisions made by national political bodies, the result is a loss of national political power. That means, in turn, the loss of sovereign political control by the member states to the union. For those whose primary allegiance is to the state, the trade-off of political power for economic advantage becomes an increasingly more questionable proposition.

This is not a new problem for the European integration movement. The British, for instance, opted out of participation in the process until 1973, when economic considerations seemed to overcome political objections. But these concerns have made the British supporters of widening rather than deepening since 1973 because widening slowed deepening (the Tony Blair Labor Government was a partial exception). Even France, one of economic integration's firmest supporters, bridles when movement seems to be providing a perceived threat to French sovereignty and thus French nationalism.

Tension between political and economic consequences has permeated the history of European economic integration since the beginning. Creating a more positive economic condition than was otherwise possible was one of the not-so-hidden parts of the agenda when ECSC was formed, because many of its supporters hoped the economic union would be, in effect, a Trojan horse for full political integration—a United States of Europe or some similar construct. Europeans have been consistently ambivalent on the subject: they wholeheartedly embrace the economic union for its economic benefits, but they are far more conflicted about extending the union to the political level.

The process of political unification of the economic union began in 1967, when the European Community was created. At the political level, the members in that year created the political infrastructure for further integration. To that end, four political institutions were formed: the European Commission, a kind of executive bureaucracy to shape and implement community-wide decisions; a Council of Ministers, composed of the heads of government or their representatives with the power to make executive branch decisions subject to national veto; a European Parliament, popularly elected but with limited power and authority; and a European Court of Justice, a body to adjudicate legal issues but, unlike the U.S. Supreme Court, with no authority to interpret statutes.

The European Community structure was a tentative step toward political union, and it has created the institutional framework for disagreement among the members ever since. In the original 1967 format, the EC firmly left power with the member states. The key institution was the Council of Ministers, which operated through a weighted veto system designed to ensure that the EC could not act in ways that were opposed by major members, thereby possibly threatening national sovereignty. The Parliament, on the other hand, was the most "European" of the institutions in its composition and orientation, and it had only advisory power. For those who wish to see greater political integration, strengthening the Parliament at the expense of the Council has always been the goal; for those who prefer to protect the national sovereignty of the members, the opposite has been the case.

The creation of the economic union through the Treaty of Maastricht, including the adoption of the *euro* as the common currency, brought this issue to a head of sorts, because the economic union required a political body to make union-wide monetary policy and the empowerment of the European bureaucracy (effectively the commission) to carry it out. While the members recognized the economic benefits of monetary and currency standardization for the economic vitality of the EU, some members also saw dire political consequences in the move. As a result, both the Netherlands and the United Kingdom among pre-Round 5 members have refused to accept the *euro* as their currency.

The debate about political integration was basically sidetracked by the end of the Cold War and the flood of new member accessions that accompanied it as first the former neutrals and then the formerly communist states clamored at the gate for admission. With the accession of the first, largest group of Round 5 states in 2004, however, a movement emerged to draft a new EU Constitution to clarify and make official the movement toward greater political union. This movement could not reach consensus and was restarted in 2007, which produced the so-called Lisbon Reform Treaty. To be implemented, that treaty required the unanimous consent of all members, and in 2008, Ireland rejected the treaty after the Irish government submitted it to a national referendum. The Lisbon Reform Treaty (more technically the Treaty on the Functioning of the European Union or TFEU) is a constitutional advancement of the Rome Treaty and 1992 Maastricht Treaty. Its effects are to strengthen the powers of EU institutions without directly undercutting national sovereignty. Thus, for instance, it modifies voting rules in the Council of Ministers to a qualified majority on some matters, mandates a stronger European Parliament, and creates the position of "President of the European Council." The treaty did, however, require universal approval of the 27 members. This unanimity was achieved in 2009, after Ireland reversed its rejection and the Czech Republic became the 27th and final member to ratify on November 3, 2009. The TFEU took effect on December 1, 2009.

The EU remains in a kind of nether region politically. It possesses some of the characteristics of a political state. As the *Factbook* points out in its rationale for including the EU in its listing of countries of the world, it has a flag, an anthem, a founding date as an entity, and its own currency. At the same time, it lacks the more important elements of power and legitimacy to make fundamental political decisions affecting the union and its citizens. Moreover, very few people living in the union have quit thinking of themselves as Germans, Frenchmen, Italians, and the like. The economic union remains a partial political union.

Pulling the Threads Together: The Future

At age 50, the EU is, in Shepherd's terms, "a European Union that has stalled at a crossroads." Part of the reason is a backlash from the rapid growth that the organization has undergone since the end of the Cold War. O'Brien describes the change: "We are in the Indian summer of European Union enlargement. European populations have grown tired of grand European projects." The French and Dutch both voted against full implementation of the union through a new constitution in 2005, although they subsequently accepted the TFEU. In the French case, the problem is wrapped in questions of *France's* place in the world: Miguet describes the French attitude as "a fear of what appears foreign: the Polish plumber (a symbol of cheap foreign labor), Turkey's proposed accession to the EU, and outsourcing by French firms." These fears have translated into growing opposition to more growth in EU membership.

The addition of Bulgaria and Romania is part of the problem. The accession of these two countries harks back to the 1980s, when there was great debate about admitting Spain and Portugal because they were poorer than the existing membership and with a very thin democratic tradition. The situation is analogous for Bulgaria and Romania, neither of which obviously or overwhelmingly meets the Copenhagen criteria for membership. The gross national product per capita for Romania is 35 percent below the EU average, and Bulgaria is 32 percent below the norm. Both countries are notoriously corrupt, and there is a fear that their corruption will infect the rest of the union.

New membership stalled for a decade after Spain and Portugal joined, and it took the end of the Cold War and a dramatic change in the political map of Europe to create a new surge in membership demand and response. New members indeed still are lined up to join, but there is no certainty that the organization is willing to embrace them in the short run.

There are basically two categories of states that have not yet joined the EU. One is composed of the western Balkan countries that are by-products, directly or indirectly, of the breakup of Yugoslavia. Two of these, Croatia and Macedonia (technically the Former Yugoslav Republic of Macedonia) are candidate members, as already noted, but others are still "potential candidates," including Bosnia and Herzegovina, Montenegro, and Serbia. All of these countries share common characteristics with Bulgaria and Romania that make skeptics wonder about their addition. The second group consists of former states of the Soviet Union. The Baltic countries (Estonia, Latvia, and Lithuania) were admitted in 2004, but these were the most westernized former republics of the Soviet Union, conquered by the Soviets in 1940, and never willing members of the USSR. The others that will likely seek admission are headed by Ukraine, but also include places like Belarus and Moldova. In addition to questionable qualifications under the Copenhagen criteria (which have blocked their applications to this point), the proximity of those countries to Russia and Russian reaction to possible adversaries on its borders adds to the reluctance to invite them to join.

The controversy surrounding these countries pales in comparison to the application of the "800-pound gorilla" in the queue and the subject of by far the most controversy—Turkey. Turkey has actively sought membership at least since it witnessed the inclusion of its historical rival, Greece, in 1981. Their desires have been thwarted on a number of grounds included in the Copenhagen criteria. Turkey's commitment to "stable democracy" has been suspect, as has the competitiveness of its economy. Moreover, the campaign of suppression of its Kurdish minority in eastern Turkey has raised questions about its adherence and commitment to human rights and the rule of law.

The Turkish case is particularly controversial for at least two other reasons. One is that it puts the EU at odds with the United States, which has been and remains a staunch supporter of Turkish membership. The United States has been a consistent supporter of the widening option, because it brings past opponents and potential future problem states (like those of Eastern Europe) into the western umbrella with minimum cost for the United States. Because Turkey is the key NATO member on NATO's Middle Eastern-oriented flank, the United States is particularly desirous of Turkey's admission to the EU. Taspinar states the basis of the U.S. case: "a stable, Western-oriented Turkey on a clear path toward EU membership would serve as a growing market for Western goods, a contributor of labor that Europe desperately needs, a democratic example for the rest of the Muslim world, a stabilizing influence in Iraq, a valuable actor in Afghanistan, and a critical ally in fighting global terrorism." It should be noted that at least four of these six advantages have essentially nothing to do with Turkey's positive impact on the EU but are benefits to the American geopolitical presence in the Middle East, a perspective that many EU members do not share.

The EU perspective is understandably different and centers on the impact that Turkey would have on the structure and dynamics of the EU. That perspective is decidedly more ambivalent and tends to rest on two grounds. One of these sources of ambivalence, the sheer size and thus potential impact of Turkey, is openly stated; the other, that Turkey is a relatively poor Muslim state, is less openly discussed.

If Turkey becomes a member of the EU, it will be the second largest and most populous country in the union, and one whose "population is almost as large as all of the newcomers put together," as Gordon and Taspinar put it. That fact puts some perspective on the impact of adding Turkey to the union: it is a qualitatively different prospect than the accession of small states in the western Balkans. Bulgaria and Romania may be poor, and their poverty may result in the immigration of many of their citizens to other EU countries as part of the principle of free movement of peoples, but that movement would not be on the scale that potential Turkish immigration might create.

This concern is made more poignant by the fact that Turkey is also Muslim, and as Rachman contends, "European skepticism about welcoming a relatively underdeveloped country, which would immediately become the second-largest member of the EU . . . is unlikely to change in the short run." This physical impact is heightened by the prospect of "70 million Muslims (the population of Turkey) looking for jobs in Europe," according to Taspinar. This problem is apparent in France, where the "Polish plumber" phenomenon certainly applies to a Turkish worker influx, and also to Germany, where James and Szabo note, "Germany's enlargement fatigue results in part from a fear of immigration and the cheap labor it brings." The German fear is particularly great because the foreign component of Germany's population currently stands at 9 percent, a figure higher than that in the United States. This concern combines the immigration and Muslim aspects of the problem, because, as Finan points out, Muslims "are the fastest growing group in the EU."

The EU decided on October 3, 2005, to launch accession talks that have resulted in Turkey being added to the candidate member list. It was an important move because, as Taspinar points out, "No country that has begun accession talks has failed to complete them." Turkey is the only wholly Muslim country to get this far in the process of accession; were the EU somehow to deny their application at this point, it would create a precedent the basis of which would be so obviously anti-Muslim as to be undeniable.

CONCLUSION

The EU is by far the most comprehensive, successful experiment in economic integration in the contemporary world. It has been a far more ambitious effort than any other attempt to transcend national boundaries economically, and it has moved much further along than other proposals and actions, none of which has moved past the initial stage of forming free trading areas. The EU has marched through free trade status to customs union, to single market, and now to full economic union with strong political implications. It has done this on a regional basis among countries that share a common civilization and were in common economic straits after World War II. Its uniqueness reflects partly the circumstances in which it was born and in which it has subsequently strived. Whether the lessons of the EU have value for future like endeavors aimed at economic integration must be measured by comparing the experiential universe in which the EU was born and has flourished with the parallel circumstances of other places and times.

What kind of future does the EU have? It can develop in two directions—economically or politically—but will it do both, or either? The economic dimension involves the completion of the economic union process, which means the inclusion of all members within the currency union and the inclusion of all new members into all aspects of the union. Since a number of the members admitted under Round 5 (to say nothing of candidate members and other aspirants) have economies that are substantially less developed than the pre-expansion core of western European states, pulling off the latter requirement will be no small feat. If completing this dimension is the most important business the EU sees for itself, the argument of the deepeners would seem to be made stronger, a position that would be particularly troublesome in the EU's relations with its most important aspirant for membership, Turkey. At the same time, deepening of the union also slows down the process of adding new members from the former Soviet Union and delays indefinitely the major question that looms on the more or less distant horizon, which is whether or what role Russia may have in the future EU.

A political perspective leads to different problems. Essentially, there are two political questions. The first is the political evolution of the EU itself: will the EU move toward becoming a full political union? Progress has floundered on this question, and reaction to the Reform Treaty suggests this concern has not disappeared. In the past, countries that very much favored and enjoyed the benefits of further integration became very skittish when the political consequences of moving forward had potentially erosive effects on national identity and prerogatives.

Finally, there is the political question of the EU's place in world affairs. The primary political role initially envisaged for the economic integration project was the stabilization of western economies to make them more resistant to communism and a more secure barrier against Soviet expansion. This political stabilizing role expanded after the end of the Cold War to incorporating the formerly communist states into the greater peace and prosperity of Europe. That process has made significant progress through Rounds 4 and 5 of membership expansion, but the process is not yet complete. Among others, the United States has been a primary champion of widening, the process by which that political goal can be achieved. Whether the wideners or the deepeners will prevail remains the significant unknown variable for the future of the EU.

A final question is whether the EU process is idiosyncratic because of the unique conditions of Europe in which it has occurred or whether the process can be extended toward other parts of the world. One way to think of the EU is as the culmination of globalization, if on a regional rather than universal scale. None of the rest of the world has achieved or is in the active pursuit of levels of association and integration even vaguely approximating that of the EU. It would take geopolitical change of massive proportions before the conditions might even conceivably be ripe for a parallel development elsewhere.

STUDY/DISCUSSION QUESTIONS

1. On what bases do economic integration schemes differ? Discuss the differences. Where does the EU fit in this scheme?
2. What are the forms of economic integration? How does each stage build on the others? How does the balance between economic and political aspects change in various steps in the process? Describe the evolution of the EU in these terms.
3. How has the birth and evolution of the EU been influenced by both economic and political motives? Elaborate.
4. Discuss the process by which the EU came into existence and the steps in its development, including the steps and dynamics of its membership growth.
5. What are "widening" and "deepening?" Apply this distinction to the evolution of the EU.
6. What are the next steps in European integration? What are the primary barriers to achieving those objectives? Explain.
7. How does the issue of new membership, and especially the membership of Turkey, define the current status of discussions within the EU?
8. Is the EU a model for future economic integration schemes around the world? Why or why not?

READING/RESEARCH MATERIAL

Alesino, Alberto and Francesca Giavazzi. *The Future of Europe: Reform or Decline.* Cambridge, MA: MIT Press, 2006.
Algieri, Franco. "A Weakened EU's Prospects of Global Leadership." *Washington Quarterly* 30, 3 (Winter 2006–2007), 106–115.

Bache, Ian and Stephen George. *Politics in the European Union.* 2nd ed. Oxford, UK: Oxford University Press, 2006.

Cohen, Lenard J. "Detours on the Balkan Road to EU Integration." *Current History* 108, 716 (March 2009), 124–130.

Dinen, Desmond. *An Ever Closer Union: An Introduction to European Integration.* 3rd ed. Boulder, CO: Lynne Rienner Publishers, 2006.

Finan, William W. Jr. "Wrestling with Euro-Islam." *Current History* 106, 698 (March 2007), 140–142.

Gordon, Philip and Omer Taspinar. "Turkey on the Brink." *Washington Quarterly* 29, 3 (Summer 2005), 57–70.

Gros, Daniel. "The Dogs That Didn't Bark: The EU and the Financial Crisis." *Current History* 108, 716 (March 2009), 105–109.

Hay, Colin and Hakan Karlsson. *Changing Atlantic Security Relations: Do the U.S., EU, and Russia Form a Strategic Triangle?* New York: Routledge, 2006.

James, Jackson and Stephen Szabo. "Angela Merkel's Germany." *Current History* 106, 698 (March 2007), 106–111.

Kauppi, Niilo. *Democracy, Social Resources, and Political Power in the European Union.* Manchester, UK: Manchester University Press, 2005.

McCormick, John. *Understanding the European Union: A Concise Introduction.* New York: Palgrave Macmillan, 2002.

Miguet, Arnauld. "France's Election-Year Disquiet." *Current History* 106, 698 (March 2007), 112–116.

Moravcsik, Andrew. "Europe, the Second Superpower." *Current History* 109, 725 (March 2010), 91–98.

O'Brien, James C. "Brussels: Next Capital of the Balkans?" *Washington Quarterly* 29, 3 (Summer 2006), 71–88.

"Q&A: The Lisbon Treaty." *BBC News* (online), February 5, 2010.

Rachman, Gideon. "The Death of Enlargement." *Washington Quarterly* 29, 3 (Summer 2006), 51–65.

Shepherd, Robin. "Romania, Bulgaria, and the EU's Future." *Current History* 106, 698 (March 2007), 117–122.

Taspinar, Omer. "Turkey's Fading Dream of Europe." *Current History* 106, 698 (March 2007), 123–129.

Watts, Duncan. *The European Union.* Edinburgh: Edinburgh University Press, 2008.

Wood, David M and Birol A. Yesilada. *The Emerging European Union.* New York: Longman, 2004.

Wood, Steve and Wolfgang Quaisser. *The New European Union: Confronting the Challenges of Integration.* Boulder, CO: Lynne Rienner Publishers, 2007.

WEB SITES

The official EU Web site is at http://ec.europa.eu

Rising Powers: China and India

PRÉCIS

One of the ways in which the international system has changed historically is through the emergence of new major powers, called "rising powers." China and India are poised and apparently ready to assume that role in the contemporary world. China was a consequential country during the Cold War, but its significance increased with the demise of the Soviet Union and its adoption of different policies, especially in the economic realm, that have raised its status among world powers. India's entrance as a rising power is more recent, dating essentially to the 1990s. World politics is never static, and one major source of its dynamism is the relative prominence that different states have in the world order. At any point in time, one or more states will possess major prominence and be viewed as the dominant powers—superpowers in twentieth-century parlance—while other powers decline as major influences and yet other countries rise in importance and, in some cases, challenge the dominance of major powers. It is the impact of these rising powers that forms the concern of this chapter.

There is certainly nothing that is new or sinister about the rising state phenomenon. If one looks back a century to the eve of World War I, the major powers were the countries of the old European Balance of Power (Britain, France, Germany/Prussia, Russia, and the Austro-Hungarian Empire), and the major rising power was the United States. Prodded by World War II, the traditional powers declined, and from the rubble, the United States and the Soviet Union rose to primary status, a position both occupied until the Soviet Union imploded in 1991 and which the United States continues to maintain.

The twenty-first century has been witness to the significant rise of two states, China and India. The world's two most populous states and Asian neighbors and rivals, their ascent has been differential. China arose first, beginning its ascent in the late 1970s as both an economic and political rival to the existing great powers, and its international challenge remains controversial. India's claim to rising power status, on the other hand, is more recent—essentially since 2000—and it has been almost exclusively economic in content, thus making it appear less threatening and controversial. Before describing and comparing the rise of the two countries, however, it is first necessary to describe the rising power concept as the framework for comparison.

RISING POWERS

One of the most certain things one can say about the dominant powers of any period of international history is that eventually their dominance will be eclipsed by the emergence of some different country or countries. This situation is not unusual. While the United States has been *a* dominant power since World War II and *the* dominant power since the end of the Cold War, this observation is undoubtedly true for the United States as well.

What does it mean to be a "rising power"? In the most general sense, a rising power refers to a country that, by virtue of increased military, economic, or other power, is or has the potential to play a more prominent role in the international system than it has heretofore played. As noted, the United States was such a rising power in the late nineteenth and early twentieth centuries, as was the Soviet Union during the middle of the twentieth century.

The impact of rising powers is important. At the level of the international system, rising powers change the relative power balance between the major powers, with ripple effects throughout the system, often in ways that are controversial and difficult to predict. Will, for instance, a rising China eventually challenge American international predominance and lead to a transformation from an essentially unipolar to a bipolar or multipolar balance? Would such a transformation be stabilizing or destabilizing? What is the impact of the Indian challenge in areas like technological and scientific leadership on American world leadership?

The degree and extent to which rising powers challenge the given order depends to a great degree on the areas in which the rising power seeks to influence the existing order and establish its own place. Traditionally, for instance, world power comparisons have largely been at least implicitly military in content. "Power" and "military power" were used more or less synonymously, and the most certain way for a rising power to assert a challenge to the existing order was by building and flexing its military muscle.

It is not clear that power status is so unidimensional in a globalized world. Economic capability has increasingly become a benchmark of global importance, and it is the primary claim both China and India have about rising power status. China, of course, is also a military power whose military might requires some concern, while India's military prowess is almost exclusively devoted to insuring its place on the Asian Subcontinent. As powers with global aspirations, however, the primary claim of both states is largely concentrated in the economic realm.

The impact of rising states creates foreign policy questions for countries affected by the rising power. The basic question is whether the impact will help or hinder the realization of interests of the affected power. Will the rising power be a looming threat to those interests or a global partner assisting in their accomplishment? Or will it be both? Like the systemic impacts, these changes are never entirely clear in advance, leading to speculation and disagreement. Europe worried about the impact of an industrially gigantic United States, and the United States worried about the impact of a militarily powerful Soviet Union. The United States ended up a strategic partner of Europe, and the Soviets emerged primarily as a threat. Where do China and India fit?

The world's oldest continuous civilization, with a history rich in both creativity and tragedy, China stood largely outside the quantum leaps in wealth and power made possible by Western-centered advances in modern science, technology, and industrialization since the eighteenth century. From the mid-nineteenth to the mid-twentieth centuries China endured its "century of humiliation," as the once grand but then defenseless country fell under the domination and exploitation of the West and of newly industrialized Japan.

India has suffered through a similar period of repression. India is also one of the world's oldest civilizations, yet it fell under colonial domination for over two centuries of British rule, and it has spent much of the period since it regained independence in 1948 trying to establish an identity in the modern world to match its history—a process that is ongoing.

China already possesses some of the trappings of superpower status: It has nuclear weapons and is one of the five permanent members of the United Nations Security Council. If its economy continues the robust growth of the past two decades, then China may truly arrive as a state capable of wielding power on a large scale. China's growth raises two questions about its future growth: Will China present a threat to the emerging international order, or will it become another major, but orthodox, member of the international system? In a similar vein, will the Indian challenge, now largely concentrated in technological innovation, expand to create a broader place for India in the international order and thus potentially a greater source of challenge?

CHINA AND INDIA AS RISING POWERS

Although rising powers challenge the given order, the changes they make are not always threatening or profound. China and India are the latest challengers to an American-dominated international order, but one should not overstate the current nature or extent of that challenge. Rather, the challenge must be put in context.

The comparisons are instructive. China, India, and the United States are the three most populous countries in the world, although there is a large gap between the two Asian giants (collectively, over a third of world population) and the United States (about 5 percent of the global total). In this case, a large population is not necessarily an indication of strength. The sheer size of both challengers' populations dilutes greatly the per capita distribution of national wealth and creates a huge underclass whose needs are not currently but must eventually be served. This group is estimated at as many as 700 million poor

Chinese living in the rural areas of China. India has a long history of ignoring the plight of its large, mostly rural peasantry and has not seriously addressed the problem as part of its growth strategy.

The most frequently cited sources of Chinese and Indian challenge are, of course, in the economic realm. Here as well, some perspective is necessary. Chinese economic modernization is longer-standing than India's and is demonstrated by comparing gross domestic products (GDP) and GDP per capita, where China's totals are more than double their Indian equivalents. The Chinese economy is approaching the size of that of the United States, although a comparison of preslump 2007 and postslump 2009 shows the American economy grew slightly, whereas that of China and India contracted. The burden of population, however, sharply differentiates both challengers from the United States and will dampen the challenge once those disparities are seriously addressed. The most invidious comparison is in growth rates, although even that is partially moderated by lower Asian baselines.

The other dimension is military spending. American totals, it should be noted, do not come close to reflecting spending on Iraq and Afghanistan in defense totals, which would widen the gap. Although the Chinese "threat" is sometimes raised, spending levels (which are admittedly controversial) do not reinforce this notion. The challenge of China and India is not, at least for now, primarily military. The more precise nature of the challenge each poses can be seen by looking at each country.

China

China endured a "century of humiliation" during the nineteenth and early twentieth centuries that reduced it to a semicolony. The situation resulted from the loss of creativity; corruption and resistance to reform within the imperial court; the obsolescence of its emperor-based political system that relied on a corps of bureaucrats chosen for their mastery of Confucian classics rather than their command of modern ideas; and the numerous unequal treaties imposed on it by foreign powers since its defeat in the Opium War with Great Britain in the 1840s. Westerners roamed throughout China. Merchants, adventurers, diplomats, and missionaries all enjoyed special privileges placing them beyond Chinese authority, a situation that was humiliating to all Chinese.

Layered atop all of China's other discontents were a split between two centers of political and military power, each of which was determined to unify, govern, and strengthen China. The Guomindang—or Nationalist—forces led by Chiang Kai-shek were generally supported by the United States. Beginning in the 1920s, an initially small upstart group of communists led by Mao Zedong articulated its own vision of mobilizing mass support to overthrow China's antiquated social order and restoring unity to the country.

As the two forces began their titanic struggle in earnest, China endured yet another devastating blow, this time from Japan's exceptionally brutal aggression, first in its invasion of Manchuria in 1931 and then throughout its bloody drive through China proper from 1937 to 1945. The defeat of Japanese forces by the United States in 1945 renewed the violent conclusive phase of the internal battle to control China between Chiang Kai-shek's Nationalist forces and Mao Zedong's communist followers. By the autumn of 1949, China's communists emerged victorious and drove Chiang's forces to the island refuge of Taiwan.

In October 1949, Mao could boast to the assembled mass in Beijing's Tiananmen Square that "China has stood up." China was at long last unified under a strong central authority and foreign intervention in its internal affairs would no longer be tolerated. Beyond unification and the reclamation of China's sovereignty, it was Mao's abiding passion to create within China a radical, egalitarian society. In so doing, China remained largely outside the international community, and terribly repressive within, with its people mired in poverty throughout his rule from 1949 to 1976, when Mao died.

Mao's death created a scramble for power among China's ruling elites. Within a year, Deng Xiaoping had effectively consolidated governing authority within his own hands. Purged three times during Mao's reign and standing less than 5 feet tall, Deng appeared at first glance a physically unlikely ruler of the world's most populous state. Deng soon implemented his famous "Four Modernizations" campaign. Undaunted by the giant shadow cast by Mao, Deng announced an audacious series of reforms designed to advance China beyond the revolutionary dogma of Maoism and to create instead a stronger, more modern country by loosening the reins of state authority; more fully embracing economic globalization in search of foreign markets, technology, and investment; and accepting income differentials in a society that had so recently been singularly animated by radical egalitarianism.

The Four Modernizations—agriculture, science and technology, industry, and military—began in the countryside, home to three-fourths of all Chinese. Gradually, socialist-style communal farming was phased out, and explicitly, peasants were now allowed to lease land individually from the state. Without quite admitting it, Deng's regime injected market—that is, *capitalist*—incentives by allowing peasants whose production surpassed their obligatory quotas to the state at fixed prices to sell any surplus that they could produce for as much money as they could get for it. A system of rural markets and distribution systems sprang up to buy farm produce and sell it to independent urban vendors. As longer land leases gave peasants new incentives to undertake capital improvements, food production soared. With it, rural incomes rose sharply, with the most successful peasant families reaping the greatest rewards.

The older norm of imposed egalitarianism was quietly shelved. What the regime today calls "Socialism with Chinese Characteristics" took its place. With the passage of time this slogan has simply become a euphemism for capitalism with state supervision, but with less direct central control. Gradually, the limited market system begun in the countryside spread to the cities. Individuals were allowed to open restaurants, shops, and factories. Workers could be hired and fired, something that had been utterly unthinkable under Mao's "people's" regime. The wheels of a more market-driven economy were thus set into motion.

The second and third modernizations—industry plus science and technology—inherently required China's leaders to turn outward to the most advanced industrial countries for investment capital, markets for Chinese goods, scientific know-how, and the most modern production technology and management skills. Four Special Economic Zones (SEZs) were established in southeastern China in which foreign corporations were allowed to form joint ventures with Chinese partners and thus transfer their leading-edge technological, manufacturing process, and managerial expertise to initially quite limited enclaves of capitalist experimentation.

As local laboratories of industrial modernity, the SEZs were intended to, among other things, create a new leadership cohort of technologically sophisticated managers whose expertise, it was hoped, would in time fan out from the SEZs themselves and help jump-start China's obsolescent and inefficient state-owned enterprises (SOEs). During Mao's era, "redness"—that is, communist ideological purity—was more highly prized than substantive expertise in filling leadership ranks. But Deng was much more of a pragmatist. In his famous aphorism, he said, "It doesn't matter if a cat is white or black, as long as it catches mice." Results, then, would be the new measure of the country's rising managers and leaders. The Deng program provided the launching pad for China's ascent into the realm of world powers, including the fourth modernization, military power. How far will it ascend? How will China use its new status?

Economic Growth, but Questions. China's economic results have been the most dramatic. Riding a boom powered by foreign capital inflows and an aggressive export strategy, China's economy grew at an average annual rate of around 10 percent from the 1980s into the 2000s, a figure reflected in Table 11.1. Not all Chinese specialists accept these astounding government-promulgated growth statistics at face value. Regardless of the figures one accepts, there is no denying the fact that China's economy has grown dramatically during the past quarter century. It is today the world's third-largest economy, ranking only behind the United States and Japan. In critical consumer sectors such as clothing, shoes, toys, and other low-technology products, China dominates world markets. As dramatic evidence of this rise, China became the world's leading producer of manufactured goods in 2008 with 17 percent of world production compared to 16 percent for the United States.

China's recent leaders—Deng Xiaoping and Jiang Zemin to Hu Jintao—have realized that for their country to develop and modernize economically, they would have to thoroughly repudiate Mao's policies of economic self-sufficiency and instead fully embrace economic globalization. The international trend toward reducing barriers to the free movement of goods and capital has very much worked to China's advantage. In recognition of this fact, China made a major initiative to gain membership in the World Trade Organization (WTO), a goal it achieved late in 2000. As a precursor to its accession to the WTO, China negotiated a complex commercial agreement with the United States that contains a number of key concessions on China's part. Especially

TABLE 11.1

Comparison of the United States and Its Challengers on Three Dimensions: Population, Economic Vitality, and Levels of Military Spending

		United States	China	India
Population	2008*	3012 mil.	1.321 bil.	1.129 bil.
	2010**	307.2 mil.	1.338 bil.	1.166 bil.
GDP	2008	$13.1 tril.	$10.2 tril.	$4.2 tril.
	2010	$14.3 tril.	$8.0 tril.	$3.3 tril.
GDP/Capita	2008	$44,000	$7,760	$3,800
	2010	$46,900	$6,000	$2,900
GDP Growth Rate	2008	3.2%	10.7%	9.2%
	2010	1.1%	9.0%	7.4%
Military Spending	2008	$539.6 bil.	$35.3 bil.	$22.3 bil.
	2010	$552.6 bil.	$46.2 bil.	$28.5 bil.

*As of September 2007
**As of October 2009
Source: 2008 and 2010 World Almanac and Book of Facts. New York: World Almanac Books, 2008, 2010.

notable among them are market-opening measures that place many of its state-owned industries at a competitive disadvantage, thus risking a substantial loss of jobs for Chinese workers. This process has produced both WTO membership and permanent trade relations for China with the United States, but at the cost of forcing China to accept international norms that tie the country more fully to the international community and limit its ability to act outside systemic rules.

China's dramatic economic ascent is also conditioned by a litany of domestic woes that, taken together, raise the alarming possibility of widespread unrest. Its internal preoccupations include a mounting political crisis of regime legitimacy in what Minxin Pei describes as the "Chinese neo-Leninist state," severe environmental degradation, immense population pressures, official corruption, a growing gap in urban versus rural incomes, high unemployment, a steady loss of arable land, a diminished social safety net for the poor and displaced, scarcity of resources like water and petroleum, and secessionist movements in Tibet and in the westernmost province of Zinjiang. Gilboy and Read concur, stating "Beijing faces serious challenges in maintaining sustainable growth and social stability, eliminating corruption, and improving government effectiveness in a one-party system."

China's rise as an economic power is thus paradoxical. China has made great strides as an industrial power, but it has done so within the confines of a political and social system that places serious constraints on the ability of China to expand, especially into a world power, if that is its desire. Thus, individually and collectively, what do these trends and problems mean, and how do they affect an assessment of China as a rising power?

Assessing China's Economic Rise. Does China's economic and technological rise pose a threat to the world power balance? The sheer potential size of an economy energized by one-fifth of mankind raises concern: If China were to become competitive structurally with the world's most advanced economies, would that size not pose a danger of simply overwhelming the global economy and establishing itself as the "800-pound gorilla" that everyone else would have to treat with care and deference? As an illustration of this possibility, China's announced intent to increase automobile production to up to 15 million vehicles per year to service its domestic market has created palpitations in the petroleum market worldwide, as such a move could greatly increase China's presence in the petroleum-buying market, and increase demand worldwide and drive up energy prices even further.

Opinions vary on this subject, based on differing assessments of the nature of the Chinese economy and the impact on the Chinese political system. Analysts critical of the notion China poses a threat often point to factors in Chinese development that limit the threats China could pose. In a recent *Foreign Affairs* article, for instance, David and Lyric Hughes Hale identify three of what they call the "dragon's ailments." The first is demographic and points to the extremely uneven character of Chinese development. There are, they point out, "great disparities between the integrated, largely urban coastal areas in the eastern part of the country and the fragmented, rural economies in the western part." In addition, there is a substantial unemployment problem, especially in western China, that results in considerable migration to the industrialized areas. China also faces the need "to find a way to support its rapidly aging population," a dilemma shared by many industrialized countries.

That is not all. Much of the prosperity associated with the SEZs is the result of foreign collaboration and investment that limit future independence for the Chinese economy, and thus potentially threatens further development. In the July/August 2004 *Foreign Affairs*, Gilboy accentuates how this attenuates the threat posed by Chinese growth. "First, China's high-tech and industrial exports are dominated by foreign, not Chinese, firms. Second, Chinese industrial firms are deeply dependent on designs, critical components, and manufacturing equipment they import from the United States. . . . Third, Chinese firms are taking few effective steps to absorb the technology they are importing." Huang and Khanna, writing in *Foreign Policy*, agree, pointing out that "[f]ew of these products are made by indigenous Chinese companies. In fact, you would be hard-pressed to find a single homegrown Chinese firm that operates on a global scale and markets its own products abroad. The Chinese economy has taken off, but few local firms have followed." In fact, most of the collaboration is between foreigners and the notoriously inefficient SOEs. Minxin Pei adds that the private sector is no more than 30 percent of the overall Chinese economy.

Most observers also agree that the emergence of a technologically competitive China requires political reform. As Orville Schell argued in the July/August 2004 *Foreign Affairs*, "Whether the PRC will be able to continue straddling the widening divide between the economic system and its anachronistic political system is the most critical question China faces." The situation is ironic, because of the likely effect political reform would have on China's role as a world power. As Gilboy puts it, "The paradox of China's technological and economic power is that China must implement structural political reforms before it can unlock its potential as a global competitor. But if it were to undertake such reforms, it would likely discover even greater common interests with the United States and other industrialized democracies." In this view, China can be antagonistic and not very threatening or competitive, vibrant, and friendly. All this leads Carlson to conclude, "at a fundamental level, China is far from directly challenging the United States."

The result is a mixed message about the Chinese economic challenge. China's economy has clearly expanded to the point of rivaling the economies of the world's major powers in sheer size, and this impact is growing. There are, however, limits to China's current growth. Most of that growth has resulted from manufacturing consumer goods that require little scientific contribution from China, and much of it is based on artificially controlled low labor costs to achieve comparative advantage. The result has been large surpluses from foreign sales that allow further expansion, but it does not add to the vibrancy of China's innovative sector, which lags behind but is critical for long-term economic health. At the same time, the huge Chinese labor pool will eventually have to be addressed in terms of things like human services, and this will produce a significant burden, as suggested earlier.

How China will continue to evolve economically remains the major point of contention. Will China become a "normal" state whose economy and political system gradually become more and more like the rest of the world? Or will China use its growing muscle to challenge the current order? The answers are, of course, speculative. Positively, China has taken a place at the G-20 forum of world economic powers (see Chapter 12), and in 2010 purchased the iconic Swedish carmaker Volvo from the Ford Motor Company. At the same time, the Chinese continue to engage in military modernization and expansion that some observers find troublesome. China's signals are mixed enough to fuel an ongoing debate.

India

The Indian experience stands in some contrast to that of China. Both are very large, populous countries with long histories, but their trajectories toward rising power status are distinct. China began earlier, and its rise has a larger military content. India's is more recent, and apart from its regional rivalry with Pakistan, has less military content. China's rise economically has been tied to its growth as a manufacturer of consumer goods, whereas the Indian education system (at least for some of its citizens) has allowed it to challenge the leaders of the world economy closer to the cutting edge of technology.

Particularly in recent years, India has been portrayed as the "poster child" of globalization, the country where the values of globalization are clearly in place, are spreading, and are bringing with them the benefits that globalization can promise for improvements in the human condition. The explosion of India onto the global scene was, for instance, the inspiration for globalization enthusiast Thomas Friedman to reexamine globalization in his 2005 book, *The World Is Flat*, because it is the Indian entrepreneurship that has provided much of the evidence of how technology generation has spread globally, thereby "flattening" both access to and the ability to produce technology. Fareed Zakaria, in his 2008 best seller, *The Post-American World*, reinforced this positive direction.

Led by its aggressive adoption of the values of globalization and fueled largely by its preeminence in high technology, the statistics of Indian growth are substantial. As *Newsweek* reported in its March 6, 2006 edition, for instance, India has had the world's second largest growth rate over the past 15 years, and that growth continues to expand; figures are reflected in Table 11.1. The result has been an unprecedented growth both of personal income and entrepreneurial activity that has helped enlarge the middle class in India to over 300 million, and this group has the second highest consumption rate in the world, trailing only the United States. Projecting from current trends (always a risky proposition), India's economy will be larger than that of Italy in 10 years and of Great Britain in 15 years. By 2050, the Indian economy could be five times that of Japan. If the details of these projections are overinflated, the fact that India has experienced and is likely to continue to have high continued growth that could make it one of the world's future superpowers is clear.

The question is what has caused India to become such an active and successful partner in globalization? India is such an enormous, diverse, and complicated place that simple explanations do not capture its dynamics. It is, for instance, about one-third the physical size of the United States, but it has a population more than three and a half times the American population. It is enormously ethnically, linguistically, and religiously diverse (there are, for instance, sizable numbers of adherents of all the world's major religions in the country). In addition to English and Hindi, there are 14 additional officially recognized languages in the country. The 300 million estimated members of the Indian middle class (the largest in the world) are matched by at least that number who fall below the world's standard for destitution, surviving on less than $2 a day, although there are efforts underway to reduce that total. Ethnic divisions have resulted in open or smoldering violence in places as diverse as the Tamil lands in the south to Kashmir in the north. The country is also beset by one of the few remaining active Marxist wars of national liberation conducted by a small but persistent Maoist guerrilla movement. All of this diversity occurs within the framework of the world's largest political democracy.

India's growth has been fed by policy reforms reminiscent of the Reagan–Thatcher initiatives of the 1980s. Under the leadership of Indira Gandhi, state control of economic activity had effectively stifled economic growth. When she left office, deregulation and privatization permitted the growth of entrepreneurial activity that is transforming India's place in the world. The situation truly changed in 1991. As Feigenbaum explains, "In 1991, leaders in New Delhi pursued policies of economic liberalization that opened the country to foreign investment and yielded rapid growth." Whether the scale of deregulation–privatization can be kept in balance remains to be seen. The alternative may be many of the same difficulties that were revealed globally in 2007 in the West.

India's entrance into and place in the globalizing economy is largely the result of its prominence in the high-technology sector that helps define globalization's parameters. Many countries have embraced and become part of globalization by becoming essentially consumers and appliers of the growing economic possibilities that globalization provides. India does that, too, but its unique place comes from its position increasingly as both a consumer *and* a producer of technology.

The city of Bangalore has become the symbol of India's evolving place in the globalization system. Often referred to as India's Silicon Valley, it has become synonymous with the country's entrance into the global economy and serves as a gathering spot for the large number of scientists and engineers produced by India's educational system. They come to this modern, cosmopolitan city to engage in the kinds of technological innovation and entrepreneurial activity associated with the San Francisco Bay area and other American concentrations of high technology. Bangalore serves as both technological innovator and consumer, as it is also the location in which much of the highly publicized "outsourcing" of lower-end technology jobs from the United States (e.g., telemarketing, service contractors) is found.

Several factors are often cited about why India has succeeded in entering the globalized economy. One is that India emerged from an economically repressive past that left the country poised for a leap forward in activity once the opportunity arose. As numerous analysts have pointed out, the country had a closed, protectionist economy with scarcely any foreign goods, especially consumer goods, available for public consumption. This was the case because tariffs on imported goods were among the highest in the world and were combined with extremely progressive tax schedules that effectively stifled entrepreneurial activity, and, according to Feigenbaum, barred "foreign investment in many sectors." This was particularly true under Indira Gandhi, who espoused a kind of socialist economic philosophy that "the Indian upper-middle class perceived . . . as a straitjacket." Policies pursued by the government of Rajiv Gandhi further depleted Indian foreign exchange and caused a crisis that resulted in reform. Those reforms opened the country to outside investment and influence and came as a significant reaction to prior overmanagement of the economy. What has become increasingly an Indian economic "miracle" dates to these reforms, although they are hardly complete (India retains relatively high tariffs against certain classes of goods).

Several other influences have helped stimulate the Indian transition. One is that India has a societal structure amenable to economic growth. That structure includes, according to *Newsweek*, "a real and deep private sector, a clean, well-regulated financial system and the sturdy rule of law." India also has a largely democratic political culture that, when combined with an entrepreneurial work ethic, results in what Max Singer and the late Aaron Wildavsky refer to as a "quality economy"(one that has the requisites for growth because it provides the economic and political incentives for people and groups to work hard and to innovate significantly).

India has at least two other advantages. One is the Indian commitment to quality education. At least for those classes that have access to it, India has some of the best schools and colleges in the world in science and technology. However, as Feigenbaum and others note, this opportunity is far less than universal, and "a UNESCO index recently ranked India 102 out of 129 countries on the extent, gender balance, and quality of its primary education and adult literacy." The Indian Institute of Technology, for instance, is a global leader in the field, and its graduates are heavily recruited worldwide, including in the United States. Many Indians have gravitated historically to the United States for the opportunity to use their economic tools, but now they are increasingly staying in or returning to India. They do, however, become Americanized during their time in the United States, which helps explain why the Indian people are among the most pro-American in the world, at least with regard to the American people.

India's headlong plunge into globalization has not been entirely smooth or devoid of criticism, although the level of opposition remains minor. The major criticism is familiar throughout the globalizing world, that globalization may indeed increase the prosperity of the country as a whole, but that improvement is not uniform for all people. Macroeconomic benefits to Indians, in other words, are incontestable in any number of measures of the economy; microeconomic benefits to individuals are not so uniform or universal.

The anomaly of growing inequity has already been suggested in Indian demographics: India has both the world's largest middle class and number of desperately poor. Due to the tradition of social castes in India's past, this disparity has not produced a sizable backlash, as the dispossessed have not—at least yet—asserted effectively the unacceptability of their meager existence. The fact that India is fast becoming two countries economically creates an anomalous situation for Indian government and one that will eventually have to be addressed. Approximately three-fifths of the population still makes its living through agriculture, for instance. On one hand, policies that encourage the accumulation of wealth as a necessary way to stimulate India's entrance into the global economy also preclude government intervention and revenue redistribution to ameliorate the living conditions of the worst-off in Indian society. On the other hand, a serious movement toward social egalitarianism would drain Indian resources to the point of jeopardizing India's continuing movement into the upper echelon of global economic power.

The result is a debate within India that is currently largely confined to the upper classes of Indian society. Defenders of globalization make an argument familiar to Americans: That the benefits of economic growth will "trickle down" to the poor eventually and that efforts to redistribute wealth will cut off that trickle altogether. In more extreme cases, the poor are even blamed for their condition, because, among other things, they have too many children. Pal, quoting Indian columnist Dilip D'Souza, counters, "Proponents of globalization say wait ten years. But the poor can't wait. They have waited 53 years (since independence). We have to have urgent measures to help them." Activism, however, is weakened because the poor are also politically weak and disorganized, and as long as they remain so, macroeconomic justifications of globalization will overwhelm and swamp their microeconomic woes.

Like China, India's path as a rising power is still partly undefined. To date, it has largely been confined to the economic sector, with particular emphasis on the technological edge that the educational system produces. The entrepreneurial underpinning has produced growth in other areas as well. The entrance of India into world automobile production is a classic example. Tata Motor Company developed the $2,500 Nano minicar for domestic and international markets, and it recently purchased British icons Jaguar and Land Rover from Ford Motor Company (a precedent of sorts for China's acquisition of Volvo from Ford). Whether India will become increasingly politically assertive in forums like the G-20 (of which it is a member) will help define its evolving role as a rising power.

CONCLUSION

The exact nature and impact of rising powers, particularly when their rise is not principally militarily threatening in content, is always somewhat difficult to project. It is always tempting to state the challenge in dramatic, even apocalyptical terms, but these descriptions are likely to overshoot the mark, and Menon argues this is likely to be the case today. As he puts it, "those who expect a quick emergence of coequal partners to the United States are mistaken in their view. But so are those who see a future of unchallenged, open-ended American dominance."

To some extent, the existing powers generally have some role in the emergence of new challengers to their dominance, even if that contribution is unintentional. Capital from British banks in the nineteenth century, for instance, was critical in American expansion westward and the emergence of the United States as a global power in the twentieth century, and there is little evidence the British either realized or nurtured that outcome consciously. As Menon explains, the same is true today. "Dominant powers—by providing security, exporting capital, selling goods and services, and creating new technologies—unwittingly enable the rise of new centers of strength. They also stir envy and the desire to emulate. The United States has done all these things."

The question that remains is what does the rise of these two powers mean for the United States and for the rest of the world? Certainly, their evolution will have a continuing impact on the structure and operation of the global economy, as discussed in the next chapter. Beyond that, each country will, in all likelihood, make its own individual, if not entirely predictable, impact as well.

China is unquestionably a rising power, and it has already ascended to a position of world economic leadership. The consequences of this ascent, however, remain uncertain and subject to varying, even diametrically opposite, interpretations. No one can reliably look into the future and know for certain how it will be: Whether China will increasingly be a looming threat, a global partner, or some of both. The facts are not terribly at odds with one another, but what they mean differs greatly, depending on the perspective one brings to the interpretation.

How China evolves as a power depends partly on how Chinese politics evolve. Minxin Pei, for instance, argues, "It is premature to dismiss the inherent instability of China's authoritarian politics," which "rests on fragile political institutions, little rule of law, and corrupt governance." On the other hand, Kishore Mahbubani admits ongoing corruption, but maintains "China is run by the best governing class in generations . . . including many young mayors who have been trained at U.S. universities."

In the end, what kind of a rising power will China be? And how does the world deal with China? Wang Jisi suggests, for instance, "China and the United States cannot hope to establish truly friendly relations. Yet, the countries should be able to build friendly ties." And yet, the outcome remains uncertain. In Minxin Pei's words, "China may be rising, but no one knows whether it can fly."

The same kind of uncertainty surrounds India's rise. As noted, India got a later start than China in the globalizing business, and it is thus at an earlier stage of evolution. Major obstacles remain to its growth, two of which are worth noting here. One is education, an area that cuts both ways. The Indian educational system is excellent for those who can avail themselves of it, but access is restricted, and that means a substantial part of the population (especially women) remain uneducated or undereducated. The consequence, as Mukherji points out, is that "economic reform has not yet benefited enough Indians for the country to harness the potential of its youthful workforce."

The second, and obviously related, example is massive poverty. India has, in Mukherji's words, "more poverty than any other nation in the world," which has very difficult consequences. On one hand, this means there is a future responsibility to uplift the population that cannot be deferred indefinitely—at great expense. It also means a large part of the population neither contributes to nor benefits from the globalization phenomenon. As Mukherji concludes, "the benefits of rapid economic growth trickle down too slowly in India."

It has become commonplace to debate what the center of political power will be in the twenty-first century. Will this new century, like the end of the last, continue to be an American century, or will the center of gravity somehow inexorably move eastward, resulting in an Asian century? The answer depends on what new powers rise, and how far; and which countries decline, and to what degree.

STUDY/DISCUSSION QUESTIONS

1. What is a rising power? Why is the concept important in understanding the nature of international politics and changes in the balance of power? As suggested in the introduction, rising powers arise periodically. To get some flavor of the process and why it is confusing and controversial, put yourself in the position of being a European in the late nineteenth century trying to assess the impact the United

States would eventually have. Would you view the United States as a looming threat or a global partner? Why?

2. A primary source of China's rise is economic. Although China's economy has indeed expanded greatly, there is disagreement about the nature of that growth and what it means. Try to construct two arguments, one that points to the emergence of China as a major competitor and rival, and one that suggests Chinese economic development is less ominous. Compare the two arguments. Where do they agree and disagree?

3. India's rise has been different than China's. How and why has this been the case? Compare the two countries' experiences in terms of their status and the direction of their rise.

4. Both India and China have positive and negative influences on their present and future growth. What are the distinctive positive and negative impacts on both, with special emphasis on the situation in India?

5. Speculate on the impact that China and India as rising powers will have on the next 10, 25, and 50 years, and how that impact will affect the United States. Explain the reasoning underlying your projections.

READING/RESEARCH MATERIAL

Abdelal, Rawi and Adam Segal. "Has Globalization Reached Its Peak?" *Foreign Affairs* 86, 1 (January/February 2007), 103–114.

Biaian, Zhang. "China's 'Peaceful Rise' to Great Power Status." *Foreign Affairs* 84, 5 (September/October 2005), 18–24.

Blinder, Alan S. "Offshoring: The Next Industrial Revolution." *Foreign Affairs* 85, 2 (March/April 2006), 113–128.

Brzezinski, Zbigniew. "Make Money, Not War." *Foreign Policy,* January/February 2005, 46–47.

Bush, Richard C. and Michael O'Hanlon. *A War Like No Other: The Truth about China's Challenge to America.* New York: John Wiley and Sons, Inc., 2007.

Feigenbaum, Evan A. "India's Rise, America's Interest: The Fate of the U.S.–Indian Partnership." *Foreign Affairs* 89, 2 (March/April 2010), 76–91.

Friedman, Thomas L. *The Lexus and the Olive Tree: Understanding Globalization.* New York: Farrar, Straus, and Giroux, 1999.

———. *The World Is Flat: A Brief History of the 21st Century.* New York: Farrar, Straus, and Giroux, 2005.

Deng, Yong and Thomas G. Moore. "China Views Globalization: Toward a Great New Power Politics?" *Washington Quarterly* 27, 3 (Summer 2004), 117–136.

Dickerson, Bruce J, Bruce Gilley, and Dali L. Yang. "The Future of China's One-Party State." *Current History* 107, 701 (September 2007), 243–251.

Fravel, M. Taylor. "China's Search for Military Power." *Washington Quarterly* 31, 3 (Summer 2008), 125–141.

Gifford, Rob. *China Road: A Journey into the Future of a Rising Power.* New York: Random House, 2007.

Gilboy, George J. "The Myth Behind China's Miracle." *Foreign Affairs* 83, 4 (July/August 2004), 33–48.

——— and Benjamin J. Read. "Political and Social Reforms in China: Alive and Walking." *Washington Quarterly* 31, 3 (Summer 2008), 143–164.

Gill, Bates. *Rising Star: China's New Security Diplomacy.* Washington, DC: Brookings Institution Press, 2007.

Hale, David and Lyric Hughes Hale. "China Takes Off." *Foreign Affairs* 82, 6 (November/December 2003), 36–53.

Huang, Yeshing. "The Next Asian Model." *Foreign Policy*, July/August 2008, 32–40.

Jisi, Wang. "China's Search for Stability with America." *Foreign Affairs* 84, 5 (September/October 2005), 39–48.

Kaplan, Robert D "India's New Face." *The Atlantic* 303, 3 (April 2009), 74–81.

Lapton, David M. "The Faces of Chinese Power." *Foreign Affairs* 86, 1 (January/February 2007), 115–127.

Legro, Jeffrey W. "What China Will Want: The Future Implications of a Rising Power." *Perspectives on Politics* 5, 3 (September 2007), 515–533.

Mahbubani, Kishore. "Understanding China." *Foreign Affairs* 84, 5 (September/October 2005), 49–60.

Menon, Rajan. "Pax Americana and the Rising Powers." *Current History* 108, 721 (November 2009), 253–260.

Mukherji, Hahul. "A Tiger Despite the Chains: The State of Reform in India." *Current History* 109, 726 (April 2010), 144–150.

The National Security Strategy of the United States of America. Washington, DC: The White House, March 2006.

Pei, Minxin. "Dangerous Denials." *Foreign Policy,* January/February 2005, 54–56.

———. "The Dark Side of China's Rise." *Foreign Policy*, March/April 2006, 32–40.

Segal, Adam. "Practical Engagement: Drawing a Fine Line for U.S.-China Trade." *Washington Quarterly* 27, 3 (Summer 2004), 157–173.

Singer, Max and the Late Aaron Wildawsky. *The Real World Order: Zones of Peace, Zones of Turmoil* (revised edition). Chatham, NJ: Chatham House, 1996.

Wolf, Martin. "Why Is China Growing So Slowly?" *Foreign Policy*, January/February 2005, 49–52.

———. *Why Globalization Works.* New Haven, CT: Yale University Press, 2004.

Zakaria, Fareed. "India Rising." *Newsweek,* March 6, 2006, 24–42.

———. *The Post-American World.* New York: W. W. Norton, 2008.

WEB SITES

A general overview of China at www.insidechina.com
A compendium of Chinese foreign affairs position papers
State Council Information Office at www.china.org.cn
Ministry of Foreign Affairs at www.fmprc.gov.cn
Systematic overview prepared by Federal Research Division of Library of Congress
China, a Country Study at http://memory.loc.gov/frd/cs/cntoc.html
http//yaleglobal.yale.edu.

Extending Globalization: From G-7 to G-20

PRÉCIS

The benefits of and participation in globalization are not currently universally enjoyed, and thus a major question is whether and how to extend globalization more globally. Part of the answer involves the current status and dynamics of globalization and how they affect the prospects and abilities for extending the phenomenon. At the same time, extension is also a major aspect of the debate and dynamics of economic and political development. After introducing these concerns as context, the case moves to its central focus on the evolving institutional structure within which the question of extension of globalization is contested. The highlight of that institutional development is the evolution of the Group of Seven (G-7) to the Group of Twenty (G-20).

Throughout most of its existence, the term *globalization* has been misleading. The implication is that the process is global, suggesting a universality of application that has not really occurred in any systematic way to all reaches of the world. Globalization does reach and have an impact on virtually every corner of the globe, but its impact varies considerably from locale to locale. In terms of the analogy most often invoked by its supporters, globalization creates a wave of prosperity that "raises all boats." Many observers less enthusiastic about the progress achieved by globalization add, however, that it raises some boats more than others. Both postures have merit.

The first three cases in this section on globalization reflect the development of globalization to this point in time. The arguable genesis of the phenomenon lies in the Bretton Woods attempt to institutionalize free trade, the motor of a globalizing economy. The Bretton Woods process was dominated and developed by Western countries that saw its benefits principally in terms of global stabilization and their own prosperity, with the universal extension of the prosperity a lesser concern to them. The most extensive application of principles of economic integration has been in highly developed Europe through the European Union. The rising of economic power in China and India represents the breakthrough of the developing world and a transition point institutionally to the case focus here on the 2009 voluntary supplanting of the developed world–dominated Group of Seven (G-7) by the more universal and encompassing Group of Twenty (G-20).

This institutional movement must be put in context for it to gain full meaning. The movement, even the interest, in extending globalization to a place where it currently does not dominate is not universal, nor is there anything like universal agreement on how to bring it about. Extending globalization to the benefit of the maximum number of people is a social and political value, and as such, it is a concern about which purely economic approaches, including theories of globalization, are neutral. The partial exception is that spreading globalization is a "good business," but approaches to globalization are steeped in capitalist economics that are conspicuously welfare valueless.

There is also disagreement on how extension should occur. Globalizers are not so much anti-extension in the sense of seeing spreading prosperity as a desirable value as they are "a-extensionist." Advocacy goes beyond their theoretical reach, but many see extension as a social as well as an economic benefit. The question is how to go about extending the benefits. Here the arguments become more value-laden, mixing advocacy of economic and political development and globalization. The development debate is complex beyond current purposes, but boils down to questions of "why" and "how." The first question centers on whether (or to what extent) alleviating the underdevelopment of poorer parts of the world is an obligation of the more developed world. The second question is about how the developed world should approach the task of development. The options include capital transfer (developmental assistance or aid) and through internal development (capitalist-based globalization), or some combination. Both questions remain contentious and are pursued and reflected in the nexus of global economic forums like the G-7 and G-20.

This introduction helps frame the discussion of extending globalization. It begins by looking at the major controversies surrounding that extension, which in turn reflect the bases of globalization and that culminate in a series of effective requirements for becoming part of globalization, symbolically known as the Washington consensus. The discussion then moves to the development question, raising concerns about both whether development represents an obligation and whether globalization is a solution. Until recently, these discussions have been dominated by the more developed states that form the core of the globalizing economy, but the ascendancy of the G-20 signals a politically significant symbolic and substantive change in the institutional setting within which discussions occur. This institutional change represents the core of the case application, although any conclusion about how this shift may affect the process of extending globalization in the long run is premature.

CONTROVERSIES AND DYNAMICS

While most analysts believe that globalization is desirable in a general sense, exactly what it means, how it is reached, and—most importantly to this chapter—how it is extended to places that do not currently enjoy its fruits are not matters so universally accepted. Unraveling the question of extending globalization thus begins by placing it in some context, looking sequentially at controversies surrounding globalization, some of the primary underlying dynamics of the process and the effective "rules of the road" by which aspiring nonparticipants can join the prosperity.

Controversies

There are a number of sources of controversy surrounding globalization, six of which will be discussed because of their relevance to the question of extending globalization. The first is that globalization is a distinctively Western construct, based on theories of economic activity that are Western at base and that reflect Western economic and political preferences and practices. The symbol of globalization is something often called the *Washington consensus*, which represents a set of rules of economic practice that govern participation in the globalized economy and that are discussed later in the chapter. These rules reflect strongly Western economic and political values, and are especially heavily influenced by the United States, which has been the leading apostle of globalization since it began to emerge in the 1990s. In order to become a full-fledged member of the globalization system and thus to reap the primarily economic benefits that it promises (largely reflections of the material prosperity of the West, and especially the United States), countries are effectively required to adopt the values and practices of the Washington consensus, which some countries and areas find inconsistent with their own values and situations and which are not uniformly practiced by the countries that espouse them.

The other sources of controversy flow from the Western intrusiveness of the first. The second controversy surrounds the cultural impacts of embracing the Washington consensus. Becoming part of the global system inevitably entails becoming *like* the countries that are members of the system: capitalist, consumer-oriented societies that eventually adopt both the cultural aspects of the West and many of its outward trappings. A prime necessity of membership in the globalization system is opening societies to outsiders for economic purposes, including foreign investment. Foreign investors in turn bring with them preferences for how things should be done that their money helps them to influence: If you become part of the globalization system, the friendly arches of McDonalds are likely not to be far behind.

This opening and cultural assault is of greater or lesser import from region to region of the world. The trade-off it requires—sacrificing established values and practices that are dysfunctional in a globalized society for values that are compatible with globalization—is more acceptable in some places than in others. The Islamic Middle East, for instance, has been more reluctant to make this bargain than other parts of the world, but even in places like parts of Latin America that initially embraced globalization, there has been a backlash against some of its effects. These values have been most readily accepted in Asia, as the case of China and India highlighted in Chapter 11 demonstrate.

The third and fourth sources of controversy are related to one another. The third is the difficulty of making the transition from a noncapitalist economy to the capitalist model built into the Washington consensus. In general terms, the consensus requires putting in place macroeconomic and microeconomic practices (detailed below) that are difficult and that can require considerable sacrifice and even privation during the transition process. As an example, one macroeconomic requirement is reduction of government expenditures in order to create something like a balanced budget that will create a healthy economic condition for low inflation and investment, among other things. Such practices may make good long-term economic sense, but they also generally entail reductions in benefits to citizens that occur in the pursuit of reduced government spending and thus cause economic privation and political opposition to the process.

This description suggests the fourth source of controversy, already raised in Chapter 9, which is the differential macro- and microeconomic impact of globalization. As noted in the discussion of free trade, most arguments made in favor of globalization are macroeconomic in character, referring to the overall benefits to societies that become part of the globalization system. While in theory such benefits accrue to individual members of the society as well (the "rising tide that lifts all boats"), those benefits are highly differential (some boats are raised more than others), and there are individuals whose boats are not only not raised but may also be swamped and sunk in the process. Although its champions argue that globalization overwhelmingly produces winners (people become better-off), it also produces losers, and those losers become the opposition. If their numbers become large enough, the result may be political shock waves that raise the controversy to significant levels.

The dynamics of these third and fourth controversies have led to, especially in Asia, a debate over the optimal political setting for inducing—or, where incentives are inadequate, forcing—change. Conventional wisdom has suggested that the authoritarian environment is a more efficient setting for economic change, but recent startling expansion of the Indian economy has raised questions about these assessments.

The fifth controversy surrounds whether the debate is purposive. The heart of this controversy is whether the process of globalization is inevitable and whether there are meaningful, non-self-destructive choices that can be exercised as to whether one participates in globalization or not. In some parts of the world, globalization has been almost wholeheartedly embraced and the question is moot, because there is no question about whether participation is valuable or not. In other parts of the world, however, the question is lively, because there is reluctance to embrace either of the core values of globalization. In places like the Islamic Middle East, this reluctance may be the result of indecision about adopting the basic rules of globalized societies (free-market capitalism or transparent banking laws, for instance) or because the secondary and tertiary effects of globalization (secularization and Westernization) are deemed undesirable. At the same time, the transition to globalization may be politically or economically so difficult that some societies believe it should or needs to be avoided, either in principle or because preliminary experience with globalization has been disillusioning.

Whether globalization is optional or inexorable is thus an important question for many countries and areas that are either outside the network of states that are partners in globalization or that have only begun to adopt some of the trappings of membership in the globalized world. Do countries have a *meaningful* choice in this matter? If globalization is indeed inexorable, as its most vocal champions (Friedman, for instance) loudly proclaim, then resistance to accession is akin to relegating one's country to the poor peripheries of the future. In that case, the "choice" is hardly meaningful, because a negative determination is openly self-destructive. If, on the other hand, there *is* a meaningful choice to be made, then the calculation differs. Can a state or region, for instance, stay completely outside the globalization system? Can it adopt some of the trappings of globalization but not all of them? Or, is globalization, as Thomas Friedman has asserted in *The Lexus and the Olive Tree*, a "one size fits all" proposition in which one must buy in altogether or be completely excluded?

The sixth controversy is over accessibility to globalization. Because of its capitalist underlying premise, the private sources of capital that provide the enabling condition for productivity and thus participation are drawn to those places where they can maximize their profits and are repelled from places where they cannot. The latter assessment is most likely to occur in the poorest, least developed countries that lack both the human (e.g., educated people) or physical (e.g., transportation, power facilities) infrastructure to be attractive to those for whom profit is the primary motive. Infrastructure enhancement, in turn, normally requires public investments that fall outside the conceptual parameters of globalization beyond insisting on austerity to self-finance developing such capabilities. The result may be simply to lock some societies out of the globalization process.

The answers to these problems help to determine both *whether* there is a real debate about globalization and *what* the parameters of that debate might be. To this point, these questions remain only partially answered, and the answers are, to some extent, contradictory. Before looking at how different places have reacted to globalization, it is necessary to first examine the nature of globalization and thus the parameters of what it means to join the globalization process.

As noted, globalization is almost exclusively a product of the evolution of the most advanced states on the globe—what is often called the developed or First World—that have provided both the technological possibility and basic values that define the system. The unfolding process of making globalization universal is thus largely a question of how to spread the globalization system and its benefits to countries outside what President William J. Clinton called the "circle of market democracies" or the developing or Third World. The results have been mixed.

What has differentiated responses? At the risk of oversimplification, one can look at two sets of factors, which also describe the nature of globalization. One involves the nature of globalization from a technological vantage point. The vast motor of globalization has been the result of the information technology revolution, and some places are better equipped to contribute to and absorb that phenomenon than others. The second are the values, notably those included in the Washington consensus, that countries entering the globalization system must conform to, and this includes accepting or rejecting the political, social, and economic consequences of those choices.

Globalization and Technology

According to *New York Times* columnist Thomas L. Friedman, humankind lives increasingly in a "flat world" whose level nature is largely technologically defined and has basically altered the economic climate in the world. The great advances in technology that have emerged in the last third of the century and that continue to evolve and become more pervasive have been the necessary precursors for developing a truly global economy in which more and more countries and regions participate. The result is that the environment has become level (flat) for all participants rather than being hierarchical or uneven: anyone can play who wants to badly enough.

The telecommunications revolution has condensed both the time and space in which interaction occurs globally, and this has had enormous impacts on the dynamics of the international economy, both in terms of how international commerce is conducted and how the production of goods and services occur. Because each can have an impact on the ability to expand access to globalization, they are worth briefly exploring.

One impact of telecommunications has been the globalization of financial markets to an extent unthinkable as little as 20 years ago. It is now possible (and even seems routine to those whose major experience is with this reality) for investors around the world to buy and sell stocks and other financial instruments 24 hours a day by virtue of electronic access to various markets (stock, commodities, etc.) around the globe in real time. These transactions can involve the movement of enormous amounts of capital instantaneously without the ability of sovereign governments to interfere with, and in some cases even monitor, the volume and nature of transactions. This ability in turn creates a high level of international interest in high-quality information about conditions worldwide in which investment may be contemplated, and a desire on the part of investors to have uniform (and understandable for them) conditions around the world to increase their confidence in investments they might make. Realizing this, countries seeking outside investment as a way to stimulate their economies are put under pressure to produce an investment environment that those investors with electronic funds to invest (what Friedman called the "electronic herd" in *The Lexus and the Olive Tree*) will find attractive. Because many of the investors are American or influenced by the United States, the result has been pressure to build a common model of economic activity to attract investment—the Washington consensus.

The internationalization of production offers a second example. Internationalization occurs in two ways. One is the movement of firms into countries with a favorable economic climate (low wages, favorable tax structures, etc.) to manufacture goods at comparative advantage (see discussion in Chapter 9). Apparel and toys are examples of this activity at the lower end of the production cycle; electronic devices are an example at the higher end. The other method of internationalization occurs in the manufacture of complex products like automobiles, with parts made in various countries (where the parts can be produced at lower costs) for assembly elsewhere, generally where labor costs are not onerous. The effect of both these permutations is to create a climate whereby countries compete with one another for the investment opportunities and incomes that accompany either form of investment, and those who judge the competition inevitably do so on the basis of their particular economic values.

In his 2005 book, *The World Is Flat*, Friedman argues that a new dynamic has crept into the globalization process. A variety of developments in the telecommunications revolution, from universally available Web browsers to excess fiber optic networks broadly available worldwide, have had an egalitarian effect on the ability to become part of the cutting edge of the high-technology phenomenon. In the early days, the defining edge of technology was the proprietary characteristic of those with the most advanced computers and educationally based centers—the "Silicon Valley" phenomenon. If one lacked access to the most advanced computers and the brightest minds, one was relegated to being a consumer of technology or, at best, a conveyor and adapter of that technology.

The "democratization" of technology through greater access to information has reduced that advantage to the point that almost any person or group with access to educational facilities and computers has the most advanced information and knowledge available and thus can become part of the technology-producing leadership in the globalization process. At this point, the countries that seem to be taking the greatest advantage of this phenomenon are places like India, which noncoincidentally also has made some of the greatest investments in science and technology education, as noted in Chapter 11. The result is that the gap between the most advanced First World countries and ambitious Third World countries is becoming narrower, meaning the competition for leadership and success in a globalizing world is changing as well.

Does technological change make the extension of globalization inevitable? Certainly, technology has created the necessary underpinning for this particular historical round of globalizing and helps define the nature of the system and competition within it. It has been a competition in which the most advanced countries have had the major advantage, because they have had both the knowledge base on which the system operates and also the necessary capital to provide the economic incentives. The former advantage (knowledge) may be changing as the nature of the telecommunications revolution changes as well. Certainly, the competition among states that are currently part of the system is changing. Principally, this means entrance into the globalized economy is expanded to those countries willing and able to make the commitment in areas like education necessary to become part of the globalization system. It is not clear that technology creates such opportunities for countries unable or unwilling to make such investments.

Policy Bases: The Washington Consensus

Countries aspiring to "membership" in the globalization system must adopt the underlying values and rules that informally govern the relationships between the members as a condition for their entrance into the expanding prosperity. Adherence to the norms contained in those rules facilitates the flow of capital between members, especially from the rich, developed countries to the less developed aspirants. The major incentive for states to accept (or at least live by) these rules is the reasonable promise that doing so will result in greater prosperity for the country and its citizens. Remaining outside the globalization system does not necessarily relegate nonparticipating states to a lessened economic status, because other dynamics (the possession of petroleum wealth, for instance) may provide an alternative means to achieve something like the prosperity that adherents to the Washington consensus enjoy. Conformance to these rules has, however, been a necessary condition for entrance into the expanding order.

The Washington consensus is the composite of a set of economic practices that reflect both the positive and negative aspects of the American experience over the past quarter century or so. These rules have evolved across time, heavily influenced by the values of privatization (turning over previously publicly performed economic functions to private enterprise), deregulation (removing governmental restrictions from economic activities), and free trade (the removal of international barriers to the movement of goods and services across national boundaries).

There is no definitive, official list of Washington consensus rules that a country must adopt to gain membership in the globalizing economy. In *The Lexus and the Olive Tree*, however, Friedman lays out a list of practices under the rhetorical device of what he calls the "golden straitjacket" that fairly represents the basic requirements involved. Friedman provides a reasonable list of requirements and points to why adoption of the rules may be easier for some places than for others. There are in all 16 requirements.

Ten of the criteria flow directly from deregulation and privatization. According to Friedman, they apply to states seeking to join the system:

1. "Making the private sector the primary engine of its economic growth";
2. "Maintaining a low rate of inflation and price stability";
3. "Shrinking the size of its state bureaucracy";
4. "Maintaining as close to a balanced budget as possible";
5. "Privatizing state-owned industries and utilities";
6. "Deregulating capital markets" to facilitate capital flow;
7. "Deregulating its economy" to promote as much domestic competition as possible;
8. "Eliminating government corruption, subsidies, and kickbacks as much as possible";
9. "Opening its banking and telecommunications systems to private ownership and competition;" and
10. "Allowing its citizens to choose from an array of competing pension options and foreign-run pension and mutual funds" as a means to protect savings.

The straitjacket also contains six criteria associated with promoting free trade:

1. "Eliminating or lowering tariffs on imported goods";
2. "Removing restrictions on foreign investment";
3. "Getting rid of quotas and domestic monopolies";
4. "Increasing imports";
5. "Making currency convertible"; and
6. "Opening its industry, stock and bond markets to direct foreign ownership and investment."

Regardless of the virtues of any of these rules or all of them collectively, they can be very difficult to adopt. They were formulated in the 1990s, when, for instance, the United States conformed to most of the rules; the same is hardly true with regard to prominent privatization/deregulation rules today, particularly in light of actions taken in response to the economic recession that began in 2008.

Countries can face at least three different kinds of problems adapting to the straitjacket. First, the rules may be contrary to accepted practices in regions or countries. Opening up national economies to outside competition, for instance, directly contradicts policy in much of Latin America aimed at avoiding having their economies swamped by the United States by restricting imports and relying on often inefficient domestic production (a policy known as "import substitution"). Second, implementation of the policies requires an austere approach to economic policy, including a reduction in government spending, the enforcement of high savings rates, and the like. The result can be a (hopefully temporary) belt-tightening that causes consumer pain and discomfort, which can be politically difficult. The institution of such policies can be politically ruinous for governments that seek to conform. This position is sometimes made more difficult by the hypocrisy of the developed states, which lack the political will to enforce on themselves much of the discipline they demand of others. Third, if countries lack comparative advantage in any significant areas, reducing barriers to trade can create a flood of imports that drains revenues but is uncompensated for by income from competitively produced domestic goods.

In the early and mid-1990s, many of the problems that have emerged in moving toward globalization were submerged in the general prosperity that seemed to be sweeping the world, and resistance was largely isolated to particular groups displaced by the process (American textile workers, for instance) or countries and regions (most of Africa) that could not compete. When the Asian financial crisis of 1997 and 1998 hit and was accompanied by downturns in a number of other areas at the turn of the millennium, more questions began to be raised about whether globalization is an equally appealing prospect for all countries and regions. The institutional adjustment currently occurring has significant roots in this reaction.

THE DEVELOPMENTAL DIMENSION

The desirability of extending globalization to places currently untouched by it or receiving less than its optimal benefits is ultimately a value question that goes beyond economic theories of economic growth. How globalization spreads addresses the question of where it extends only indirectly, arguing that extension essentially will occur in places that either have or can develop some form of comparative advantage and that it will bypass or ignore places that do not. Questions of equity, justice, or moral and political desirability of expansion to some places but not to others simply is not part of purely economic discussions.

The extension of globalization cannot, however, be divorced from those value concerns, because it impinges upon and affects the patterns of interaction between those states that are currently part of and helped by globalization—the wealthier states of the developed world and ambitious and successful developing world states—and the generally poorer states outside the general prosperity of the most prosperous—the so-called developing states. The extension of globalization implies raising some states out of the economic morass of the developing world and into the more rarified atmosphere of globalization. As a result, extending globalization is part of a more general discussion of development.

Globalizers generally do not like to phrase the process of globalization in these terms for several reasons. First, it removes the process from the supposedly more objective level of the application of the capitalist model applied internationally to the "softer" realm of economic and social equities, and economic analysis is uncomfortable with these kinds of distinctions. Second, because developmental efforts generally have a (generally prominent) public component, moving the extension of globalization into the development framework moves the discussion more toward the role of government in economic affairs, a question for which most globalizers have a jaundiced answer. Third, the equation of globalization and development has strong international political implications in the area of most general conflict between the developed and developing worlds—the obligations of the developed to the developing world. For all these reasons, many supporters of globalization would object to the very inclusion of development into a discussion of globalization.

Nevertheless, the developmental question needs to be addressed, because it is a part of the ongoing debate and especially a major part of the underlying dynamic about the evolving international institutionalization of globalization. One of the primary reasons for expanding the G-7 to the G-20 is to include members of the developing world that have become globalizers into world economic councils, and one of the agenda items they add to the mix is that of development.

Why Development? The Moral Obligation?

The problem of economic and political development in much of Asia, Africa, and, to a lesser degree, parts of Latin America is an artifact of the dissolution of the European worldwide empires after the end of World War II. The process began in the latter 1940s in places like the Asian subcontinent and effectively culminated when Portugal granted independence to its remaining African colonies in the middle 1970s. The result of decolonization was an explosion of new sovereign states that nearly quadrupled the number of such states in 1945. The Bretton Woods conference, as noted in Chapter 9, consisted of 45 states; the current number of independent entities is close to 200.

One of the characteristics that almost all the newly independent states shared was a lack of economic development. Their poverty stood in stark contrast to the conditions of their former colonial rulers after those countries recovered from World War II. This disparity, so obvious as to be unmistakable, created an understandable desire on the part of the formerly colonized countries to emulate the prosperity of their former rulers. Economic (as well as political) development thus became the major agenda item in the relations between what became known as the developed and developing worlds. It is a problem that now spans over a half-century and remains vital and cogent.

In order to raise the economic standards of the former colonies to those of the rich countries required a difficult, expensive process for which the developing states lacked adequate resources of their own, meaning such resources would have to come from elsewhere for development to occur. The obvious candidates were the rich countries—and especially the colonial powers that had held them in bondage. The developing states, however, lacked much effective leverage to extract necessary resources—principally money and expertise—to encourage development. If the developed state refused requests or demands for assistance, what could the developing states do to force them to comply? The general answer was, "not very much."

One response to this situation was to phrase the question in moral terms: the rich states had a moral obligation to uplift the poor states. The moral basis of this argument was the immorality of colonialism and the perversity of its effects. Colonial rule was often harsh, inhumane, degrading, and reprehensible (see George Orwell's *Burmese Diaries* for a personal, vivid description), and the former oppressors thus "owed" the formerly oppressed for these indignities. More to the point, colonialists were economically exploitive (appropriating natural resources in the colonies and forcing subjects to consume products from the ruling country, for instance), and the exploitation inhibited economic development in the colonies. While this latter claim was arguable, it did serve as an explanation for both why there was disparity and why the former oppressors were obliged to do something about it.

The moral—or other—responsibility for development and actions to moderate differences remain prominent issues on the international agenda and are manifested in the institutional efforts discussed in the following section. Before turning to that effort, however, it is instructive to inspect one other aspect of the development debate: the question of which approach to development is most appropriate. The parameters of that debate are familiar in the American domestic debate about economic policy.

Approaches to Development

There are essentially two basic approaches to obtaining and applying the resources necessary for development. One, which has been historically dominant, is through the application of public sources of funds—what is generally referred to as developmental assistance or foreign aid. The other, and more recent, is the application of private sector resources, an approach that has become associated with globalization. At the applied level, the two approaches are frequently applied in tandem.

The most basic economic problem that most developing countries have is infrastructural underdevelopment (many have multiple additional difficulties such as corruption as well). The infrastructure refers to the basic human and physical building blocks on which development of a more sophisticated and productive economic system is premised. As suggested earlier, basic physical elements can include such things as roads and railroads, power generation facilities, urban areas that can accommodate a working class population, and mineral, energy, or agricultural resources that can be developed and exploited for developmental purposes. Human resources can include an educated, trained workforce, political stability, congenial economic policies, and other conditions specified in Friedman's golden straitjacket. As that construct suggests, the absence of such conditions makes countries unappealing to the kind of private investment that is the core of globalization.

The question for developing countries aspiring to a more prosperous future is how to develop the infrastructure necessary to ascend to the world economic stage. The answer—and in some ways the rub—is that the very economic resources these countries lack are the enabling mortar to cement the building blocks on which prosperity is based. But where can and should these resources come from?

As suggested at the beginning of the section, there are two broad potential sources—public and private. Particularly from the vantage point of the developing states themselves, foreign public sources have great appeal. For one thing, there is the matter of entitlement: the rich former oppressors "owe" help to the poor they oppressed. That moral appeal, however, is often less than persuasive to the rich countries. The other appeal of public resources arises from the nature of infrastructure investment in economic terms. Borrowing from the vocabulary of developmental assistance, many (even most) infrastructure development is not "self-liquidating," meaning that regardless of the benefits of a particular infrastructure project, it does not directly generate the revenue to pay for itself. Schools are a particularly clear example. They are clearly necessary parts of the human infrastructure needs on which a productive economy is based, but their direct contribution cannot be measured so that the "profits" from their activities can be used to pay off the costs incurred to build and operate them. There are a number of other elements of the infrastructure that are of a similar nature in virtually all societies that are treated as publicly supported public goods.

The globalization question revolves around where the sources of public funds should be. The traditional answer from the developing world has been the transfer of resources from the developed to the developing world on a government-to-government basis (foreign aid). The developed states have never formally repudiated this appeal, but they have generally been unwilling to honor it at levels anywhere near what is needed to meet the demands of the developing states. Resource transfer has been a perpetually inadequate source for the development demands of the developing world.

Globalization encourages a movement toward an alternative source of public funding: internal resources. To produce the wealth needed to underwrite economically non-self-liquidating infrastructure development, the globalization response is fiscal and monetary austerity, as specified in the straitjacket, to wring developmental resources from the developing countries themselves. Developing countries find shifting the discussion to this ground objectionable on three grounds. First, it shifts the debate away from the moral grounds of a developing world obligation to assist in the developmental process. Rather than providing the resources that could stimulate development, the former oppressors adopt the position of setting and monitoring standards in the developing countries.

Second, it is an approach that is too politically dangerous for Third World countries to embrace. Austerity, which is at the heart of much of this approach, means enforced savings at the expense of current consumption, which is politically unpopular. Moreover, as already noted, the insistence is to some extent hypocritical, since it demands that developing states adopt and enforce odious restrictions that the states demanding them often lack the political courage to enforce on themselves. Third, it is not clear that the adequate domestic resources are available in many countries even if a maximum husbanding effort is undertaken. The paucity of developmental resources is, after all, the very problem that developmental efforts seek to change. Reliance on this method is intolerably slow under the best of circumstances and impossible physically at the worst.

The issues involved in the developmental debate are, of course, complex beyond the ability to detail here, but there is little disagreement that infrastructure is a sine qua non for development. Neither pure approach is adequate or acceptable to all parties: the developed states have never shown an adequate commitment to developmental assistance to suggest outside public funding will solve the problem, and the non-self-liquidating nature of much infrastructure development means a purely private approach will not maximize outcomes either. The result is that only a mixed approach can probably work. The gist of a mixed approach is that public funds, largely provided by the developed world, must be employed to create basic human and physical infrastructure environments into which the private sector can then move and provide the investment that can create the prosperity associated with the globalized world.

There is not, however, consensus either on the mechanics or on the pace at which such progress should proceed. Historically, much of the formal interaction between the developed and developing worlds on the subject has occurred in generalized international forums like the United Nations through advocacy groups on one side or the other like the Group of 77 (see below). Forums like the United Nations have not proved adequate or congenial for making much progress on the problem. The movement from G-7 to G-20, however, provides another and potentially more fruitful venue for such discussions.

FROM G-7 TO G-20

Reconciling the problems and contradictions within the global economy to the mutual satisfaction of all or most of its members remains a work in progress. As already suggested, there are fundamental disagreements about how the system should be organized and to whose benefit and advantage. Historically, the discussions have been dominated largely by the wealthiest countries, which had an adequate stranglehold on resources to be able to dictate the context and outcomes on such important matters as development and the extension of globalization.

Globalization is changing the equation of these discussions. Newly powerful states like China, India, and others have broken the monopoly once concentrated in North America, Europe, and Japan. The result is new faces and voices with different messages demanding a seat and voice at the economic table. Their appeals for inclusion are increasingly proving ineluctable.

These changes are increasingly being manifested institutionally. The original framework devised at Bretton Woods (see Chapter 9) produced a structure of institutions like the IMF and IBRD that continue to be dominated by the traditional powers. This pattern was continued in developed world-dominated forums like the Organization of Economic Cooperation and Development (OECD) and culminated in the formation of a kind of executive directorate in 1985, the G-7.

While all this was congealing, the developing world emerged from colonialism and brought with it the developmental agenda, which was first formally articulated and came to center on forums like the G-77 and the G-20 developing states (an organization separate from the G-20 that is the focus of the study). Developing world demands, however, fell on at least partially deaf ears until the process of globalization began to move the center of economic power away from its traditional mooring to a broader and more inclusive base. The culmination of that process to date was the late 2009 announcement that the G-7 would supplant itself with the more broadly based G-20, a body the G-7 created.

This case application looks at the history and dynamics of this significant change. It begins with a brief overview of the historical development of a maze of institutions on both sides of the developmental divide. It then moves to the changing world economy and how those changes have militated toward a shift in institutional arrangement that is currently capture in the movement from G-7 to G-20. The chapter concludes with some speculation about what these changes may mean.

Economic Institutions since World War II

As noted in Chapter 9, a major concern of post–World War II planners was how to avoid another calamity resembling the economic conditions that heralded the second global conflagration of the twentieth century. Their major goal was economic stabilization, first among themselves and later toward emerging parts of the world. One device the creators of the original Bretton Woods institutions—the IBRD and the IMF—employed to maintain control was weighted voting formulas in each based on the initial subscriptions of the founding members to the organization (in the case of the United States, about 1/3 of the funds and thus votes). The developing states continue to try to reduce or repeal these formulas, since they relegate them to minority status, and succeeded in doing so with the WTO.

From an operational standpoint, the solidarity of the developed world on economic issues falls to the OECD. This organization was originally instituted in 1948 as the Organization of European Economic Cooperation (OEEC) at

American insistence as a device to dispense Marshall Plan assistance to war-torn Europe. In 1960 it was reconstituted as the OECD with the aim, stated on its Web site, to act as a "forum of countries committed to democracy and market economies." The headquarters of the 30-member organization include the three major states of North America, most of the countries of the European Union, and several important Pacific rim states (Japan, South Korea, Australia, and New Zealand), and Turkey. All members of the G-7 are OECD members, and since the European Union is the twentieth member of G-20, most other OECD members are part of G-20 as well.

A parallel group of organizations emerged among the members of the developing world to champion their position in the economic order. The original meeting of developing world states expressing what became the developmental agenda was the Bandung Conference of 1955. This movement did not gain momentum until 1964, however, when the first UN Conference on Trade and Development (UNCTAD) adjourned on June 15 in Geneva, Switzerland, with 77 developing country participants declaring the formation of the Group of 77 (G-77). This organization, whose membership has swollen to 130 states, held its first meeting and declared itself permanent organization with the Charter of Algiers (site of the meeting) in October 1967. The G-77 now meets annually at the beginning of each regular session of the UN General Assembly.

The purpose of G-77 is to further the developmental agenda of its membership, which encompasses most of the developing world. As stated on its Web site, the G-77 provides a "means for the countries of the South to articulate and promote their collective economic interests and enhance their joint negotiating capacity." In 2003, the G-77 was joined by the creation of the G-20, or group of 20 developing states, an organization including 23 members in 2008. The organization was spearheaded by Brazil, India, and South Africa, whose foreign ministers brought it into existence on June 20, 2003, with the Brasilia Declaration. Other prominent members include Argentina, China, Indonesia, and Mexico, all members of the more prominent G-20.

The operation of the G-77 highlights the leverage problem the developing world has had in achieving developed world status. In the 1970s, the G-77 issued a call for a New International Economic Order (NIEO), the most prominent feature of which was call for the developed countries to transfer 1.5 percent of their annual wealth to the developing world annually to facilitate the developmental process. This figure was wildly in excess of the amount the developed countries were willing even to contemplate. In 2009, for instance, the GDP/PPP of the United States stood at $14.3 trillion, meaning a 1.5 percent transfer would have been over $200 billion; the U.S. developmental assistance budget is about 1/10 of that amount. Considerable moral exhortation by G-77 was unsuccessful in convincing the developed states to adopt the NIEO, which died a silent, unfulfilled death.

This brief discussion lays the groundwork to discuss some of the institutional setting in which the evolution from G-7 to G-20 exists. The context is one of institutional multiplicity. The Bretton Woods framework offers an umbrella set of institutions that are basically universal in membership (all members of the G-20 are members of the WTO except Russia, for instance, which has candidate status), but are largely dominated by the developed states, and their status is reinforced by organizations like the OECD. The G-77 provides some of the same function for the developing world, as does the G-20 developing world group. Both sides of the institutional divide on globalization and its extension are thus represented in a debate that now centers on the move from G-7 to G-20.

The G-7/G-20 Transition

The G-7 has existed since 1985, when a group of finance ministers from the countries that would form its membership met at the Plaza Hotel in New York to discuss mutual efforts to coordinate foreign exchange intervention to drive down the value of an overinflated U.S. dollar. From this meeting, G-7 evolved as a series of regular annual or semiannual meetings among what Elliott describes as the "rich G-7 countries."

The membership of G-7 (and also G-20) and some of its pertinent characteristics are depicted in Table 12.1.

The G-7 countries are a homogenous lot. All are well established economic powers with strong democratic traditions. Except for Japan, all are traditional Caucasian with some colonial background (except for Canada). Their economic homogeneity is best shown through their uniformly high GDP/capita figures and low economic growth rates. All belong to the OECD and the Bretton Woods institutions.

When the G-7 was formed, its members arguably were the world's premier economic powers, the seven states including the North American economic giants, the core of the EU, and Japan. In terms of standards of living measured by GCP/capita, they remain at or near the top, challenged only by a few oil-rich states that are otherwise economically unexceptional and Australia. In terms of gross size and pace of economic growth, however, the G-7 countries are no longer the unassailable world standard, and it is in partial recognition of changing economic importance that the shift from G-7 to G-20 is based.

The G-7 no longer encompasses the world's largest economies. Using that standard—reflected in the Global GDP Rank column of Table 12.1—three current members (France, Italy, and Canada) would no longer qualify, replaced by China, India, and Russia. All three of these latter countries, however, are unlike the original G-7. Only India, for instance, is meaningfully democratic, and all have significantly lower standards of living and higher growth rates than the G-7 countries. India and China in particular share the common characteristic of having been prominent members of the organizations that have advocated the developmental agenda *and* being states that have succeeded extravagantly in entering the globalization system.

Russia, with its roots in the Soviet Union, stands apart from the rest. In 1998, it was given what amounted to honorary membership in the G-7 (some described the G-7 with Russia as the "G-7 $^1/_2$"), although it is dissimilar to the other G-7 countries by all measures save physical size of its economy. Indeed, Russia is the only member of the G-20 that is not a member either of the

TABLE 12.1

G-7, G-20 Characteristics (2008)

Country	GDP/ PPP*	GDP Global Rank**	GDP/ Capita	Economic Growth
G-7 Members				
Canada	1.30 T	12	$39,300	0.6
France	2.1 T	8	$32,700	0.7
Germany	2.86 T	5	$34,800	1.3
Italy	1.82 T	10	$31,000	−0.7
Japan	4.34 T	3	$34,200	−0.4
United Kingdom	2.23 T	6 Tie	$36,600	0.7
United States	14.3 T	1	$47,000	1.3
G-20 Additions				
Argentina	675 B		$14,200	7.1
Australia	801 B		$38,100	4.7
Brazil	1.99 T	9	$10,100	5.2
China	7.8 T	2	$6,000	9.8
India	3.2 T	4	$2,800	6.6
Indonesia	916 B		$3,900	6.1
Korea, South	1.28 T	13	$26,000	2.5
Mexico	1.56 T	11	$14,200	1.4
Russia	2.23 T	6 Tie	$15,800	6.0
Saudi Arabia	583 B		$20,100	4.2
South Africa	490 B		$10,000	2.8
Turkey	906 B		$12,000	1.5
European Union	14.9 T		$32,900	−0.4

*GDP/PPP = Gross Domestic Product/Purchasing Power Parity
**For countries with economies of over $1 trillion (US)
Source: All figures from Infoplease, Economic Statistics by Country, 2008.

OECD or the G-77 and is the only member of G-20 that is not a full member of the WTO (it has candidate status). The institutional membership pattern is shown in Figure 12.1.

The G-20 is the creation of the G-7 at their meeting of finance ministers on September 25, 1999 at Cologne, Germany. Like so many economic institutions, it came into being as the result of the financial crisis of 1997–1998 "to promote international financial stability" by broadening participation in the alleviation of the crisis. The first chair of the G-20, Canadian finance minister Paul Martin, said at the time that the new forum "will focus on translating the benefits of globalization into higher incomes and better opportunities everywhere" (quoted in Kirton). The G-20, in other words, would promote the globalization model of development.

G-20 broadens the scope and heft of the G-7 considerably. According to its Web site, "member countries represent 90 percent of global gross national

Country	G-7	G-20 (developing)	OECD	G-77	WTO
Argentina		X		X	X
Australia			X		X
Brazil		X		X	X
Canada	X		X		X
China		X		X	X
France	X		X		X
Germany	X		X		X
India		X		X	X
Indonesia		X		X	X
Italy	X		X		X
Japan	X		X		X
S. Korea			X		X
Mexico		X	X		X
Russia					
Saudi Arabia				X	X
S. Africa		X		X	X
Turkey			X		X
U.K.	X		X		X
U.S.	X		X		X
EU					

FIGURE 12.1 G-20 Institutional Memberships.

product, 80 percent of world trade (including EU intra-trade)), as well as two-thirds of world population." The countries added also make the G-20 entirely more diverse than G-7 in a variety of ways.

There are 19 countries that are members (the seven G-7 states plus 12 others); the twentieth "state" member is the EU, which provides indirect membership for EU countries not otherwise represented in G-20. The 19 countries represented are all prominent economically but are not the 19 largest economies in the world. At $490 billion GDP/PPP, South Africa has the smallest economy of the G-20, a figure exceeded by at least three nonmembers: Iran at $842 billion, the Netherlands at $670 billion, and Poland at $667 billion (figures are from 2008 and are provided by Infoplease). The Dutch and Poles, of course, have indirect membership through the EU. Other economically prominent states that are not members include Pakistan ($453 billion), Egypt ($442 billion), Belgium ($390 billion), Malaysia ($386 billion), Nigeria ($381 billion), Sweden ($348 billion), and Venezuela ($338 billion).

The G-20 nonetheless adds enormous diversity to the G-7 and injects a significant number of proponents of extension of globalization into the ranks. At one obvious level, it corrects an anomaly of a G-7 that does not totally represent the world's largest and most influential economies by incorporating not only the rising powers—China and India but also the slightly smaller but increasingly important countries like Brazil, South Korea, and Mexico among trillion-dollar-plus economies. It accomplishes this without depriving G-7 countries no longer at the top of their premier status.

In terms developed in this chapter, the new membership includes two categories of states. The first group includes highly developed states that are members of OECD but whose economies have historically been less central internationally than the G-7 members: Australia, Mexico, South Korea, and Turkey. These four countries are comparatively wealthy and developed, with relatively high per capita GDPs (higher for Australia and Korea, lower for Mexico and Turkey). None of the four are members of G-77, and only Mexico is part of the G-20 developing country group.

The other seven members of the G-20 clearly represent the developing world and its network of associations. All are members of both the G-20 developing countries and the G-77, and most have been vocal proponents of the developmental agenda. Generally speaking, they meet the economic criteria of aspiring developing countries: comparatively low standards of living (per capita GDP from $2,800 to $20,100) and comparatively high economic growth rates (2.8–9.8 percent). They vary considerably in size (China has the world's largest population and second largest economy, while South Africa has the 25th largest population and 20th largest economy) and thus geopolitical influence. What they share, beyond their aspiration to globalization prosperity, is a history of advocacy of the developmental agenda.

CONCLUSION

A truly global globalization process requires the extension of the system and its benefits to large reaches of the globe into which it has not yet protruded. Extension of globalization has occurred, but it has been limited, and it certainly has not spread to all the places that aspire to its status. The primary barrier to a greater dispersion of the prosperity is the lack of the kind of economic development that makes nonparticipating aspirants attractive to the globalizers. The globalized world is, after all, a rich man's club, and until outsiders gain the characteristics and values of the members, they are not going to be allowed to join.

Not all countries, of course, want to join. There is, for instance, little clamoring for inclusion within many Middle Eastern countries fearful of the westernization that is part and parcel of the process. Among those who do want to join, the problem is how to gain the resources to develop in ways that will make them attractive. The developed countries inside the globalized world and the developing countries on the outside have disagreed on how development should be financed. Since the globalizers have possessed the necessary resources, they have until recently been able to control the outcome.

The rising economic powers are changing the environment. Like the proverbial oasis camel, countries like China and India have poked their heads under the tent flaps of the major powers symbolized by the G-7, and they have become full members of the discussions that will ensue. The G-20 is now *their* forum as well as that of the traditional powers, and they will add the developmental agenda to future discussions about extending globalization.

The G-20 has become a fixture of the landscape since its inception in 1999 as, in the words of its Web site, the "premier forum" for promoting "open and constructive discussions between industrial and emerging market countries on key issues related to economic stability." The decision by the G-7 countries to suspend regular meetings (while retaining the option of special ad hoc conclaves) and the convening of the G-20 "summit meeting" in Seoul, Korea, in November 2010 suggest the permanence of the institutional shift that has occurred.

Where all this will lead substantively in terms of the outcome of the process of extending globalization is, of course, anybody's guess. The institutional movement from G-7 to G-20 is both a recognition that change has happened and a platform and framework for future change. The platform itself is a dynamic, not a static, construct. It is, for instance, almost certainly only a matter of time until some of the emerging countries outside G-20 are admitted, and when they are, the structure and direction of the effort may shift as well.

STUDY/DISCUSSION QUESTIONS

1. What is the concept of extending globalization? What is its place in the discussion of international economics, including development?
2. What are the dynamic bases of globalization? Describe them. How are these bases reflected in the Washington consensus?
3. Describe the process of globalization as a developed world–developing world competition. How has this been manifested in contending visions of how globalization should be extended?
4. Describe the developmental agenda of the developing world and why it has historically been less than successful.
5. How has the institutional underpinning of the international economy evolved over time? How have the positions of the two sides in the debate over globalization been represented institutionally?
6. How does the shift from G-7 to G-20 represent an important shift in the institutional setting over extension of globalization? Include in your response relevant comparisons and contrasts of the characteristics of G-7 countries and the countries added to forum G-20.

READING/RESEARCH MATERIAL

Abdelal, Rawi and Adam Segal. "Has Globalization Reached Its Peak?" *Foreign Affairs* 86, 1 (January/February 2007), 103–114.

Ahmia, Monrad. *The Group of 77 at the United Nations*. New York: Oxford University Press, 2006.

Blinder, Alan S. "Offshoring: The Next Industrial Revolution." *Foreign Affairs* 85, 2 (March/April 2006), 113–128.

Elliott, Larry. "G-7 Elite Group Makes Way for G-20 and Emerging Nations." *Guardian* (online), October 4, 2009.

Friedman, Thomas L. *The Lexus and the Olive Tree: Understanding Globalization*. New York: Farrar, Straus, and Giroux, 1999.

———. *The World Is Flat: A Brief History of the 21st Century*. New York: Farrar, Straus, and Giroux, 2005.

Kirton, John. "What Is G-20?" University of Toronto: Munk Centre for International Studies, November 30, 1999.

Orwell, George. *Burmese Days: A Novel*. London: Secker and Wartburg, 1986.

Singer, Max and the Late Aaron Wildawsky. *The Real World Order: Zones of Peace, Zones of Turmoil* (revised edition). Chatham, NJ: Chatham House, 1996.

Snow, Donald M. and Eugene Brown. *International Relations: The Changing Contours of Power*. New York: Longman, 2000.

Wolf, Martin. *Why Globalization Works*. New Haven, CT: Yale University Press, 2004.

Zakaria, Fareed. "India Rising." *Newsweek,* March 6, 2006, 24–42.

———. *The Post-American World*. New York: W. W. Norton, 2008.

WEB SITES

General Sources
http://www.globalpolicy.org/globaliz/econ.htm
http://yaleglobal.yale.edu
CIA World Factbook
http://www.cia.gov/cia/publications/factbook/print/ve.html
G-20
http://www.g20.org/about_what_is_g20.aspx
http://www.g20.utoronto.ca/g20whatisit.html
G-77
http://www.g77.org/doc/
G-20 (developing countries)
http://en.wikipedia.org/wiki/G20_developing_nations
WTO membership
http://www.wto.org/english/theWTO_e/whatis_eif_e/org6_e.thm
Global economic statistics (Infoplease)
http://www.infoplease.com/world/statistics/economic-statistics-by-country.html.

Human Security

There are some international problems that affect people and their well-being across borders that cannot adequately or fully be solved by individual states acting on their own. Sometimes these kinds of problems are referred to as transnational or transstate issues. Because they have large implications for safety, sense of safety, and even survival of individuals, groups, and even states, they are lumped together as matters of human security.

The four chapters in this part address various aspects of this problem that are important in contemporary international relations. Chapter 13, "Global Warming," provides an overview and analysis of the global warming phenomenon and debates surrounding the existence or severity of the problem. Looking at the global effort to deal with the problem through the UN framework and the Kyoto Protocols, it seeks to extrapolate responses to the plans laid out in the 2007 Bali convention on climate change that were supposed to be formalized in Copenhagen in 2009. These efforts largely failed for reasons discussed in the case. Chapter 14, "International Immigration," looks at the global movement of people between countries, a phenomenon primarily associated with migration from the developing to the developed world today. Current trends are likely to continue or even be accentuated by demographic change and globalization. The case study focuses on the U.S.-Mexican border as a prominent example of this phenomenon.

The final two chapters deal with more direct threats to human security and even existence. Chapter 15, "Failed States and Failing States," looks at the dynamics and consequences of the effective cessation of national sovereign control of territory by states and how this may affect life within countries and their relations with other countries. State failure is a relative condition, and Pakistan is examined in terms of its potential to become a failed state. Chapter 16, "Terrorism," attempts to define and describe the problem of terrorism and, based upon that discussion, to find its solution. The chapter culminates in a discussion of possible future directions of the so-called "war on terror" that has been the centerpiece of American and other efforts to suppress the problem.

Global Warming: Facing the Problem after Copenhagen

PRÉCIS

Global warming represents one of the clearest, yet most controversial, issues facing the world. It is clearly a problem that cannot be solved by the individual efforts of states, but must be done collectively if it is to be done successfully at all. It is controversial because there is substantial disagreement both about the nature and severity of the problem and over the structure and content of proposed solutions to climate change that is the clear by-product of global warming.

This case study looks at the problem from two related vantage points. The first is an examination of the controversial process surrounding international efforts to deal with global warming. The lightning rod for this effort has been the Kyoto Protocol of 1997, set to expire in 2012. Attempts to implement and move beyond the actions prescribed in that treaty, in 2007 at Bali, Indonesia, and in Copenhagen in 2009 have failed. The second is on the nature and extent of the problem and thus what does and does not require controlling. The two emphases are related because the nature of the problem has a clear relationship to the kinds and extent of remedies that are proposed for it.

The issue of global warming—the extent to which the climate of the Earth is gradually increasing in temperature due to human actions or natural processes—is one of the most controversial, divisive, and yet consequential problems facing international relations in the twenty-first century. No one, of course, favors a gradual or precipitous change in global climate because the consequences could be catastrophic. Having said that, amateurs and experts, some disinterested, some self-interested, disagree on almost everything about the phenomenon. While some question whether global warming exists at all, others predict dire consequences unless drastic measures are taken to curb the contributors to warming the Earth (mostly the burning of fossil fuels in support of a broad variety of human activities). The fact that fossil fuels are used to produce energy and that the chief fossil fuel used in that endeavor is petroleum inextricably links global warming to the energy question, the subject of Chapter 2. There are significant differences on the parameters of the problem (exactly what will be affected and how much), and on the quality of the science underlying claims on either side (especially when extrapolations are made far into the future).

Regardless of how serious the problem is, global warming is clearly a classic, full-blown transnational issue. As Eileen Claussen and Lisa McNeilly put it, "Climate change is a global problem that demands a global solution because emissions from one country can impact the climate in all other countries." Global warming, in other words, will be curbed internationally or not at all.

The underlying dynamic, if not its seriousness, can be easily stated. Global warming is the direct result of the release of so-called greenhouse gases into the atmosphere in volumes that are in excess of the capacity of the ecosystem to eliminate them naturally. Although there are a number of these gases, the vast majority of the problem comes from the burning of fossil fuels such as petroleum, natural gas, coal, and wood, which release carbon dioxide, methane, and nitrous oxide (what the Kyoto Protocol calls the "three most important" contributors to pollution) into the air in large quantities. The natural method of containing the amount of carbon dioxide (which is the major culprit) in the atmosphere is the absorption and conversion of that gas in so-called carbon sinks, which separate the two elements (carbon and oxygen) and release them harmlessly back into the atmosphere. In nature, the equatorial rain forests have been where these sinks have historically done most of the work.

The problem of excessive carbon dioxide comes from both sides of the production and elimination process. The burning of fossil fuels, which are essential for much energy production and thus economic activity worldwide, has increased steadily over the last century (and at current rates will continue to do so). Thus, there is more carbon dioxide in the atmosphere than there used to be, and because carbon dioxide has a half-life of roughly a century, that which is emitted today will be around for a long time. At the same time, cutting down trees in the rain forests has reduced the number and quality of natural sinks, thereby reducing nature's ability to capture and convert carbon dioxide into innocuous elements.

The cumulative effect is that there is more carbon dioxide in the atmosphere than there used to be, and it acts as a greenhouse gas. What this means is that as heat from the sun radiates off the Earth and attempts to return in an adequate amount into space to maintain current climate, carbon dioxide acts as a "trap" that retains the heat in the atmosphere rather than allowing it to escape. This blanketing effect keeps excess heat in the atmosphere, and the result is a warmer atmosphere and the phenomenon of global warming—net increases in atmospheric temperatures in specific locales and worldwide.

Responsibility for causing global warming and thus primary liability for doing something about it is also controversial. Significantly, the problem has become a mainstay of the global debate between the more industrially developed countries mostly located in the Northern Hemisphere and the less developed countries, many of which are located in the Southern Hemisphere. One aspect of this debate has to do with causation of the problem and hence responsibility. Fossil fuel burning is at the heart of warming; clearly, much of the problem was created in the North, which has already gone through an industrializing process for which fossil fuel-based energy was and remains an important component. From the vantage point of developing countries that aspire to the material success of the developed countries, this creates two points of contention. On one hand, they view developed countries as the cause of the problem and thus believe those countries should solve the problem by reducing emissions. At the same time, developed countries ask them to refrain from the same kind of fossil fuel-driven growth that they underwent, because doing so will simply make the greenhouse gas effect worse. The call for self-abnegation (under the banner of "sustainable development") by those countries that were fossil fuel self-indulgers strikes many in the developing world as hypocritical, to say the least. Currently, this aspect of the problem centers primarily on India and more particularly on China, which is now the world's second largest producer of carbon dioxide.

The Kyoto Protocol of 1997 (so named after the city where it was finalized) has been the most visible symbol of the global warming process and has become the lightning rod of the procedural and substantive debate over it. The protocol is a very technical, complicated document (see the next section), the heart of which is a series of guidelines for the reduction of emissions by various countries according to a timetable established in the document. The requirements of the agreement have raised controversy because of the differential levels of reduction they impose; this has been especially true in the United States. Support for or opposition to the Kyoto Protocol has also become, in many quarters, emblematic of how one feels about the issue of global warming.

The Kyoto Protocol will expire in 2012, creating a sense of concern among supporters of international attempts to control global warming through international regulation and a sense of relief among skeptics of global warming and opponents of provisions of the protocol. The process of modifying and extending the protocol began formally in Bali, Indonesia, on Kyoto's 10th anniversary on December 1, 2007, which laid out the principles to guide negotiations for a new, stronger accord in Copenhagen, Denmark, during December 2009. The Copenhagen summit failed to move the process forward, leaving the future of global climate control in limbo.

This introduction has laid out some of the basic underlying issues about global warming and the Kyoto Protocol as its symbol. The next section will briefly examine the process by which the international community moved to the formalization of the effort to contain and reverse global warming and where that effect appears to be heading. Since the urgency (or even the need) to engage in such a process depends on whether or to what extent the problem exists, positions on global warming are then presented. The case concludes by looking at the prospects for global warming and the institutionalization of efforts to contain it.

THE ROAD TO KYOTO—AND BEYOND?

Although the Kyoto Protocol has been the most visible symbol (or target, depending on one's perspective), it was in fact an evolutionary step in a process that was begun well before the protocol was adopted and has continued to evolve since (notably with the Bali and Copenhagen conferences). Kyoto became the lightning rod for support or opposition because it provided the most comprehensive set of regulations and guidelines that had occurred to that point; in a very real sense, the rhetoric of global warming turned into a concrete plan and program in 1997. The process continues.

Several points can be made about the road to Kyoto by means of introduction. First, concern about climatic change had been going on for a long time before the protocol was adopted, and the formal international process that resulted in the document began almost 20 years earlier. Second, the document and its requirements are complicated and technical, making a detailed description impossible within the confines of this case format. Third, the United States has had a special role in the evolution of this process, as is so often the case in international initiatives. In this case, the United States has, as in the case of the International Criminal Court, vacillated on the issue, with one administration (Clinton) serving as a major architect, with its successor (Bush) reversing that position completely, and the current administration (Obama) reasserting support. The United States is the world's largest producer of greenhouse gases, and thus the protocol's provisions have questionable effectiveness without American participation. Fourth, the protocol is over a decade old, and some critics maintain that it is based in science that has been overcome by events, meaning its provisions are of declining relevance.

The Kyoto Process

The chronology of global warming as a formal international concern is described by the United Nations Framework Convention for Climate Change (UNFCCC) Secretariat in a 2000 publication, *Caring for Climate*. According to that document, the first step in the process occurred in 1979, when the First World Climate Conference was held. That meeting brought together international scientists concerned with the effects of human intervention in the climate process and the possible pernicious effects of trends that they observed. This meeting also provided the first widespread recognition of the greenhouse gases phenomenon, which was largely known only within the scientific community before then.

The international momentum began to pick up in 1988 with two events. First, the United Nations General Assembly adopted a resolution, 43/53, urging the "protection of global climate for present and future generations of mankind." The resolution was sponsored by Malta. In a separate action, the World Meteorological Organization (WMO) and the United Nations Environmental Programme created the Intergovernmental Panel on Climate Change (IPCC) and charged this new body with assessing the scientific evidence on the subject. As requested, the IPCC issued its First Assessment Report in 1990, concluding that the threat of climate change was real and worthy of further study and concern. Also in 1990, the World Climate Conference held its second meeting in Geneva, Switzerland, and called for a global treaty on climate change. This call in turn prompted the General Assembly to pass another resolution, 45/12, which commissioned negotiations for a convention on climate change to be conducted by the Intergovernmental Negotiating Committee (INC). This body first met in February 1991 as an intergovernmental body. On May 9, 1992, the INC adopted the UNFCCC, which was presented for signature at the Rio De Janeiro United Nations Conference on the Environment and Development (the Earth Summit) in June 1992. The requisite number of signatures was obtained in 1994 and the UNFCCC entered force on March 21, 1994. The process leading to the Kyoto Protocol was thus officially launched.

One express feature of the UNFCCC was an annual meeting of all members of the Convention (which numbered 199 members and observers in 2010) known as the Conference of the Parties (COP). The first COP was held in 1995 in Berlin. The third COP was held in Kyoto, Japan; the result was the Kyoto Protocol.

The Protocol

The Kyoto Protocol is a complicated document (references to the whole treaty can be found in the Web sites section of this chapter) the details of which go beyond present purposes. Several elements can, however, be laid out that provide a summary of what the protocol attempts to do and, based on those purposes, the objections that have been raised to it.

The overarching goal of the protocol is a net reduction in the production and emission of greenhouse gases and thus the arrest and reversal of the adverse effects of climate changes caused by these gases. The protocol identifies six gases for control and emission reduction. Three of these gases are "most important": carbon dioxide (CO_2), methane (CH_4), and nitrous oxide (N_2O). This importance comes from the large relative contribution of these gases to the problem: Carbon dioxide accounts for fully half of "the overall global warming effect arising from human activities" in UNFCCC's language, followed by 18 percent for methane and 6 percent for nitrous oxide. For the United States in 2002, for instance, the percentages were 83 percent carbon dioxide, 9 percent methane, and 6 percent nitrous oxide, according to David Victor. The other three specified categories, the "long-lived industrial gases," are hydroflurocarbons (HFCs), perfluorocarbons (PFCs), and sulfur hexafluoride (SF_6).

The goal of the protocol is a global reduction in the production of targeted gases of 5 percent below the baseline year for measuring emissions, 1990, by the period 2008–2012. The baseline year establishes how much each developed country contributed to emission levels. These levels were then used for two purposes: to determine how much reduction each targeted country must accomplish, and to provide a measuring stick for determining when the protocol comes fully into effect. For determining these contributions, the protocol further divides the countries of the world into three different categories (what it calls Annexes) in terms of the obligations that are incurred.

Since the overwhelming source of greenhouse gases is fossil fuel consumption (gasoline, coal, and natural gas) for energy production for economic activity and transportation, it comes as no surprise that the countries most clearly identified and targeted are those in the developed world, and indeed, Annex I contains these countries. Using 1990 baseline figures for CO_2 emissions as its yardstick, these countries are listed by the amount of emissions they produced and the percentage of the world's total emissions this amount represents. Leading the list by a wide margin is the United States, which was responsible for 36.1 percent of global emissions. Aggregated as a whole, the European Union followed with 24.2 percent, followed by the countries of the Russian Federation with 17.4 percent, and Japan with 8.5 percent (for a total of 86 percent of global emissions). The next largest polluter after these was Australia with 2.1 percent.

The protocol also created two other Annex categories. Annex II contains all the members of the Organization of Economic Cooperation and Development (OECD) but excludes the Economies in Transition (EIT) countries (basically the Annex I countries minus the old communist world). Countries designated in Annex II are "required to provide financial resources to enable developing countries to undertake emissions reduction activities and to help them adapt to adverse effects of climate change," according to the UNFCCC. The final category is Non-Annex I countries. These are the developing countries whose economies are not yet developed enough to contribute meaningfully to global warming and are thus excluded from participating in reduction activities. This category contains some significant economic powers (South Korea, for instance) and the world's two largest countries in population, China and India, whose potential contribution to the global warming problem are enormous and have been the source of much concern.

The baseline for Annex I countries provides the specifications for reductions of emissions levels. These differ by country. Switzerland, most central and eastern European countries, and the European Union are targeted at 8 percent reductions (individual EU countries have different standards to reach the total); the United States' target is 7 percent; and Canada, Hungary, and Japan have 6 percent targets. Russia, New Zealand, and the Ukraine are ordered to stabilize their emissions at 1990 levels, and Norway, Australia, and Iceland can actually increase their emissions levels.

If all these provisions are not complicated enough, the protocol adds another source of complications in terms of what UNFCCC calls "three innovative mechanisms" for meeting goals by means other than straight reductions. These are joint implementation, the clean development mechanism (CDM), and emissions trading. Each deserves at least brief mention, if only to illustrate the convoluted nature of the entire process.

Joint implementation (technically, emission reduction units in the protocol) allows Annex I countries to gain credits against their emission reduction quotas by undertaking projects with Non-Annex I countries either to help those countries reduce their emissions or increase carbon sinks. The CDM provides emissions credits for Annex I countries that invest in projects in Non-Annex I countries, especially in the private sector, that contribute to emissions reductions or in other ways that support the general principle of sustainable development (developmental projects that do not add to pollution of the environment). Emissions trading allows countries that exceed their emissions goals in effect to sell that excess to Annex I countries, which can then apply the excess purchased toward reaching their own required reductions.

As this discussion suggests, the mechanisms and procedures included within the Kyoto Protocol process are indeed complicated, intricate, and difficult to comprehend and implement. They create very different requirements for different states and categories of states, as well as complicated means of compliance through the addition of the "innovative" methods already discussed. As a result, it should not be surprising that this process has also resulted in a certain level of controversy. That controversy, in turn, centers on the United States, which has emerged as the most vocal and important opponent of the protocol.

American and Other Objections

Both because of extent of American contribution to greenhouse gas emission (about 25 percent of all the affected gases and 36 percent of carbon dioxide) and the related formula for implementing the Kyoto Protocol, American participation in the effort is virtually a sine qua non for the global warming effort to succeed. When the movement began, the United States was an enthusiastic participant in the process leading to Kyoto, and the Clinton administration was among the early signers and supporters of the protocol and its implementation.

That position changed when the Bush administration entered office. During the 2000 campaign, Bush favored legislation that would require power plants (one of the major sources of carbon dioxide, along with transportation vehicles) to reduce their emissions by adding "scrubbers" to emissions leaving plants and entering the atmosphere. After he assumed office, he quickly changed course, siding instead with power industry opponents of Kyoto and announcing on March 13, 2001, that he no longer favored U.S. participation in the Kyoto Protocol. In the process, the administration publicly stated that it would not send the treaty signed by Clinton to the Senate for ratification. As a result, the United States has remained the most important country in the world that is not a party to the protocol and thus does not consider itself subject to its requirements, although it remains a party to the UNFCCC. The Obama administration's position is much closer to Clinton's, including enthusiastic (if ultimately unsuccessful) support for the Copenhagen summit.

Bush administration objections to the protocol, which reflected the views of opponents generally, tended to focus on two basic themes. The first is cost and burden to the United States. Although some other countries have higher percentage reduction quotas than the United States, treaty opponents argue being to bearing 7 percent of 36 percent of the total required reductions is too great a burden. In addition, U.S. emissions were already 15 percent above the 1990 level by the end of the millennium and, according to Victor, rising at 1.3 percent per year, thereby demanding even further reductions. Thus, the United States is being asked to do too much proportionately to the rest of the world. In the view of critics, compliance would be economically ruinous in terms of the additional expenses of doing business and the loss of comparative advantage to industries in other countries that are not regulated by these requirements. American conformance to Kyoto standards that do not apply universally thus unfairly imbalances the "playing field" of economic competition.

This leads to the second objection, which is the exclusion of developing countries from the requirements of the protocol. In most cases, this exclusion is innocuous, as most of these countries do not and will not contribute meaningfully to greenhouse gas in the foreseeable future.

The Bush administration directed its criticism of developing-world exclusion principally at two countries, China and India. China has become a major greenhouse gas emitter, as already noted (it is the second-largest emitter in the world), and this situation will continue and intensify as China further develops (thereby requiring additional energy) and continues to promote automobile ownership among its huge population base. India does not pose quite as urgent a threat, but with a population roughly the size of China's and an emerging technological and industrial capacity, the sheer magnitude of the country's potential suggests it should be part of the solution before it becomes an overt part of the problem. One of the few evidences of progress at Copenhagen was a joint Chinese–American accord to address this problem.

A third, more contemporary objection to the protocol is that it is essentially dated. The argument here is the march of technology and change may have simply outgrown its provisions. John Browne, writing in *Foreign Affairs*, summarizes this argument: "First, Kyoto was simply the starting point of a very long endeavor. Second, we have improved, if still imperfect, knowledge of the challenges and uncertainties that climate change presents. . . . Third, many countries and companies have had experience reducing emissions that have proved that such reductions can be achieved without destroying competitiveness of jobs. Fourth, science and technology have advanced on multiple fronts. Finally, public awareness of the issue has grown."

A fourth objection, related to the third, is that the protocol and all its provisions are simply too complicated and unwieldy to be administered in any enforceable, objective way. The various "innovative" ways of substituting means of compliance are a case in point. This complexity suggests to some critics of the protocol that the effort should be scrapped and a new, comprehensive approach grounded in contemporary realities should replace it (this argument is often made by opponents with energy industry credentials). Environmentalists argue this is essentially a cop-out to avoid implementing greenhouse gas emission standards. This opposition comes with a price; it can be argued that it is bad for America's interests for the United States to be seen as the rogue nation of greenhouse gas pollution. As the chief of opponent of Kyoto, the United States becomes the leader in blocking the only binding international agreement for fighting global warming, while offering no alternate path to protect the planet.

Finally, there is an objection from the other end of the spectrum that says the fatal flaw of the Kyoto Protocol is not that it requires too much of countries and the world but that it requires too little. In this argument, the problem is not the degree of sacrifice demanded, but the need to cut greenhouse gas emission much more drastically, in the range of 50 percent rather than the roughly 5 percent demanded in the Kyoto Protocol.

Bali, Copenhagen, and Beyond

The 10th anniversary of the Kyoto accords was marked by a major UNFCCC conference in Bali, Indonesia in December 2007. Nearly 10,000 delegates attended the meeting, the purpose of which was to draft a follow-on agreement that would improve upon the results of the Kyoto Protocol. Gaining American participation and support were major objectives of the conferees.

The conference produced two documents of note. One, known as the Bali Road Map, laid out a process for finalizing a new, binding agreement in time for the 2009 meeting in Copenhagen. The other document was the Bali Action Plan, a set of principles to guide deliberations leading to the agreement.

Major issues introduced at the Bali meeting, to which the United States sent a delegation, included future targets for carbon dioxide emissions reductions and the participation of countries excluded under the annexes of the Kyoto agreement. Mindful of Bush administration objections, the conferees agreed in principle (in the Action Plan) deep cuts in global emissions will be required, but, according to Fuller and Rivkin, the plan "contains no binding commitments." The American delegation insisted that developing economies must likewise act, and China and India agreed to include alterations of their status in negotiations. These outcomes were sufficiently satisfying to the Bush administration that its delegation endorsed the Bali outcome, a major accomplishment for its supporters.

Turning the general agreement into a specific, binding, and effective accord has proven to be the hard part—the "devil in the details." Among enthusiasts of global warming control (which included President Obama), there were high hopes for the December 2009 Copenhagen summit. Technically, the Copenhagen conclave was a series of meetings, most prominently the 15th meeting of the Conference of Parties of the UNFCCC (COP15) and the 5th convening of the Meeting of the Parties of the COP members of the Kyoto

Protocol (COP/MOP5). The summit was attended by 115 heads of state and generated much anticipation prior to its beginning on December 8.

By all accounts, the Copenhagen summit was a failure. It neither formally proposed or enacted any binding, mandatory agreements to supersede Kyoto after its 2012 expiration, nor did it succeed in creating the framework for a global treaty by 2012, which was its goal as specified by the Bali Road Map. As the meeting wound down threatening to produce no agreements at all, a group of major countries, including the United States, China, India, Brazil, and South Africa, convened what the UNFCCC Web site called an "Informal High Level Event" on December 18, the day before the summit was to adjourn. The result was something called the Copenhagen Accord calling for a goal of no more than a 2 degree Fahrenheit increase in global temperatures. This accord was noted but not adopted by the conference. Although UNFCCC continued in 2010, the fate of a follow-on agreement to the Kyoto Protocol remains very much in doubt.

The reasons for the failure are debatable. Part of the problem is that public perceptions of global warming have become less intense, particularly in the United States. A major reason has been the impact of skeptics about the problem that proponents have not entirely countered. International difficulties include continuing complaints about different levels of sacrifice necessary to slow or reverse the phenomenon, although this concern has been partially mitigated by the more positive attitudes of countries like China and India at Copenhagen. At the same time, many of the proposed solutions like the CDM are so complex and nebulous that they create a certain level of cynicism about the crafting of enforceable standards.

WARM AND GETTING WARMER: BUT HOW MUCH?

The urgency and importance of a new global warming accord depends vitally on the urgency and importance of the problem. The debate over global warming is essential and contentious. There have been at least three related factors that make a calm, rational debate over the extent and consequences of global warming difficult to conduct. The first is the absence of immediate consequences of whatever change is occurring. Over the past quarter century or more, climate change in the form of warming has indeed been occurring worldwide, but the effects have been so gradual and generally miniscule that either they have gone unnoticed by most people or have not been easily attributable to the phenomenon. Were there dramatic events that could be associated with climate change (or equally convincing absences of predicted changes), it would be easier to make the case one way or the other. Certainly global warming is blamed for a number of contemporary events from the melting of polar ice caps to recent patterns of violent weather, but there is disagreement about whether the global warming that underlies them is the result of natural change or human behavior.

Second, there are abundant scientific disagreements about the parameters of the problem and its solution. Some of the disagreement is honest, some

possibly self-interested, but for every dire prediction about future consequences, there is a rebuttal from another part of the scientific community. This
debate often becomes scientifically shrill and accusatory, leading to confusion
in the public about what to believe. In this confusion, the citizenry has a difficult time making reasoned assessments and consequent demands on policymakers to adopt standards.

Third, almost all the projections have until recently been sufficiently far in
the future to allow considerable disagreement and to discourage resolution.
One can argue that the scientific evidence to date is very strong one way or the
other on various consequences of warming; the actual consequences are distant enough, however, that the extrapolation is subject to sufficient variation
that scientists can take the same data and reach diametrically opposed conclusions. These extrapolations are often 50 or even 100 years in the future, when
most of the people at whom they are aimed will not even be alive to witness or
be held accountable for them. Attempts to add urgency to the issues by public
figures like former U.S. vice president Al Gore reinforce those who already
believe in the problem but do not convert skeptics.

The often acrimonious debate over the melting of polar ice caps provides
an example of this disagreement. There is no disagreement over the fact that
ice caps are melting; the disagreement is about why and what this means.
Those most worried about global warming argue the burning of fossil fuels is
the culprit, and the consequences include rising ocean levels (mostly from
melting in Antarctica) and ecological change (especially in the Arctic). Critics
contend there is little evidence that the changes are not natural and dispute the
notion of an accelerated rise in sea levels (they argue, for instance, that most of
the melting is of floating ice—ice already in the water—that does not affect
ocean levels one way or the other). Environmentalists counter that greater
melting of floating ice accelerates the melting of ground ice (ice on land),
which *does* raise ocean levels, and so on. How is the layman to gauge these
arguments?

Getting Too Warm?

That global climate is changing is not contested on any side of the debate over
global warming. The Intergovernmental Panel on Climate Change has investi-
gated the extent to which this has happened in the past and has concluded that
the average surface temperature of the Earth increased by about 1 degree
Fahrenheit during the twentieth century and "that most of the warming
observed over the past 50 years is attributable to human activities." (Much of
the IPCC material in this section is from the 2001 report of Group I–III of the
IPCC, cited in the suggested readings.) Extrapolating from trends in the last
century, the IPCC predicts additional warming between 2.2–10 degrees
Fahrenheit (1.4–5.8 degrees Celsius) in this century. The primary culprits are
the greenhouse gases cited in the Kyoto Protocol that result from deforestation
(and its destruction of carbon sinks), energy production from the combustion
of fossil fuels (natural gas, oil, and coal), transportation (primarily cars and

trucks, but also trains and other modes), cattle production (methane gases), rice farming, and cement production.

A variety of effects have been observed and attributed to these changes. In some areas, birds are laying eggs a few weeks earlier than they used to, butterflies are moving their habitats farther up mountains to avoid lowland heat, and trees are blooming earlier in the spring and losing their leaves later in the fall. Any of these changes can be dismissed as of low relative concern, but there are more fundamental changes alleged with more obvious consequences. Warming, the IPCC II reports, shows that snow accumulation is decreasing worldwide, as is the global supply of ice pack. At the same time, glaciers are retreating worldwide (some of the most dramatic American examples are in places like Glacier National Park in Montana), sea levels and ocean temperatures have risen, and rainfall patterns in many regions have changed as well. In addition, there is evidence that permafrost is thawing in the polar regions, that lakes are freezing later and thawing earlier, and that even some plant and animal species have declined and may disappear due to changes in climate.

Some of the most dramatic examples involve the effects on coastal regions. The projected problems arise both from the gradual rise of oceanic levels and the warming of ocean waters. Both are a concern because of the large and growing portion of populations residing in coastal locations (it is, for instance, a major demographic reality in the United States that the population is gradually moving out of the central parts of the country toward more temperate coastal regions).

The extent of these effects, of course, depends on the amount of change caused by global warming. IPCC II data project an average rise of between 6 and 36 inches in sea levels by 2100. Using the higher figure, the impact on some countries would be dramatic. A 36-inch rise would inundate territory in which 10 million people live in Bangladesh alone, forcing their relocation to scarce higher land. The same increase would cover 12 percent of the arable land of the Nile River delta in Egypt, which produces crops on which over 7 million people are dependent. Some estimates suggest the island country of Vanuatu in the South Pacific would simply disappear under the rising waters. Worldwide, it is estimated that 45 million people would be displaced.

Warming of ocean water could also have dramatic effects, for instance, by affecting ocean currents that now have an influence on climate in various parts of the world. The Atlantic Gulf Stream, for instance, could be affected by warmer water coming from polar regions, changing patterns for the coastal United States and Europe. As an example, Gulf Stream effects that tend to keep major hurricanes off parts of the American coast (e.g., the South Carolina Lowcountry) could be diverted, resulting in a new pattern of hurricane, tornado, and storm patterns. Large-scale changes in patterns of ocean circulation are possible worldwide. The cumulative effect, according to the IPCC, could be "a widespread increase in the risk of flooding for human settlements (tens of millions of inhabitants in settlements studied) from both increased heavy precipitation and sea level rise" (IPCC II).

Not So Fast

Scientists disagree about the accuracy of these projections and the direness of the consequences that they project. There is little disagreement about the historical record (e.g., the amount of climate change in the last century) because that is based on observable data that can be examined for accuracy, although there is some disagreement on the precise causes of change (e.g., scientists affiliated with the power industry tend to downplay the impact of energy production). There is, however, disagreement on projections of trends and effects extrapolated into the future. The main source of this disagreement is the fact that any projections are based in observations of effects in a future that has not yet occurred, but are instead based on projections of historically grounded observations (and hence scientific inference) into a future the exact dimensions of which cannot be known or entirely predicted. Extrapolation becomes more uncertain the farther predictions are cast into the future, and thus there is an increased level of disagreement the farther into the future one goes. Since the deleterious effects of global warming are argued to be cumulative and thus more serious the farther into the future one projects; the basis for lively, at times acrimonious, discussions are thus built into the debate.

There tend to be three criticisms of global warming scientists that can be phrased in terms of questions. The first is the factual content of the warnings: How much effect will global warming have? A second, corollary question is how much those effects will accumulate under different assumptions about natural and man-made adjustments to these effects? Third, how difficult are the solutions?

These are good questions that, depending on how they are answered, define both the dimensions of the problem and the urgency and forms that dealing with it should take. The question of how much is clearly the driving dynamic. If the amount of change will be great and the consequences large and damaging, that makes the problem more urgent and sacrifices to solve it both urgent and important.

The problem, of course, is that there is disagreement on these matters. Take, for instance, the projections on how much average surface temperatures will increase in this century if action is not taken. Estimates range from 1 to 10 degrees Fahrenheit, and that is a considerable range in terms of the consequences to the world and mankind. If the actual figure is at the upper end of that spectrum, then things like snow pack, glacier, and polar ice cap melting will be considerable, with oceans rising at the upper limits of predictions (around three feet). Parts of Tampa Bay and New Orleans, among other places, will be under water unless levees are constructed to keep the water out, and Vanuatu may become the next Lost City of Atlantis (an analogy often made by global warming scientists). If the rise in mean surface temperature is closer to or at the lower extreme (a degree or so), however, the consequences are probably far less dire.

Who knows which part of the range is correct? The answer is that with any scientific certitude, no one does. The amount of warming is necessarily an extrapolation into a future that does not exist, after all, not an observation of something that does. Clearly, it is in the interests of those who either do not believe in the more severe projections or who would be most adversely affected by concerted efforts to reduce emissions to believe in the lower projections and thus to deny the more severe reactions. At the same time, those who believe the problem to be dire have an interest in accepting the higher estimates, either as a hedge against uncertainty (if one plans for the worst, then anything else may be more manageable) or because of a sincere belief in the higher numbers.

The layman is left up in the air. Because the effects are not immediate and unambiguous, the average person has little way to answer the second question: What does all this mean? Is the world headed for an environmental catastrophe if something is not done to slow, stop, or reverse global warming? The scientists on both sides of the issue are passionate and self-convinced, but they have not, by and large, made a case to the world's publics that is compelling, understandable, and convincing—one way or the other. In a world of more instantly consequential problems, it is hard to bring oneself to develop the passion that the advocates, regardless of scientific credentials, have on the issue.

This leads to the third question, which brings the concern full circle and returns to the Kyoto Protocol and beyond: What should be done about the problem? The immediate answer, of course, is that it depends on how bad the problem is. Most of the world has accepted the basic science of those warning about the more dire consequences of not solving the global warming problem, and the United States has until recently been prominent among major powers (and greenhouse gas emitters) in denying or downplaying the problem and resisting the Kyoto solution. Admittedly, the major source of official U.S. objection is not the veracity of global warming science, but is instead directed at the differential obligations for solving it that Kyoto prescribes: reductions with economic consequences that would make the American economy less competitive and the exclusion of developing-world countries with large pollution potentials from regulation. If, however, the American government fully accepted the direst projections of the consequences, these objections would probably pale in comparison to the dictates of solving the problem. Implicitly or explicitly, American opposition to the Kyoto Protocol also reflects a belief the problem is not great (or, more minimally, that the solution can be deferred without significant consequences).

There is, of course, a hedge in answering the third question that reflects a deep American trait in viewing problems. That hedge is a belief that technology will somehow find a way to ameliorate the problem, either by finding a way to decrease the emission of greenhouse gases or to increase the ability to absorb and neutralize those gases and their consequences. That is the position often taken by the American energy and transportation industries, and it is an approach that has worked to solve other problems at other times. Whether adherence to that belief is a blind leap of faith or a sound scientific prediction is, like so much of the debate over global warming, a question of perspective.

CONCLUSION

No one disagrees that global warming is taking place or that its effects are not pernicious to some degree. There are no pro-global warmers. However, there is considerable reluctance to attack and eradicate the problem, and this has been especially true in the United States, whose participation in the effort is absolutely critical to its solution. Why?

The answer lies in two phenomena, one only hinted at to this point and one discussed more fully. One problem is the contrast between the short term and the longer term regarding global warming and its effects. In the short term (say, the next 10–20 years), it is not absolutely clear that there will be major negative worldwide or local events that can be attributed unambiguously and consensually to global warming. If, as many maintain, the spate of extremely destructive hurricanes of 2005 (Katrina and Rita) could unambiguously be tied to global warming, that might have been cause to act. But is warming clearly the cause? Those who warn about the prospects of global warming are, quite correctly from their viewpoint, insisting that remedial actions need to be taken now to avoid disastrous effects in the short and longer term. These actions include personal and societal sacrifices on the altar of cleaner air, including reductions in emissions from power plants, automobiles, and the like which will incur costs that will be passed along to all of us.

The longer view reverses this perspective. According to those most concerned with the damaging effects of global warming, the failure to act in the short run condemns those who will experience the negative effects. As cities are inundated a 100 years from now, for instance, it will likely not be difficult to convince people they need to make those sacrifices as the water laps at their front doors, but by then it may be too late to take the corrective actions that need to be taken now to prevent that future fate.

Can these two contrasting perspectives be reconciled? In the abstract, they can. If humankind *knew* that the failure to take action today would condemn those who follow to a specific negative fate, then people might be able to agree to make those sacrifices. That reconciliation flies in the face of the second phenomenon, uncertainty of the nature of the future and a consequent reluctance to act when the consequences of acting or not acing are not precisely knowable.

The first part of this difficulty has been discussed extensively already and need not be reiterated. The simple fact is that there is indeed disagreement about the parameters and severity of the global warming situation, and those who are reluctant to counsel sacrifices that would be politically unpopular can and do use that uncertainty to justify inaction. Those who warn of global warming counter the irresponsibility of ignoring what they are convinced is inevitable, but such arguments fall on at least partially deaf ears in the absence of incontrovertible evidence that the warnings are true.

Until that undeniable evidence is produced, there is precedent to believe humankind will simply defer the problem. In some ways, the global warming problem and its solution are like deficit spending. No one believes spending more than is taken in is good and responsible policy, and everyone knows in the abstract that some time in the future, someone else is going to have to pay off the debt that is being accumulated. At some point, the piper will have to be paid, but exactly when this will occur and what exactly the piper will exact are matters of disagreement that help us justify not taking the corrective action of balancing budgets. Why should global warming be any different?

At the beginning of the case study, global warming was described as a true transnational issue, and one with unique aspects. That uniqueness has at least three significant angles. First, global warming is truly a global issue that affects the entire planet and can only be solved by essentially universal actions by the countries of the world. This observation accentuates the role of American opposition to the Kyoto Protocol; if global warming is indeed the problem it is advertised to be, the United States will bear unique responsibility globally for failing to address and solve it. Second, responding to global warming will have direct impacts on two of the most important motors of the global economy: energy production and use, and transportation. Disruptions to either or both of these industries could have catastrophic economic effects for the world generally. The problem of global warming, in other words, is important to everyone's well-being. Third, global warming is the only environmental change problem that intensifies or is intensified by other major environmental problems. Rising water levels affect the ability of the Earth to produce food, and desertification is increased by warming, to cite two problems created. The effects of global warming are, in other words, pervasive.

How warm is the world getting, what does that matter, and what should or must be done or not done about it? These are the questions asked throughout this case study, and they are all questions that have potentially vital answers for the good of all of us individually and collectively. What, then, are those answers?

STUDY/DISCUSSION QUESTIONS

1. Describe the global warming problem. What causes it? What are the short- and long-term consequences of global warming?
2. Describe global warming as a North–South political and climatic problem. Who bears responsibility for creating and solving the problem?
3. Describe the process leading to the Kyoto Protocol. What are the major provisions of the protocol? Which provisions are most controversial? Why?
4. Why does the United States have a unique place in the global warming and Kyoto Protocol process? What are the major U.S. objections to the protocol? Why can the protocol not be effective without American participation in its implementation?
5. The Kyoto Protocol will expire in 2012. Discuss efforts to negotiate a follow-on agreement at Bali and Copenhagen. Why have these meetings failed to produce new accords? What are the implications for the future?
6. What are the major claims made by those who believe that global warming is a major worldwide problem? How do skeptics counter these assertions?

7. Explain the major dilemma of the global warming debate in terms of short- and long-term effects. Are the prospects sufficiently dire that you believe we should endure short-term sacrifices to guard against long-term dangers?
8. Why is global warming unique as a transnational issue? Explain.

READING/RESEARCH MATERIAL

Ackerman, John T. *Global Climate Change: Catalyst for International Relations Disequilibria.* PhD Dissertation. Tuscaloosa, AL: University of Alabama, 2004.

Anderson, Terry and Harry I. Miller, eds. *The Greening of U.S. Foreign Policy.* Stanford, CA: Hoover Institution Press, 2000.

Beyond Kyoto: Advancing the International Effort Against Climate Change. Arlington, VA: Pew Center on Global Climate Change, 2003.

Black, Richard. "Copenhagen Climate Summit Undone by 'Arrogance.'" *BBC News* (online), March 16, 2010.

Browne, John. "Beyond Kyoto." *Foreign Affairs* 83, 4 (July/August 2004), 20–32.

Claussen, Eileen and Lisa McNeilly. *Equity and Global Climate Change: The Complex Elements of Global Fairness.* Arlington, VA: Pew Center for Global Climate Change, 2000.

Crook, Clive. "The Sins of Emission." *The Atlantic* 301, 3 (April 2008), 32–34.

Diehl, Paul R. and Niles Peter Gleditsch, eds. *Environmental Conflict.* Boulder, CO: Westview, 2001.

Fuller, Thomas and Andrew C. Rivkin. "Climate Plan Looks Beyond Bush's Tenure." *New York Times* (online), December 16, 2007.

Gupta, Joyeeta. *Our Simmering Planet: What to Do about Global Warming.* New York: Zed Books, 2001.

Intergovernmental Panel on Climate Change. A Report of Working Groups I–III. *Summary for Policymakers—Climate Change 2001.* Cambridge, UK: Cambridge University Press, 2001.

Luterbacher, Urs and Detlef F. Sprinz, eds. *International Relations and Global Climate Change.* Cambridge, MA: MIT Press, 2001.

Michaels, Patrick J. and Robert C. Balling Jr. *The Satanic Gases: Clearing the Air about Global Warming.* Washington, DC: CATO Institute, 2000.

Pirages, Dennis C. and Theresa Manley DeGeest. *Ecological Security: An Evolutionary Perspective on Globalization.* New York: Rowman and Littlefield, 2004.

Podesta, John and Peter Ogden. "The Security Implications of Climate Change." *Washington Quarterly* 31, 1 (Winter 2007–2008), 115–138.

Schelling, Thomas C. "The Cost of Combating Global Warming: Facing the Tradeoffs." *Foreign Affairs* 75, 6 (November/December 1997), 8–14.

Stern, Todd, and William Antholis. "A Changing Climate: The Road Ahead for the United States." *Washington Quarterly* 31, 1 (Winter 2007–2008), 175–187.

Victor, David C. G. *Climate Change: Debating America's Options.* New York: Council on Foreign Relations Press, 2004.

Vidal, John, Allegra Stratton, and Suzanne Goldenberg. "Low Target, Goals Dropped: Copenhagen Ends in Failure." *Guardian.co.uk* (online), December 19, 2009.

Whitty, Julia. "The Thirteenth Tipping: 12 Global Disasters and 1 Powerful Antidote." *Mother Jones* 31, 6 (November/December 2006), 45–53, 101.

Wirth, Timothy. "Hot Air over Kyoto: The United States and the Politics of Global Warming." *Harvard International Review* 23, 4 (2002), 72–77.

WEB SITES

Assessment of state of environment

Yale Center for Environmental Law and Policy at http://www.ciesin.columbia.edu/indicators/ESI

Text of Kyoto Protocol at http://unfccc.int/resource/convkp.html

Third Assessment Report of IPCC at http://www.ipcc.ch.

International Migration: The U.S.-Mexican Border

PRÉCIS

The movement of people across national borders to resettle—immigration—is a major international phenomenon, and one that dates back to the beginnings of humankind. People move for a variety of reasons, from the hope of economic betterment to the fear of political repression or extinction; the common theme is and has been the attempt to improve the human condition. Today there are roughly 200 million refugees worldwide, with the majority being people from the developing world (Africa, Asia, and Latin America) seeking new homes in the developed world (Europe and North America). The case study application of the movement of Mexicans and Central Americans across the U.S.-Mexico border illustrates the underlying dynamics of worldwide immigration, while adding some unique variables in the form of drug trafficking and terrorism.

Migration is one of the oldest and most enduring aspects of the human experience. At some level of remove, essentially everyone is an immigrant or the descendant of immigrants; the only humans who can rightfully claim nonimmigrant status are direct descendants of the earliest humans from the Great Rift Valley in Africa (where the ancestors of today's human population are believed first to have emerged) who still live there. The immigrant status is especially true for North Americans: even those peoples to whom the appellation "Native Americans" is applied arrived here from Asia, probably walking across the then land bridge between Asia and North America in the Bering Straits. Peoples moving from place to place are thus a very enduring part of history.

Immigration is a large, important, and controversial contemporary phenomenon. In 2005, the United Nations Department of Economic and Social Affairs reported that there were 191 million international immigrants (people residing in countries other than that of their birth). That figure fluctuates from year-to-year, as some immigrants are repatriated and others leave voluntarily or flee their native lands. The reasons they move are various and complicated, but the net result is a constant flow of people across borders. As Koser points out in a 2009 article, today approximately 1 in every 35 people in the world is an immigrant. The arrival of new peoples has always been a source of controversy of greater or lesser intensity depending on who was trying to settle where in what numbers and for what reasons. No two cases are identical.

The immigrant question has always been important for the United States. As the admonition to "bring me your tired, your huddled masses" on the Statue of Liberty heralds, the United States is a quintessential immigrant state, with waves of immigrants from various places arriving at different times in the country's history to constitute one of the world's most nationally and ethnically diverse populations. Sometimes the process of new immigrant waves has been orderly, open, and noncontentious, but as often as not it has been surrounded by considerable disagreement and rancor.

Immigration has, of course, become particularly contentious over the last two decades because of the large-scale movement of Mexicans and Central Americans across the U.S.-Mexican border. The actual numbers involved are difficult to estimate actively, because many of the immigrants have been so-called "irregular" or illegal immigrants who, by definition, are unaccounted for when they arrive. Using the 2005 UN figures, it is estimated that about 20 percent of immigrants in the world are in the United States, over half of which have entered across the U.S.-Mexican border, mostly illegally. The result has been an enormous political controversy in the United States over what to do about this problem, the dimensions and dynamics of which form the case application in this chapter.

While the American situation is the currently most public manifestation of concern over immigration, it is by no means the only place where the question sits on the public agenda. Europe, for instance, is host to a considerably larger immigrant population than the United States, especially in a few select countries like Germany. To understand the nature of the concern—and to place the current U.S. debate into a global context—it is necessary to look at the immigration question more broadly, which is the purpose of the next section.

PARAMETERS OF IMMIGRATION

Immigration is a normal, daily occurrence in much of the world. Some countries are more permissive about letting citizens leave (emigrate) or enter from other countries (immigrate), but some population movement is a regular part of international activity, and one that is arguably increasing in a globalizing world in which international commerce of all kinds is increasing. Employing an accepted definition used by Koser that an international immigrant is "a person who stays outside his usual country of residence for at least one year," the global total of immigrants today is around 200 million people.

Immigrants are often subdivided into more or less controversial categories. Regular international immigrants consist of those individuals who have migrated to a country through legal channels, meaning their immigration is recognized by the host government. Countries allow such immigrants into the country for a variety of reasons and in different numbers depending on the needs or uses they may have for such populations. Parts of Europe—notably Germany—have long admitted workers from places like Turkey to augment a shrinking workforce as its population ages (see discussion below), and the United States has historically given priority status to people with particularly needed education and technical skills, such as scientists and engineers from developing countries like India.

There are, however, other categories of immigrants that are more controversial. In the contemporary debate (and especially the U.S.-Mexican case), the most controversial are so-called *irregular immigrants*. The UN Department of Economic and Social Affairs defines this class of people as "those who enter a country without proper authorization or who have violated the terms of stay of the authorization they hold, including by overstaying." Acronyms for irregular status include illegal, undocumented, and unauthorized immigrants. As Koser points out, "there are around 40 million irregular immigrants worldwide, of whom perhaps one-third are in the United States." The most publicized, and largest, part of that total are irregular by virtue of illegal entry into the country; some of the most problematical, however, are individuals who have entered the country legally but have overstayed the conditions of their residence, as in not leaving after student or temporary work visas have expired. This latter category is troublesome because of possible connections to anti-American activities such as terrorism.

A special category of immigrants are refugees. Broadly speaking, refugees are the most prominent example of what the UN Commission on Human Rights (UNCHR) calls "forcibly displaced people," who, according to 2009 UNCHR figures, number about 42 million. The largest numbers of people within this category are refugees (displaced people living outside their native countries) at about 15.2 million, internally displaced persons or IDPs (refugees within their own countries) at about 26 million, and asylum seekers (people who have sought international protection but whose applications have not been acted upon), who numbered 827,000 in 2008. The Refugee Act of 1980 in the United States borrows its definition from the 1951 UN Convention Relating to the Status of Refugees (and its 1967 Protocol), saying a refugee is "a person outside of his or her country of nationality who is unable or unwilling to return because of persecution or a well-grounded fear of persecution on account of race, religion, nationality, membership in a particular social group, or political opinion." Those who seek refugee status often come from developing countries where human misery is both economic and political, meaning that it is sometimes difficult to determine why a particular refugee or group of refugees seek to migrate. As Koser points out, "though an important legal distinction can be made between people who move for work purposes and those who flee conflict and persecution, in reality the two can be difficult to distinguish."

International and internal refugees are most prominently associated with conflict zones and especially civil conflicts. One of the world's most well publicized instances of refugee dynamics is the Darfur region of Sudan and surrounding countries like the Central African Republic and Chad, as discussed in Chapter 8. In terms of sheer numbers, the largest concentrations of refugees are people fleeing the wars in Afghanistan and Iraq: 1.8 million Afghan refugees in Pakistan, 1.1 Iraqi refugees in Syria, and 980,000 Iraqi and Afghan refugees in Iran.

The dynamics of immigration as a global issue requires looking at the phenomenon from at least three vantage points. The first is the motivation for immigration: Why do people emigrate from one place to another, and what roles do they fulfill when they become immigrants? The second is where the phenomenon of immigration is the most and least evident on a global scale. While it is generally true that the global pattern is one of people moving from the developed to the developing world, the pattern is selective and regionally distinctive. The third concern is immigration as a problem, both globally and locally. Are there distinctive problems that are created by current, ongoing patterns, and are these likely to get better or worse in the future? The answers to these questions, in turn, help frame the context of the problems associated with immigration across the Mexican border into the United States.

Immigration Motivations and Functions

People migrate for a variety of both positive and negative reasons, and immigration is more or less positively received by the people of the places to which they migrate depending on the role and need the receiving country has for the particular migrants that are arriving. Both the motivations for migrating and the reactions to being asked to receive migrants are sufficiently numerous and complex that it is difficult to generalize across the board.

The most obvious—virtually tautological—reason for international migration is to improve one's living conditions by relocation. People decide to leave for both political and economic reasons: politically to avoid conflict or discrimination in their home land, and economically in the hope or promise of a materially better life in the country to which they immigrate. This basic statement of motivation has numerous variations, as Choucri and Mistree enumerate: "the most obvious patterns of international migration today include the following: migration for employment; seasonal mobility for employment; permanent settlements; refugees who are forced to migrate; resettlement; state-sponsored movements; tourism and ecotourism; brain drains and 'reversals' of brain drains; smuggled and trafficked people; people returning to their country of origin; environmental migration and refugees from natural shortages or crises; nonlegal migration; and religious pilgrimage."

History's most dramatic migrations have had political upheaval as an underlying theme. As Koser points out, "large movements of people have always been associated with significant global events like revolutions, wars, and the rise and fall of empires; with epochal changes like economic expansion, nation-building, and political transformations; and with enduring challenges like conflict, persecution, and dispossession." While these dramatic kinds of events are still at play, the current surge of immigration has a more subtle economic theme that is part of globalization and modern demographic changes in the world.

The economic motivation, to move somewhere where economic opportunities are better than where one lives, is nothing new. As Choucri and Mistree summarize, "during good times people migrate to find better opportunities; during bad times people migrate to escape more difficult circumstances." In either situation, the motivating factor is opportunity, which is manifested in the availability of jobs because, as Choucri and Mistree add, "To the extent that population growth exceeds a society's employment potential, the probability is very high that people will move to other countries in search of jobs."

Demographics enter the picture here. Population growth rates are highest in developing countries, and that means the numbers of rising job seekers is greatest in these countries relative to the number of jobs available. In the developed world, on the other hand, population growth rates are much lower (in some cases below levels to maintain current population sizes), the overall population is aging, and thus the percentage of citizens in the active workforce is diminishing. Goldstone explains the consequence: "the developed countries' labor forces will substantially age and decline, constraining economic growth in the developed world and raising demands for immigrant workers." Indeed, there are estimates that the developed countries that will be most successful in the future are those who are best able to augment their shrinking workforces with immigrant labor. This simple dynamic dictates pressure for population migration from developing to developed countries globally, and that pressure is often in fairly dramatic excess of immigration quotas and the like that many developed countries (including the United States) have. The United States is the only developed country with a direct land border with a developing country, making that interplay most obvious in the Mexican-American case.

The kinds of talents that immigrants can contribute come in different categories that make acceptance of immigrants more or less enthusiastic. The smallest and most welcome category of immigrants is what the United Nations refers to as "highly skilled workers." These workers, generally highly educated and possessing scientific or engineering expertise at the cutting edge of the global economy, are the subject of so-called "brain drains" in one direction or the other. Countries of origins of these individuals are often anxious to restrict their emigration or, for those who have moved, to encourage their return (reverse brain drains, a phenomenon introduced with regard to India in Chapter 12). Countries like the United States that have historically been the beneficiaries of the movement of the highly skilled people make special provisions to make immigration possibilities attractive for these groups (see Martin for a discussion).

The far more problematical category of economic immigrants is those who have comparatively low skill levels. They are a double-edged sword for the countries into which they move. On one hand, they provide labor when it is in short supply, and particularly in areas that are low paying or undesirable. Koser refers to these kinds of jobs as "3D jobs: dirty, difficult, or dangerous." He points out that "in the majority of advanced economies, migrant workers are overrepresented in agriculture, construction, heavy industry, manufacturing, and services—especially food, hospitality, and domestic services." Martin adds that these kinds of jobs are "the work magnet that stimulates illegal immigration."

Unskilled immigrants—especially irregular immigrants—pose a particular moral and practical dilemma for receiving states. These immigrants do jobs that the citizens are either unwilling to do or that they will not do at the lower wages that migrants will accept (especially irregular migrants). Thus, without a pool of such laborers, vital services either would not get done or would only be done at higher costs. The alternative to migrant labor is more expensive indigenous labor, which would demand higher wages (federal minimum wages in the United States at least), which would ripple upward through the wage system (there would be relatively fewer laborers for traditional jobs, making them more valuable). The dilemma is that quotas on legal immigration are far too restrictive to produce an adequate sized legal migrant pool to do the jobs migrants do, and if the current "underground" economy went above board and hired only legally registered immigrants, they would have to pay them higher wages, provide benefits, and do other things that would raise the costs of their labor. The moral dimension is that this situation often leads to a public denunciation of irregular immigrants by those employers who most depend on them and who would be most economically damaged were there to be no irregular immigrants.

The acceptance or rejection of economic immigrants thus operates at two levels. Highly skilled immigrants are almost always welcome, because they augment the receiving country's talent pool and add intellectual or physical capabilities that might not otherwise be present in adequate numbers or at all. It is estimated, for instance, that fully one-half of the scientists and engineers practicing in the United States are of foreign birth. Under the Immigration Act of 1990, the United States allows 140,000 immigrants with needed skills into the country annually. The country's intellectual and technological base would be seriously compromised were they to leave or be evicted.

The system operates differently regarding less skilled immigrants, which, of course, includes most of the irregular immigrants. As suggested already, there is some hypocrisy that taints the question of such economic immigrants. For the most part, the immigrants themselves are impoverished people fleeing great economic deprivation personally and motivated to improve the lots of themselves and their extended families. Indeed, remittances from these workers back to their relatives in their countries of origin are a significant part of the economies of some of these countries. The fact that these workers lack proper documentation, however, means they are here illegally, and this fact triggers sentiment against them. At the same time, their status leaves them particularly vulnerable to unscrupulous employers who can pay them at very low rates because they have no leverage against exploitation. Complicating matters is that since illegal employment typically also means that wages are not taxed (they are paid on a cash basis), any demands that this category of people makes on community resources (health care and education, for instance) is not offset by payments they have made into those systems. It is not clear whether the blame in this case lies with the workers or with employers who do not withhold and submit parts of earnings to appropriate government entities.

Refugees present a separate problem. Generally, they can also be divided into skilled and unskilled groups, with the skilled often constituting professionals from the country from which they flee, and the unskilled composed mainly of subsistence farmers and the like. The skilled parts of the population are more likely to be absorbed into the country to which they flee (although generally at much lower standards of living), while the unskilled generally cannot be absorbed and become a burden on the country or on international bodies like the United Nations Commission on Human Rights (UNCHR). Moreover, most refugees are from developing countries and flee to adjacent countries, which are also poor and thus lacking the resources to tend for their new citizens. Darfurians, for instance, have fled to Chad and the Central African Republic, both of which are desperately poor and incapable of providing much succor to the refugees.

There is another category of generally irregular immigrants that should be mentioned: criminals who move to new countries in order to carry out illegal activities of one sort or another. Human traffickers and smugglers are one instance of this form of immigration. Another is the movement of drug traffickers into the countries in which they do business or through which they transit. This form of irregular immigration is a particular problem along the U.S.-Mexican border and the source of a disproportionate amount of the concern with immigrants that anti-immigration forces mount. As will be suggested in the case study section, there is often not a great deal of effort within the anti-immigration movement to differentiate between criminal and purely economic immigrants.

The World Situation

There are two basic and overlapping trends in worldwide immigration. The first is that the burden of this immigration is shifting geographically from the developing to the developed world, and especially to Europe and North America. (Asian migration is actually greater than migration to North America, but it is intra-developing world movement.) The other trend is that immigration is increasing numerically: there are more immigrants worldwide than there have been. Part of this latter trend can be at least partially explained by the overall increase in world population. A significant element, however, is demographic, based in aging populations in the developed world and the consequent need to import younger workers both to sustain economic activity and to support an aging and unproductive population.

The UN Department of Economic and Social Affairs/Population Division presents a statistical summary of the immigration trends in its *International Migration Report 2006: A Global Assessment* (hereafter IMR). The report provides comparative data for 1990 and 2005 that are representative of the migration problem. Between 1990 and 2005, overall global migration increased from 154.8 million in 1990 to 190.6 million in 2005, a statistically small increase of from 2.9 to 3.0 percent of world population. The distribution of that migration, however, was significant. The IMR divides the destinations of immigrants between the more and least developed countries. In 1990, the more developed countries were the destination of 82.4 million immigrants (53.2 percent of the world total). By 2005, that number had increased to 115.4 million, or 60.5 percent of the total.

These destinations are geographically distinct. Europe and North America are the destinations of most of the immigrants to the developed world (not entirely surprising given that the two continents encompass most of the developed world). Europe bears the brunt of this migration, followed by North America. As the IMR summarizes, "the proportion of migrants living in North America rose from 18 percent in 1990 to 23 percent in 2005, and the share of Europe rose from 32 to 34 percent. In 2005, one in every three international migrants lived in Europe and about one in every four lived in North America." The growth rate of international migrants is greatest for North America, where the "migrant stock" rose by an annual rate of 3.2 percent between 1990 and 2005. Most North American immigrants come from Mexico and Central America, whereas immigrants to Europe come primarily from Africa and Asia.

These figures are particularly noteworthy for the United States, which has the largest number of international migrants of any country in the world (20.1 percent of the world total in 2005, according to the IMR). The U.S. Department of Homeland Security Office of Immigration Statistics provides estimates of the distribution and number of immigrants. For 2008, it reports that there were 1,107,126 immigrants with permanent legal resident status in the country, but also estimated that there were 11,600,000 "unauthorized immigrants." Slightly over seven million of those residents were from Mexico, with approximately another one million each from El Salvador and Guatemala.

These trends are likely to increase in the future. As Goldstone points out, "the developed countries' labor forces will substantially age and decline, constraining economic growth in the developed world and raising the demand for immigrant workers." The rate at which populations are aging, and how governments respond to this problem, varies greatly, with different consequences. Japan, for instance, has one of the world's most rapidly aging populations and has, for cultural reasons, been very reluctant to allow non-Japanese immigrants into the country. This is already having two effects.

First, it means that a shrinking portion of the population is part of the productive workforce that must, among other things, produce the wealth needed to support older, retired Japanese. Second, it means a contraction in productivity and also population. The cumulative effect of these dynamics is the projection of a smaller and less economically prominent Japan in the future. In contrast, the American population is aging more slowly, and the effects have been attenuated by the influx of younger immigrant workers to do jobs that aging Americans either cannot or will not do (3D jobs in particular). Europe also has this problem, which especially features low fertility rates, and is wrestling with acceptable rates or immigration to deal with it, a problem made more acute by the relatively high percentage of immigrants who are Muslim.

The scale of immigration, especially from the developing to the developed world, is not going to go away. If anything, it will increase in the future. As Goldstone suggests, "Current levels of immigration from developing to developed countries are paltry compared to those that the forces of supply and demand might soon create across the world." The degree to which this likely trend is a concern depends on whether one views immigration as a problem or not.

The Immigration Problem

Most of the discussions of immigration in the popular debate tend to focus on the problems associated with the phenomenon. The breaching of sovereign national borders is one manifestation of the concern many have with immigration, and underlying many concerns is a sort of "nativism" that seeks to protect the racial or other purity of particular countries from the polluting of countries by the outsiders. The desire to "secure" borders, one of the most frequent ways in which immigration opposition is voiced, also collides with the dynamics of globalization. Both these factors are present in the American debate about immigration from Mexico.

The question of migration needs to be put in some historical perspective, especially in the United States, where the debate has become loudest and most shrill. The United States is, and basically always has been, an immigrant country, with different national groups arriving in waves during the over two centuries of the American experience. In the nineteenth century, for instance, much of the immigration was from Europe, as Europeans sought to flee physical (e.g., the Irish potato famine) or other economic and political distress (e.g., large Italian migration that, according to Martin, reached 285,000 in 1907 alone). Those immigrant waves have been selective and have provoked reactions: the National Origins Act of 1924, for instance, limited Italian legal immigration to 4,000 annually. The twentieth century saw the placing and then removal of bans or highly restrictive limits on Asian immigration. The current reaction to Latin American immigration must take into account that it is, in some important ways, part of a broader historical pattern of rejection and embrace of different immigrant groups.

Large-scale, and especially irregular, immigration does pose problems conceptually for governments. While the instances of truly effective "Great Wall" of China solutions to keeping borders sacrosanct are historically few, high levels of border porosity do pose the question of national control of their own territory. As Choucri and Mistree put it, "perhaps in no other arena is countries' lack of effective control of borders and national access so striking as in the realm of international migration." According to Koser, this is particularly a problem with illegal migrants: "One legitimate risk is irregular immigrant's threat to the exercise of sovereignty."

The result is an essential ambivalence. Breaches of sovereignty are a matter of concern in principle among those to whom national sovereignty is a particular obsession, but it is also a practical concern if those who may breach sovereign boundaries are individuals—such as terrorists—about whom the country has legitimate concerns in national security of other terms. The problem, of course, is that creating boundaries that cannot be breached—the most extreme form of making boundaries secure—is probably impractical or impossible (the direct American–Canadian border, excluding the Alaska–Canada border, is over 3,900 miles long) and would have other undesirable consequences. Chief among these would be the effect of slowing or strangling the flow of goods, services, and people across national boundaries, the essence of globalization. Choucri and Mistree, once again, capture the basis of the problem: "the evident inability to regulate and control access across national borders is one legacy of the current phase of globalization."

This dynamic is most often overlooked in the debate over secure borders and immigration control. Restriction of movement across national boundaries is directly antithetical to the promotion of free trade which, as pointed out in Chapter 9, is the heart of globalization. While cutting off the flow of Mexican and Central American peasants across the southern border of the United States may seem to have no direct impact on global economic activity, the underlying dynamics of such a movement can have such an impact. The movement of labor from places where it is abundant to places where it is not is indeed part of the globalization phenomenon. Goldstone argues that the two forces need not be at fundamental odds with one another, however. "Correctly managed, population movement can benefit developed and developing countries alike. . . . Immigration to developed countries can provide economic opportunities for the ambitious and serve as a safety valve for all."

The brunt of this discussion has been that international immigration is a large and complex phenomenon. The movement of people from one area to another began with the migration out of the Great Rift Valley that began human population of the globe, and it continues to this day. The growing size of the global population, the increased unacceptability of great disparities between people in the developed and developing world, and contemporary forces like those associated with globalization help shape the contemporary issue. Nowhere is that issue more poignant or prominent than in the case of the U.S.-Mexican border.

THE U.S.-MEXICAN BORDER PROBLEM

Immigration policy has always been a matter of disagreement and ambivalence among Americans. One pole in the disagreement is and always has been the self-image Americans have of themselves as a nation (and essentially a nationality) of immigrants who have escaped oppression from an otherwise tainted world and hold their arms open for others like themselves. The Statue of Liberty's welcome to the oppressed captures this popular sentiment. The other pole, however, suggests a more selective attitude, the idea that some peoples are more welcome than others. Immigrant nationalities as widely disparate as the Irish and Italians from Europe and the Chinese and Japanese from Asia have been the objects of exclusion. In terms of the current controversy, it is symbolically significant that one of the derogations heaped upon Italian immigrants of the late nineteenth and early twentieth century was to refer to them as "wops," an acronym for "without official papers." In important ways, the current reaction against Mexican and Central American irregular immigrants (or "wops") is simply the contemporary manifestation of this historical strain.

The current crisis along the U.S.-Mexican border is also part of the global migration trend from the developing to the developed world already introduced. The basic dynamics that are causing a surge in African and Middle Eastern migration to Europe are present in the United States as well, and for most of the same reasons. The existence of an aging population that is not replenishing itself rapidly enough to sustain an adequate workforce to fill needed functions (especially 3D jobs) afflicts both North America and Europe, tying together immigration and prosperity in the process. The dictates of globalization, moreover, demand an increased flow of productive workers into the country if the national edge in the global economy is to be maintained.

The current crisis has its own unique, exacerbating characteristics as well. As a developed–developing world phenomenon, the U.S.-Mexican border case is intensified by the nature of the border. At 1,933 miles of mostly desolate, rural topography, it is a very long and difficult frontier to "seal," as its proponents advocate, without debilitating levels of resource expenditure that might prove inadequate in the most optimal circumstances. At the same time, the U.S.-Mexico boundary is the world's only direct land border between the developed and developing worlds. While G-20 member Mexico may chafe at its continuing designation as a developing world, the per capita income of Mexicans is only about 30 percent that of Americans statistically, meaning the economic lure of migration is present. Citizens from Central America migrate through Mexico and across the border, a more direct form of developing world migration. Migrants to Europe, in contrast, have no equivalent of the U.S.-Mexico boundary as a symbol of obstruction to their entrance.

The U.S.-Mexican case is also distinguished by its sheer volume and the accompanying complexity of the problem. No one, of course, knows exactly how many irregular immigrants are in the United States, and those who voice the greatest concern would argue that official estimates of 11.6 million cited earlier are probably too low (one sees estimates ranging from about 10–20 million depending on the source). This is a larger number than for any other country, although there are several countries such as Germany that have a higher percentage of immigrants in the population than the United States. Moreover, the problem is geographically distinct within the United States: About one-quarter of all estimated irregular immigrants in the United States in 2008 were in California (2.85 million), followed by Texas (1.68 million), and Florida (840,000). Arizona, whose actions to restrict irregulars caused great political commotion in 2010, is fifth on the list at 560,000.

The issue is also a complex one. The concern about the U.S.-Mexican border not only pertains to immigration, although it is certainly that. In addition, however, the question of the integrity of the frontier has strong implications for the trafficking of illicit drugs into the United States. Indeed, it will be argued that much of the concern about criminality associated in the popular debate is not about immigration so much as it is about the U.S. "war on drugs." In addition, the frontier is also important because foreign terrorists who are intent on doing harm to the United States must enter across the U.S. border in either Mexico or Canada. One irony of the current fixation with the Mexican border is that it may have the unwanted effect of making the Canadian border more permeable and thus easier for terrorists to penetrate than it was before.

This introduction suggests the direction of the rest of the case. The discussion will first move to describing the nature of the physical dimension of the American border and whether or how that border can be "secured." With that rejoinder in mind, the discussion will then move to the nature of the various prongs of the threat itself posed by a porous border: illegal immigrations, drugs, and terrorists. Each discussion will include some analysis of whether making the border more or less impermeable solves each aspect of the problem and what other forms of effort might be equally or more effective. One suggestion that will be raised is the possible hypocrisy of some claimed solutions.

The Physical Problem

Almost all the solutions proposed for the U.S.-Mexican border revolve around some better way to "secure" it, which means roughly to make it more difficult for unauthorized people to come across the border into the United States. The most extreme advocacies call for "sealing" the border, which generally equates to making it impossible physically for unwanted outsiders to intrude on American soil. Before examining the desirability of such a policy and what it would entail, it is necessary first to examine the physical problem posed by the unique nature of the American border.

Border security is, of course, a problem for all sovereign states. How much and what kind of a problem depends largely on two aspects of the problem: whether the border's function is to keep people from leaving (emigration) or entering (immigration), and the physical qualities of the border: its length and complexity, for example. Keeping émigrés from leaving the United States has never been a particular problem (except for criminals fleeing prosecution, for instance); the emphasis has always been on regulating who and how many people enter the country. The U.S. problem has thus focused on the physical qualities of the border to be secured.

The territorial boundaries of the United States are among the most extensive, complex, and difficult to secure of any country on Earth. These borders can be divided into sea and land boundaries, each of which poses different priorities and problems. Moreover, the land borders of the United States are shared with two contiguous neighbors, Canada and Mexico. While the current dispute centers on the Mexican border, both are concerns: treating one as a problem and not the other is discriminatory and diplomatically untenable, and sealing the Mexican border but not the Canadian border runs the risk that some of the nefarious activity associated with a porous Mexican border would simple be transferred to the Canadian border (the entrance of terrorists or illicit drugs into the country, for instance).

The land and sea borders are extensive. The land border between the United States and Canada, for instance, is slightly more than 5,500 miles long (the boundary between Canada and the 48 contiguous states is 3,987 miles and between Canada and Alaska is 1,538 miles). Added to the 1,933 mile land border between the United States and Mexico, the total American land border is 7,358 miles. While not the longest in the world (Russia's border with 14 other countries is approximately two-thirds longer), it is nonetheless a very long and forbidding stretch of territory to secure. In fact, most of the U.S.-Canadian border is hardly secured at all, particularly the extensive stretch between Lake Superior and the Pacific Ocean and the Alaska–Canada border. As a practical matter, it would be impossible to do so and, happily, for the most part such security is unnecessary.

The sea borders of the United States are even more extensive. Two measures are normally used to describe these borders: coastline and shoreline. The coastline generally refers to a line drawn along the intersection of the coast and the ocean, not allowing for bays, inlets, and other coastal features. The shoreline measures the topography of the coast, including the shores of bodies of water that empty into the oceans and seas. Using figures supplied by the National Oceanic and Atmospheric Administration, the coastline of the United States is 12,383 miles, and the shoreline is 88,633 miles. Almost 42 percent of the U.S. coastline (5,580 miles) and 35 percent of shoreline (31,383 miles) are Alaskan and have not been a major concern since the Cold War. The 1,350 miles of Florida coastline and 8,426 miles of its coastline, however, are important security concerns regarding drugs importation and, to a lesser extent, the smuggling of irregular immigrants.

Effectively securing these borders is clearly a formidable task that is complicated by three other factors. One is the availability of assets to accomplish the task. The current effort concentrates on the 1,933 mile Mexican border and two forms of security: a border fence and larger numbers of Border Patrol and other human assets to monitor activity. It is not clear where the funds are to meet both these demands, and expanding the effort to include the Canadian and sea boundaries of the United States beyond current (and quite limited) proportions would be a further drain on available resources.

A second problem is whether such efforts can be entirely effective against determined attempts to breach the boundary. Illegal entry across the Mexican frontier is already largely orchestrated by illegal agents (so-called "coyotes") who exact significant fees to sneak immigrants across the border, and the result of enhanced security efforts might simply be to increase their sophistication, as well as the expense and thus profit of their illegal enterprise. Moreover, it is not clear that an "immigrant-proof" solution is possible. As former New Mexico Governor Bill Richardson has been quoted as saying, "If we put up a ten-foot fence, somebody is going to build an eleven-foot ladder."

Finally, there is the question of unintended consequences of increased security. These are most marked in the case of the impediment to movement of goods and peoples across the borders, a question of the impact of border security on globalization, raised earlier. As Flynn has noted, an attempt to better control the border between the United States and Canada (especially the bridges between Detroit and Ontario) a decade ago had catastrophic effects on U.S. productivity, and any serious attempt to screen effectively something as simple as truck traffic at major crossing points with either country would create an enormous economic dislocation. This, of course, is a major problem regarding both the land and sea borders, and one that is generally underemphasized in discussions of border security.

The Border Threats

As already noted, the question of the U.S.-Mexican border is really more than one threat. Its most prominent feature has been the level and consequences of irregular immigration across the border, and that aspect will be most prominently examined. It is also, however, a question of the movement of illicit narcotics and the consequent criminal behavior they bring with them and of the possible penetration of the United States by terrorists. It is not entirely clear that the most extensive and most important of these threats are the same thing.

The Immigration Problem.   Immigration is, and always has been, an integral part of the American experience. While for most times and purposes, it has been one of the proud elements of the American heritage, it has had its dark side in the form of negative reactions to the migration of some people to the United States at some times. Throughout American history, what is now referred to as illegal immigration has always been a part of the pattern, and the history of immigration politics is largely an attempt to regulate both the quantity and quality (measured both in point of origin and skill levels) of immigration to the country. In the current context, the immigration problem along the U.S.-Mexican border is the most dramatic and contentious manifestation of a worldwide pattern of international immigration which, if authorities to which allusion has already been are correct, will only increase in the future.

The sheer volume of irregular immigrants in the United States is the heart of the perceived problem in the American political debate. There is some minor disagreement about the terms of legal immigration into the country as it affects the flow of highly skilled and talented people into or out of the country, largely reflected in immigration quotas and the like. The heart of the debate, however, is about irregular immigration by Mexicans and Central Americans into the countries in numbers that exceed 10 million and may be much higher. Efforts to secure the border are aimed at reducing or eliminating the flow of irregulars into the country; efforts to apprehend and deport irregular immigrants already in the country are aimed at reducing those numbers.

Why is this immigrant flow a problem? Generally speaking, two reasons are cited, which help illuminate the actual parameters of the concern. One concern is the criminality that is associated with illegal residents. Whether crime is greater in places where there are concentrations of irregular immigrants is contested, but those who hold this concern point particularly to greater incidents of violent crime, normally by members of the irregular immigrant population against other members of that community, but sometimes spilling over and affecting the broader communities in which they are located. The other concern is the demands on social services (e.g., schools and medical facilities) made by irregular immigrants and their families, a concern accentuated by the fact that most irregular immigrants pay only user taxes (e.g., sales tax) but do not contribute to the social security fund or through payroll deduction, for instance.

These are two distinct problems that point to a basic division within the irregular immigrant population. There are, in essence, two groups that make up that community. By far the most numerous are *economic immigrants,* individuals who migrate to the United States in the same manner and for the same reasons that people in the developing world generally migrate to the developed world: the hope of providing a better life for themselves and their families. There is no systematic indication that their participation in or contribution to crime is any greater than that of the population at large; indeed, the knowledge that their arrest can lead to their deportation probably inhibits much criminal activity toward which they might be drawn. The other group is comprised of *criminal immigrants,* individuals who enter the country to engage in criminal behavior. Most prominent within this group are people engaged in narcotics trafficking in one way or another. This group brings with it the violent crime that has ravaged Mexico in particular, and is the source of virtually all the concern over the impact of immigration on crime.

Dividing the irregular immigrant community into these two categories helps understanding the problem and what to do about it. One must begin by asking the question, why do immigrants come illegally to the country? In the case of the vast majority—the economic immigrants—the answer is economic opportunity: jobs. This should not be surprising, given the disparity of wealth between the United States and Mexico and Central America, but this is also why economic immigrants migrate worldwide. In the case of irregular immigration into the United States, one explanation of why this has occurred—and especially why it has occurred to the extent it has—is found in the impact that the North American Free Trade Agreement (NAFTA) had on Mexico.

As discussed in the third edition of this book (Chapter 9, "Evaluating Globalization: The Case of NAFTA"), one of the perverse effects of that agreement was to flood Mexico with cheap, subsidized American corn the price of which undercut Mexican peasant growers, bankrupting them and forcing them off their farms. Many of these displaced peasants have become part of the flood of irregular immigrants to this country. Before NAFTA came into effect in 1994, there were an estimated 4.2 million illegal Latin American immigrants in the United States, compared to current totals.

The irony of this situation is that NAFTA was supposed to have exactly the opposite effect: it was supposed to create jobs in Mexico that would reduce the need of Mexicans to come north seeking employment. As Governor Richardson put it, "The whole idea that NAFTA would create jobs on the Mexican side and thus deter immigration has just been dead wrong." In a 2005 Center for Immigration Studies (CIS) report, Krikorian argues that what happened was virtually the result of American politics that forced acceptance of agribusiness-friendly farm subsidies as a part of gaining acceptance of NAFTA (that included corn subsidies). As Krikorian puts it, "the massive growth of immigration pressures was not a failure of NAFTA, but an inevitable consequence." Why? "Economic development, especially agricultural modernization, *always* sets people on the move, by consolidating small farms into larger, more productive operations. . . . The problem with NAFTA was that neither country did anything meaningful to make sure the excess Mexican peasantry moved to Mexico's cities instead of ours."

All of this, of course, took place within the context of the global economy of the 1990s and how that economy affected North America. Martin suggests the dynamics at work: "The economic situation in both countries in the 1990s—a boom in the United States, a very slow recovery from a 1994 bust in Mexico—led record numbers of Mexicans to enter the United States during the second half of the decade."

Without suggesting that NAFTA is the only reason that a large number of economic immigrants have entered the United States, nonetheless the vast majority of irregular migrants have been displaced Mexicans and Central Americans who have come to the United States in the pursuit of economic advancement, including the accumulation of enough money to send remittances back to their local communities and families at home, as already noted. Their migration is like economic migration everywhere, moving from where there is no economic opportunity (jobs) to where such opportunities exist.

The immigration problem and its solution take on a different complexion put in these terms. If there are jobs available that irregular immigrants fill, then there must be a labor need that these immigrants fulfill. Generally, this means low-skill, low-paying jobs, often with one or more of the 3D characteristics of being dirty, dangerous, or difficult. If there were Americans willing to do these jobs at wages that employers were willing to pay, there would not be jobs, and there would be no incentive for migrants to immigrate. That they have done so and continue to do so indicates not only that such opportunities exist, but that they have not been sated. That is simple supply and demand.

Moreover, the dynamics suggest that there is not only a market for immigrant labor but also a continuing market for irregular immigrant labor. Given the reaction against irregular immigration, this assertion seems anomalous, but it is nonetheless true. The simple fact is that illegal workers have advantages to employers over legal immigrants: They will work at lower wages (they have no bargaining ability on wages), they will work longer (they are covered by no labor laws or contracts), and they do not require employers to pay benefits like social security taxes or health insurance. For highly labor-intensive work like lawn care, roofing, or garbage collection, hiring irregular laborers has economic advantages for employers that allow them to maximize profits while minimizing costs. Moreover, if the kinds of jobs that irregular immigrants typically perform became part of the regular economy, labor costs would increase (to minimum wage, at the least), which in turn would drive up the wages of other lower end jobs.

This places the problem in a different context than those who simply call for expelling irregular immigrants like to frame the question. Do all the advocates *really* want to get rid of irregular immigrants? Since they are doing jobs that either would not get done at all or only at higher labor costs otherwise, the answer is not clear. If all employees, including current irregulars in the underground economy, were to enter the mainstream, then suddenly these workers would be paying all taxes (rather than just regressive levies like sales taxes), thereby contributing to things like social security and Medicare/Medicaid and making themselves less of a social services burden. But doing so would mean employers would have to increase their own efforts and expenses, which they clearly are reluctant to do. There is a high level of hypocrisy in the contention that people oppose illegal immigration but employ irregular immigrants.

If irregular economic immigrants are the heart of the border problem, then any solution aimed at reducing or eliminating them must begin with the incentives they have to migrate and to stay. That means an emphasis on the elimination of the illegal jobs in the underground economy that are the mainstay of and magnet for irregular immigrants. Assuming the country is willing to bear the consequences of such a policy succeeding (which is not clear), then the heart of border policy should have a significant component that seeks to reduce the numbers who seek to breach the border. A core part of such a strategy necessarily involves reducing the availability of jobs that irregulars occupy. An avenue to do so already exists in American law and could be implemented simply by enforcing penalties against those who hire irregular immigrants. Reducing the number of available job opportunities would probably not, in and of itself, eliminate irregular immigration (it would, for instance, take a while for the word to circulate to potential immigrants), but it could reduce the flow, thereby making efforts to secure the border by other means more plausible.

This solution is so obvious that one wonders why it is not more prominently mentioned in solutions to irregular immigration. The reason at least partially reflects a certain degree of ambivalence, even hypocrisy, in the debate.

Many people oppose illegal immigration on the grounds that their actions are illegal, that they represent an assault on national sovereignty, and that they are a burden on social services. At the same time, however, many of these same people support the functions these same workers perform (3D labor at low costs,) and some even benefit personally from the presence of these workers (primarily employers). It is particularly this latter group that may be enthusiastic denouncers of illegal immigrants but not want to prosecute those who hire them, since they are the lawbreakers in this part of the problem.

There is some indication that the same demographics that combined to create the immigrant surge may also alleviate it with time. In a June 7, 2010 *Newsweek* article, Campos-Flores points out that fertility rates in Mexico have declined dramatically "from 6.7 children per woman in 1970 to 2.1 today," according to World Bank figures. The result will be a gradual reduction in the number of young people entering the Mexican labor market, from over 850,000 per year in the early 2000s to about 300,000 per year in 2030, a number the Mexican economy can more adequately absorb. Some of this is already occurring (projected new members of the labor force this year are down to 750,000), but with a rub: "Mexican migration will taper off further just as baby boomers begin retiring in 2012," according to Campos-Flores.

The other form of irregular immigration for which no one has official sympathy is *criminal immigration*, the movement of individuals into the country who are parts of criminal enterprises and whose reason for immigration is to further their criminal activities. In some cases, such immigrants may be associated with things like human trafficking, but the most prominent form that criminal immigration takes on the U.S.-Mexican border is the illicit drug trade, which is the second prong of the border problem.

The Narcotics Problem.   The drug trade across the U.S.-Mexican frontier is both an immigration and narcotics policy problem. Most of the illegal drugs that enter the United States are shipped through Mexico and then across the border, making it a border issue. At the same time, many of those who carry drugs into the United States (so-called "mules") are irregular immigrants who are more or less reluctantly brought into the trade. As Shifter explains, "Mexico is the transit route for roughly 70 to 90 percent of the illegal drugs entering the United States. . . . Along the U.S.-Mexico border, the kidnapping trade, clearly tied to the drug trade, is flourishing." Andreas points out that increased American border security efforts exacerbates the drug problem: "adding thousands new Border Patrol agents has had the perverse effect of entrenching smugglers rather than deterring immigrants since the problem of breaching the border is more difficult and requires help for some immigrants," some of which is provided by drug traffickers. Moreover, the drug and immigration efforts come into conflict with one another, since they are conducted by different government agencies (e.g., the Border Patrol and the Drug Enforcement Agency) with different priorities and different cultures. Adding National Guardsmen to this mix, as was begun in 2010, can only add to the jurisdictional confusion.

The drug and immigration issues intersect when members of the various drug syndicates move across the border into the United States to better control their illicit operations. There is considerable evidence that Mexican drug cartels are now active in most large American cities and that they bring with them the drug-related violent crime that has become endemic on the Mexican side of the border. The numbers of immigrants who are part of criminal immigration are quite small compared to the economic immigrants, but their presence is amplified because of the spikes in violent crime that occur where they are present. This violence is mostly between members of various drug cartels, but inevitably it spills over into broader communities, inflaming anti-immigrant sentiments that are at least partially misdirected. These kinds of problems have already destabilized Mexican national and local politics, and there is a fear that the same thing could happen on the U.S. side of the border.

Responses to the drug and immigration problems are similar. The major response to the drug problem has been interdiction—trying to stop the transit of drugs across the border—but that is a largely impossible tack. As Andreas suggests, "The amount of cocaine necessary to satisfy US customers for one year can be transported in just nine of the thousands of large tractor-trailers that cross the border every day." The logic of globalization contained in instruments like NAFTA make detailed monitoring of cross-border traffic more difficult and, because such monitoring and inspection takes time, is clearly counterproductive in globalization terms. It is not at all clear that such "supply-side" approaches to the flow of drugs across the border can be effective.

A more comprehensive view of drugs breaching the border includes an emphasis on reducing the market for drugs in the United States. Just as the availability of jobs has fueled economic immigration, so too has the demand for drugs fueled the growing flow of drugs into the country. If the demand for illegal drugs among Americans were to decrease (analogous to drying up jobs for irregular immigrants), then the supply coming across the border would also likely decrease, since there would be a decreased market. During the height of the so-called "war on drugs" during the late 1980s and early 1990s, this approach was known as "demand-side," and while hardly anyone suggested it was a comprehensive solution to the problem, it could help by making the volume of trafficking across the border more manageable.

The Terrorism Problem.   While there is some analogy between the immigration and drug problems, this comparison largely does not extend to the problem posed by the penetration of the United States by terrorists. For one thing, the terrorism threat is not a specifically U.S.-Mexican border problem. Terrorists can enter the United States from Mexico, but also from Canada or at airports or seaports anywhere in the country. Indeed, it is arguable that the greater emphasis placed on the Mexican border may mean a diminution of personnel and effort at other points of entry, making them more likely transit points than they would be in the absence of an immigration emphasis.

The terrorism threat, unlike the other two, is also more of a qualitative than a quantitative problem, and one that is managed in a distinctive way.

Irregular economic immigration is a question of a very large volume of people breaching the border, but where each individual poses little if any threat to the United States or its citizens. The problem that people perceive is the result of the overwhelming numbers of irregular immigrants and the collective burdens and problems they create. In contrast, there are relatively few terrorists against whose entry the United States must prepare, but the potential havoc that any one poses means that efforts must be essentially airtight or they can yield disastrous results. Thus, for instance, a boundary system that reduces the flow of economic immigrants across the Mexican border by 90 percent would have an enormous impact on the border issue, but the same effectiveness against terrorist penetration might be entirely unacceptable.

Because the goal of terrorist interception is absolute, the methods employed to prevent the entrance of terrorists into the country is multilayered and more extensive than it is for irregular economic immigrants, as suggested in Chapter 16. The U.S. government operates elaborate intelligence networks to monitor the movement of potential terrorists toward the U.S. border, something it does not undertake for the movement of Mexican peasants. This means, of course, a high level of interaction between government agencies to coordinate antiterrorist activities that are present to some extent in the pursuit of criminal immigrants but not for economic immigrants.

CONCLUSION

The question of irregular immigration across the U.S.-Mexican border has become an explosive, emotional political issue in the United States, where emotions have arguably oversimplified and distorted the nature of the phenomenon. The purpose of this case study has been to place the American situation in its global context and to point out that the U.S. problem is more variegated and complex than simple depictions suggest.

Migration is and has always been a global phenomenon. As noted, 1 in every 35 people alive today is an immigrant in one sense or another and for one reason or another. In many cases, the motivations are economic, and in others they are political. In the most extreme cases, people are forced to flee their regions or countries and to become refugees. People have been migrating since humankind's forebears left the Great Rift Valley of Africa, and they have done so for a variety of reasons. Escaping a less favorable condition in hopes of finding a better situation has always been the deep underlying motivation.

The U.S.-Mexican border situation mirrors many of the broader global trends. People have been coming across this junction between the developed and developing worlds in large numbers since the early 1990s. Most have been irregulars—the people without official papers ("wops")—of this generation. They have come for the variety of reasons that immigrants always move, but their situation has been complicated because this form of immigration has been augmented and admixed with criminal immigration associated with the flow of illicit narcotics into the United States and the fear of terrorist penetration of the country's borders. Each of these sources of breaches of American national sovereignty as represented by a porous border has different bases and probably different solutions. While an understanding of immigration as a global problem may not offer the solutions to all these problems, it does at least provide some context within which to consider them.

STUDY/DISCUSSION QUESTIONS

1. What is immigration? Into what categories are immigrants normally placed? Especially describe the categories of "irregular immigrants" and refugees.
2. Discuss immigration in terms of why people immigrate, where they immigrate (and why), and why these patterns represent a national and international problem.
3. What are the basic categories of economic immigrants? Why is the distinction important in understanding the current controversy in the United States?
4. Summarize the world situation in terms of immigration. What are the basic trends? Why are they likely to continue? What dilemmas do attempts to restrict immigration present and face?
5. Discuss the general parameters of the physical border security problem facing the United States and the unique problems of the U.S.-Mexican border in that context.
6. What are the three distinct aspects of the U.S.-Mexican border threat? Discuss each, including how each might be solved.
7. Is the United States truly sincere about ending and reversing irregular immigration? What would the consequences of that success be economically and otherwise in the United States? Are Americans really willing to accept these consequences?

READING/RESEARCH MATERIAL

Andreas, Pete R. "Politics on Edge: Managing the U.S.–Mexico Border." *Current History* 105, 695 (February 2006), 64–68.

Campos-Flores, Arian. "Don't Fence Them In: The Arizona of the Future Won't Suffer from Too Many Immigrants—But from Too Few." *Newsweek*, June 7, 2010, 34–35.

Choucri, Nazli and Dinsha Mistree. "Globalization, Migration, and New Challenges to Governance." *Current History* 108, 717 (April 2009), 173–179.

Flynn, Stephen. *America the Vulnerable: How Our Government Is Failing to Protect Us from Terrorism.* New York: Harper Perennials, 2005.

Goldstone, Jack A. "The New Population Bomb: The Four Megatrends That Will Change the World." *Foreign Affairs* 89, 1 (January/February 2010), 31–43.

"International Migration Levels, Trends, and Policies." *International Migration Report 2006: A Global Assessment.* New York: United Nations Department of Economic and Social Affairs/Population Division, 2006.

Kehoe, Timothy J., and Kim J. Ruhl. "The North American Free Trade Agreement after Ten Years." University of Minnesota: Center for Urban and Regional Affairs, 2004 (http://www.econ.umn.edu/~tkehoe).

Koser. Khalid. "Why Immigration Matters." *Current History* 108, 717 (April 2009), 147–153.

Krikorian, Mark. "Bordering on CAFTA: More Trade, Less Immigration." *National Review Online*, July 28, 2005 (http://www.cis.org/articls/2005/mskoped072805.html).

Krauze, Enrique. "Furthering Democracy in Mexico." *Foreign Affairs* 85, 1 (January/February 2006), 54–65.

Martin, Susan F. "Waiting Games: The Politics of US Immigration Reform." *Current History* 108, 717 (April 2009), 160–165.

O'Neil, Shannon. "The Real War in Mexico." *Foreign Affairs* 88, 4 (July/August 2009), 66–77.

Payan, Terry. *The Three U.S.–Mexico Border Wars: Drugs, Immigration, and Homeland Security.* Westport, CT: Greenwood, 2006.

Rockenbach, Leslie J. *The Mexican–American Border: NAFTA and Global Linkages.* Abingdon, England: Routledge, 2001.

Rozenthal, Andres. "The Other Side of Immigration." *Current History* 106, 697 (February 2007), 89–90.

Shifter, Michael. "Latin America's Drug Problem." *Current History* 106, 697 (February 2007), 58–63.

Snow, Donald M. *Cases in International Relations.* 3rd ed. New York: Pearson Longman, 2008.

2008 Global Trends: Refugees, Asylum-seekers, Returnees, Internally Displaced and Stateless Persons. New York: United Nations High Commission on Refugees, June 16, 2009.

"Unauthorized Immigrant Population, 2000, 2008." Office of Immigration Statistics, U.S: Department of Homeland Security, 2009. Reprinted in *World Almanac and Book of Facts, 2010.* New York: World Almanac Books, 2010.

Van Hear, Nicholas. "The Rise of Refugee Diasporas." *Current History* 108, 717 (April 2009), 180–185.

Failed and Failing States: The Case of Pakistan

PRÉCIS

A major contemporary problem of the international system involves unstable member states, especially states that may cease to function effectively as internal or international actors, or other states that are or might move in the direction of dysfunction. The prototype for total state failure is Somalia, and a number of other states show some indications of the kind of loss of function that could constitute failure. This case study views the problem of state failure through its indicators and what various observers have tried to construct as indices of failure. It applies that information to the case of Pakistan, a major world power and participant in U.S. efforts in Afghanistan that has shown some of the indicators of potential failure.

The heavy involvement of the United States and much of the rest of the international system in the Persian Gulf and Southwest Asian area has brought with it intimate contact with some of the most volatile, unstable countries of the world, places like Iraq, Afghanistan, and Pakistan. All these states have or have been alleged to have some connection to international religious terrorism, or what President Barack Obama prefers to call "violent extremism" (a designation with roots in the Bush administration Obama succeeded). The major gist of American interest in this region, of course, has been that it has provided a breeding ground and safe haven for terrorists harboring the avowed intent to wreak havoc in the United States and other developed world countries. The major thrust of western policy has been to make these areas inhospitable to violent extremists by uprooting existing

285

terrorists and transforming the countries involved so that they will no longer be prone to produce or sustain terrorists. Among the major obstacles bedeviling these efforts is the fact that a number of target countries fall into the general category of failed or failing states.

The term *failed state* became widely used in the early post-Cold War period. The prototype for the designation was Somalia, the governance of which essentially collapsed in 1991 with the overthrow of the country's dictatorial leader, Siad Barre, and the inability of warring factions in the drought-stricken country to find a replacement leader who could rule and bring some form of order in the country. This condition has continued to the present in the East African country, meaning it has lacked an effective central government for roughly two decades—a situation in no immediate likelihood of changing. Among the artifacts of Somali anarchy is the inability of any authority to suppress pirates using Somalia as their base of operations.

The designation *failed state* has been extended to encompass other countries of the world. Since 2005, the journal *Foreign Policy*, acting in cooperation with the independent think tank Fund for Peace has produced an annual global assessment of states that have, by its criteria, failed or shown vulnerability to failure. The result is an index of failure in rank order. The 2009 rankings of the top 20 countries on the list (those countries with the highest failure scores) are as follows:

1. Somalia	11. Ivory Coast
2. Zimbabwe	12. Haiti
3. Sudan	13. Burma/Myanmar
4. Chad	14. Kenya
5. Democratic Republic of Congo	15. Nigeria
6. Iraq	16. Ethiopia
7. Afghanistan	17. North Korea
8. Central African Republic	18. Yemen
9. Guinea	19. Bangladesh
10. Pakistan	20. East Timor

The list is both geographically and geopolitically interesting. Of the 20 countries listed, 11 are African, including the top 5 and 7 of the top 10. Africa is, of course, the poorest and arguably most contentious and unstable part of the world. Among that top ten, all three of the countries involved in the crisis in Darfur (Sudan, Chad, and the Central African Republic) are prominently included (see discussion of Darfur in Chapter 8). Of the rest, eight are in Asia, evenly divided between the Middle East and other parts of Asia, and one is in the Western Hemisphere (Haiti). Within the Asian total, three particularly volatile countries, Iraq, Afghanistan, and Pakistan, all of enormous importance to American foreign policy and the global contest over Islamic religious extremism, are included (the other major country in the area, Iran, ranks 38th on the list). These geographic and geopolitical concentrations provide some of the basis for why the phenomenon is of more than academic interest.

THE NATURE AND PROBLEM OF FAILED STATES

Although varying degrees of disorder and chaos within social and political communities are certainly not new characteristics of the contemporary world, the extent and consequences of the phenomenon are arguably more important than they have been at many other times. The failure of states has both internal and external manifestations and consequences. Domestically, failure tends to occur in the poorest countries and regions of the world (notably in Africa and parts of Asia) and makes bad human conditions worse, gives rise to concerns about possible or actual humanitarian disasters (see Chapter 8), and makes amelioration of those conditions extremely difficult, in some cases arguably impossible in terms of local resources. Internationally, state failure can lead to destabilizing regional power vacuums of greater or lesser international concern. Failure in its various guises in different places thus poses different kinds and depths of problems for the areas directly affected and for the broader world community.

The Nature of Failed States

Definitions of failed states vary, but all contain as their core the notion of the collapse of legitimate authority and the inability to replace that authority, thereby resulting in a governmental void that destabilizes the places it occurs. Helman and Ratner, for instance, offered one definition in 1992 to classify events in Somalia, the first prominent failed state, calling it "a state utterly incapable of sustaining itself as a member of the international community." This definition, of course, emphasizes the international dimension of state failure, whereas other definitions emphasize the internal dimension. The free encyclopedia *Source Watch*, for instance, refers to a failed state as "a shattered social and political structure," whereas the Crisis Watch Workshop (London) offered the description of a "condition of state collapse" in 2006. The shared core of these distinctions is the collapse of meaningful governance and the order it entails in failed states.

States can evince varying levels of failure. A totally failed state would be a situation of utter and complete anarchy and disorder throughout the territory of the state. Such a level of failure is an "ideal type" of sorts that is only approximated by degrees in the real world. There is, for instance, general agreement that Somalia is and has been the most totally failed state in the world for some time, but that does not mean, for instance, that all its territory is ungoverned and chaotic. In many areas, local tribal warlords maintain a modicum of order, but their authority is neither entirely legitimate nor does it extend to anything like the total sovereign territory of the country. Indeed, one of the generally ascribed characteristics of a legal state in the international system is that it a physical territory over which sovereign control is maintained, meaning that a country like Somalia, which has no government that can maintain control over its territory, is not entirely sovereign. The absence of a universal authority does not, however, mean the kind of total failure suggested by the "ideal" form of failure.

Because there are degrees of state failure, there have been attempts to differentiate between the amounts of failure that different states experience. *Foreign Policy*, for instance, has an elaborate quantitative set of measures by which it ranks different countries in developing its ordinal scheme (the methodology and measures are available at the *Foreign Policy* Web site). In a rougher fashion, the Crisis Watch Workshop has adopted a three-fold scheme for comparing countries in their relative descent into state failure, a categorization fundamentally similar to my own scheme found in *National Security for a New Era*, third edition. State failure, of course, is the penultimate condition, but it can be preceded by less extreme degrees as well.

The least severe case of failure occurs in what the Crisis Watch Workshop calls "fragile states," and which I have called failure-prone states. A fragile state is one that is "susceptible to crisis in one or more of its subsystems." A number of states on the *Foreign Policy* list, for instance, have demonstrated political characteristics such as strongly authoritarian rule, the suppression of human and minority rights, and the inability to sustain electoral regularities that could be manifested in the breakdown of effective rule at sometime in the future. A significant part of the reason for Iraq's inclusion as high on the list as it is, for instance, arises from the fact that the various religious and ethnic divisions in the country have never been able historically to reach a peaceful political accord that allows them to coexist in anything like a mutually satisfactory political order, a problem that could become acute after the removal of all American and other outside forces from the country.

The next classification is what the Workshop calls the "crisis state" (or, in my terms, "failing state"). Such states not only show the potential for failure but also have evinced adequate deterioration in one or more sectors to be moving toward total failure. The crisis state is, in other words, a "state under acute stress, where institutions face a serious contestation and are potentially unable to manage conflicts and shocks." Thirty years of war and turmoil in Afghanistan have created a state of affairs there where it is unclear that the system could in fact manage itself without considerable outside interference.

The most serious condition, of course, is full state failure. While no other state has reached the utter lack of sustainability achieved by Somalia, a number of others have problems of potentially equivalent magnitude. The Fund for Peace offers four primary criteria by which a state may reach the designation of failed.

The first criterion is a "loss of physical control of territory or monopoly of the legitimate use of force therein," or, in other words, the breakdown of internal order normally associated with self-policing and a military monopoly indicating the activity of armed opposition in the country. The second criterion is a failure of government decision making, the "erosion of legitimate authority to make collective decisions." The third criterion is the breakdown of public services, the "inability to provide reasonable public services" that are expected from government and which form part of the reason for supporting the government when they are provided. Finally, the Fund lists the ability to act internationally, arguing a failed state has the "inability to interact with other states as a full member of the international community." In addition, the Fund suggests other characteristics that may accompany these core problems: widespread corruption and criminality, the existence of internal or external refugees and the involuntary movement of populations, and a sharp economic decline. The purpose of the Failed State Index (FSI) is an attempt to indicate what kinds of factors can lead to the various conditions of failure.

The Failed State Index

No two states fail (or approach failure) in exactly the same way, and the profiles of failed states are not identical. This does not mean, however, that there are no agreed-upon categories and indicators that generally define the phenomenon. The FSI is the most elaborate of the schemes publicly devised to measure state failure, and it is worth describing both because it suggests the number and variety of factors that can contribute to failure, and because the index reveals the inherent limits on the ability to measure and particularly to compare state failure across states.

The index is composed of 12 factors divided into 3 categories. There are four social indicators, two economic indicators, and six political indicators. The four social indicators include demographic pressures (e.g., a growing population), refugees or displaced persons (e.g., citizens forced from their homes to other locations either inside or outside the country), group grievances (e.g., the perception of some ethnic, religious, or clan group that it is the victim of systematic discrimination), and human flight (e.g., people who feel compelled to leave the area of their residence). The two economic indicators are uneven development (e.g., great and growing disparities in wealth between groups) and economic decline. The political indicators include delegitimization of the state (e.g., the withdrawal of support for authority), public service decline, human rights violations, problems with the security apparatus (e.g., ineffective or selective repression of illegal or dissident activity), factionalized elites, and external intervention in the country. Collectively, the indicators "provide snapshots of state vulnerability or risk of violence for one time period each year," according to the 2009 survey. While the indicators "measure vulnerability to collapse or conflict," according to *Foreign Policy*, the "ratings do not necessarily predict when states may experience violence or collapse." The index, in other words, is an example of descriptive, not inferential, statistics.

Each indicator in the survey is rated on a 1–10 scale (further refined to tenths) on the basis of data accumulation and analysis, and each of the 177 states included in the survey receives a score on each dimension. The 12 scores for each state are added together to produce a state's individual score or profile. These cumulative scores are then displayed in decreasing order to provide the global index and rank order of states. The higher the score on each variable and thus its accumulation, the greater the degree of failure.

The index is beguilingly elegant and apparently precise because of its mathematical character, but the extent of that precision can be deceptive.

First, the 12 factors in the index are equally weighted (each contributes 1–10 points, or roughly one-twelfth, of a country's score). The result implies that each indicator is equally important across countries and factors (e.g., the impact of the number of internally displaced persons in one country has the same quantitative effect as economic underperformance in another), when that may or may not be the case in fact. Second, the index implies that its data are in fact interval level—that the differences between values is uniform across values and indicators (e.g., the difference between a one and a two score and between a six and a seven is the same within each indicator and across measures), and this is almost certainly not true. Third, asserting the interval level of the data is necessary for the index to possess additivity, the meaningful ability to add the various values together to produce a sum that is precise and meaningful and can thus be used to describe precise differences in levels of failure across countries. In the 2008 index, for instance, Somalia leads the list with a score of 114.2 (out of a possible 120 points for "perfect" failure), whereas Pakistan, in ninth place, has a score of 103.8, a difference of 10.4. What exactly that difference means is not at all clear.

The purpose of this discursion is not to disparage the index or the efforts of those who compile it. Rather, it is to suggest that the reader not be hypnotized by the apparent elegance and precision of representations that are really more imprecise than the numbers may imply. Even if one does raise some questions about the precise nature of the FSI, it does not discredit either the general or the specific dynamics that it seeks to capture. The general categories of social, economic, and political indicators are certainly useful in organizing thinking about and measuring failure, and the indices indeed capture important parts of the dynamic of state failure. One should not, however, overdo interpreting differences one finds.

Problems of Failed States

Asking what problems failed states create is another way of asking if or why having nonfunctioning, even dysfunctional states within the world system creates difficulties with which members of the international order must cope. Looking at this question requires first recognizing that the designation of "failed state" is generally viewed as stigmatizing, which means that states will deny or downgrade their own designation as such. It is, however, generally recognized that there are both internal and international consequences that accompany the varying levels of state failure, and that these consequences vary in severity depending on the country in which they occur.

Since calling a state "failed" has the effect of stigmatizing that entity, it is a status that states unsurprisingly want to avoid and actively deny if it is bestowed on them. This is particularly true for leaders in failed states, since their leadership is generally considered to be part of the basis for failure. Indeed, the Fund for Peace, in assessing responsibility for state failure, lists "corrupt leaders, dysfunctional societies, bad neighbors, global recession, unfortunate history, and geography" as recurring causes. Of those reasons, the quality of leadership is one of the purely human causes, and dysfunction in society is at least strongly related to the quality of leadership. Since failure tends to occur disproportionately in the most isolated and destitute countries, the stigma presumably has less impact on the masses in those countries, who must recognize their suffering but for whom the international sobriquet of failed state has little discernible impact.

If, or how much, the designation matters tends to depend on two additional factors: the degree of failure and the varying consequences of failure regionally and internationally. Clearly, a state that is fragile or failure prone is less problematic than one that is in crisis or failing, and a fully failed state creates more difficulties than one that is "merely" in the throes of failure. Fragile or even failing states have yet to plunge entirely into political and other chaos and are thus presumably more redeemable than failed states, assuming the willingness of regional or international actors to try to avoid that fate.

The other, and clearly related, consideration is the consequence that failure has to other states. Zimbabwe, for instance, is second on this year's list of failed states, and conditions in that country are clearly deplorable and certainly extraordinarily difficult for the people who live there. The miseries that have created state failure in Zimbabwe, however, have had limited carryover to other places, mostly the movement of refugees to neighboring countries. The spillover effect, on the other hand, can have an impact regionally. Take Sudan as an example. As noted already, it ranks third on the 2009 list, in no small measure because of the ongoing Darfur crisis. The external refugee problem created by Darfurians fleeing Sudanese suppression, however, has spread across the border and helped infect the situations in Chad (number four on the list) and the Central African Republic (number eight).

The consequences of state failure are particularly dire when they infect larger and more consequential states. Three of the world's most populous countries, Pakistan (6th in population, 10th on the failure index), Bangladesh (7th in population, 19th in failure), and Nigeria (8th in population, 15th in the failure index) are examples. Pakistan, which combines a large population with a geopolitically important position between Afghanistan and India and the possession of nuclear weapons, stands out particularly, which is why it is the subject of the case study.

The various forms and degrees of state failure create both internal and international problems for themselves and the rest of the international system. Domestically, the most important result of state failure is the resulting loss of whatever public services that may have been available. These are notable both in the area of security, where there is little or no coercive authority available to maintain the public order or to control the activities of more or less organized criminal factions, and in the provision of public services. Sometimes this loss of authority is countrywide, and in others the absence of legitimate rule is regional. This is certainly the case in places like Afghanistan, for instance, where the central government exercises authority primarily over Kabul and its environs, whereas such control as exists elsewhere is exercised by tribal organizations (some of which are associated with the opium trade) or insurgent groups like the Taliban. In either case, there is little sense of uniform security, justice, and the like. In most cases, public services—from schools to running water and electricity to roads and airports or public health—are rudimentary to begin with (since failure tends to occur in the most destitute, least developed countries), and the failed state proves even less capable of providing for public needs, thereby worsening the wretched human conditions associated with failure. Although the failure was to some large degree caused by the Americans in the first place, the chaos of early post-invasion Baghdad, where there was a near-total loss of public services for months after the American arrival, is emblematic of this condition.

The internal consequences vary depending on the degree of failure a particular country is undergoing. In the prototype state, Somalia has suffered nearly two decades of essential national loss of authority, with the only sense of internal order provided by different tribal or clan groupings that exercise differing kinds and degrees of social order in the parts of the country they govern. It has been, however, the pattern and tragedy of Somalia that no group or coalition has emerged capable of uniting the country under a single regime. In Zimbabwe, an order of sorts exists under the capricious rule of Robert Mugabe, but it is essentially a reign of terror that has systematically destroyed the national economy and the underlying social fabric. Lesser degrees of disorder may produce serious but less dire consequences.

The "shattered social and political structure" of failed states (the *Source Watch* definition) can have other pernicious effects that arise from the internal power vacuum accompanying and defining failure. One is that it can provide the conditions in which pernicious organizations can arise, because there is no governmental authority to suppress them as they are forming or after they have formed. It is not, for instance, at all surprising that international piracy is centered in Somalia: There is no central government that can control the activities or existence of pirate groups within Somali territory, and the extreme poverty and despair of Somali existence creates conditions in which piracy may seem a rational solution to personal poverty.

Such vacuums may also provide the seedbed for radical groups to form or for existing groups to seek refuge and safe haven. It is often suggested, for instance, that should combined American–Afghan–Pakistani efforts ever progress to the point of threatening the safe haven of Al Qaeda in remote areas of Pakistan such as Baluchistan and also prevent the migration of Al Qaeda back into Afghanistan, the group might seek refuge in Somalia. The presumed attractions of such a connection would be the inability of a nonexistent Somali authority to deny Al Qaeda entrance into the country and the economic benefits the terrorists might bring with them. Ironically in this case, however, the 2009 Failed States Index article in *Foreign Policy* suggests that previous Al Qaeda experience in Somalia makes such a migration there unlikely. Al Qaeda has tried to conduct operations there in the past, but they have concluded that Somalia is so chaotic that the terrorists "had an awful experience trying to operate" there, because of the "terrible infrastructure, excessive violence and criminality, and few basic services." If a state has failed so totally that even the world's most notorious and pursued organization will not seek to use it for protection, then one can imagine the formidable barriers to trying to elicit the support of legitimate international enterprises and states in uplifting such places from their failure.

The extent of state failure is an international problem and concern similarly varies depending on the extent of relative failure and the regional or international importance of the state that is failing. Except in the most isolated kinds of places (e.g., Haiti, certain parts of central Africa), the degree of state failure reflects the extent that a given state's problems can infect its neighbors. Countries like Chad and the Central African Republic would be in some degree of failure because of their inherent poverty and lack of resources for success under any circumstances, but the civil unrest in Sudan most dramatically represented by Darfur almost certainly elevates those countries' place on the list. Were Darfur not such an international cause célèbre, however, the plight of those countries would hardly be noteworthy. A place like Bangladesh, on the other hand, is certainly on the boundary between failed and failing status, but it is relatively isolated in the world and causes few regional or international difficulties. Thus, its failure is of lesser consequence than is the case for Pakistan (of which Bangladesh was formerly a part, as noted later), whose location and status as a nuclear-weapons state make its degree of difficulties much more important for both the region and the international order as a whole.

The international consequences of state failure flow directly from the domestic problems associated with it. The failure of state authority not only creates dilemmas of internal governance but it also generally means the inability to control borders and frontiers and may well lead to troublesome refugee flows across borders out of states that are failing into states where this influx adds to the fragility or even crisis that those states may be undergoing. The Darfurian situation is an example, and the inability (or unwillingness) of either Afghanistan or Pakistan to effectively control movement across their long shared border adds to the sense of crisis in those countries.

Similarly, the existence of internal power vacuums in failed or failing states may attract the presence of criminal or politically undesirable elements that cause regional or more broadly international difficulties. The problem of controlling international piracy in the Arabian Sea and western Indian Ocean, for instance, would be much easier if there were a Somalian national authority to which international authorities could call upon for aid or to which they could provide assistance in the suppression of pirate havens in Somali territory.

In the contemporary situation, of course, the international problem highest on the agenda is the attractiveness that failed states may provide to politically dangerous and objectionable groups, most notably terrorists. It should not, for instance, be a particular surprise that all of the places where Al Qaeda has successfully sought refuge at one time or another are on the FSI list (e.g., Afghanistan, Pakistan, and Sudan), are places where Al Qaeda affiliates are notable (Iraq and Yemen, for example), or are the list of potential safe havens for the organization (Somalia).

The connection between failed states and international terrorism gives the phenomenon a prominence and sense of importance it would not likely otherwise possess. If international religious terrorism is to be isolated and destroyed, then it follows that part of the strategy for doing so involves removing those conditions in which terrorism breeds and where terrorists find sympathetic environments to exist and prosper. It is generally assumed that the kinds of environments that nurture terrorism and state failure are similar to one another, and thus part of the strategies of antiterrorism are also strategies with an antistate failure intent or effect. While it is not entirely clear what exactly needs to be done to alter those environments, the question of what to do about state failure will likely remain lively as long as international religious terrorism is a problem, and the urgency of the effort will be related directly to the importance of the places where state failure and the existence of potential for terrorism are greatest.

The extent of the international consequences of state failure varies depending on the importance of a particular country on the global system. While there is no agreed formula or set of criteria for assessing importance, three factors stand out for exemplary purposes. One is the size of the failing country: the larger a country is in physical size and population, the more consequence its actions, including state failure, are likely to have on the world around it. State failure in Nigeria, Africa's most populous and one of its physically largest countries, has more of a ripple effect than the same phenomenon in Guinea. Second, some countries are more geopolitically consequential than others. Factors such as geopolitical location or special relationships with other countries are examples. Third, there may be special characteristics making a country more important than it might otherwise be.

In contemporary terms, there is no place in the world where the conjunction of circumstances and consequences is greater than in Pakistan. Pakistan is the sixth most populous country in the world and the world's second most populous Muslim state (after Indonesia, although there are more Muslims living in India than either Indonesia or Pakistan). Its location between India and Russia has made it a historically important buffer area (along with Afghanistan), and it borders on the Arabian Sea, thus potentially giving it the ability to influence the world's oil flow. Its "special circumstance" is that it is currently the only Islamic state to possess nuclear weapons. For these reasons, the potential failure of Pakistan is an important problem worthy of consideration.

PAKISTAN: A FAILED STATE?

As already noted, Pakistan occupies the 10th spot on the 2009 FSI, down one position from 2008. In one sense, the Pakistani state has already failed once: As a result of the secession of Bangladesh in 1971, the original Pakistan created by the partition of the Indian subcontinent in 1947 was essentially cut in half, with the original eastern part of the country becoming Bangladesh and the western half remaining Pakistan. Had the original Pakistan remained intact, it would today have a population of over 320 million, making it slightly larger than the population of the United States and thus the world's third most populous country. The centrifugal possibility of further disintegration, however, remains one of the vulnerabilities that places Pakistan on the failed state list.

The Pakistanis, of course, deny the prospect of their failure and demonstrate righteous indignation when their country is considered in the same breath as obviously precarious places in the world. That said, the risk of violence and state vulnerability that mark various aspects of the failed states is apparent in Pakistan. Before applying the general categories of the FSI to the Pakistani situation, however, a brief look at the country will help provide some context for the assessment.

A Thumbnail Sketch of Pakistan

The state of Pakistan is one of the consequences of the breakup of British colonial rule of the Indian subcontinent (the so-called "Raj") after World War II. When it became apparent that Great Britain could no longer carry on the role of colonial master after the war and that the various groups living there demanded independence that Britain was unable or unwilling to resist, the question became the form in which that independence would be granted.

It was a complicated problem because of the enormous diversity of peoples who lived on the subcontinent, many of whom demanded their individual independence, an assertion often contested by others. The British attempted to solve the problem by creating two states that would be organized around the region's two dominant religions, Islam and Hinduism. Hindu was the original religion of most of the subcontinent, but successive invasions over nearly a millennium had also spread Islam to great parts of the region, and indeed the British colonial imposition displaced the Muslim Mughal Empire in a good bit of the subcontinent (not including southern India). In the process, a good bit of religious intermingling occurred, making it impossible neatly or easily to create separate sovereign enclaves for practitioners of the two religions. Moreover, there were sizable parts of the region that did not desire to be a part of either of the denominationally defined states.

It was in these circumstances that a British commission headed by wartime hero Lord Mountbatten negotiated the partition of the subcontinent. In 1947, two major states, India and Pakistan, came into existence, and over 100 smaller political entities (many of them so-called princely states) were given the choice of joining one or the other. In numerous cases, the status of these entities and their wishes were either contested regarding the country they would join, or the majority preferred an independence that was not one of their options. The most famous of these situations surrounded and continues to plague Jammu and Kashmir.

Indian nationalism was well established, making the formation and development of the Hindu state of India comparatively easier than the similar process in Pakistan. Part of the reason for this was that India had pre-existed the British colonial period and thus a national sense of identity existed for most of the citizens. Pakistan, on the other hand, was a much more recent idea that lacked the deep roots in the minds and hearts of many of the people who became part of the country.

The "idea of Pakistan" to borrow Cohen's title, was born in 1933 by a group of expatriate Muslim students at Cambridge University in England in a pamphlet called *Now or Never*. According to Cohen, "the concept of a separate Indian Muslim political entity was first put forward by Choudhary Rahmat Ali." The name Pakistan is an acronym, with the letters in its name deriving from the various physical areas that constituted Muslim "homelands" (roughly, areas from which Pakistanis had migrated or were original inhabitants): Punjab, Afghania (the North-West Frontier Province), Kashmir, Iran, Sindh, Turkharistan, Afghanistan, and Baluchistan. The acronym means "land of the Paks," and it translated from Urdu as "pure (Pak) country (stan)." The core of all these regions, and the true dynamic and rationale of Pakistan, was to draw under one national umbrella the Muslims of the subcontinent.

The new state of Pakistan was born with several difficulties, most of which continue to place a burden on the Pakistani state. The first of these was that habitation patterns were not neatly divided, meaning it was impossible to draw boundaries creating a state in which the various Muslim populations exist. Dispersion of Muslims was one aspect of this problem, and after partition, the result was massive and often quite violent migration of Hindus out of what became Pakistan and of Muslims out of India, especially in 1948. The other, and most dramatic, aspect was that Pakistan was divided into two parts, east and west, separated by over 1,000 miles of sovereign Indian territory. This problem unraveled in 1971 with the secession of the eastern part of Pakistan as Bangladesh.

The second problem was ethnic diversity within the Pakistani population. The original Pakistan was dominated by two ethnic groups, the Punjabi in the west and the Bengali in the east, and much of the reason for Bangladeshi secession arose from Bengali perception of inferior status in the country. After 1971, the Punjabi, with about 45 percent of the population in 2009 (figures from the *CIA World Factbook*), became the clearly dominant ethnic group in Pakistan, with other major ethnic groups including the Pashtuns (Pathans) at 15.42 percent, the Sindhi, 14 percent, and the remaining roughly one quarter divided among Sariaki, Muhagirs, Baluchis, and others. Each of the ethnic groups retains some ethnic ties at odds with a common Pakistani nationalism.

The third problem, which derives from the first two, is a lack of common nationalism that has crippled attempts to develop a coherent Pakistani state and polity. Although all but about 5 percent of Pakistanis share Islam as their religious faith (a positive nationalistic factor), that commonality is often overridden by other, more negative influences. For one thing, there is sharp disagreement within the Islamic majority (75 percent of the population is Sunni and 20 percent Shiite) about the role and pervasiveness of Islam in the country, ranging from those who prefer a largely secular society to those who prefer a highly Islamist Pakistan. More fundamentally, however, is the ethnic division within the country. In the original Pakistan, the major ethnic division was between provincially based ethnic groups. As Cohen explains it, "Each of its provinces is associated with a single ethnolinguistic group: Punjab with Punjabis, Sindh with Sindhis, Baluchistan with Baluchs, and the Northwest Frontier Province (NWFP) with Pashtuns. Pashtuns and Punjabis are found throughout the country." While all the ethnic groups present differing challenges to the Pakistani polity, one stands out in particular. Again, Cohen explains, "The separatist group that poses the largest threat to Pakistan today is perhaps the Pashtun nationalist movement. It was active well before Pakistan's creation, then faded for twenty years, and now is experiencing a resurgence." The Pashtun (more specifically, the Ghilzai Pashtuns) live on both sides of the Afghanistan–Pakistan border (the Durand Line), form the core of both the Afghan and Pakistani Taliban, and have periodically advocated the formation of an independent state of Pashtunistan encompassing Pashtun tribal lands in both countries. Moreover, the government in Islamabad (notably the Inter-Services Intelligence Directorate or ISID) was active in both forming and sustaining the Taliban as a way to weaken the government of Afghanistan, a historic Pakistani foreign policy priority.

Fourth has been the role of the military in Pakistani society. As Hassan Haqqani has detailed eloquently in his seminal *Pakistan between Mosque and Military*, there has been an uneasy alliance throughout Pakistani history between the professional military and Islamic elements in society that has generally been arrayed against democratizing elements within the country. Lacking any strong traditions at national birth, the question of governance of Pakistan has always been tenuous and usually has been dominated by the military, which either rules directly or looms behind civilian governments as a specter should they falter. The military's strength is derived largely from the fact the Pakistan exists as a kind of national security state due to the constant (and partially self-generated and self-sustaining) military rivalry with India, and its alliance with various religious factors has made it the most important factor in Pakistani politics across time. Haqqani, writing in *Current History*, explains this impact of "the perception among Pakistan's national security elite that the country is surrounded by enemies determined to dismember it. . . . Until that sense of siege is gone, it will be difficult to strengthen civilian institutions in Pakistan."

These factors and others coalesce to produce a tenuous political situation that has continued to exist from the formation of Pakistan to the present. Haqqani summarizes the situation in his 2005 book, "Pakistan is far from developing a consistent system of government, with persisting polarization along three major, intersecting fault lines: between civilians and the military, among various ethnic and provincial groups, and between Islamists and secularists." All these factors coalesce to form the backdrop against which to assess whether (or the extent to which) Pakistan should be thought of as a failing or failed state.

Pakistan and the Failed State Index

The discussion of failed states generally provides a framework within which to examine the status of Pakistan. The vehicle for such an examination can be centered on the three categories of the *Foreign Policy/* Fund for Peace Failed State Index: social, economic, and political indicators.

The current regional international terrorist crisis centered on Afghanistan and significantly overflowing into Pakistan has raised the problem of state failure by exposing the vulnerability of the country to the conflict in Afghanistan. As Haqqani (in *Current History*) explains, "The government of Pakistan has been unable to retain control of its own territory and population. . . . Afghanistan in many ways has replaced Kashmir as the main arena of the still-unresolved struggle between Pakistan and India." The relationship between the Pakistani government and the tribal groups (largely Pashtun) living within the mountainous regions along the Durand Line has always been delicate and imperfect—with tribal groups exercising considerable autonomy from Islamabad—but the American-led battle against the Taliban has created outside pressure on Pakistan to increase its control over these areas, resulting in a strain between Islamabad and places like the NWFP and hence more general political trauma. No small part of outsider—read American—concern about potential Pakistani failure derives from the extent to which American pressure on Pakistan may push that country to the brink of failure or over it, a daunting prospect given Pakistan's nuclear capability. Cohen, however, counsels caution in reaching extravagant projections about Pakistani failure: "Each time Pakistan has been declared a 'failed state' it has come back from the grave—albeit with a weakened economy, a more fragmented political order, less security in relations to its powerful neighbor, and disturbing demographic and educational trends." How many of these weakening impacts of rebirth can be sustained before failure becomes a reality is the question to which an examination of the Failed States Index categories can be directed.

Social Indicators. The social problems reflected in the index apply strongly to Pakistan. In essence, the index uses two kinds of indicators to measure social distress. One of these is internal pressure, found in such things as demographic difficulties and the grievance of different social groups. The other is in pressures caused by movements of peoples either internally or from outside the country.

Pakistan suffers from the kinds of demographic difficulties that plague so much of the Middle East: a rapidly growing, youthful population and the general lack of educational and employment opportunities to produce a satisfied population. Cohen summarized this situation in 2004, and his description holds today: "In the long run, the lack of economic activity, the booming birth rate [2.7 percent in 2009, according to the *CIA World Factbook*], the youth bulge, intensive urbanization, and a hostile regional environment could leave Pakistan with a large, young, and ill-educated population that has few prospects for economic advancement and could be politically mobilized." The educational situation is exemplary: Pakistan spent 2.6 percent of gross domestic product (GDP) on education is 2006 (the most recent figures reported by the CIA), which ranked it 155th among world countries. The overall literacy rate is almost exactly half the population, with an average "school life expectancy" of seven years. Given the shortage of public expenditures on education, many Pakistanis are forced to educate their children privately, largely in the religious *madrassah* schools that have been a hotbed of radicalization. At the micro level, the result is members entering the workforce educationally prepared for only the most rudimentary kinds of jobs (which are inadequately available); at the macro level, the country is gradually losing its educated elite, leaving it progressively behind countries like neighboring rival India in the pursuit of advanced industry and service professions. In 2008, the unemployment rate in Pakistan ranked 146th in the world.

International religious terrorism and responses to it have resulted in refugee and internal displacement problems as well. *The World Almanac and Book of Facts* 2010 edition, for instance, cites the U.S. Committee for Refugees and Immigrants *World Refugee Survey 2009* that there are 1,775,600 external refugees in Pakistan, mostly displaced Pashtuns from Afghanistan residing in the Pashtun frontier provinces that are also the safe haven and recruiting ground for the Taliban both in Afghanistan and Pakistan. Reporting in the online *Huffington Post* in October 2009, Patrick Duplat reports that there have been as many as 700,000 internal displaced persons (IDPs), principally in South Waziristan, largely the result of population flight as the Pakistani Army swept areas such as the Swat and Buner districts to displace Taliban as part of the country's commitment to aid the United States and to relieve pressure from Pakistani Taliban and Al Qaeda elements.

Economic Indicators. Pakistan is a poor country by any measure. It has a comparatively weak economy (its GDP per capita was estimated at $2,600 in 2008), over three quarters of its underemployed workforce is in either the agricultural or service sectors, and the less than one-quarter involved in industry is mostly employed in relatively low skill, poorly paying occupations such as textiles and food processing. "Pakistan has no highly desired product or service to offer except textiles," according to Cohen, and textiles represent the most rudimentary form of development, particularly from a foreign investment vantage point. A weak economic base, in turn, provides inadequate opportunities for the quantity of young people entering the labor market as a result of the youth bulge, and the failing educational system means most of those workers are only prepared for relatively menial jobs that cannot contribute to the development of more sophisticated economic endeavors that would improve Pakistan's economic standing in the world—"a decline in Pakistan's technological base," in Haqqani's estimation.

Haqqani (in *Current History*) further summarizes the dismal state of the Pakistani economy: "Pakistan's gross domestic product stands at about $75 billion in absolute terms and $295 billion in purchasing power, making Pakistan's economy the smallest of any country that has tested nuclear weapons thus far. Pakistan suffers from massive urban unemployment, rural underemployment, illiteracy, and low per capita income. One-third of the population lives below the poverty line, and another 21 percent subsists just above it." This set of factors represents a cauldron of potential sources of instability.

The Pakistani economy is further exacerbated by its *rentier* status, the idea that much of Pakistan's economy derives from foreign sources of income. The term was originally coined to describe states whose income was largely derived from selling ("collecting rents") on the exploitation of natural resources like petroleum rather than through more basic domestic, jobs-related activities, and was originally applied primarily to Middle East and other oil producers. It has been extended to incorporate income derived from the provision of services for foreign providers, in the case of Pakistan foreign assistance provided for Pakistani participation in antiterrorist activities. When governments become dependent on these rents for government operations rather than taxes from individual labor and production, a state can gain rentier status. Shaikh explains this phenomenon and its application to Pakistan: "Political scientists generally use the term 'rentier state' to describe states that finance more than 40 percent of their expenditures through 'revenue accrued from abroad.' Recently, the term has also come to refer to any state that hires out its services to the highest bidder. Pakistan qualifies neatly on both counts." In the case of Pakistan, American assistance since 2002 (the first full year of the "war on terror") has contributed to Pakistan's growing dependence on outside funding. As Tellis points out in an Autumn 2008 *Washington Quarterly* article, 57 percent of American aid has been for antiterrorism activities, 18 percent for military procurement (mostly buying American equipment), and 25 percent for economic activities, 16 percent of which "took the form of budgetary support through direct cash transfers," a direct rentier application. All of these factors combine in Shaikh's estimation to Pakistan's condition where "the nation seems adrift, in danger of capsizing."

Political Indicators. The social and economic woes afflicting Pakistan are inevitably manifested in terms of political dissatisfaction with the Pakistani state, and state actions can and have made these conditions better or worse. The political burden facing the Pakistani political system is further exacerbated by the country's turbulent political history, which has produced no solid, firm consensus about who should govern or how, and these conditions are made worse by the current external and internal pressures on the country related to international religious terrorism, problems related to Pakistan's ethnic mosaic and to conscious policies of past Pakistan governments (particularly toward Afghanistan) that have, in significant ways, come home to roost for the Pakistanis. The result is considerable potential for violence and instability, the stuff of political failure.

Some of Pakistan's political problems are clearly self-inflicted. Pakistan has failed to resolve fundamental political problems along two dimensions. The first is agreement on how Pakistan should be ruled and by whom. Advocates of democracy have vied across time with more authoritarian elements, mostly associated with the military, and an accommodation between the two has never been reached, leaving the country alternating between military rule opposed by democrats charging those in charge with heavy handed authoritarian rule, or civilians in charge of a government with the military lurking in the background in opposition to the corruption of the civilian rulers. Unfortunately, the suspicions of both groups against the other have had merit, and a consequence has been, in the words of Tellis, "the absence of strong and legitimate centers of moderation and modernity."

The second dimension is the failure to overcome regional and ethnic differences within the country, an affliction common to the region. Pakistan remains a multinational state (a political entity containing multiple ethnic— or national in an anthropological sense—groups) whose loyalties are, in important ways, more closely associated with their tribal roots than they are with the well-being of Pakistan, and the politics of the country often pits the Punjabi plurality that rules against the various tribal groups on the peripheries of the Punjabi center. This problem is exacerbated by the regional concentration of minority groups in different physical sectors of the country, as already noted.

These factors combine with the country's economic weakness as centrifugal influences on the "idea" of Pakistan. As Cohen puts it, "The causes of separatism in Pakistan are fairly clear: uneven development, inequitable distribution of resources, a lack of representative political institutions, and an oppressive state apparatus." All of these factors act as a toxin against the emergence of a stable political system in Afghanistan.

Assessment and Consequences

The State Failure Index provides useful categories for examining the situation in Pakistan, and the mosaic that emerges from examining the country within this framework is arguably ominous. It is probably excessive to argue that the Pakistani state either has failed or is in imminent danger of failing: The central government does indeed maintain control over most of the country, and those areas where its domain is not well established—the tribal lands along the Afghan frontier—are areas where that situation has been historical and purposive. As Haqqani concludes about the Federally Administered Tribal Areas, "the FATA is kept underdeveloped and overarmed as a barrier against invaders." Indeed, the government has long adhered to a bargain with the residents that they will remain largely autonomous as long as they pose no threat to the political center.

What makes the Pakistani situation poignant has been the overflow of the Afghanistan war into Pakistan through the movement of Pashtun Taliban and Al Qaeda personnel back and forth from Afghanistan into areas of Pakistan over which the government does not exercise more than nominal authority. Pakistani historic sponsorship of the Taliban through the ISID as a way to keep Afghanistan weak creates a perceived bond between the two groups and makes more difficult Pakistani responses to American and other western demands to regain control over the border areas and to suppress the Taliban and other extremists operating in the region. A major and obvious impact of Pakistani efforts to please the Americans is to alienate its own Pashtun minority and thus further potentially to destabilize the regime. The 2009 Pakistani campaign into the Swat Valley to root out Taliban and Al Qaeda elements there (only 60 miles or so from Islamabad) and the subsequent spate of suicide bombing attacks against Pakistani urban targets illustrates the destabilizing impact of these dynamics. With regard to the regional situation, the Pakistanis are in a literal "damned-if-they-do-and-damned-if-they-don't" situation that is partially of their own doing.

This current situation regarding Afghanistan both feeds concerns about further destabilization and potential failure and makes the consequences more vital. This teetering on the brink is not new, as noted by Cohen earlier. Pakistan is and always has been a fragile, artificial country that survives despite any real tradition of cohesion, and it did, after all, survive the loss of half its population and territory with the 1971 secession of Bangladesh. The central reality is that Pakistan has always come back from the brink, although Cohen warns that "the failure of Pakistan as a state cannot be ruled out."

The consequences of this possibility are what activate international concern about Pakistan. Pakistan is by almost any measure the largest and most important country in the world to face the possibility of failure: is it, like assessment about large American banks leading to their "bailout" in 2008, too large to be allowed to fail? Who would be drawn into the resulting vacuum, and how? More importantly, can the world afford to have a nuclear power fail, with possible resultant loss of control of the nuclear arsenal in an atmosphere where terrorists might attempt to control those weapons? One can argue that the breakup of the Soviet Union was a massive case of state failure by a nuclear state, and the result was not the loss of control of the arsenal. The analogy, of course, is incomplete: the Soviet Union disintegrated, but there were successor states (Russia, etc.) in place to maintain order, and that would not necessarily be the case if Pakistan were "unable to retain control of its own territory and population," a possibility raised by Haqqani and at the heart of the definition of state failure.

CONCLUSION

State failure, in its differing degrees, is an important dynamic of modern international politics. It is a problem particularly associated with the less developed and hence more unstable areas of the world, with countries in Africa and Asia particularly vulnerable and prone to the prospect of different levels of the dysfunction the concept attempts to capture. When failure occurs in marginalized areas and countries the status of which do not have strong ramifications elsewhere in the world (e.g., much of Africa), state failure is viewed as regrettable, but it is usually not the subject of much concerted action by countries more concerned with more immediate and immediately consequential problems. Even when the problems bubble up in horrifying vividness, as they did in Somalia in 1992 and in the Darfur region of Sudan since 2003, reactions are inconclusive and unsuccessful (Somalia) or half-hearted and irresolute (Darfur). Moving states away from the precipice of various levels of failure involves addressing a complex set of intractable problems, as the elaboration of the FSI categories reveal, and it has so far been beyond the efforts of the rest of the states of the world.

Sometimes, however, the prospects of state failure are more difficult, even impossible, to ignore, because of the prominence of the potentially failing state and the consequences of its failure. Pakistan is such a state, both because of its size, its geopolitical importance, and the special circumstance of its possession of nuclear weapons. Were Pakistan instead Guinea, the world would take little heed of its difficulties, but Pakistan is not Guinea. When important states begin to show signs of crumbling, the world takes notice, and that prospect makes Pakistan a fitting case of the dynamics of state failure or its potential.

STUDY/DISCUSSION QUESTIONS

1. What is a failed state? What are the different degrees of state failure? Discuss.
2. What is the Failed State Index (FSI)? What geographic regions are most represented on the list? Why?
3. Discuss the categories and indicators on the FSI. Include in your discussion an assessment of the utility and precision of the index.
4. What are the domestic and international consequences of state failure for the victim country and the international system? What characteristics make the failure of some states more consequential for the international system than others?
5. Why is Pakistan a matter of concern when discussing the failed state phenomenon? Discuss those aspects of the Pakistani experience that are relevant to the discussion of its inclusion on the FSI.
6. Discuss the FSI status of Pakistan as a potential failed state in terms of the categories of the index.
7. Based on the discussion of Pakistan, should it be considered a failed, failing, or failure-prone state? Why does its status matter to the world outside its boundaries?
8. How has Pakistan's involvement in Afghanistan made the factors contributing to state failure both worse than it might otherwise be but also the result of Pakistani self-infliction?

RESEARCH/READING MATERIALS

Central Intelligence Agency. *CIA World Factbook*. Washington, DC: Central Intelligence Agency, 2009 (http://www.cia.gov/library/publications/the-world-factbook/geos/country).

Cohen, Stephen Philip. *The Idea of Pakistan*. Washington, DC: Brookings Institution Press, 2004.

Duplat, Patrick. "Pakistan: Inconvenient Truths." *Huffington Post* (online), October 29, 2009.

Fair C. Christine. "Time for Sober Relations: Renegotiating U.S. Relations with Pakistan." *Washington Quarterly* 32, 2 (April 2009), 149–172.

"Failed States." Crisis Watch Workshop. London, March 2006 "The Failed State Index." *Foreign Policy*, July/August 2008, 64–73.

"The Failed State Index 2009: FAQ and Methodology." *Foreign Policy* (online), July 2009 (http://foreignpolicy.com/articles/2009/06/22/2009_failed_state_index_faq_methodo . . .).

Haqqani, Husain. *Pakistan Between Mosque and Military.* Washington, DC: Carnegie Endowment for International Peace Press, 2005.

———. *"Pakistan and the Islamists."* Current History 106, 699 (April 2007), 147–152.

Helman, Gerald B., and Steven R. Ratner. "Saving Failed States." *Foreign Policy* 89 (Winter 1992/1993), 3–20.

Hussein, Zahid. *Frontline Pakistan: The Struggle with Militant Islam.* New York: Columbia University Press, 2007.

Khan, M. Asghar. *We've Learned Nothing from History: Pakistan–Politics and Military Power.* Oxford, UK: Oxford University Press, 2005.

Reidel, Bruce. "Pakistan: The Critical Battleground." *Current History* 107, 712 (November 2008), 355–361.

Rubin, Barnett R. and Ahmed Rashid. "From Great Game to Grand Bargain." *Foreign Affairs* 87, 6 (November/December 2008), 30–44.

Shakih, Farzana. "Pakistan's Perilous Journey." *Current History* 107, 712 (October 2008), 362–368.

Tellis, Ashley J. "The Merits of Dehyphenation: Explaining U.S. Success in Engaging India and Pakistan." *Washington Quarterly* 32, 4 (Autumn 2009), 21–42.

———. "Pakistan's Record on Terrorism: Conflicted Goals, Compromised Performance." *Washington Quarterly* 31, 2 (April 2008), 7–32.

The World Almanac and Book of Facts, 2010. New York: World Almanac Books, 2010.

Terrorism: The Changing Global Threat

PRÉCIS

The terrorist attacks of September 11, 2001, are now a decade in the past, but the problem of terrorism remains a vital international and national concern. Terrorism had been building as a force for the better part of two decades but previously had not achieved the level of notoriety that the attacks evinced. Efforts to respond to the actions of Al Qaeda (the principal international terrorist group) have, in turn, caused the nature of the threat itself to change, and efforts to adapt to and counter new permutations remain a major agenda item for terrorism suppressors.

The purpose of this case is to investigate the nature of the terrorist problem, how it is changing, and what can be done about it. It begins by examining briefly the dynamics of terrorism: What is it; what do terrorists seek to do; who are they; and what causes people to become terrorists? It then moves to how terrorism has evolved structurally as a problem since September 11 and what efforts have been mounted against it. It concludes by examining the current decentralized nature of the threat and social problems posed by so-called lone wolf terrorists.

The tragic terrorist attack by the Islamic terrorist group Al Qaeda against the World Trade Center towers and the Pentagon 10 years ago on September 11, 2001, was a seminal international and national event. Internationally, it signaled a new and frightening escalation of a problem that had troubled Europe and other parts of the world for a long time, and it produced an enormous outpouring of sympathy and support for the United States as the newest victim. Nationally, the attacks traumatized an American population suddenly aware of its vulnerability and spawned a major national priority to deal with this problem under the official sobriquet of the "global war on terrorism" (GWOT).

The GWOT is now roughly a decade old as well. It has had some successes, capturing or otherwise suppressing elements of the old Al Qaeda network, to the point that Scott Atran suggested in 2005, "remnants of the mostly Egyptian hardcore around bin Laden have not managed a successful attack in three years," an observation that still arguably holds. Others like Hoffman disagree: "not only is Al Qaeda alive and kicking, it is actively planning, supporting, and perhaps even directing attacks on a global canvas." Regardless of which side of the debate is correct, the perceptions of the terrorism problem have by no means diminished, much less abated. The monolithic threat posed by Al Qaeda itself may be different than it was in 2001, but the problem of terrorism remains: New permutations have arisen that are, if anything, more provocative and dangerous. Most share radical Islam as a foundation, but from Chechnya to Indonesia, new and different organizations have emerged as new challenges: International terrorism has become a hydra-headed beast, with Al Qaeda as its vital organ.

Some of the ardor and intensity associated with the early post-9/11 period has weakened in recent years. In some ways, this reaction is entirely natural and justifiable. For one thing, the intensity has dissipated as time has passed and no equivalent attacks have followed. Terrorist activities, including some well-publicized attacks and attempts worldwide, continue, but none have risen to a level of violence and atrocity even closely approaching 9/11, and there are widespread suspicions that terrorists may simply lack the resources necessary to replicate the attacks on New York and Washington, DC by Al Qaeda. The possibility that terrorists might gain access to weapons of mass destruction (WMDs) is the signal exception to this train of analysis. The absence of major terrorist follow-on activities against the United States, despite a series of botched attempts, is particularly exemplary in this regard. At the same time, the GWOT has been questioned by some because of its association with some dubious actions like the war in Iraq.

None of this means the problem of terrorism has disappeared, of course. Terrorism remains a major and, in some ways, more pervasive force that may or may not pose individual threats of the calamity of 9/11 but which has spread to infect greater parts of the world. Still based in particularly militant, unorthodox interpretations of Islam as its core, the threat has morphed from an apparently concentrated, hierarchical Al Qaeda directed by Osama bin Laden and his associates to a more diffuse movement directing its mayhem internally in places like Pakistan and India and more broadly to European targets like London.

The changes, examined more systematically later in the chapter, are partially organizational and structural. Al Qaeda is no longer a monolithic, hierarchical entity directing terror; rather, it is a loosely associated series of "franchises" bound by some ideological affinity. Acts of terror now include highly public acts by independent individuals known as lone wolves. The Internet sometimes serves as a connector between these demented individuals and purveyors of venomous, murderous hatred via so-called virtual networks or leaderless resistance groups.

WHAT IS TERRORISM?

The first step in coming to grips with terrorism is defining the term. It is an important consideration, because so many phenomena in the contemporary international arena are labeled terrorist. This makes a definition particularly important as a means to measure whether a particular movement, or act, is terrorism or not. Without a set of criteria defining what does and does not constitute terrorism, it is hard to tell.

This is not a merely semantic exercise. Take, for instance, the recent emphasis on Chechen separatists and their separatist campaign, which the Russian government has called terrorist. Certainly, actions, such as enlisting suicide terrorists to blow up two Russian airliners and the brutal siege of the school in Beslan in the Caucasus, were hideous, brutal acts that comport with an understanding of terrorism, but is it correct to label the movement that commissioned and carried out the acts terrorist as a result? In context, when the Russian government of the then president Boris Yeltsin used the Russian army to attack Chechnya in 1995 to wipe out the secessionist movement there (among other things, leveling the capital of Grozny) and former president Vladimir Putin renewed the campaign in 1999, there were widespread international accusations that the Russian government was terrorizing the Chechens and engaging in crimes against humanity (acts of state terrorism). So who is the terrorist here?

Having an agreed-on definition of terrorism helps answer defining questions; unfortunately, such a consensus does not exist. Rather, there are virtually as many different definitions as there are people and organizations making the distinctions. There are also some commonalities that recur and will allow the adoption of a definition for present purposes. A few arguably representative examples will aid in drawing distinctions.

The U.S. government offers the official definition in its 2003 *National Strategy for Combating Terrorism:* "premeditated, politically motivated violence perpetrated against noncombatant targets by subnational groups or clandestine agents." In *Attacking Terrorism,* coauthor Audrey Kurth Cronin says terrorism is distinguished by its political nature, its nonstate base, the targeting of innocent noncombatants, and the illegality of its acts. Jessica Stern, in *Terrorism in the Name of God,* defines terrorism as "an act or threat of violence against noncombatants with the objective of exacting revenge, intimidating, or otherwise influencing an audience." Alan Dershowitz (in *Why Terrorism Works),* offers no definition himself, but notes that definitions typically include reference to terrorist targets, perpetrators, and terrorist acts.

These definitions, and similar ones from others in the field, have common cores. All of them share three common points of reference: terrorist acts (illegal, often hideous and atrocious), terrorist targets (often innocent non-combatants), and terrorist purposes (political persuasion or influence). The only difference among them is whether they specify the nature of terrorists and their political base: The State Department, Cronin, and Dershowitz all identify terrorist organizations as nonstate-based actors. Cronin in particular emphasizes that "although states can terrorize, by definition they cannot be terrorists."

For the rest of this case study, terrorism will be defined as "the commission of atrocious acts against a target population normally to gain compliance with some demands the terrorists insist upon." It does not specify that terrorism must be committed by nonstate actors, because that may be a characteristic of modern terrorism, but not of terrorism per se. Terrorism thus consists of three related phenomena, each of which must be present in some manner for something to be considered an act of terrorism. The fourth element in other definitions, perpetrators of terrorism, is implicit in the three criteria. Discussing each helps enliven an understanding of what constitutes terrorism.

Terrorist Acts

The first element of the definition encompasses *terrorist acts,* which are the visible manifestation of terrorism and the part of the phenomenon with which most people are most familiar. Several comments can be made about terrorist acts.

One comment is that what distinguished terrorist acts from other political expressions is that they are uniformly illegal. Terrorist acts upset the normalcy of life through destructive acts aimed at either injuring or killing people or destroying things. Regardless of the professed underlying motives of terrorists, the actions they commit break laws and are subject to criminal prosecution. By raising the rhetoric of terrorist actions to acts of war (currently holy war or *jihad*), terrorists may seek to elevate what they do to a higher plane ("one man's terrorist is another man's freedom fighter"), but the simple fact remains that terrorist acts are criminal in nature.

A second comment is that the general purpose of terrorist acts is to frighten the target audience: The word *terrorism* is derived from the Latin root *terrere,* which means "to frighten." The method of inducing fright is through the commission of normally random, unpredictable acts of violence that induce such fear that those who witness or experience the acts will conclude that compliance with terrorist demands is preferable to living with the fear of being future victims themselves. With the exception of explicitly targeted acts like assassinations, acts of terrorism are not particularly aimed at the actual victims themselves (who are often randomly selected and whose fate does not "matter" to the terrorist) but at the audience who views the actions. As Brian Jenkins once put it, *"Terrorists want a lot of people watching and a lot of people listening, and not a lot of people dead."* (Emphasis in original.) The dynamic of inducing this fright is the disruption of the predictability and safety of life within society, one of whose principal functions is to make existence predictable and safe. Ultimately, a major purpose of terrorism may be to undermine this vital fiber of society.

Terrorists may, of course, act for a variety of other reasons. Jenkins provides a list of six other, generally less lofty, purposes for terrorist actions. Terrorist actions may be aimed at exacting special concessions, such as ransom, the release of prisoners (generally members of the terrorist group), or publicizing a message. Gaining the release of political prisoners was the stated reason that Hizbollah kidnapped Israeli soldiers in summer 2006, triggering the widespread violence there. Indonesia's Jemaah Islamiyah carried out its 2004 attack on the Australian embassy and promptly announced that it would perpetrate similar attacks if its leader, Abu Bakar Bashir, was not released from prison.

Terrorists may act to gain publicity for their causes. Before Palestinian terrorists kidnapped a series of airliners and then launched an attack on the Israeli compound at the Munich Olympics in the 1970s, hardly anyone outside the region had ever heard of the Palestinian cause; the terrorist actions got them that global awareness. The publicity may be intended to remind a world that has shifted its attention away from a particular group and its activities that it is still active and that it is still pursuing its goals.

Another, and more fundamental, purpose of terrorist acts is to cause widespread disorder that demoralizes society and breaks down the social order in a country. This, of course, is a very ambitious purpose, and one that presumably can only be undertaken through a widespread campaign that includes a large number of terrorist acts. The suicide terror campaign by Hamas against Israeli civilians (and the Israeli counterattacks against Palestinians) could be an example of terrorism for this purpose.

A more tactical use of terrorism is to provoke overreaction by a government in the form of repressive action, reprisals, and overly brutal counterterrorism that may lead to the overthrow of the reactive government. This was a favorite tactic of the Viet Cong in the Vietnam War, and evoked the ironic analogy of building schools during the day (as a way to pacify the population) and then bombing those schools at night (because they became the source of Viet Cong actions after nightfall).

Terror may also be used to enforce obedience and cooperation within a target population. Campaigns of terror directed by the governments of states against their own citizens often have this purpose, which is often assigned to a secret police or similar paramilitary organizations. The actions of the KGB in the Soviet Union, the Gestapo and other similar organizations in Nazi Germany, and the infamous death squads in Argentina during the 1960s and 1970s are all examples of the use of government terror to intimidate and frighten their own populations into submission. At a less formal governmental level, many actions of the Ku Klux Klan during the latter nineteenth and early twentieth centuries against black Americans would qualify as well.

Jenkin's last purpose of terrorist action is punishment. Terrorists often argue that an action they take is aimed at a particular person or place because that person or institution is somehow guilty of a particular transgression and is thus being meted out appropriate punishment for what the terrorists consider a crime. Although the Israeli government would be appalled at the prospects of calling its rescinded counter terrorist campaign to bulldoze the homes of the families of suicide terrorists (or bombing the homes of dissident leaders) as acts of terror, from the vantage point of the Palestinian targets of the attacks, they certainly must seem so.

Stern (in *Terrorism in the Name of God*) adds a seventh motivation that is internal to the terrorist organization: morale. Like any other organization, and especially terrorist groups in which the "operatives" are generally young and not terribly mature, it may be necessary from time to time to carry out a terrorist attack simply to demonstrate to the membership the continuing potency of the group as a way to keep the membership focused and their morale high. As Stern puts it, "Attacks sometimes have more to do with rousing the troops than terrorizing the victims." Improving or maintaining morale may also have useful spin-off effects, such as helping in recruiting new members to the group or in raising funds to support the organization's activities.

What this discussion seeks to demonstrate is that terrorists commit their actions for a variety of reasons. Some of these are more purposive and "noble" than others, but it is rarely immediately clear what may motivate a particular action. Moreover, different reasons may motivate different groups at different times and under different circumstances. Knowing that a terrorist attack has occurred, in other words, does not necessarily tell one why it has been committed or whether and how to guard against its repetition.

Terrorist Targets

The targets of terrorists can be divided into two related categories. The first is people, and the objective is to kill, maim, or otherwise cause some members of the target population to suffer as an example for the rest of the population. The second category is physical targets, attacks against which are designed to disrupt and destroy societal capabilities and to demonstrate the vulnerability of the target society. The two categories are related in that most physical targets worth attacking contain people who will be killed or injured in the process. Attacking either category demonstrates the inability of the target population to protect its members and valued artifices, thus questioning the efficacy of resisting terrorist demands.

There are subtle differences and problems associated with concentrating on one category of target or the other. Clearly, attacks directly intended to kill or injure people are the most personal and evoke the greatest emotion in the target population, including the will to resist and to seek vengeance. From the vantage point of the terrorist, the reason to attack people (beyond some simple blood lust) is to attack their will to resist the demands that terrorists make. Dennis Drew and I refer to this as *cost-tolerance,* the level of suffering one is willing to endure in the face of some undesirable situation. The terrorist seeks to exceed the target's cost-tolerance by making the target conclude that it is less painful (physically or mentally) to accede to the terrorist's demands than it is to continue to resist those demands. This goal is achieved by maximizing the level of fear and anxiety that the target experiences because of the often hideous effects of attacks. If the target group becomes so afraid of being the next victim that they cave in and accept the terrorist demands, the terrorist wins; if the target remains resolute, the terrorist fails.

Overcoming cost-tolerance is not an easy task, and it often fails. For one thing, terrorist organizations are generally small with limited resources, meaning that they usually lack the wherewithal to attack and kill a large enough portion of the target population to make members of that population become individually fearful enough to tip the scales (blowing up people on airplanes may be a partial exception). One of the great fears associated with terrorist groups obtaining and using weapons of mass destruction is that such a turn of events would change that calculus. For another thing, attacking and killing innocent members of a target group (at least innocent from the vantage point of the group) may (and usually does) infuriate its members and increase, rather than decrease, the will to resist. That has certainly been the case in the reaction to the 9/11 attacks, which both awakened the public to the threat of terrorism and created a steely resolve to resist those who committed them. The reaction of Indians to the Mumbai attack has been similar.

When the targets are physical things rather than people per se, the problems and calculations change. When the target of terrorists is a whole society, the range of potential targets is virtually boundless. In attacking places, the terrorist seeks to deprive the target population of whatever pleasure or life-sustaining or -enhancing value the particular target may provide. The list of what used to be called *countervalue* targets when speaking of nuclear targeting (things people value, such as their lives and what makes those lives enjoyable) covers a very broad range of objects, from hydroelectric plants to athletic stadiums, from nuclear power generators to military facilities, from highways to research facilities, and so on. Compiling a list for any large community is a very sobering experience.

It is unreasonable to assume that the potential list of physical targets for any country can be made uniformly invulnerable. There are simply too many targets, and the means of protecting them are sufficiently discrete that there is little overlap in function (protecting a football stadium from bombers may or may not have much carryover in terms of protecting nuclear power plants from seizure). As a result, there will always be a gap between the potential threats and the ability to negate all those threats, and the consequence is a certain level of risk for which there are simply inadequate resources to cancel.

Terrorist Objectives

The final element in the definition of terrorism is the objectives, or reasons, for which terrorists do what they do. For present purposes, the discussion of terrorist objectives will refer to the broader outcomes that terrorists seek (or say they seek) to accomplish. Objectives are the long-range reasons that terrorists wage campaigns of terrorism. In the short run, terrorists may engage in particular actions for a variety of reasons, as already noted (group morale or recruitment, for instance). What they seek ultimately to accomplish is the province of terrorist objectives.

The ultimate goals of most terrorist groups are political. To paraphrase the Clausewitzian dictum that war is politics by other means, so too is terrorism politics by other, extreme, means. Likewise, the objectives that terrorists pursue are extreme, at least to the target population, if not to the terrorists themselves. Sometimes, terrorist objectives are widely known and clearly articulated, and at other times they are not. Ultimately, however, campaigns of terror gain their meaning in the pursuit of some goal or goals, and their success or failure is measured to the extent that those goals are achieved.

Terrorism is the method of the militarily weak and conceptually unacceptable. The extremely asymmetrical nature of terrorist actions arises from the fact that terrorists cannot compete with their targets by the accepted methods of the target society for success. Terrorists lack the military resources to engage in open warfare, at which they would be easily defeated, or in the forum of public discourse and decision, because their objectives are unacceptable, distasteful, or even bizarre to the target population.

The fact that terrorist objectives are politically objectionable to the target sets up the confrontation between the terrorists and the target. Normally, terrorist goals are stated in terms of changing policies (Palestinian statehood or the right to repatriation within Israel, for example) or laws (releasing classes of detained people) that the majority in the target state find unacceptable. Because the terrorists are in a minority, they cannot bring about the changes they demand by normal electoral or legislative means, and they are likely to be viewed as so basically lunatic and unrealistic by the target audience that it will not accord seriousness to the demands of those who make them. To the terrorists, of course, the demands make perfect sense, and they are frustrated and angered by the treatment their demands are given. The stage is thus set for confrontation.

Terrorists achieve their objectives by overcoming the cost-tolerance of the target population to resist. The campaign of terrorist threats and acts is intended to convince the target population that acceding to the terrorist demands is preferable to the continuing anxiety and fear of future terrorism.

Determining whether terrorists achieve their goals or fail is complicated by the contrast between the tactical and strategic levels of objectives, making the compilation of a "score card" difficult. Modern terrorists have rarely been successful at the strategic level of attaining long-range objectives. Al Qaeda has not forced the United States from the Arabian Peninsula (although the American presence is declining), Russia has not granted Chechnya independence, and Jemaah Aslamiyah has yet to achieve a sectarian Islamic state in Indonesia. At the same time, the terrorist record at achieving tactical objectives (carrying out terrorist attacks) is, if not perfect, not a total failure either. As long as terrorists continue to exist and to achieve some of their goals, they remain a force against the targets of their activities. Thus, the competition between terrorists and their targets over the accomplishment of terrorist objectives continues to exist within a kind of nether world where neither wins nor loses decisively and thus both can claim some success.

The history of terrorism, moreover, suggests its ability to endure. Different terrorist groups with different objectives come and go, but the use of terrorism as a tool to achieve *some* goals has endured for at least 2 millennia (most historians of terrorism—see Rapaport, for instance—date the practice to the resistance to Roman rule over Palestine during Biblical times). Thus, efforts to suppress terrorism may be more realistic if their goal is to determine a "tolerable" level of terrorist activity and to try to keep instances of terrorism at or below that level rather than adopting the more comprehensive but historically daunting task of eradicating terrorism.

EVOLVING TERRORISM SINCE SEPTEMBER 11

The events of September 11 understandably riveted national attention on a specific terrorist threat posed by Al Qaeda. The focus was natural given the audacity and shock value of the actual attacks and by the novelty of an organization such as Al Qaeda. To the extent that Americans had much of any previous understanding of terrorism, it was associated with more "classical" forms, such as highly politicized anti-colonialist movements like the Irish Republican Army (IRA); with state terrorism in the form of suppression by totalitarian regimes like Hitler's Germany or Stalin's Soviet Union; or with isolated anarchist assassinations or individual acts like the bombing of the Murrah Federal Building in Oklahoma City.

Understanding the nature of the current threat has been difficult for at least two reasons. First, the contemporary form of terrorism is very different from anything encountered before, certainly by Americans. It is nonstate-based terrorism that does not arise from specific political communities or jurisdictions but instead flows across national boundaries like oil slipping under doors. This makes it conceptually difficult to understand and to counter. It is also religious, showing signs of fanaticism that are present in all religious communities but that are alien to most people's ability to conceptualize. Slaughter in the name of God goes beyond most of our intellectual frameworks. It is also fanatically anti-American and thus in sharp contrast to the general pro-Americanism that Americans at least believed dominated the end of the twentieth century. In addition, it employs methods such as suicide terrorism that, if not historically unique, are deviant enough to go beyond most abilities to conjure.

Second, our understanding is made more difficult by the extremely changeable nature of contemporary terrorist opponents. The Al Qaeda of 2001 was hard enough to understand, but it has evolved greatly since then. Partly this is because international efforts since 2001 have been quite effective in dismantling the old Al Qaeda structure by capturing and killing many of its members. This success, however, has caused the threat to disperse and transform itself into forms that we find even less recognizable and thus more difficult to identify and attack. Thus, a discussion of organizational evolution is necessary to clarify the nature of the current terrorist threat.

The Traditional Threat

Stern, in *Terrorism in the Name of God*, lays out the requirements for a successful terrorist organization. The effectiveness of a terrorist organization is dependent on two qualities: resiliency (the ability to withstand the loss of parts of its membership or workforce) and capacity (the ability to optimize the scale and impact of terrorist attacks). The larger the scale of operations that the terrorist organization can carry out without large losses to its members through capture or death, the more effective the organization is. Conversely, if an organization can only carry out small, relatively insignificant acts while having large portions of its membership captured or killed, it is less effective.

Resiliency and capacity are clearly related to one another. For a terrorist group to carry out large operations like 9/11, it must devise a sophisticated, coordinated plan involving a number of people or cells who must communicate with one another both to plan and to execute the attack. The Achilles' heel in terrorist activity is penetration of the organization by outsiders, and the key element is the interruption of communications that allows penetration into the group and movement through the hierarchy to interfere with and destroy it and its ability to carry out attacks (in other words, to reduce its resiliency). The most effective way for the terrorist groups to avoid penetration is to minimize communications that can be intercepted, but doing this comes at the expense of the sophistication and extent of its actions (reduction in capacity).

The result is a dilemma that is changing the face of contemporary terrorist organizations. Historically, according to Stern and others, most terrorist groups have followed an organizational form known as the *Commander-Cadre* (or *Hierarchical*) model. This form of group is not dissimilar to the way complex enterprises are structured everywhere: Executives (commanders) organize and plan activities (terrorist attacks) and pass instructions downward through the structure for implementation by employees (cadres). In order to try to maintain levels of secrecy that improve resiliency, terrorist groups structure themselves so that any one level of the group (cell) knows only of the cell directly above and below it.

Commander-cadre arrangements have advantages: They can coordinate activities maximizing capacity (the African embassy bombings, for instance); can organize recruitment and absorb, indoctrinate, and train recruits; and can carry out ancillary activities such as fund-raising, dealing with cooperative governments, and engaging in commerce and other forms of activity. The disadvantage of these organizations is that they may become more permeable by outside agencies because of their need to communicate among units. Modern electronics become a double-edged sword for the terrorist: Things like cell phones facilitate communications in executing attacks, but those communications can be intercepted, leading to resiliency-threatening penetration. In fact, electronic surveillance of terrorist communication has been extremely helpful in the pursuit of Al Qaeda to the point that the old structure of the 1990s, which basically followed the commander-cadre model, has been reduced greatly in size from its zenith. While exact membership numbers are highly elusive, the active membership of Al Qaeda is probably no more than a few thousand.

The result of the campaign against Al Qaeda has been to cause it to adapt, to become what Stern refers to as the "protean enemy" that has "shown a surprising willingness to adapt its mission" and to alter its organizational form to make it more resilient. Al Qaeda is no longer a hierarchically organized entity that plans and carries out terrorist missions. Instead, it has adopted elements of the alternate form of terrorist organization, the *virtual network* or *leaderless resistance* model and has dispersed itself into a series of smaller, loosely affiliated terrorist organizations that draw inspiration from Al Qaeda. If it ever was a monolithic dragon, Al Qaeda has mutated into a hydra-headed monster.

The virtual network organizational model was apparently developed in the United States by the Aryan Nation hate group. Its problem was that its membership was constantly being penetrated and disrupted by law enforcement organizations like the FBI, which used extensive electronic surveillance (wiretapping) to uncover and suppress illegal Aryan Nation activity and to prosecute both the planners and executioners of its actions. The solution for Aryan Nation, recently adapted and adopted by international terrorist organizations like Al Qaeda, is the virtual network/leaderless resistance.

The core of this model is to reduce direct communications between the leadership and its members. Rather than planning operations and instructing operatives to carry out plans, leaders instead exhort their followers to act through public pronouncements (for instance, through the use of Web sites). Leaders may issue general calls to action, but they have no direct communications with followers that can be intercepted or used as the basis for suppression or conspiracy indictments. The leader has no direct knowledge or control of individual terrorist acts, which he or she may inspire but not direct. The hope is that a devoted follower like Eric Rudolph (convicted of killing an off-duty policeman in an attack against a Birmingham, Alabama, abortion clinic in 2000 and for hate killings in Atlanta) will be inspired to carry out the mission. The advantage of this model is that it maximizes the resiliency of the organization and protects its leadership from capture or prosecution; its principal drawback is reduced capacity to order specific "desirable" actions. It has become, however, a major part of the changing environment of the terrorist threat and responses to it.

The traumatic attacks of 9/11 created an overwhelming response worldwide in which governments and international organizations came to focus on the nature of the threat and how to respond to it. Because the attacks occurred on American soil, the responses were particularly fervent and robust here. The analogy that was quickly adopted was that of war: The United States was now engaged in a "global war on terror." An understanding that policy response and the efforts enlisted in its support are necessary before one can assess the current state of the "battle."

DEALING WITH TERRORISM: THE GWOT

If the assault on terror is indeed a war, what does that robust rhetoric mean? Is the GWOT really a war at all, or something else (in the immediate wake of September 11, French president Jacques Chirac suggested calling it a "campaign" to remove some of the military emphasis)? Is it really possible to make war, as the term is generally used, against a method or idea, as opposed to some identifiable group of people? How does one attack and defeat a non-state-based enemy organization that has no territory or identified population base that can be subjected to and subdued by military actions? In addition, what does "victory" mean in this context? Is it the destruction of the opponent, or its containment? What kinds and levels of resources are necessary for the task?

All of these are valid questions for which definitive, consensually agreed answers do not exist. Begin with the war analogy. It is frequently argued that it makes no sense to talk about war against an abstraction, and the idea of terrorism is the application of an idea. Can you "kill" an idea in some concrete or abstract manner? If so, how do you know you have accomplished the task? Wars, at any level, are contests between members of different groups to assert control. People and their ideas are not the same things.

The war analogy suffers even if one switches emphasis and says the GWOT is a war on global terrorists. Switching the emphasis at least has the virtue of making a war of people against other people, but it still retains two problems. First, warfare against terrorists is war against asymmetrical warriors, a problem introduced in Chapter 5. That means the countries seeking to defeat terrorism are militarily superior in conventional terms and that terrorism is the means by which terrorists seek to create a situation in which they have a chance to succeed. The problem lies in the criteria for success for those seeking to snuff out terrorists and for the terrorists themselves. For any country engaged in terrorism suppression, the criterion is very exacting: The war cannot be won until terrorists everywhere specified by the war have been defeated. Those seeking to suppress terrorists must crush their opponents; in a phrase, they can only "win by winning."

The situation is different for the terrorists. Terrorists know that they cannot win in the traditional sense of crushing their enemies, but equally, they know their enemies cannot validly claim victory as long as the terrorists can continue to operate. Thus, terrorists realize that their criterion for success is to avoid being defeated by their opponents, and that the longer they remain a viable force, the more likely they are to becoming a sufficient irritant that their opponents conclude acquiescence to their demands is preferable to continuing the frustrating struggle against them. The terrorists, in other words, can "win by not losing."

A second problem associated with modern asymmetrical warfare is that contemporary international terrorist organizations are nonstate actors. If most of the contemporary religious terrorists are Muslims who come from or have connections to parts of the Islamic Middle East, not all Muslims in the Middle East support the terrorists or what they do, and no state government has claimed association with major terrorist organizations since the overthrow of the Taliban in Afghanistan. These nonstate actors generally imbed themselves within physical areas and among people sympathetic to them; they move around, including across international borders; and they rarely establish public physical symbols that can be identified with them (some Islamic charities that serve as fronts for terrorist activities such as recruitment and fund-raising are partial exceptions).

The problem this creates for a "war" on terrorists is finding and specifying targets that can be attacked and defeated. When Al Qaeda was openly running training camps in Afghanistan, this was not so much of a problem, and occasionally a military attack would be made on one of these facilities (for instance, cruise missile attacks on Al Qaeda training camps in 1998 in retaliation for the bombings of American embassies in Africa). Since the fall of the Taliban and the dispersal of Al Qaeda into greater nonstate anonymity, military actions directly against it have become more difficult. The military problem is the inability to find and target the most vital parts of the terrorist existence—the so-called centers of gravity on which the terrorists rely for the continued viability. The result, according to Audrey Kurth Cronin, is "that it is virtually impossible to target the most vulnerable point in the organization." Moreover, even when a terrorist presence can be reasonably located and defined, attacking it is difficult to do and to explain. The general location of Al Qaeda along the Pakistan–Afghanistan border area is well known. Attacking these areas angers the nonterrorist populations and local governments, and at worst such attacks serve as terrorist recruiting aids. Moreover, the statelessness of terrorists means that if attacks against them are successful, they will simply move their operations to less vulnerable locations.

The problem of dealing with terrorists is both physically and intellectually very difficult, and any simple, sweeping antidotes to solving the problem of terrorism are likely both to be inadequate and to result in failure. That does not mean the task is hopeless or that things cannot be done to manage or mitigate the problem. Certain forms of terrorism suppression are available, and the discussion turns to introducing these. The threat has, as already suggested, changed in recent years, and so some of the clear contemporary forms of terrorist activity will be examined.

Suppressing Terrorists: Antiterrorism and Counter Terrorism

In conventional terrorism suppression circles, two methods for dealing with the terrorist problem are most often invoked: antiterrorism and counter terrorism. The two terms are sometimes used interchangeably, although each term refers to a distinct form of action with a specific purpose. Any program of terrorist suppression will necessarily contain elements of each of them, but failing to specify which is which generally or in specific applications only confuses the issue.

Antiterrorism refers to defensive efforts to reduce the vulnerability of targets to terrorist attacks and to lessen the effects of terrorist attacks that do occur. Antiterrorism efforts thus begin from the premise that some terrorist attacks will indeed occur, and that two forms of effort are necessary. First, antiterrorists seek to make it more difficult to mount terrorist attacks. Airport security to prevent potential terrorists from boarding airliners or the interception and detention of possible terrorists by border guards are examples. Second, antiterrorists try to mitigate the effects of terrorist attacks that might or do occur. Blocking off streets in front of public buildings so that terrorists cannot get close enough to destroy them is one approach, while civil defense measures (i.e., hazmat operations) to mitigate the effects of an attack is another way to deal with the problem.

There are three related difficulties with conducting an effective antiterrorist campaign. One is that antiterrorism is necessarily reactive; terrorists choose where attacks will occur and against what kinds of targets, and antiterrorists must respond to the terrorist initiative. A second problem is the sheer variety and number of targets to be protected. As suggested earlier, the potential list of targets is almost infinite, and one purpose of attacks is randomness so that potential victims are always off guard and antiterrorists will have trouble anticipating where attacks may occur. The third problem is target substitution: If antiterrorist efforts are sufficiently successful that terrorists determine their likelihood of success against any particular target (or class of targets) is significantly diminished, they will simply go on to other, less well-defended targets.

The other form of terrorist suppression is *counter terrorism,* offensive and military measures against terrorists or sponsoring agencies to prevent, deter, or respond to terrorist acts. As the definition suggests, counter terrorism consists of both preventive and retaliatory actions against terrorists. Preventive acts can include such things as penetration of terrorist cells and taking action—including apprehension and physical violence against terrorists—before they carry out their acts. Retaliation is more often military and paramilitary and includes attacks on terrorist camps or other facilities in response to terrorist attacks. The purposes of retaliation include punishment, reducing terrorist capacity for future acts, and hopefully deterrence of future actions by instilling fear of the consequences.

Counter terrorism is inherently and intuitively attractive. Preventive actions are proactive, taking the battle to the terrorists and punishing them in advance of creating harm. In its purest form, preventive counter terrorist actions reverse the tables in the relationship, effectively "terrorizing the terrorists." Pounding a terrorist facility as punishment after enduring a terrorist attack at least entails the satisfaction of knowing the enemy has suffered as well as the victim.

The problem with counter terrorism, like antiterrorism, is that it is insufficient on its own as a way to quell all terrorism. Preventing terrorist actions requires a level of intelligence about the structures of terrorist's organizations which is quite difficult to obtain, and it has been a central purpose of terrorist reorganization to increase that difficulty. The effect is to make a terrorist network difficult to penetrate, learn of its nefarious intentions, and interrupt those activities. The absence of a state base that can be attacked means it is more difficult to identify terrorist targets whose retaliatory destruction will cripple the organization, punish its members, or frighten it into ceasing future actions.

Ideally, antiterrorism and counter terrorism efforts act in tandem. Counter terrorists reduce the number and quality of possible attacks through preventive actions, making the task of antiterrorist efforts to ameliorate the effects of attacks that do succeed less difficult. Counter terrorist retaliation then can hopefully reduce the terrorists' capacity for future mayhem. The result is a more manageable threat confronting the antiterrorists. In practice, however, these efforts sometimes come into operational conflict. The antiterrorist emphasis on lessening the effects of attacks may lead to publicizing the possibility of particular attacks as a way to alert citizens (the color-coded warning system, for instance), whereas counter terrorists prefer to keep operations as secret as possible to facilitate clandestine penetration and interruption.

The Contemporary Threats

Largely due to the success of terrorism suppression efforts since September 11, 2001, the shape of the threat has undergone a protean transformation. Al Qaeda still exists, and its most villainous figures, like bin Laden himself, still remain at large, but the monolithic, commander-cadre structure has largely disintegrated under a relentless assault that has killed or captured much of the old network. In its place, the threat has dispersed among a much more diffuse set of loose organizations and individuals. Stern describes this new face of terrorism in a 2010 *Foreign Affairs* article, "The destructive ideology that animates the al Qaeda movement is spreading around the globe, including, in some cases, to small-town America. Homegrown zealots, motivated by al Qaeda's distorted interpretation of Islam, may not yet be capable of carrying out 9/11-style strikes, but they could nonetheless terrorize a nation."

Part of this dispersion has been the result of actions taken by bin Laden and his associates in the 1980s and 1990s. During the period when Al Qaeda operated terrorist training camps openly in Afghanistan, the organization trained thousands of recruits from countries around the globe, and many of these individuals returned to their homes and have organized affiliated movements that now carry out many of the terrorist activities associated with Al Qaeda.

Hoffman argues that the result has been an Al Qaeda-based terrorist threat with four distinct dimensions. What he calls Al Qaeda Central contains the remnants of the 9/11 organization. Al Qaeda Affiliates and Associates consist of the spinoff organizations; Al Qaeda in Iraq (Mesopotamia) is a prime example. Al Qaeda Locals are virtual network organizations in different locations; terrorist activity in Yemen is exemplary. Finally, there is the Al Qaeda Network, which is composed of "homegrown Islamic radicals"; much of the so-called lone wolf activity is of this nature.

Two of these permutations are particularly prominent and troublesome in the contemporary scene. One is the problem of the "lone wolf" terrorist, an individual who commits acts of terror without apparent outside assistance or motivation. The other is the activities associated with virtual networks, a phenomenon greatly accentuated by the exploitation of the Internet to further their activities. The two are connected because Internet appeals may activate both lone wolves and members of virtual networks. Both are troublesome because they are extremely difficult to identify and counter before they act.

Lone Wolf Terrorists. The phenomenon of individuals apparently unconnected to any organized terrorist group has been a recurring part of the terrorism problem for a long time. Because their actions are idiosyncratic, isolated, and often erratic, they do not receive the level of attention that more systematic, organized movements do. Rather, attention is drawn to the lone wolves when particular actions capture public attention.

Interest in lone wolves in the United States peaked in the 1990s with the unrelated cases of Unabomber Theodore Kaczynski (the deranged university professor who killed 3 and wounded over 20 others with letter bombs between 1978 and 1995) and Timothy McVeigh, who killed 159 people in the truck bombing of the Murrah Federal Building in Oklahoma City in 1995. Since these highly publicized cases, there have been episodic instances of domestic lone wolves, such as the pursuit and capture of abortion clinic bomber Eric Robert Rudolph between 1996 and 1998, the May 2009 shooting spree by James von Brunn at the U.S. Holocaust Memorial Museum in Washington, DC, and even the action of Joseph Andrew Stack III, who crashed a small airplane into the Internal Revenue Service office in Austin, Texas, on February 18, 2010.

Three apparent lone wolf attacks connected loosely to radical Islamic terrorism galvanized interest again in 2009–2010. The first was the massacre of over 30 fellow soldiers by Major Nidal Hasan at Ft. Hood, Texas, in fall 2009. This heinous act was followed by one during Christmas 2009, when Omar Farouk Abdulmuttalab attempted to detonate a bomb concealed in his underwear aboard a plane en route from Europe to Detroit. Finally, Faisal Shahzad, a naturalized American citizen of Pakistani descent, attempted to explode an amateurishly fashioned bomb on Times Square in New York in April 2010. Each instance pointed to the difficulty of getting a precise handle on terrorism committed by autonomous individuals in advance of their acts; these individuals were, of course, captured, tried, and sentenced for their crimes.

What are the characteristics of the lone wolf terrorist? The European Union *Instiotuut voor Veilgheids-en Crisismanagement* offers a useful set of interrelated characteristics in a 2007 study. First and foremost, lone wolves act individually rather than as parts of more or less well-organized groups. Second, lone wolves do not belong to any organized terrorist group or network. Third, they act without the direct influence of a leader or hierarchy. Fourth, the tactics and methods they employ are conceived and conducted by the individual without "any direct outside command or direction." Lone wolf terrorist activities are conceived by individuals who act autonomously in designing and carrying out their acts.

The nature of lone wolf acts speaks to why they are simultaneously so difficult yet marginal in the greater scheme of terrorism. On one hand, the autonomy of the lone wolf makes him or her extremely difficult, if not impossible, to identify in advance, since, by definition, these individuals are usually antisocial loners. Belonging to no terrorist groups, they have no communications that can be intercepted and traced back to them, and they may be able to evade detection for a long time after they commit their acts, unless they make some crucial mistake that leads to their apprehension. The Unabomber, after all, evaded identification and capture for 17 years before his brother recognized his identity through the text of one of his manifestos and turned him in to authorities. On the other hand, acting alone generally limits the sophistication and extent of the destruction the lone wolf can inflict. The Murrah attack by McVeigh or the machine-gunning of a Hebron mosque by Israeli right-wing extremist Baruch Goldstein on February 24, 1994 (which left 29 praying Muslims dead) may well represent the outward limits of mayhem lone wolves can inflict. Blowing up an airplane in flight or car bombings like Times Square may also serve as outer limits.

Lone wolf attacks are frequent enough, however, to cause concern. The EU study, for instance, catalogued instances conforming to its criteria between 1968 and 2007 in the developed world. According to this report, 30 lone wolf attacks occurred in the United States, followed by 9 in Germany, 7 in France, 6 in Spain, 5 in Italy, 3 in Canada, 2 each in Australia, the Netherlands, Russia, and the United Kingdom, and 1 each in Denmark, Poland, Portugal, and Sweden. From a U.S. view, it is not only the most frequent victim but the vast majority of indigenous attacks within its boundaries are also by lone wolves.

Two other factors make the isolation and categorization of lone wolf terrorism problematical. One is whether a particular act meets the criteria for terrorism laid out earlier in this chapter, or whether it is an instance of pure depravity. This difficulty is particularly relevant when trying to determine the objective of a lone wolf attack. McVeigh, in his twisted way, had the apparent objective of avenging the Branch Dravidians who had died at Waco, Texas. What, on the other hand, was the objective of von Brunn in gunning down a security guard at the Holocaust Museum other than an insane expression of anti-Semitism?

The other factor is the degree of autonomy and independence of the apparent lone wolf. Groups with diverse messages of hate indeed publicize their causes and exhort their followers on the Internet, and it is often unclear whether apparently independent acts have been influenced by such appeals. There is evidence, for instance, that Rudolph was "inspired" by extreme antiabortion appeals on the Internet, and both Hasan and Abdulmuttalab were influenced by the violent preachings of American-born, Yemen-based Muslim cleric Anwar al-Awlaki. These kinds of connections muddy sharp distinctions between lone wolves and virtual networks.

Virtual Networks. The virtual network/leaderless resistance and protean hybrid forms of terrorist organizations are the adaptations that terrorists have had to make in the face of the increased sophistication of terrorist suppressors against traditional commander-cadre groups. They represent ways to deal with the ability of terrorism suppressors to intercept communications and to penetrate terrorist hierarchies as a result. The primary adaptation has been to cease direct communications between terrorist leaders and followers in locations where communications interception is most active and thus where traditional terrorist forms are most vulnerable.

As noted, the genesis of this adaptation was apparently the reaction of Lopuis Beam and his Aryan Nation followers to government discovery and harassment of their activities based on wire taps. The response was to cease direct communications among group members. One advantage of severing communications was to deprive the government of advanced knowledge of Aryan Nation plans; another was to shield Beam from direct responsibility for illegal actions. As adapted by others, it has also made penetration of terrorist organizations more difficult.

The heart of this model is to eliminate a direct link between leaders and followers. Direct contact is replaced by indirect communication, often in the form of Internet postings that seek to attract new members, spread the group's message, and even exhort members to actions. The posting of sermons by al-Awlaki from Yemen, for instance, effectively served to help radicalize lone wolf terrorists like Hasan and Abdulmuttalab. Given the vastness and portability of Internet access, it is an effective tool to protect the identity and location of leaders and thus to reinforce resiliency in the organization. For example, despite concerted efforts to capture and eliminate al-Awlaki, he remains at large in the mountainous desert of Yemen.

Operating virtual networks has both advantages and disadvantaged. The advantages are primarily in increasing resiliency, particularly in places where the government's electronic surveillance capabilities are greatest. It should, for instance, come as no great surprise that the model was spawned in the United States where, over the years, American authorities (notably the FBI) have developed very sophisticated means of penetrating subversive organizations of all kinds, including terrorists. Eliminating virtual organizations, however, is much more difficult, especially for identifying terrorist followers and their plans in advance. Since leaders exhort or suggest attacks rather than organizing and ordering them, the timing and nature of any specific act is largely left to the individual follower, who is effectively acting as a lone wolf, albeit one with outside inspiration. Regardless of who inspired the Times Square bombing attack by Shahzad, for instance, the act itself was largely his own.

Increased resiliency, however, comes at a price in terms of capacity, a trait shared by lone wolves. Individuals generally cannot plan and execute operations on the same scale as larger groups. As University of Michigan analyst Juan Cole put it in a *Foreign Policy* article, "they cannot hope to accomplish much. At most, they can carry bombs on trains (a reference to the 2004 Madrid train bombings)." This limit on capacity has in turn helped inspire a hybrid form by combining elements of both traditional and virtual network models.

The hybrid model seeks to combine the "best" of both models. In an October 2005 speech, President George W. Bush summarized this new form. "Many militants are part of global borderless terrorist organizations like Al Qaida, which spreads propaganda and provides financing and technical support to local extremists and conducts dramatic and brutal operations. They are found in regional groups associated with Al Qaida. . . . Still others spring up in local cells inspired by Islamic radicalism but not centrally directed." Where conditions permit (some of the tribal areas of Pakistan, for instance), these hybrids may function as near-traditional organizations; where they cannot, they necessarily become more like virtual networks.

The point is not so much the forms that are most prevalent as the process they represent. Terrorists and their organizations practice a form of asymmetrical warfare and, as discussed in Chapter 5, a major characteristic is the adaptability of such movements. Asymmetrical warfare is a methodology, not a method, and so is terrorism. Stern's protean analogy is apt. The Greek god Proteus, after all, was noteworthy for his ability to take on various forms or appearances, and so do terrorists. The protean analogy thus suggests that the terrorist challenge is dynamic, not static. Like Proteus, terrorists adapt to challenges to their existence and abandon forms and practices that prove dysfunctional or self-destructive. The implication is clear: Today's terrorist threat is different than the threat that existed in 2001, and the challenge of the future will not be the same as it is today.

CONCLUSION: WHENCE THE THREAT

The problem of international religious terrorism has changed and gained dubious celebrity since 9/11. Before the attacks, acts of terror were considered a horrible aberration, not an integral part of international existence. The single most deadly terrorist act in history changed that perception. The threat of terrorism is now considered ubiquitous and efforts to suppress it a pervasive part of everyday life. The war on terrorism—whether the war analogy is apt or not—is now an accepted, institutionalized part of the political environment nationally and internationally.

The terrorism environment is clearly changing. While Al Qaeda remains the central threat with which many people identify, the problem has become less centralized and more diffuse as the efforts of terrorism suppressors have forced terrorists to adopt different forms and approaches to attaining their lethal goals. At the same time, the absence of follow-on attacks on the order of magnitude of 9/11 has also eroded some of the urgency that surrounds the terrorism issue.

In this atmosphere, whence the war on terror? Will the emphasis continue to erode in the popular minds if there is not another major attack in the United States? Has the terrorism suppression effort become adequately proficient that a major breakdown is decisively less likely than it was in 2001, when such efforts were more modestly sized and prioritized? If the current threat continues to appear increasingly impotent, will support (or the need) for high priority, expensive terrorism efforts decline? Will there be a slow retreat in the threat and efforts to contain it to pre-9/11 levels, as international religious terrorism recedes and before another wave of terror takes its place?

The terrorism future is hard to predict. If history is a faithful guide, the current spate of international religious terrorism will indeed fade away eventually, although it is not clear how long that will take. History also suggests that a new cycle of terrorists will emerge with different, and as yet unknown, reasons for being. Terrorists come and go, but terrorism persists. The effort and desire to eradicate both terrorists and their methods is both laudatory and understandable, but it may be hopelessly utopian and unrealistic. Terrorism has been so enduring because its practitioners have indeed emulated Proteus; today the emphasis is on lone wolves and virtual networks. But who knows about tomorrow?

STUDY/DISCUSSION QUESTIONS

1. Define terrorism. What are its common elements? How does the elaboration of the elements help us understand the nature of terrorism?
2. What do terrorist acts seek to accomplish? In what circumstances do they succeed or fail?
3. What kinds of targets do terrorists attack? What is cost-tolerance? How does it factor into resistance to terrorism and terrorist success?
4. Why do terrorists engage in terrorist activities? What do they seek to accomplish? Why do terrorists adopt asymmetrical means to achieve their objectives?
5. How has international terrorism changed since 9/11, notably in terms of terrorist organization? What are the implications of these changes for dealing with terrorists?
6. What are the three ways of dealing with terrorism discussed in the text? Describe each as an element in lessening or eliminating the problem of terrorism.
7. What are the prospects for terrorist future? Specifically, what threats are posed by lone wolf terrorists and virtual terrorist networks? What does it mean to describe the terrorism threat as protean?

READING/RESEARCH MATERIAL

Art, Robert J and Kenneth N. Waltz. *The Use of Force: Military Power and International Politics.* 7th ed. London: Rowman and Littlefield, 2008.

Atran, Scott. "Mishandling Suicide Terrorism." *Washington Quarterly* 27, 3 (Summer 2004), 67–90.

———. "The Moral Logic and Growth of Suicide Terrorism." *Washington Quarterly* 29, 2 (Spring 2006), 127–147.

Benard, Cheryl. "Toy Soldiers: The Youth Factor in the War on Terror." *Current History* 106, 696 (January 2007), 27–30.

Bergen, Peter and Swati Pandrey. "The Madrassas Scapegoat." *Washington Quarterly* 29, 2 (Spring 2006), 117–125.

Burke, Jason. "Think Again, Al Qaeda." *Foreign Policy,* May/June 2004, 18–26.

Bush, George W. "Transcript: Bush Discusses War on Terrorism." *Washington Post* (online), October 6, 2005.

Clarke, Richard A., ed. "Terrorism: What the Next President Will Face." *Annals of the American Academy of Political and Social Science*, 618 (July 2008), 4–6.

Cole, Juan. "Think Again: 9/11." *Foreign Policy*, September/October 2006, 26–32.

Cronin, Audrey Kurth. "Sources of Contemporary Terrorism." In Cronin, Audrey Kurth and James M. Ludes, eds. *Attacking Terrorism: Elements of a Grand Strategy*. Washington, DC: Georgetown University Press, 2004.

Dershowitz, Alan M. *Why Terrorism Works: Understanding the Threat, Responding to the Challenge*. New Haven, CT: Yale University Press, 2002.

Fleishman, Charlotte. "The Business of Terror: Conceptualizing Terrorist Organizations as Cellular Businesses." Washington, DC: Center for Defense Information, May 23, 2005.

Gunaratna, Rohan. "The Post-Madrid Face of Al Qaeda." *Washington Quarterly* 27, 3 (Summer 2004), 91–100.

Hoffman, Bruce. "From the War on Terror to Global Insurgency." *Current History* 105, 695 (December 2006), 423–429.

———. *Inside Terrorism*. 2nd ed. New York: Columbia University Press, 2006.

Jenkins, Brian. "International Terrorism." In Robert J. Art and Kenneth N. Waltz, eds. *The Use of Force: Military Power and International Politics*. New York: Rowman and Littlefield Publishers, 2004, 77–84.

Laqueur, Walter. "The Changing Face of Terror." In Art and Waltz, eds. *The Use of Force*. New York: Rowman and Littlefield Publishers, 2004, 451–464.

"Lone Wolf Terrorism." *Instituut voot Veilgheids-en Crisismanagement* (online), June 2007. (http://www.transnationalterrorism.eu/tekst/publications/Lone-Wolf.%20 Terrorism.pdf)

Nacos, Brigette. *Terrorism and Counterterrorism: Understanding Threats and Responses in the Post-9/11 World*. New York: Penguin Academics, 2006.

National Strategy for Combating Terrorism. Washington, DC: The White House, 2003.

The 9/11 Commission Report: Final Report of the National Commission on Terrorist Attacks Upon the United States (authorized ed.). New York: W. W. Norton, 2004.

Pillar, Paul D. "Counterterrorism after Al Qaeda." *Washington Quarterly* 27, 3 (Summer 2004), 101–113.

———. "Dealing with Terrorism." In Art and Waltz, eds. *The Use of Force*. New York: Rowman and Littlefield Publishers, 2004, 469–476.

Rapaport, David C. "The Four Waves of Terrorism." In Cronin and Ludes, eds. *Attacking Terrorism*. New York: Rowman and Littlefield Publishers, 2004, 46–73.

Sloan, Stephen. *Beating International Terrorism: An Action Strategy for Preemption and Punishment*. Montgomery, AL: Air University Press, 2000.

Snow, Donald M. *National Security for a New Era: Globalization and Geopolitics after Iraq*. 3rd ed. New York: Pearson Longman, 2008.

———. *September 11, 2001: The New Face of War?* New York: Longman, 2002.

———and Dennis M. Drew. *From Lexington to Baghdad and Beyond: War and Politics in the American Experience*. 3rd ed. Armonk, NY: M. E. Sharpe, 2009.

Stern, Jessica. "Mind over Martyr: How to Deradicalize Islamic Extremists." *Foreign Affairs* 89, 1 (January/February 2010), 95–108.

———. *Terrorism in the Name of God: Why Religious Militants Kill*. New York: ECCO, 2003.

———. "The Protean Enemy." *Foreign Affairs* 82, 4 (July/August 2003), 27–40.

Yew, Lee Kwan. "The United States, Iraq, and the War on Terror." *Foreign Affairs* 86, 1 (January/February 2007), 2–7.

WEB SITES

Official U.S. government Web sites dealing with terrorism

The Department of Homeland Security at http://www.Whitehouse.gov/homeland

The State Department at http://www.state.gov

Text of bin Laden "Epistles" http://msanews.net/MSANEWS199610/19961012.3.html

Reports on Future Trends from Federal Research Division http://www.loc.gov/rr/frd/terrorism.html

UN action against terrorism http://www.un.org/Docs/sc/committees/1373/

RAND Corporation on terrorism, homeland security http://www.rand.org/research_areas/terrorism/

Terrorism Research Center at http://www.terrorism.com/.

INDEX

Note: The letters 'f' and 't' following the locators refers to figures and tables.

Absolute sovereignty, 6–7. *See also* Sovereignty
Afghanistan/Afghanistan war. *See also* Al Qaeda
  American military effort in, 94
  anti-Al Qaeda mission, 99
  campaign against bin Laden, 94
  civil war and US participation, 94
  COIN strategy (US), 98–99
  current civil war in, 98
  dual nature of, 98
  ethnic groups of, 96
  foreign invaders of, 95–96
  geographic bases, importance of, 95
  mujahidin elements in, 97
  Pashtun's role, in governance, 96–97
  Pashtunwali protection to bin Laden, 97
  resource deployment (US), 94
  Soviet expulsion, consequences of, 97
  Soviet occupation (1979–1988), 97
  Taliban activities in, 96–97
  Taliban government's rule, 97–98
  Taliban's asymmetrical forces, 95
  tribal structure of, 96
African Union (AMIS), 151, 162
African Union Mission in Sudan (AMIS), 159
African Union-UN Mission in Darfur
  (UNAMID), 159, 162–164
Ahmadinejad, Mahmoud, 136, 141
Al Aqsa, 70
Al Qaeda, 88, 92, 306, 312, 314
  affiliates and associates, 315
  central, 319
  destruction goal, 94
  locals, 319
  network, 315
  and Taliban, distinctions, 98
  training camps, 317
American Civil War, 44–45, 89
American Jewish Council, 73
American Revolution, 15
Amnesty International, 161
Amnesty International, 161
Annex I countries, Kyoto Protocol, 250
Annex II countries, Kyoto Protocol, 250
Annexes, fossil fuel consumption, 250
Anti-Americanism, 124, 132
Antiterrorism, 317–319
Arab-Israeli War. *See* Six Day's War of 1967
Arafat, Yasser, 74
Argentina, 309
Armenia, 35, 46
Articles. *See* United Nations charter
Aryan, 131
Aryan Nation, 315

Asia-Pacific Economic Cooperation (APEC), 188–189
Asian financial crisis, (1997, 1998), 230
Aslamiyah, Jemaah, 312
Asylum seekers, 265
Asymmetrical warfare, 83–86, 87–93. *See also*
  Afghanistan/Afghanistan war; Warfare
  conflict environment, 87–89
  definition, 85, 91
  Iraqi precedence, 93
  new/old war, 86–87
  peace, post-conflict, 93–94
  physical structure of, 89–91
  quasi-military situations, 92–93
  symmetrical *vs.*, 91–92
  symmetrical warfare, defined, 84–85
Attacking Terrorism, 307
Australia, 11, 63, 113, 250, 309
Austria, 197
Austro-Hungarian Empire, 206
Authoritarian regimes, 6
Axis powers, 29, 44
Azerbaijan, 33–34, 132

Bali Action Plan, 253
Bali conference
  major issues, 253
Bali Road Map, 253–254
Balkans states, 198, 201
Band-Aid analogy, 163
Bandung Conference, 236
Bangladesh, 256
Bangalore, 216
Barak, Ehud, 72, 76
Baseyev, Shamil, 38
Bashir, Abu Bakar, 309
Bashir, Omar Hassan al-, 159
Begin, Menachem, 70
Belarus, 201
Belgian Congo, 9, 150
Belgium, 194, 196
Benelux countries, 194
Berkowitz, Bruce, 87–88
Billiard ball theory, 5
bin Laden, Usama, 92. *See also* Al Qaeda
  Al Qaeda operation and, 319
  foreign fighters recruitment by, 97
  "global war on terrorism" (GWOT) *vs.*, 306
  quasi-military attacks of, 92
  US campaign against, 94
Birmingham, abortion clinic attack, 315
Bodin, Jean, 4
Bosnia, 41–42
  Croats, 49, 198
  ethnic cleansing, 51

327

Bosnia (*continued*)
Muslims, 49
war crimes and, 48–49
Boutros-Ghali, Boutros, 49
Brain drain, 266
Brazil, 127
Bretton Woods conference, 173–177, 180–182,
193, 222, 231, 235, 237
Brierly, J. L., 13
British empire, 130
Browne, John, 252
Bulgaria, 201
Burmese Diaries (Orwell), 232
Bush administration, 10, 14, 31–32, 161, 251.
See also Iran, U.S. relations with
about Darfur situation, 148, 159
ICC jurisdiction and, 54, 56
Iranian nuclear weapon issue, 138
Iraq invasion, 12–13, 31
Israel-Palestine, peace process, 69, 76
Kyoto Protocol, objections to, 248, 251–253
preventive war, Doctrine of, 14
proliferation problem, North Korea, 115,
117–119
Proliferation Security Initiative (PSI), 113
Rome Treaty, unsigning of, 52
terrorism, handling, 285, 323
torture issue, captives, 55
UN PKOs, US participation, 158, 161, 165
Bush, George W., 12–13, 32, 52, 64,
69, 113, 323

Cambodia, 8, 148
Camp David I, 70–71
Camp David II, 71–75
Camp David Accords, 70–72
Canada, 29–30
Capitalism, 210, 225
Carbon dioxide (CO2), 246–247, 249
Care International, 161
Caribbean, 15
Caring for Climate (UNFCC publication), 248
Carter, Jimmy, 69–71, 134
Caspian Sea oil, 30–31, 33–35
Central African Republic, 266, 269,
286, 291, 293
Central America, 15
Chechnya, 2, 37, 307, 312
Cheney, Richard, 55
Chiang Kai-shek, 209–210
China
automobile production, 213
century of humiliation, 208–209
"Chinese neo-Leninist state," description, 212
communism, emergence of, 208–209
economic challenges of, 213–214
economic growth, 211–212
Four Modernizations, impact on, 210
Four Special Economic Zones (SEZs) of, 211
GDP per capita comparison with India, 209
global warming and, 247
greenhouse gases and, 252–253
growing to superpower, 208
Mao's regime, 209–210
market domination, 211
as neo-Leninist state, 212
oil and, 22, 29
political system in, 213–214
Socialism with Chinese Characteristics, 210
status, 208
UN security council member, 208
US comparison with, 212t
WTO and, 211–212
Chirac, Jacques, 316
CIA World Factbook, 194, 200
Circle of market democracies, 226
Civil wars, 101–102, 279–280, 282
Claussen, Eileen, 246
Clean development mechanism
(CDM), 251, 254
Climate change. *See* Global warming
Clinton administration, 52
Camp David II convention, 72
Copenhagen summit, 252
genocide convention, 48
ICC jurisdiction and, 52
Israeli-Palestinian peace process and, 72
Kyoto Protocol, 248, 251
pivotal states, power and, 127
proliferation problem (North Korea), 114–117
Treaty of Rome and, 52
UNCAT ratification, 56
Clinton, William, 52, 69, 226
CNN, 48–49
Cold War, 8, 10, 47–48. *See also* Post-Cold War
Commander-cadre model, 314–315
Common (single) market, 190
Communism, 192
Complex interdependence, 178
Concerning the Law of War and Peace, 44
Conference of the Parties (COP), 249
Conflict environment, 87–89, 95–97
Conflicts, 60–80. *See also* Israeli-Palestinian
conflict
environment, 87–89, 95–97
irresolvable, 61–64
Consultation, 176
Control and emission reduction, of gases, 249
Council of Ministers (European Community), 199
Convergence policy, 78
Copenhagen criteria, 197
Coroalles, Anthony M., 89
Cost-tolerance, 310–312
Counter terrorism, 310, 317–319
Countervalue, 311
Croatia, 198, 201
Cronin, Audrey Kurth, 307
Cuba, 112
Cultural impact of globalization, 224
Current History, 22
Customs union, 190
Cyprus, 150, 197
Cyrus the Great, 130
Czech Republic, 197

Darfur, 158–164
Darfur Peace Agreement (DPA), 159
Darfur situation, 148
Chinese support, Sudan, 161
civil war (2003), 151

crisis, aspects of, 159–160
 Human Rights Watch, report on, 160
 international effort, lacking in, 161
 UNAMID's role, 162–164
Deepeners, 194
Democratic People's Republic of Korea (DPRK
 or North Korea), 104
Democratic Republic of Congo, 9
Democratic Republic of Korea. *See* North Korea
Democratization, 228
De Nevers, Renee, 87
Deregulation, 229
De Republica, 4
Dershowitz, Alan, 307
Deterrence, 109–113
Developed countries, 226
Developed world *vs.* developing world, 223,
 231, 235
Developing countries, 226
Diamond, 137–138
Diamonds, 19
Diplomacy, 70
Dispute settlement, 176
Dispute Settlement Body (DSB), 181
Dispute Settlement Understanding (DSU), 181
Doctors without Borders, 161. *See also*
 Medecins sans Frontieres (MSF) (Doctors
 without Borders)
Dome of the Rock, 70
Drew, Dennis, 310
Dutch, 200

East Timor, 11
Economic development, 167
Economic globalization. *See also* North
 American Free Trade Agreement (NAFTA)
 basis of, 223
 environmental concerns and, 182–183
 free trade objections, 177–182
 India and, 214–218
 integration, extent of, 188
 petroleum scarcity and, 27
 physical dimensions of, 188
 technology and, 227–228
 Washington basis for, 229–230
Economic union, 191
Economies in Transition (EIT) Parties, 250
Eden, Anthony, 7
Egypt, 69–70, 150, 129
Electronic herd, 227
Electronic surveillance, 315
Elliott, Larry, 237
Energy cycles, and oil, 25–26
Energy security, 29
Estonia, 197, 201
Ethnic cleansing, 42, 51
Euro, 191, 199–200
European Atomic Energy Community
 (EURATOM), 195
European Coal and Steel Community (ECSC),
 192, 195
European Commission, 199
European Common Market, 192
European Community (EC), 199
European Court of Justice, 199

European Economic Community (EEC), 195
European Parliament, 199–200
European Union, 167
 cross-national experience, 194
 birth and early evolution, 195–196
 future of, 200–203
 integration process, 189–194
 membership criteria and process, 196–197
 membership growth, 196t
 ongoing issues, 196–198
 overview of, 188–189
 political implications of, 193, 198–200

Failed State Index (FSI), 289–290
Failed states, 9–10, 90–91. *See also* Pakistan,
 case study
 failure scores, country-wise ranking, 286f
 index of, 289–290
 problems of, 290–294
Fair Traders, 171, 183–175
Fascist regimes, 6
Fast track procedures, and WTO, 176–177
Fatah, 77
Feigenbaum, Evan A., 215, 216, 217
Fence, The, 77
Field Manual, 93
Finland, 197
First World. *See* Developed countries
First World Climate Conference, 248
Ford Motor Company, 218
Forcibly displaced people. *See* Refugees
Foreign Affairs, 127, 213, 252, 319
Foreign direct investment (FDI), 180
Foreign Policy, 213
Fossil fuels, 246–247, 250. *See also* Carbon
 dioxide (CO2); Oil; Global warming
Four Modernizations (China), 210
Four Special Economic Zones (SEZs), 211
Fourth Geneva Convention on War, 54
France, 194, 200–201
Franco-Prussian War of 1870, 192
Fravel, M. T., 191
Freedom, 94
Free trade. *See* North American Free Trade
 Agreement (NAFTA), World Trade
 Organization (WTO)
Free Trade Area of the Americas (FTAA), 127
Free Traders, 170
French Revolution, 5
Friedman, Thomas, 22, 226, 227, 229

G-7
 characteristics, 238t
G-20. *See also* Globalization, extension of
 characteristics, 238t
 China's role, 214
 India's role, 218
 institutional membership, 239f
 Mexico and, 273
G-77. *See also* Globalization, extension of
 annual meeting, 236
 developmental agenda, developing world,
 235–236
 formation of, 235
 institutional membership, 239

G-77 (*continued*)
  Missile Technology Control Regime, 112
  New International Economic Order (NIEO)
    and, 236
  non-members of, 240
  purpose of, 236
Gandhi, Indira, 215–216
Gandhi, Rajiv, 216
Gaza Strip, 67, 71
General Agreement on Tariffs and Trade
    (GATT), 174–176
Geneva Briefing Book, 181
Geneva Convention, 44
Geopolitical issues, 29–30, 75
Georgia, 37
Germany, 194
Gestapo, 309
Gilboy, George J., 212, 213, 214
Global Exchange, 180–181
Globalization, 184. *See also* Economic
    globalization; India; Venezuela; Technology;
    Washington Consensus
  role of telecommunication, 227–228
  technology and, 227–228
Globalization, extension of, 235–237. *See also*
    Washington consensus
  controversies regarding, 224–227
  developed world *vs.* developing world, *000*
  developmental agenda, 241
  developmental dimension, 230–231
  economic institutions, 235–237 (*See also*
    individual institutions)
  funding sources, developing countries, 232–233
  G-7/G-20, transition, 234–235, 237–240
  institutionalization of free trade (*See* Bretton
    Woods conference)
  moral obligation, colonial countries, 231–232
Global warming, 245–260. *See also* Kyoto
    Protocol
  developed country *vs.* developing country, 247
  greenhouse gas emission (2008–2012),
    249–250
  IPCC II reports on, 256
  issues of, 247–248
  Kyoto Protocol, expiration (2012),
    245, 247, 254
  of ocean water, 256
  projection, limitations, 254–255, 257–258
  as transnational issue, 246
  US international initiative, regarding, 248
Global war on terrorism (GWOT), 306. *See also*
    Terrorism; Terrorists
Golan Heights, 67
Goldberg, Jeffrey, 73
Golden Horde, Genghis Khan's, 95
Golden straitjacket, 229
Goldwyn, David L., 22
Gonzalez, Alberto, 55
Great Depression, 172
  in Europe, 170
  free trade and, 172–173
  institutionalizing trade, 172–173
Great Satan, 136, 149
Greenhouse gases, 246–249, 251–254
  defined, 246

emission, American contribution to, 251
fossil fuel use and, 247
Grotius, Hugo, 4–5, 44
Group of 77. *See* G-77
Group of Seven. *See* G-7
Group of Twenty. *See* G-20
Guantanamo Bay, 56
Guardian Council, 136
Gulf War. *See* Persian Gulf War
Guomindang forces (China), 209

Hague Convention, 44
Haiti, 15
Hale, Lyric Hughes, 213
Hamas, 77
  and the Palestinian election, 64
  and terrorism, 309
Herzegovina, 201. *See also* Bosnia
Hertzog, Chaim, 77
Hertzog, Michael, 77
Hierarchical model. *See* Commander-cadre
    model
Hindu Code of Manu, 44
Hirsch study, 29
Hitler, Adolf, 173, 313
Hizbollah, 309
Hobbes, Thomas, 4
Holocaust (Nazi Germany), 8, 44
Holy Land, 60, 65
Huang, Yeshing, 213
Hughes, David and Lyric, 213
Humanitarian disasters. *See also* Darfur
    situation
  causes for, 147
  description, 146–149
  instances of, 148–149
  international actions, enforcement, 147
  UN's role, as mediator in, 149
Humanitarian intervention principle, 9–10, 49
Human Rights Watch, 159–161
Hungary, 197
Hussein, Saddam, 32, 43, 45–46, 108, 119, 138,
    141, 147, 150
Hutu people, 49
Hybrid Symmetrical-Asymmetrical War, 91
Hydroflurocarbons (HFCs), 249

Ia Drang, battle of, 91
IBRD (International Bank for Reconstruction
    and Development), 174, 235
Iceland, 250
IDPs (internally displaced persons), 265
IMF (International Monetary Fund), 174, 235
Immigrant, international
  categories of, 265
  definition, 265
  irregular, 265
Immigration. *See also* U.S.-Mexican border
    problem
  categories, 267–268 (*See also* Migration)
  functions, 266–269
  global issues, 266
  motivation, 266–269
  problems in, 271–272
  worldwide, 269–271

Imperial Preference System, 173–174
Improvised explosive devices (IEDs), 91
India, 202–206, 242–243, 291
    economic liberaliztion (1991), 215–216
    education system, impact on, 214, 217
    entrepreneurial work ethic, 216–217
    ethnic divisions, 215
    GDP per capita comparison with China, 209
    globalization, benefits of, 214–215
    global warming and, 247
    as G-20 member, 218
    growth projection (2050), 215
    outsourcing, 216
    poor people in, 217–218
    Tata Motor Company in, 218
    technological innovation, 208
    US comparison with, 212t
Indian Institute of Technology, 217
India's Silicon Valley, 216
Independent actors, pivotal states as, 143
Indo-Pakistani War, 61
Indonesia, 129
Industrial Revolution, 162
"Informal High Level Event" (UNFCC web site), 254
Intergovernmental Negotiating Committee (INC), 249
Intergovernmental Panel on Climate Change (IPCC), 249, 255–256
Intergovernmental Negotiating Committee (INC), 249
Intergovernmental organizations (IGOs), 169
Intergovernmental Panel on Climate Change (IPCC), 249, 255
International Bank for Reconstruction and Development (IBRD). See World Bank
International Convention on the Prevention and Punishment of the Crime of Genocide (United Nations). See United Nations Convention on Genocide
International Court of Justice (ICJ), 53
International Criminal Court (ICC), 42, 50–54, 160
Internationalists, 171–172
International Military Tribunal, 45
International Monetary Fund (IMF), 174
International Trade Organization (ITO), 174–175
Internationalization, 227
Internet, 7
Intervention, in civil wars, 3, 9, 11
Intifadas, 67
Iran, 136–143. See also White Revolution
    ethno-religious aspects of, 130
    nuclear weapons and, 138–140
    limits of power and, 140–143
    oil reserves, 29
    overview of, 127–128
    as pivotal state, 128
    political evolution of, 133–137
    as unique state, 130–133
    as revolutionary state, 135–137
    Shah, 133–135
    as theocratic state, 135
    U.S. relations with, 137

Iranian hostage situation, 135
Iranian Revolution, 135–137
Iraq
    American invasion, 1, 13, 31, 45, 88
    asymmetrical warfare and, 93
    Bush administration and invasion, 12–13, 31
    oil reserves, 29–33
    sovereignty and, 12-16
    US confrontation after, 88
    War (1990), 30–31, 84
Iraq War (1990), 30–31, 84
Ireland, 200
Irish Republican Army (IRA), 313
Islamic Republic of Iran, 128, 135–136
Islamiyah, Jemaah, 309
Isolationism, 172
Israel independence, war, and displacement, 65–76
Iran and, 139
    Six Day's War of, 66
    Yom Kippur War of 1973, 68–69
    peace process, 69–70, 76
    Camp David I, 70–71
    Camp David II, 71–75
Israeli Defense Forces (IDF), 75
Israeli-Palestinian conflict, 64, 76–78
Italy, 194

Jalili, Ali A., 94
Jammu, 61. See also Kashmir
Janjaweed (rebels), 151, 159–160
Japan, 43–44, 209, 250
Jemaah Islamiyah, 309, 312
Jenkins, Brian, 308–309
Jerusalem, 66, 68, 70–74, 78
Jihad, 308
Jisi, Wang, 219
Johnson, Samuel, 8
Jordan, 66–67, 69
Justice and Equality Movement (JEM), 159, 160

Kadima Party, 78
Kashmir, 61, 63
Katanga (Shaba), 150
Kazakhstan, 33–34
Kellogg-Briand Pact, 103
Kerry, John, KGB, 309
Khan, Genghis, 43, 83
Khamenei, Ayatollah Ali, 148–149
Khatami, Mohammed, 148
Khmer Rouge, 8
Khomeini, Ayatollah Ruhollah, 134–135
Kibbutzes, 67
Killing Fields, The, 148
Kirton, John, 238
Kodmani, Basma, 73, 77, 140
Kosovo, 50, 152
Ku Klux Klan, 309
Kurds, 131–132
Kuwait, 29, 45, 84. See also Persian Gulf War
Kyoto Process, 248–249
    mechanisms and procedures, 249–251
Kyoto Protocol. See also Global warming
    American participation, 248
    American and other objections, 251–253

Kyoto Protocol (*continued*)
Annex categories of, 250
components, 249–251
contemporary objections to, 248–253
evolution of, 248–254
goal of, 249–250
overview, 245
process, 248–249 (*See* Kyoto Process)
regulations and guidelines, global warming, 248
10th anniversary, 253

Latvia, 197, 201
Leaderless resistance model. *See* Virtual network
Lemkin, Richard, 43
Lexus and the Olive Tree, The (Friedman),
226–227, 229
Libya, 29
Lind, Michael, 170
Lisbon Reform Treaty, 200
Lithuania, 197, 201
Little Wall, 74
Legitimate authority, 3
Locke, John, 5
London Agreement (1945), 45
Lone wolf terrorists
activities, nature of, 319
characteristics of, 320–321
definition, 319–320, 319–321
EU study report, 321
examples, 320
radical Islamic terrorism and, 320
terrorist organization *vs.*, 320
Timothy McVeigh's case, 320
Unabomber Theodore Kaczynski's case, 320
virtual network operations and, 322
Luxembourg, 194
Lynch, 161–162

Macedonia, 198, 201
Macroeconomic practices, 196–197, 206, 208
Mahbubani, Kishore, 219
Medvedev, Dmitry, 37
Makovsky, David, 77
Malaysia, 239
Maloney, 138
Malta, 197–198
Mao Zedong, 209–210
Map of
Azerbaijan, 36f
Iran, 131f
Jerusalem, 68f
Maugeri, Leonardo, 22
McNeilly, Lisa, 246
Medecins sans Frontieres (MSF) (Doctors
without Borders), 161
Mediterranean island countries, 197
Menon, Rajan, 218
Methane (CH4), 249
Mexico, 182, 184, 189
Microeconomic practices, 225
Middle Eastern oil, 21–22, 26, 29
Migration, 263–283
Military Balance, The, 76
Milosevic, Slobadan, 46
Moldova, 201

Monetary union, 190
Monnet, Jean, 192, 195
Mossadeqh, Mohmmad, 133
Mozambique, 116
MSF. *See* Medecins sans Frontieres (MSF)
(Doctors without Borders)
Mukherji, Hahul, 219
Multinational corporations (MNCs), 180
Mumbai attack, 311
Munich Olympics (1970), 309
Muslims, 49, 65, 316. *See also* Hamas, and the
Palestinian election; Israeli-Palestinian
conflict
My Lai, 48

Nagorno-Karabakh, 35, 37
Nano, 218
Nationalist (China). *See* Guomindang forces
(China)
National Security for a New Era, 32, 288
National Security Strategy, 138
National Strategy for Combating Terrorism, 307
Naxcivan, 35
Nazis, 3, 43, 309
Neoisolationism, 172
Netherlands, 194, 200
Newsweek, 16, 74–75, 203, 205
New York Times, 69, 198, 227, 280–281
New Zealand, 250
NGOs. *See* Nongovernmental organizations
(NGOs)
Nicaragua, 15
Nigeria, 29
Nile River, 256
Nitrous oxide (N2O), 249
Non-Annex I countries, Kyoto Protocol, 250
Nondiscrimination, 176
Nongovernmental organizations (NGOs), 160
North American Free Trade Agreement (NAFTA)
controversy, 191
illegal immigration, 202
impact on jobs, 171
impact on overall economy, 171–172
income equality, 171–172
North American Treaty Organization (NATO),
165–166, 221
Northern Alliance, 91–92
North Korea
deterrence and, 109–113
proliferation and, 104–109, 113–119
security and, 103–104
Norway, 198
Nuclear fusion, 26
energy cycles and, 25
power plants, and oil production, 25
Nuclear Non-Proliferation Treaty (NPT),
103–104, 112–113
Nuclear proliferation. *See* Proliferation
Nuclear weapons, 138–140
Iran and, 138–140
Nuremberg, war crimes trials, 2, 45–46

Obama administration
violent extremism, international religious
terrorism and, 285–286

Copenhagen summit, 251–253
diplomatic policy, Iran, 140–141, 143
ICC ratification and, 56–57
Iranian nuclear program and, 138
Kyoto protocol and, 248
nuclear agreement, negotiation, 119
peace process, Middle East conflict, 70
West Bank settlement issue and, 73
Obama, Barack, 119, 141, 285
Oil. *See also* Middle Eastern oil; Scarcity, of
   resources
   conflicts and, 140, 30–38
   domestic effects of, 28–29
   energy cycles and, 25–26
   as energy source, 25
   future consequences, 26–27
   geopolitical issues and, 29–30
   global warming and, 245
   importance and value of, 23–25
   political implications, 27–30
   reserves, World ranking, 27t
   rich reserves of, 129
Oil and Gas Journal, 26
Oil card, 31
Oklahoma City bombing, 313, 320
Old City (East) Jerusalem capitals, 71, 76
Olmert, Ehud, 76, 78
On the Law of War and Peace, 5
Operation Desert Storm. *See* Persian Gulf War
Operation Iraqi Freedom, 85. *See also* Iraq
   War (1990)
Operation Restore Hope (Somalia), 15
Opium War, 209
Opponents, identification of, 85,
   91–93, 98–99
Organization of Economic Cooperation and
   Development (OECD), 235–239, 250
   members of, 236
Organization of Petroleum Exporting Countries
   (OPEC), 24
Orwell, George, 232
Ottoman Empire, 38, 46

Pahlevi, Muhammed Reza, 25,
   128, 130, 133
Pakistan, case study, 61, 63, 111–112
   Bangladesh, creation of, 296
   common nationalism, lack of, 296–297
   dispersion of Muslims, 296
   economic indicators, 299–300
   ethnic groups of, 296
   as failed state, 294–295
   Failed State Index, 297–298
   formation and development of, 295–297
   international concern about, 302
   Military, role of, 297
   Muslim political entity of, 296
   political indicators, 300–301
   political situation of, 297
   social indicators, 298–299
   Taliban Movement and, 301–302
Pal, Amitabh, 206
Palestinian Authority (PA), 72
Palestinian Legislative Council, 13, 77
Palestinian Liberation Organization (PLO), 72

Palestinians, 312. *See also* Hamas, and the
   Palestinian election; Israeli-Palestinian
   conflict, 64
Panama, 15
Peace enforcement, 155–157
Peace imposition (PI), 154–155, 157
Peacekeeping, defined, 151
Peacekeeping operations (PKOs), 151, 152–153,
   156–157
   ambiguity in, 151–152
   American position in, 157–158
   Chapter Six of, 151, 153, 156
   contemporary cases, 153–154
   Half operations, 151, 156
   parameters, 152–153
   tasks and forces in, 154–157
   theory and practice, 151–153
Peacekeeping practices. *See also* Peacekeeping
      operations (PKOs)
   evolution of, 149–150
   UN's role, 149–151
Peace of Westphalia, 4
Peace operations, 151
Peacock Empire. *See* Persian Empire
Pei, Minxin, 212–213, 219
PEMEX, 21
Pentagon attack. *See* Global war on terrorism
   (GWOT); Terrorism; September 11th attacks
People's Republic of China. *See* China
Perfluorocarbons (PFCs), 249
Perle, Richard, 14
Persia, 128
Persian Empire, 128, 130, 134–135
Persian Gulf War, 9, 11, 85, 149
Petrolists, 28–29
Petroleum. *See* Oil; Middle Eastern oil
Philippines, 88
Pivital states, defined, 127
PKOs. *See* Peacekeeping operations (PKOs)
Platoon, 48
Pol Pot, 8
Poland, 197
Politics, defined, 191
Political ideology, 47, 172, 195, 211
Populist/fascist regimes, 6
Portugal, 201
Post-American World, The, 215
Post-Cold War, 10
Post-war peace, conditions of, 85, 93
Post-World War II, 24, 43, 54, 173
Powell, Colin S., 52, 159
Power, exercise in, 7
Privatization, 229
Proliferation
   as international problem, 138–140
   measures towards, 104, 112–113
Protean enemy
   contemporary threat and, 319
   future challenges, terrorists, 323
   virtual network operations, 321–322
Protectionism, 170
Putin, Valdimir, 37

Quasi-military situations, 92–93
Qurei, Ahmed, 80

Rabin, Yithak, 72
RAND Corporation, 102
Rape of Nanking, 44
Reagan, Ronald W., 135
Reagan-Thatcher initiatives, 215
Refugees, 265
  civil conflicts and, 266
  migration, reasons for, 265–266
Repatriations, 74–75, 80
Reserves, of oil, 27
Resource conflict, 19–38
Revolutionary Guards and Courts, 136
Reza Khan, 130, 133
Ricardian principle, 178
Rice, Condoleezza, 137, 141
Rights, of the people, 6
Rio de Janeiro United Nations Conference on
  the Environment and Development (the
  Earth Summit), 249
Rising powers, 206–219. *See also* China; India
  definition, 207
Romania, 197, 201
Rome Conference of 1998, 52
Rome Treaty, 195
Roosevelt, Franklin D., 174
Rothgeb, John, 176
Rounds, and GATT, 175
Rousseau, Jean-Jacques, 5
Rudolph, Eric, 315
Russia. *See also* Soviet Union
  oil and, 28–29, 35
  sovereignty, 3
Russian pipeline, 36
Rwanda, 41–42

Sadat, Anwar el, 70
Saudi Arabia, 129, 142
SAVAK, 134
Scarcity, of resources
  defined, 20
  as global dilemma, 263–259
  petroleum, 23–30
  political importance of, 20
  solutions for, 21–22
Schell, Orville, 213
Schuman, Robert, 195
Scrubbers, emissions and, 251
Security
  human, 243–244
  international, 157–158
Self-help, 7
September 11th attacks, 10, 305–306, 313. *See
  also* Terrorism
  asymmetrical warfare, 84–85
  Bush's military priorities, before, 13
  international terrorism, rise of, 158
  Iraqi's (confrontation of US) after, 88
  NPT (non proliferation treaty), 113
  terrorism, global threat, 305, 313–315, 316,
    319
Serbia, 198
Shah of Iran, 133–135
Sharon, Ariel, 75–76
Sheffer, David, 52
Sherman, William Tecumseh, 44

Shifter, Michael, 280
Shiites, 130–132, 134–135. *See also* Iran
Sierra Leone, 50
Siegman, Harry, 71
Silicon Valley, 228
Sinai Peninsula, 67, 71
Singer, Max, 216–217
Single market. *See* Common market
Six Day's War of 1967, 66–67
Slovakia, 197
Slovenia, 197
Snow, Donald M., 13, 31–32, 93, 142
Socialism, in China, 210
Somalia, 9, 11–12, 15, 49
South Africa, 236, 239–240, 254
South Korea, 45
Sovereignty
  assault on, outside the UN, 10-11
  assault on, through UN, 8–9
  American response, 12–16
  concept of, 3–4
  external relations, 4
  internal relations, 4
  intervention response, 11–12
  objections to, 6–8
  old-time conceptualizations, 7
  origins and evolution, 4–6
  sources and extent of, 6
  Soviet Union, 15–16, 149. *See also* Russia;
    specific countries
  Shah of Iran abdication and, 130
Soviet Union, 8, 34–35, 48, 65, 69, 84, 95,
  105–106, 108–110, 112, 148–149, 188,
  194–195, 197–198, 201, 203, 206–208, 237,
  302, 309, 313
Spain, 201
Stable peace, 154
Stalin, Joseph, 313
Star Wars. *See* Strategic Arms Limitation Talks
  (SALT)
State-owned enterprises (SOEs), 211
State sovereignty. *See* Sovereignty
Status of Force Agreement (SOFA), 31
Stern, Jessica, 307, 310, 314
Strategic Arms Limitation Talks (SALT), 105
Strategic Arms Reduction Talks (START), 105
Substitution, of resources, 21
Sudan, 158–159
Sudanese Liberation Army/Movement (SLA/M),
  159–160, 162
Sulfur hexafluoride (SF6), 249
Sullivan, Gordon, 89
Sunnis, 132, 135
Superpowers, 126
Supreme authority, 4
Sweden, 197
Swiss banking system, 197
Switzerland, 198
Symmetrical warfare, 84–85, 88–91. *See also*
  Warfare
Syria, 66, 109, 131, 142

Taiwan, 61
Taliban, 91. *See also* Al Qaeda
  and Al Qaeda, distinctions, 98

activities in Afghanistan, 96–97
asymmetrical forces of, 95
government's rule in Afghanistan, 97–98
in Pakistan, 301–302
Task force, peacekeeping, 154–157
Tata Motor Company, 218
Technological advances, 227–228. *See also*
Warfare
Technology, 227–228
Telecommunications revolution, 227
Temple Mount, 74–75
Terrorism, 37, 305–324. *See also* Global war on
terrorism (GWOT); *individual organizations*
Terrorism in the Name of God, 307, 314
Terrorists
acts, 308–310
attacks of September 11th, 30,
305–306, 313
evolution of, 313–314
GWOT and, 316–323
objectives, 311–313
targets, 310–311
Third World, 226. *See also* Developing countries
Thirty Years War (1684), 1–2, 87
Tiananmen Square uprising, 210
Tibet, 212
Tony Blair Labor Government, 199
Top-down theory, 5
Torture, 54–56
Trade promotion authority, 176
Transnational issues
global warming, 248–254
resource conflict, 19–38
terrorism, 305–324
Transparency, 176
Treaty of Maastricht, 195–199
Trinidad, 50
Truman administration, 175
Truman, Harry S., 174
Turkey, 198, 201–203
Turkish pipeline, 37
Turkmenistan, 33
Turtles, countries as, 180
Tutsi people, 49

Uganda, 116
Ukraine, 198, 201
UN Commission on Human Rights
(UNCHR), 265
UN Convention Relating to the Status of
Refugees, 265
refugee, definition, 265
UNCTAD (UN Conference on Trade and
Development), 174, 236
New International Economic Order (NIEO)
and, 236
United Arab Emirates, 29
United Kingdom, 113, 321
United Nations, 11
peacekeeping role of, 146–165
United Nations charter, 10–13, 151, 173
United Nations Conference on the Environment
and Development (the Earth Summit), 249
United Nations Conference on Trade and
Development (UNCTAD), 174

United Nations Convention Against Torture
(UNCAT), 43, 54
United Nations Convention on Genocide, 43,
47–49, 159
United Nations Declaration on Human Rights,
47, 54
United Nations Department of Economic and
Social Affairs
irregular immigrants, definition, 265
United Nations Department of Peacekeeping
Operations (UNDPKO), 151, 153, 156
United Nations Diplomatic Conference on the
Establishment of a Permanent International
Criminal Court, 52
United Nations Emergency Force (UNEF),
66, 150
United Nations Environmental Programme, 249
United Nations Forces in Cyprus (UNFICYP),
150
United Nations Framework Convention for
Climate Change (UNFCCC), 248–252,
253–254
Bali conference, 253
United Nations General Assembly, 248
United Nations in Somalia (UNISOM), 9
United Nations International Force in East
Timor (INTERFET), 11
United Nations International Law Commission, 50
United Nations Operation in Congo
(ONUC), 150
United Nations Security Council Resolution
(UNSCR), 11, 13–14, 16, 53
United States Chamber of Commerce, 174
United States Department of Energy, 25
United States Foreign Policy, 32, 128, 286
United States, oil reserves, 29
Unstable peace, 154
U.S.-Mexican border problem
baby boomers, retirement (2012), 280
border security, 274–276
criminal activities, immigrants, 274
current crisis in, 273
drug trafficking and, 274, 280–281
illegal immigrants, 264
immigration parameters, 264–266
immigrants percentage, 273–274
immigration policy, 273–274
irregular immigrants, 276–280
physical problems, 274–276
terrorist immigrants, 281–282
UN immigration figures (2005), 264
Uzbekistan, 33

Valero, 21
Venezuela, 28–29, 239
Versailles Peace Conference, 173
Victor, David, 249
Viet Cong, 88, 309
Vietnam, 48, 87–91, 148, 309
Virtual network, 315

Wahhabi sect, 135
Wailing Wall, 74
War crimes, 41–57
Bosnia, 49. *See also* Bosnia

War crimes (*continued*)
  defined, 45
  evolution of, 47–49
  overview, 41–43
  media, role of in, 49
  Rwanda, 49–50, 53
  torture and, 54–56
  tribunals for, 50–56
  impact of World War II, 44–47
Warfare, 83. *See also* Asymmetrical warfare;
    Symmetrical warfare
  environment, 87–89, 95–97
  identification of opponents, 85, 91–93
  oil and, 29
  overview, 83
  physical structure of, 89–91, 97–98
  postwar peace, 85–86, 93–94, 99–100
  preemptive, 14
  preventive, 14
War planning. *See also* Asymmetrical warfare
  definition, 84
  electronic innovations in, 85
  21st century
    basic considerations, 85
Warsaw Pact, 197
Washington Conference on naval fleet sizes, 103
Washington Consensus, 224–225,
    227, 229
  defined, 224
  free trade promotion, criterion, 229–230
  membership, basic requirements, 229
  policy bases of, 229–230
Washington Post, 114, 161–162
Washington Quarterly, 300
Weapons of mass destruction (WMD), 14, 117
Web sites
  China, 221
  Darfur, 166
  defense issues, 102
  environmental concerns, 262
  European Union, 205
  globalization, 242
  Israeli-Palestinian conflict, 82
  military matters, 102

  national security issues, 102
  peace summit, 82
  terrorism, 102, 326
  war crimes, 58
  WTO, critical views of, 186
Webster, Daniel, 14
West Bank, 13–14, 65, 68–75
What After Iraq?, 13, 31, 142
White Revolution, 134
Why Terrorism Works, 307
Wideners, 194–196
*2010 World Almanac and Book of
    Facts, The,* 26
World Bank, 174
World Climate Conference, 248–249
World Food Program, 160–161
World Is Flat, The (Friedman), 215, 228
World Meteorological Organization
    (WMO), 249
World Trade Center attack. *See* Global war on
    terrorism (GWOT); Terrorism; September
    11th attacks
World Trade Organization (WTO), 169–184,
    190, 211–212, 235, 237–239
World War I, 192
World War II, 44–47. *See also* Post-World War II
World War III, 87
Wounded Knee, 46

Xiaoping, Deng, 210–211

Yeltsin, Boris, 307
Yergin, Daniel, 22
Yom Kippur War (1973), 68–69
Yoo, John, 55
Yugoslavia, 197–198

Zaire, 9
Zakaria, Fareed, 215
Zarqawi, Abu Musab al-, 93
Zemin, Jiang, 211
Zimbabwe, 286
Zionist movement, 65–66
Zweig, David, 22